Critical Essays on
EDMUND SPENSER

CRITICAL ESSAYS
ON
BRITISH LITERATURE

Zack Bowen, General Editor
University of Miami

Critical Essays on
EDMUND SPENSER

edited by

MIHOKO SUZUKI

G. K. Hall & Co.
An Imprint of Simon & Schuster Macmillan
New York

Prentice Hall International
London Mexico City New Delhi Singapore Sydney Toronto

G. K. Hall & Co.
An Imprint of Simon & Schuster Macmillan
866 Third Avenue
New York, New York 10022

Library of Congress Cataloging-in-Publication Data

Critical essays on Edmund Spenser / edited by Mihoko Suzuki.
      p.   cm.—(Critical essays on British literature)
    Includes bibliographical references and index.
    ISBN 0-7838-0019-3
    1. Spenser, Edmund, 1552?–1599—Criticism and interpretation.
2. Spenser, Edmund, 1552?–1599. Faerie queene. 3. Epic poetry, English—History and criticism.   I. Suzuki, Mihoko, 1953–
II. Series.
PR2364.C69 1995 1996
821'.3—dc20
                                               95-18184
                                                CIP

10   9   8   7   6   5   4   3   2   1

Printed in the United States of America

Contents

◆

General Editor's Note

♦

The Critical Essays on British Literature series provides a variety of approaches to both classical and contemporary writers of Britain and Ireland. The formats of the volumes in the series vary with the thematic designs of individual editors and with the amount and nature of existing reviews and criticism, augmented, where appropriate, by original essays by recognized authorities. It is hoped that each volume will be unique in developing a new overall perspective on its particular subject.

Concentrating on contemporary scholarship, Mihoko Suzuki sees the 1980s as a decade of innovative theoretical approaches to Spenser. These supersede the critical opposition of earlier historical and New Critical schools of criticism, prevalent in the 1960s and 1970s. The emphasis on psychoanalytic and feminist theory from the 1980s to the present principally incorporates historical tenets in seeking to place Spenser in his culture. Suzuki's selection of essays, while concentrating on *The Faerie Queene*, also includes three works on *The Shepheardes Calender*.

Zack Bowen
University of Miami

Publisher's Note

◆

Producing a volume that contains both newly commissioned and reprinted material presents the publisher with the challenge of balancing the desire to achieve stylistic consistency with the need to preserve the integrity of works first published elsewhere. In the Critical Essays series, essays commissioned especially for a particular volume are edited to be consistent with G. K. Hall's house style; reprinted essays appear in the style in which they were first published, with only typographical errors corrected. Consequently, shifts in style from one essay to another are the result of our efforts to be faithful to each text as it was originally published.

Acknowledgments

♦

I thank Zack Bowen for inviting me to edit this volume, and the contributors who graciously allowed their work to be collected here. Special thanks are owed to Judith Anderson, Stephen Greenblatt, Richard Helgerson, David Lee Miller, Patricia Parker, Anne Lake Prescott, and Lauren Silberman for various acts of assistance and for facilitating the inclusion of their essays; and to Susanne Wofford, as always, for helpful conversations. I also thank the members of my graduate seminar on "Spenser and Critical Theory" for their enthusiasm about both, as well as the late A. Bartlett Giamatti for first introducing me to Spenser's "play of double senses." The Research Council of the University of Miami provided financial assistance. Finally, Frank Palmeri, in this as in everything else, gave me and continues to give me invaluable encouragement and advice. "You frame my thoughts and fashion me within."

Introduction

◆

In his analysis of twentieth-century Spenser criticism, Paul Alpers described the field as "moribund" until the publication of C. S. Lewis's *The Allegory of Love* (1936); and it was not until the 1960s that Spenser became "a normal subject of critical and scholarly investigation."[1] This development in Spenser studies laid the groundwork for the publication of two important collections of essays on Spenser, one edited by Harry Berger, Jr., in 1968 and the other edited by A. C. Hamilton in 1972.[2] Berger characterized in the introduction to his collection the varied critical methods brought to Spenser criticism of the 1960s as "the rhetorical, the allegorical, the numerological, the iconographic, and the archetypal (or mythological)."[3] The 1970s produced several important book-length studies that sought to give an overview of *The Faerie Queene*, especially in terms of its allegory—for example, A. Bartlett Giamatti's *Play of Double Senses: Spenser's "Faerie Queene"* (1975), Isabel MacCaffrey's *Spenser's Allegory: The Anatomy of Imagination* (1976), and James Nohrnberg's *The Analogy of "The Faerie Queene"* (1976).

Not only did the 1980s see a significant summation of scholarship in Hamilton's monumental *The Spenser Encyclopedia* (1990); with the introduction of New Historicist and feminist theories, as well as psychoanalytic and other theoretical and interdisciplinary approaches, the 1980s also witnessed a transformation of Spenser studies from the one Berger described in 1968. In fact, Spenser studies, as much as Shakespeare studies, have been one of the fields in the literature of the English Renaissance most receptive to innovative theoretical approaches. To take just one example, the originators of the New Historicism in Renaissance studies, Stephen Greenblatt and Louis Adrian Montrose, both wrote influential essays on Spenser in the early 1980s that set the terms of the debate.[4] The present collection aims to give representative examples of theoretical and interdisciplinary criticism for undergraduates and graduate students alike, while attempting to give some

1

coverage to *The Faerie Queene* without repeating essays that have already been anthologized in other collections.[5]

Alpers noted in 1969 a split in Spenser criticism between those who studied an "esoteric" Spenser accessible only to initiates and those who saw in his poetry a "common wisdom" comprehensible to sympathetic and patient readers.[6] This opposition, which I would rephrase as that between interpretation based on historical particulars and interpretation based on transhistorical insights, no longer characterizes Spenser studies of the 1980s. Literary theory, especially psychoanalytic and feminist theory, has often been criticized in the abstract for being transhistorical in its claims and not sufficiently historicized; but critics of Spenser using these approaches have been alive to contemporary contexts, such as Reformation iconoclasm and Spenser's negotiation of a female sovereign and patron. And the New Historicism, while often deploying little-known historical material, aims to elucidate the embeddedness of Spenser in his own culture in ways that are generally accessible. Even the most learned examples of Spenser criticism, then, have not been consigned to the "esoteric," but have brought new contexts to the text in illuminating ways.

Criticism of *The Shepheardes Calender* in the 1980s has been notable in demystifying the genre of the pastoral, taking it out of the purely literary and aesthetic registers. In a series of influential essays, Louis Montrose set forth his theories concerning Spenser's negotiation of what he called the "pastoral of power." Here his essays are represented by one of the earliest, which first called attention to the social and political aspects of Spenser's pastoral as an expression of his courtship of Elizabeth as sovereign and dispenser of patronage. The selections reprinted here focus on the *Aprill, October* and *November* eclogues. Harry Berger, Jr., whose essays on *The Faerie Queene* were extremely influential for an entire generation of students of Spenser, turned his attention to *The Shepheardes Calender* in the 1980s.[7] The essay reprinted here, "The Mirror Stage of Colin Clout," is inflected by psychoanalytic theory, as its title's reference to Jacques Lacan's well-known essay "Le stade du miroir comme formateur de la fonction du Je" suggests, and focuses on the *Januarye* eclogue to interrogate the relationship between nature and art; rather than the poem functioning as an imitation of nature, Berger reverses the direction of the representation and shows that nature in fact serves as a narcissistic projection for the poet. He thus discerns an ironic relation between Colin and Spenser rather than an identity, and a "metapastoral critique" in Spenser's writing of pastoral.

Finally, Jonathan Goldberg, who in *Endlesse Worke: Spenser and the Structures of Discourse* (1981) read Spenserian narrative through poststructuralist theory, has recently turned his attention to theories of sexuality. The essay reprinted here raises the "exorbitant question" of "disorderly love" between Colin and Hobbinol to discuss more generally the "place" of homosexuality in Renaissance England as an "open secret." In contrast to Berger, who read the mirror as a figure for narcissism, Goldberg interprets it as one representing "reciprocity, similarity, and simulation" of a pedagogical as well as an erotic relationship; the homoerotics that is denied (by Colin) and policed (by E. K.) in favor of the heterosexual courtship of Rosalind paradoxically enables the production of *The Shepheardes Calender*.[8]

David Lee Miller's essay on Spenser's poetics, while focusing on Book 1, also gives a useful overview of the entire *Faerie Queene* from a psychoanalytic and political perspective. Referring to Ernst Kantarowicz's theory of the "king's two bodies," Miller posits two versions of the "ideal body": a texual one, whose synecdochic traces constitute *The Faerie Queene* itself, and a political one, which authorizes the defective natural body of the monarch.[9] Anne Lake Prescott's article on Book 1 demonstrates its relationship to *The Travayled Pylgrime*, a chivalric allegory by a noncanonical contemporary writer, Stephen Bateman. Prescott reminds us of Spenser's embeddedness in contemporary literary culture, an embeddedness that needs to be recovered in order to counterbalance the almost exclusive focus on Spenser's relationship to classical, Continental, and English canonical writers.

The essays on Book 2 group together two influential and complementary theoretical approaches to the Bower of Bliss. Stephen Greenblatt's chapter from *Renaissance Self-Fashioning* reads the episode through reference to Freud's *Civilization and Its Discontents*, seeing the violent destruction of the Bower, which figures sexual renunciation, as the price exacted by civility. Greenblatt further suggests contemporary contexts for the episode: European colonialism in the New World and English colonialism in Ireland as well as Reformation iconoclasm. Patricia Parker's chapter on the Bower of Bliss from *Literary Fat Ladies* extends her theory of dilation in romance narrative, first put forward in *Inescapable Romance: Studies in the Poetics of a Mode* (1979). Reading this episode through the tradition of lyric—from the biblical psalm to Sannazaro and Petrarch—Parker shows how the lyric, associated with the feminine, and in this episode the enchantress Acrasia, threatens to suspend the forward quest of the hero Guyon.

The three essays on Books 3 and 4 all deal with the question of gender from various perspectives and demonstrate the importance of feminist theory and criticism for Spenser studies. In the selection from *Milton's Spenser: The Politics of Reading* (1983), Maureen Quilligan conjoins reader-response theory with feminist theory, focusing on the "overtly inscribed female readers" of Book 3 and the female perspective of its characters. Quilligan sees Book 4's cancellation of Book 3's ending—the hermaphrodite embrace—and Book 4's revision of Amoret's story in Book 3 as symptomatic of what she calls the "failure of Orpheus," as marking a "self-mutilation" prompted by censuring (male) readers of Book 3. Lauren Silberman's essay on the Hermaphrodite reads the displacement of that image from the middle of Book 1 to the end of Book 3 as symptomatic of the structural and thematic shift from Book 1 to 3. Like Quilligan, Silberman sees Ovid as a crucial subtext for Spenser's figuration of gender and sexuality. Judith H. Anderson's essay elucidates the centrality of the queen in Books 3 and 4 of *The Faerie Queene*, combining the New Historicist focus on the queen as a site of political power in the text and the feminist focus on the queen as a powerful woman. Despite Spenser's apparent encomium of the queen, Anderson detects a "more complexly shaded" representation of Elizabeth as early as Book 3, which prepares the way for the more explicit criticism of the later books.

Book 5, long excoriated and seldom taught (at least in undergraduate courses), has received renewed attention owing to critical interest in politics and history. My own essay on Radigund, while placing Britomart in the tradition of classical epic heroes, deploys anthropological theories of sacrifice and scapegoating to reveal the contradictions in Spenser's so-called "moderate Puritan position," which regarded Elizabeth as the exception to the general prohibition against female sovereignty. Susanne Wofford's essay on giants also investigates the intersection between classical and contemporary contexts—giants as classical figures of rebellion but also as representations of the body politic in civic pageants. She argues for *The Faerie Queene*'s ambivalence toward the giants' destruction, which at once establishes legitimate political order and reveals the function of these violent and grotesque others as versions of the self.

With Richard Helgerson's essay we move from the context of classical epic to that of Italian Renaissance epic. His focus on the politics of literary form, particularly its concern with nation and nationalism, explains his juxtaposition of Spenser with Tasso, rather than with the more familiar Ariosto, whose relationship with Spenser has received much attention in the past.[10] Helgerson contrasts Tasso's subordination of the private to the public and of the romance to the epic with Spenser's continuous deferral in representing a powerful sovereign order. Spenser instead counterposes the chivalric romance and the aristocratic power it celebrates to Tasso's epic telos and its inscription of the modern centralized state.[11]

Two essays on Book 6, one in relation to the pastoral lyric to which Spenser returned and the other in relation to the Mutabilitie Cantos, conclude the volume. Paul Alpers, the author of a body of influential work on Spenser's pastoral, argues that the pastoral form to which Spenser returned at the end of his career, in Book 6 of *The Faerie Queene* and in a series of what Alpers calls "public lyrics"—*Colin Clouts Come Home Againe* and *Prothalamion*—offers alternatives to Spenser's epic endeavor. Alpers's article thus has affinities not only with Montrose's political reading of *The Shepheardes Calender* but also with Parker's focus on the interplay of lyric and epic and its implications for narrative. The selections from Kenneth Gross's book on idolatry and iconoclasm focus on the two endings of the poem—Book 6 and the Mutabilitie Cantos. Gross explicates the Blatant Beast as a "demonic iconoclast" who functions as Spenser's projection of the poem's own violence and aggression. On the other hand, Faunus from the Mutabilitie Cantos Gross calls a "prophetic iconoclast" whose irony and satire offer an alternative to the Beast's indiscriminate destruction at the end of Book 6.

In the preface to his collection, A. C. Hamilton quoted J. E. Hankins's statement that "the 1960s will be remembered as a great period of Spenser scholarship."[12] It is hoped that this volume demonstrates the continuation into the 1980s of what Hamilton called the "developing critical tradition in Spenser studies," especially in its movement to include theoretical and interdisciplinary approaches.

Notes

1. Paul J. Alpers, ed., *Edmund Spenser* (Harmondsworth, England: Penquin, 1969), 179–80.

2. Harry Berger, Jr., ed., *Spenser: A Collection of Critical Essays* (Englewood Cliffs, N.J.: Prentice Hall, 1968), and A. C. Hamilton, ed., *Essential Articles for the Study of Edmund Spenser* (Hamden Conn.: Archon, 1972). For a history of Spenser scholarship, see Herbert E. Cory, *The Critics of Edmund Spenser* (1911; reprint, New York: Haskell House, 1964); Edwin Greenlaw et al., eds., *The Works of Edmund Spenser: A Variorum Edition*, 11 vols. (Baltimore, Md.: Johns Hopkins University Press, 1932–57); Jewel Wurtsbaugh, *Two Centuries of Spenser Scholarship* (Baltimore, Md.: Johns Hopkins University Press, 1936); Paul J. Alpers, ed., *Edmund Spenser* (Harmondsworth, England: Penguin, 1969); R. M. Cummings, ed., *Edmund Spenser: The Critical Heritage* (New York: Barnes & Noble, 1971); and A. C. Hamilton, ed., *The Spenser Encyclopedia* (Toronto: University of Toronto Press, 1990), s.v. "Scholarship, 1579–1932."

3. Berger, introduction to *Spenser*, 1. Berger, however, eschewed a focus on critical method in his collection: "But most commentators worth their salt do not take rigorous stands within classifiable 'positions' except when they are functioning poorly; they work more or less *ad hoc* with whatever equipment they bring to the poem and whatever 'method' they feel any particular poem calls for."

4. Stephen Greenblatt, *Renaissance Self-Fashioning from More to Shakespeare* (Chicago: University of Chicago Press, 1980); the chapter on Spenser is reprinted in this collection. See also his "Murdering Peasants: Status, Genre, and the Representation of Rebellion," *Representations* 1 (February 1983): 1–29. Louis Adrian Montrose, "'The perfecte paterne of a Poete': The Poetics of Courtship in *The Shepheardes Calender*," *Texas Studies in Literature and Language* 21, no. 1 (Spring 1979): 34–67, is partly reprinted in this volume. See also his "Of Gentlemen and Shepherds: The Politics of Elizabethan Pastoral Form," *ELH* 50.3 (Fall 1983): 415–19, and "'Eliza, Queene of shepheardes,' and the Pastoral of Power," *ELR* 10.2 (Spring 1980): 153–82.

5. Anne Lake Prescott and Hugh Maclean, eds., *Edmund Spenser's Poetry: Authoritative Texts and Criticism*, 3rd ed. (New York: Norton, 1993). This edition contains a comprehensive and up-to-date bibliography. The Festschrift for A. C. Hamilton, *Unfolded Tales: Essays on Renaissance Romance*, ed. George M. Logan and Gordon Teskey (Ithaca, N.Y.: Cornell University Press, 1989), contains several important essays on Spenser. In the collection edited by Harold Bloom, *Modern Critical Views: Edmund Spenser* (New York: Chelsea House, 1986), most of the articles come from the 1960s, two from the 1970s, and a handful from the 1980s.

6. Alpers, *Spenser*, 186.

7. Berger's essays have now been collected in *Revisionary Play: Studies in Spenserian Dynamics* (Berkeley and Los Angeles: University of California Press, 1988).

8. This essay originally appeared in a special issue of *South Atlantic Quarterly* entitled "Displacing Homophobia" and now forms part of *Sodometries: Renaissance Texts, Modern Sexualities* (Stanford, Calif.: Stanford University Press, 1992).

9. This essay has been incorporated into *The Poem's Two Bodies: The Poetics of the 1590 "Faerie Queene"* (Princeton, N.J.: Princeton University Press, 1988).

10. See especially Paul J. Alpers, *The Poetry of the Faerie Queene* (Princeton, N.J.: Princeton University Press, 1967), 160–99.

11. This essay now forms part of *Forms of Nationhood: The Elizabethan Writing of England* (Chicago: University of Chicago Press, 1992), which won the 1992 James Russell Lowell Prize awarded by the Modern Language Association.

12. *Essential Articles*, xi.

The Shepheardes Calender

◆

"The perfecte paterne of a Poete": The Poetics of Courtship in *The Shepheardes Calender*[1]

Louis Adrian Montrose

First among the verses which commend Spenser's heroic poem to its royal audience is Ralegh's graceful vision of "The grave, where Laura lay":

> All suddenly I saw the Faery Queene:
> At whose approach the soule of *Petrarke* wept,
> And from thenceforth those graces were not seene.
> For they this Queene attended; in whose steed
> Oblivion laid him downe on *Lauras* herse.[2]

Ralegh envisions Spenser as overgoing not Vergil or Chaucer but Petrarch—not the epic poet of the *Africa* but the visionary love poet of the *Canzoniere* and *Trionfi*. The Faerie Queene supplants Laura as the supreme image of the poet-lover's power to sublimate desire. Ralegh does not envision *The Faerie Queene* as an exemplary heroic poem but as the verbal courtship of an exalted female whose patronage can satisfy the poet's material ambitions and whose Idea is a spur to his moral and poetic aspirations. In other words,

From *Texas Studies in Literature and Language* 21, no. 1 (March 1979): 34–67. © 1979 by the University of Texas Press. Reprinted by permission of the author and the University of Texas Press.

Ralegh is suggesting that *The Faerie Queene* and his own *Cynthia* poems are parallel in strategy and purpose. Spenser had declared a public, Vergilian vocation in his *Letter* to Ralegh; by transforming Spenser's declaration into intimate Petrarchan terms, Ralegh illuminates a characteristic stance of the Spenserian persona: a humble poet celebrates a sublime female figure—a Petrarchan mistress, great lady, goddess, or saint. This *topos* is a conspicuous one in Spenser's poetry. He uses it to express a dialectic of poetic aspirations and constraints, to articulate his awareness of a discrepancy between the myth of the Poet's high calling and the functions to which his skills are relegated in his own society. These Spenserian preoccupations appear in incipient form in *The Shepheardes Calender*, shadowed in the pastoral simplifications of Colin Clout's "great misadventure in Love" (*Aprill*, Argument). My object is to explore the implications of Ralegh's conceit for an understanding of Colin's role in the *Calender*. Colin's courtships unfold a sequence exemplifying "the perfecte paterne of a Poete" set forth in the dialogue of *October*. He enacts an amorous courtship of Rosalind, a social courtship of Eliza, a spiritual courtship of Dido. Each of Colin's wooings is also Spenser's exploration of a particular mode of poetic power and form; each is a manifestation of the arduous courtship of the Muse.

I

In *The Shepheardes Calender*, Spenser inventories and analyzes the heritage of the English poet; he assesses the aims and resources, the limitations and dangers, of the poetic vocation. The poem is a vehicle for the highest personal aspirations and public significance a poet can claim: a vatic role, sanctioned by the artistic and ethical idealism of Renaissance Humanism but frustrated by the constraints of a social order controlled by powers for whom poetry is, at worst, morally corrupting and politically subversive; at best, a useful instrument of policy or an innocuous diversion. Colin's courtships of Rosalind, Eliza, and Dido are permutations of the *Calender*'s recurrent attempt to transform language into power, to animate the word as a force in the world, to create the personal and social harmony which, for Renaissance poets and rhetoricians, is figured in the responsiveness of nature to the music of Orpheus.

The Shepheardes Calender is something more than a skillful poetic restatement of ethical, political, and religious orthodoxies. Its publication in 1579 demonstrated the capacity of the vernacular to produce a poetry "well grounded, finely framed, and strongly trussed up together" (Epistle). Spenser's conspicuous concern with the creation and projection of a poetic persona and his thematic emphasis on erotic desire and social ambition proffered to readers a range of verbal strategies that could give formal expression to the complexity and ambivalence of an emergent generational consciousness. The *Calender*'s catalytic power is attested by the vigorous growth of an Elizabethan pastoral tradition in its wake; by its immediate and continued popularity during the 1580s and 1590s; and by other poets' elevation of Spenser's Colin to the status of *genius loci* in their pastoral worlds. Colin is a poet, lover, and courtier; a would-be mover of trees and waters, mistresses and rulers, in a world in which the degree of success to which he aspires is beyond reach.[3] Colin can be identified neither as a simple allegorical projection of Spenser nor as a pathetic and unenlightened antithesis to his sage and serious creator. "Immerito," the persona of the poet who has written the *Calender*, presents himself within the eclogues in the persona of "Colin Clout." "Touching the generall dryft and purpose" of Immerito's self-presentation, E. K. writes that "his unstayed yougth had long wandred in the common Labyrinth of Love, in which time to mitigate and allay the heate of his passion, or els to warne (as he sayth) the young shepheards .s. his equals and companions of his unfortunate folly, he compiled these xii Aeglogues" (Epistle). Colin's pattern of prodigality and misfortune has its origin precisely in his successful embrace of the Renaissance poet's pastoral role; the literary shepherd's otiose environment of eroticism and poetry is being viewed through the stern spectacles of Tudor patriarchal morality. In a Reformation society whose ideology reinforces strict control by personal, political, academic, and ecclesiastical fathers, sexual passion and love poetry signify waste and idleness, a dangerous lack of bodily and spiritual self-discipline, a potential threat of insubordination and rebellion.[4]

The Vergilian progression puts pastoral at the beginning of the poet's career; the principle of decorum puts it at the bottom of the hierarchy of poetic kinds. Pastoral is persistently associated with new poets and with poets who are young. In the Epistle to the *Calender*, E. K. speculates on Immerito's motives for writing eclogues:

> doubting perhaps his habilitie, which he little needed, or mynding to furnish our tongue with this kinde, wherin it faulteth, or following the example of the best and most auncient Poetes, which devised this kind of wryting, being both so base for the matter, and homely for the manner, at the first to trye theyr habilities: and as young birdes, that be newly crept out of the nest, by little first to prove theyr tender wyngs, before they make a greater flyght. . . . So finally flyeth this our new Poete, as a bird, whose principals be scarce growen out, but yet as that in time shall be hable to keepe wing with the best.

This conjunction of humility and pride exemplifies the pastoral poet's capacity to strike ambivalent poses. Spenser articulates a tense relationship to literary and social patriarchy shared by many in his literary generation: poetic progenitors have shaped a literary tradition within which the new poet must find a place by creative imitation; the elder Tudor generation has shaped and still controls the social institutions and cultural values within which the young, educated gentleman or would-be gentleman must live and write and try to advance himself.

Tensions between generations and between cultural values that are observable in later Elizabethan society are mirrored in the uneasy mixture of two currents within the *Calender.* Spenser's moral eclogues persistently oppose youth and age, ambition and contentment, recklessness and caution, insolence and deference, eroticism and asceticism. The youthful figures in the moral eclogues manifest crude analogues of Colin's refined obsessions, though they can in no way emulate his verbal skill. E. K.'s Epistle suggests that the way to unify one's moral experience of this heterogeneous poem is to read the relationship between Immerito and Colin in terms of the moral eclogues' dichotomies: the sage, serious, and mature moral poet confronts and condemns the image of his own unstayed youth, turning the unfortunate folly of his past to the public good and redeeming poetry from wantonness. But the debates in the moral eclogues are between limited perspectives.[5] Spenser does not provide an easy validation of his reader's stock homiletic responses; he encourages them to interpret and evaluate dialectically. The relationship between Immerito and Colin involves a similar strategy. Spenser's work fuses the sober Tudor Humanism of his rigorous formal education at the Merchant Taylors' School and Cambridge with the elegant romanticism, restless expansiveness, and troubled introspection that characterize the later Elizabethan cultural milieu. In both *The Shepheardes Calender* and *The Faerie Queene,* Spenser attempts to transcend the cultural opposition that he is articulating; the poems repeatedly evidence the strains and contradictions involved in this attempt. In *The Faerie Queene,* erotic and poetic fertility come to be celebrated as complementary heroic virtues that have emanated from the pastoral environments of The Garden of Adonis and Mount Acidale. But Spenser must continue to defend his celebratory vision against "these Stoicke censors" (*FQ,* IV. Proem. 3) and against The Blatant Beast. Colin's life within the *Calender* projects a poetic vocation of the kind upon which Spenser himself is ambitiously embarking—but one which runs its course toward that failure which the aspiring minds of Elizabethan society are forever being warned to expect. Spenser readies for his greater flight by apprising himself of its hazards, not by eliminating them.

II

E. K. divides the eclogues "into three formes or ranckes. For eyther they be Plaintive . . . or recreative, such as al those be, which conceive matter of love, or commendation of special personages, or Moral: which for the most part be mixed with some Satyrical bitternesse" (Generall Argument). The eclogues that E. K. classifies as "Moral" depict potential conflicts between narrow self-interest and common profit, and explore the difficulty of creating an effective, morally motivated rhetoric to do battle against the perversions of language that can mislead the susceptible human will. "Recreative" poetry is celebratory. It commends the virtue of its subject and signifies a harmonious relationship between subject and poet; it creates a joyful circumstance in which poetry itself can be celebrated. "Complaint" is the poetry of frustrated desire, unfulfilled longing, alienation; it is a protest against an irremediable reality that obtrudes into a vision of happiness, harmony, perfection. Colin's complaints bemoan the absence, loss, or irretrievability of the recreative state in its idealized personal form, as the fulfillment of sexual love. The refinements of mood and expression in Colin's plaintive poetry transform its subject—the loss of recreative experi- ence—into a new form of recreative experience; the frustration of erotic desire offers an occasion for the perfection of imaginative form. Colin is not the image of a man in history but rather the image of a poet in literary history. He experiences the joys and sorrows of aspiration and suffers conflict and desire in the intimate terms of love and poetry. It is largely through Colin's experience that Spenser relates poetics to the other forms of verbal expression and coercion that the *Calender* mirrors. The moral mode complements the plaintive, for it originates in the denial or loss of erotic recreation's authentic social form: a community organized on the principle and practice of charity.

Immerito begins his cycle of eclogues with Colin's plaintive invoca- tion: "Ye Gods of love, that pittie lovers payne, / (If any gods the paine of lovers pittie:)," and with the initial allusion to the poem's underlying plaintive/recreative myth: "And Pan thou shepheards God, that once didst love, / Pitie the paines, that thou thy selfe didst prove" (*Januarye*, 13–14, 17–18). Pan is an archetype of the creative power of the human spirit, for he accomplishes his own transformation of what the Olympian gods have already transformed: Syrinx is metamorphosed into reeds; Pan makes a musical instrument from the reeds, turns nature into art, creates culture.[6] Pan brings forth music from the artifact he has made; he is able to transform erotic frustration into the consolation of an art that can recreate the senses and the spirit, that can turn the plaintive into the recreative and turn sorrow into celebration.

In *Januarye*, the irony of Colin's situation is that he is unable to transform the pain of love into the plaintive solace of poetic creation. Colin's poetry has been the expression of his love and the medium of his courtship. The disappointment of his erotic aspirations manifests the rhetorical failure of his erotic poetry: "She deignes not my good will, but doth reprove, / And of my rurall musick holdeth scorne" (63–64). The pain of longing and denial impels Petrarchan creativity, but it renders Colin poetically sterile:

> Wherefore my pype, albee rude *Pan* thou please,
> Yet for thou pleasest not, where most I would:
> And thou unlucky Muse, that wontst to ease
> My musing mynd, yet canst not, when thou should:
> Both pype and Muse, shall sore the while abye.
>
> (67–71)

It is conventional for oncoming night to end an eclogue. Here nightfall implies an ironic relationship between Colin and Apollo: "So broke his oaten pype, and downe dyd lye. / By that, the welked *Phoebus* gan availe" (72–73). The transition from "rude *Pan*" to "the welked *Phoebus*" is the *Calender*'s initial, oblique allusion to the singing contest between Pan and Apollo. It suggests Colin's failure to accomplish a critical vocational transition from the pastoral already mastered and outgrown to the higher poetic calling which remains above his reach. Colin's Apollonian aspirations are frustrated, and this frustration is beyond the powers of Pan to sublimate into recreative pastoral art.[7]

III

The *Aprill* eclogue, which E. K. classifies as "Recreative," interrelates "matter of love" and "commendation of special personages," transforms sexual into social courtship, and connects the celebratory mode to the plaintive and moral modes which frame Colin's lay by providing the circumstances of its performance and reception. It is a historical circumstance of immense political and cultural significance that, for the second half of the sixteenth century, England's sovereign is a virgin queen who is governor of both state and church, and whose personal mythology is contrived to be a national and Protestant substitute for a cult of the Blessed Virgin. One literary consequence is the production of royal encomia which assimilate to the public celebration of an earthly ruler both the sacred psalm or hymn of praise and the private love sonnet, which itself was often classed as a species of encomiastic poetry.[8] The relationship between courtier-poet and Queen is idealized as a love that has been purified of physical desire; its erotic energy has been transformed into art and service. The public ritualizations of intimate relationship in encomia of Elizabeth serve effectively as instruments of policy, as romantic mystifications of the motives of the Queen and her councillors. But they can also function as idealizations of the motives of courtier-poets. The rhetoric of royal encomium provides an allowable occasion for the cultivation of love poetry, and a purified medium for the pursuit of socio-economic advancement. The Elizabeth cult can serve the personal aesthetic and material ends of her worshippers.

The crux of the *Aprill* eclogue's strategy is in the second stanza of Colin's song. Here the poet metamorphoses an Ovidian aetiology into a Tudor genealogy: "For shee is *Syrinx* daughter without spotte, / Which *Pan* the shepheards God of her begot" (50–51). E. K. glosses Pan variously as God, Christ, and Henry VIII. Spenser's myth alludes to the immaculate conception of a blessed virgin, cleverly countering Catholic insinuations of Elizabeth's bastardy with an insinuation of her divinity. If we follow out the Ovidian logic of the myth, which E. K. retells concisely in his gloss, it becomes obvious that Elisa is also a personification of pastoral poetry: the "offspring" of the love chase and the nymph's transformation were the reeds from which Pan created his pipe.[9] The myth of *Aprill* is a variation on the myth of *Januarye.*

Sannazaro, one of the "excellent . . . Poetes, whose foting this Author every where followeth" (Epistle), has re-created the myth of the origins and history of pastoral poetry in the Tenth Prose of his *Arcadia.* There the shepherds are led to a sacred grove by a priest who is the genius of the pastoral world. They see a great pipe of seven reeds hung up before a cave: it is the pipe of Pan. The priest narrates the myth of Syrinx's metamorphosis and Pan's creation of the pipes from the reeds into which she had been changed, the descent of the pipes into the hands of Theocritus ("a shepherd of Syracuse") and thence into the hands of Vergil ("Mantuan Tityrus"). The priest alludes to Vergil's fourth eclogue: the celebration of an unborn child and a new age of peace and plenty, subsequently interpreted as a prophecy of the Advent of Christ. The priest concludes by recounting Vergil's restlessness within the pastoral's narrow and lowly confines, and his progression from eclogues through georgics to epic. The implication of the episode is that the pipes of Pan have passed into the hands of Sincero, Sannazaro's Petrarchan persona, who is only sojourning in the pastoral world.

Spenser's fourth eclogue incorporates and complicates Sannazaro's strategy; it re-creates the myth of Pan and Syrinx in the context of a royal encomium which is being advanced as an English and Protestant fulfillment of Vergil's fourth eclogue. The myth of Elisa's generation from the union of Pan and Syrinx is a re-creation of the original Ovidian myth, in which the desire for sexual union was first frustrated, then sublimated into a union of Pan's breath with the reeds into which Syrinx had been changed. The subject of Colin's recreative encomium is an act of poetic re-creation. The first stanza is an invocation to the Muses; the second stanza expresses the conception of an image through a genealogical procreation myth; in the third stanza, the unfolding of the image commences with the imperative, "See, where she sits upon the grassie greene" (55); the final stanza bids the perfected image to go forth into the world, to be received by the Queen: "Now ryse up *Elisa*, decked as thou art, / in royall array" (145–146). The poet has transformed *Eliza* into *Elisa*. Elisa, the special personage which has been the subject of his celebration, he commends to Elizabeth, the special personage from whom he hopes a commendation in return: "Let dame *Eliza* thanke you for her song" (150). Spenser emphasizes Elisa's status as an ideal image created by the poet, rather than her status as a poetic reflection of Elizabeth: "So sprong her grace / Of heavenly race, / No mortall blemishe may her blotte" (52–54). The effect is to discriminate the ideal image from the actual personage who is the nominal subject of celebration.

The genealogical myth is repeated from a different perspective in the seventh stanza, the numerical center of the encomium:

> *Pan* may be proud, that ever he begot
>   such a Bellibone,
> And *Syrinx* rejoyse, that ever was her lot
>   to bear such an one.
> Soone as my younglings cryen for the dam,
> To her will I offer a milkwhite Lamb:
>   Shee is my goddesse plaine,
>   And I her shepherds swayne,
> Albee forswonck and forswatt I am.
>
>   (91–99)

The lowly pastoral deities, shepherd-poet and muse, have engendered a great goddess. The poet shifts into a suppliant style of courtship. At the center of the idealizing form within which the poet has boldly re-created the human personage of Elizabeth in his own inspired image, the courtier humbly worships his Queen. In *Aprill*, the triumphant first occurrence of the myth of Pan and Syrinx blazes the praise of the Orphic poet who articulates a vision of perfection toward which humanity may strive. In its poignant recurrence, the myth ushers in a pastoral image of the poet's status in the actual social order; it suggests the subservience of poetic to political power, and the poet's economic dependency on the patronage system manipulated by the Queen and her regime. The poet's gift is a rhetorically powerful symbolic form, an illusion that sanctifies political power; the poet's expectation is a reciprocal, material benefit. Spenser qualifies a visionary conception of poetry by placing it within the context of his own historical and social existence and by expressing it as the erotic idealization of a power relationship.

Colin's "laye of Fayre *Elisa*" is a poem-within-a-poem, a framed performance; the responses of the fictional auditors within the eclogue condition the reader's responses to Colin's song. According to its prefatory "Argument," the eclogue's intention is encomiastic; it is recreative, in E. K.'s sense of the term, and its subject is the Queen. Within the eclogue's fiction, however, Hobbinoll's purpose in singing Colin's song is to celebrate not the subject but the poet, not Elisa but Colin. The occasion of composition was recreative but the occasion which gives rise to Hobbinoll's performance is plaintive. The poem lives in the memory of those who have heard and admired it; it is now a public trust, a document of cultural history. The poet himself is now lost in love melancholy, alienated from his creative sources and from the society which he has endowed: "Hys pleasaunt Pipe, whych made us meriment, / He wylfully hath broke" (14–15). In the ambiguous commentary of the shepherds which follows Colin's song, Spenser insinuates that Colin's relationships to Rosalind and Eliza are permutations of an underlying problematic of desire:

THENOT.

Ane was thilk same song of *Colins* owne making?
Ah foolish boy, that is with love yblent:
Great pittie is, he be in such taking,
For a naught caren, that been so lewdly bent.

HOBBINOLL.

Sicker I hold him, for the greater fon,
That loves the thing, he cannot purchase.

(154–59)

The poetic power manifested in the song is now lost because love for Rosalind is debilitating. But there is also the implication that the song *itself* was the manifestation of a reckless aspiration for which Colin now suffers. Within the fiction of the *Aprill* eclogue, Colin's recreative song is being revived in a plaintive pastoral world where love breeds pain as well as joy. *Januarye's* plaintiveness provides the context for our experience of *Aprill's* recreation.

. . . .

IV

The thematic nucleus of the *October* eclogue is formed out of the poet's inability effectively to refashion his audience "in vertuous and gentle discipline," and his failure to elicit the gracious and bountiful thanks which the ideals of courtesy proclaim to be his due. Colin's plaintiveness is parodied in the disappointment impeding Cuddie's production of the verbal confections that pleasure his fellow shepherds. Like Colin's love songs, Cuddie's rhymes and riddles have not elicited from their audience the return which his own poetic gift was devised to procure:

The dapper ditties, that I wont devise,
To feede youthes fancie, and the flocking fry,
Delighten much: what I the bett for thy?
They han the pleasure, I a sclender prise.

(13–16)

Cuddie is a purely recreative versifier; his appeal to the baser instincts of youth befits the baseness of his own conception of the poet's proper reward.[10]

Piers responds to Cuddie's complaint with the moralized Elizabethan defense of poetry and poets: the right poet is a persuader to virtue who seeks only the reward of honor. This initial opposition of poetic stereotypes—purely recreative and debased by materialistic ambitions; purely moral and elevated by virtuous aspirations—generates a dialectic of reformulated positions at successively higher generic levels. The absolute values of the initial positions become more ambivalent as the dialogue unfolds. Cuddie's first response is to deflate Piers' idealism by a commonsensical insistence on life's material necessities:

> But who rewards him ere the more for thy?
> Or feedes him once the fuller by a graine?
> Sike prayse is smoke, that sheddeth in the skye,
> Sike words bene wynd, and wasten soone in vayne.
> (33–36)

Piers' counter-response is to counsel poetic aspirations synonymous with vicarious social elevation: the more elevated the poetic kind, the more elite its subjects and audience. Cuddie is advised to abandon "the base and viler clowne," whom Piers has previously declared to be the object of the moral poet's reforming power. Now Cuddie is to sing of love and war in an encomiastic epic which celebrates the heroic virtue of Eliza and "the worthy whome shee loveth best" (47)—Elizabeth and Leicester, as E. K.'s gloss informs us.

As the poet's subject becomes more exalted, his audience more powerful, and his own chance for fame and material reward more tangible, his Orphic powers become correspondingly confined. The higher the poet aspires, the more he becomes encomiast rather than teacher and reformer. The idealistic Piers attributes this phenomenon to the identity of moral and social hierarchies. The crucial change conditioning the poetic subject is in the nature of the poet's audience: the base and vile clown must be instructed; virtuous and gentle lords and princes elicit only praise. The modern poet's situation is seen from a less idealizing perspective in *The Teares of the Muses*. There Polyhymnia laments the Elizabethan poet's decline in power from his prototypes:

> Whilom in ages past none might professe
> But Princes and high Priests that secret skill,
> The sacred lawes therein they wont expresse,
> And with deepe Oracles their verses fill:
> Then was shee held in soveraigne dignitie,
> And made the noursling of Nobilitie.
> But now nor Prince nor Priest doth her maintayne.
> (*TM*, 559–65)

In the beginning was the word. In an ideal mythic past, poetry was the profession of society's leaders; and, by implication, poets enjoyed the perquisites of a social elite. Intellectual and imaginative power were then synonymous with political and metaphysical power. The historical conditions of Spenser's society have reduced the Poet-Priest to an inferior and dependent position in relation to the aristocratic patron and poetaster.

Queen Elizabeth, of course, is lauded as "Most peereles Prince, most peereles Poetresse" (577). And

> Some few beside, this sacred skill esteme,
> Admirers of her glorious excellence,
> Which being lightened with her beawties beme,
> Are thereby fild with happie influence:
> And lifted up above the worldes gaze,
> To sing with Angels her immortall praize.
>
> (*TM*, 583–88)

The Queen's perfection inspires the poet's praise—but does not the poet's praise create her perfection? A rhetorical strategy of the encomiastic poet is to establish his own greatness through his praise of the prince's greatness. Becoming one with the angels, he restores to himself the title of high priest. Yet the wailing burden of *The Teares of the Muses* is that the poet's claim to his inheritance goes unrecognized, and that its material fruits are not forthcoming. The Muse of epic, Calliope, laments,

> For noble Peeres whom I was wont to raise,
> Now onely seke for pleasure, nought for praise.
>
> Their great revenues all in sumptuous pride
> They spend, that nought to learning they may spare;
> and the rich fee which Poets wont divide,
> Now Parasites and Sycophants doo share.
>
> (*TM*, 467–72)

In the clear view from Parnassus, the Muse can distinguish Sycophant and Poet as antitheses; for the poet who invokes his queen as his muse, the distinction becomes profoundly problematic.

Cuddie's response to Piers in *October* echoes the complaint of Calliope in *The Teares of the Muses*. The patronage of Maecenas drew Vergil from pastoral and georgic to the epic song of which Augustus was worthy. But the moral virtue which was once synonymous with temporal power has fallen off:

> But after vertue gan for age to stoupe,
> And mighty manhode brought a bedde of ease:
> The vaunting Poets found nought worth a pease,
> To put in preace among the learned troupe.
> Tho gan the streames of flowing wittes to cease,
> And sonnebright honour pend in shamefull coupe.
> And if that any buddes of Poesie,

Yet of the old stocke gan to shoote agayne:
Or it mens follies mote be forst to fayne,
And rolle with rest in rymes of rybaudrye:
Or as it sprong, it wither must agayne:
Tom Piper makes us better melodie.

(67–78)

Cuddie implies that, at least in part, the debasement of poetry into idle fripperies is the result of the political and socioeconomic constraints placed upon the poet. The predicament of the heroic poet in the present age is that he has no subject worthy of celebration and is not free to reprehend his audience so as to refashion them into subjects worthy of praise. Heroic poetry's lack of a worthy subject becomes the subject of moral pastoral mixed with some satirical bitterness. Such pastorals must use allegory, "to insinuate and glaunce at greater matters, and such as perchance had not bene safe to have beene disclosed in any other sort."[11] In *A Discourse of English Poetrie* (1586), William Webbe lauds the *Calender* as the equal of Vergil's *Eclogues*, and calls Spenser "the rightest English Poet that ever I read." In addition to its "many good Morall lessons . . . there is also much matter uttered somewhat covertly, especially the abuses of some whom he would not be too playne withall: in which, though it be not apparent to every one what hys speciall meaning was, yet so skillfully is it handled, as any man may take much delight at hys learned conveyance, and pick out much good sense in the most obscurest of it."[12] Allegory is not only a veil to prevent the profanation of spiritual mysteries but also an obfuscation of meaning and intention necessary to circumvent governmental hostility to all expressions of dissent or controversy.

. . . .

V

The pastoral elegy sung by Colin in *November* is filled with echoes of the previous eclogues in which he has had a role. Thenot urges Colin to awake his sorrowful Muse, "Whether thee list thy loved lasse advaunce, / or honor *Pan* with hymnes of higher vaine" (7–8). But Colin remains steadfast in his rejection of the recreative, Panic persona: "Thenot, now nis the time of merimake. / Nor *Pan* to herye, nor with love to playe" (9–10). In challenging Colin to overgo his performance of the *August* sestina (43–46), Thenot is also challenging him to transcend the situation that the sestina distills. The *Aprill* lay and the *August* sestina were rehearsed by other shepherds because Colin no longer sang; the *November* elegy is a spontaneous creation sung by Colin in the eclogue's narrative present. Colin now refrains from the sublimated eroticism of *Aprill* and the frustrated eroticism of *August.* In this public performance, the poet includes himself within the poem among those who have been formed into a community of mourners by Dido's death: "So well she couth the shepherds entertayne, / . . . Als *Colin cloute* she would not once disdayne" (95–101). Dido is remembered as a public fulfillment of the private audience Rosalind refused to be: "She deignes not my good will, but doth reprove, / And of my rurall music, holdeth scorne" (*Januarye*, 63–64); and as a courteous and bounteous fulfillment of the public audience that Colin hoped Eliza would be: "Let dame *Eliza* thanke you for her song" (*Aprill*, 150).

Why is the subject of this crucial elegy within Spenser's neo-Vergilian poem named Dido? The *November* eclogue has been thought to be an obscure topical allegory. It has been proposed that, because Vergil's Dido is also named Elissa, Spenser's Elisa and Dido are projections of Elizabeth.[13] Little attention has otherwise been paid to the significance of the name change in Spenser's imitation of Marot's *elegie* for Loyse de Savoye. The effect, however, is to make Spenser's pastoral elegy a conspicuous allusion to and revision of the critical episode of recreative truancy in Vergil's epic. Vergil's Dido embodies all those passionate, private needs and desires that must be repudiated by the hero who is destined to refound civilization on principles of law and reason; Aeneas' private person must be subsumed by the public role and its collective burdens. After her suicide, Dido wanders among the shades of other unfortunate lovers in the fields of mourning. Aeneas passes the fields of mourning on his journey to the Elysian fields, the exclusive preserve of heroes, where he is to receive prophetic knowledge from the spirit of his father. Aeneas greets Dido and is spurned by her; she is now reunited with her first husband. In the *November* elegy, Colin's Dido has found her own rightful place in the field of heroes, where the poet hopes to join her. Dido's apotheosis inspires in Colin the desire for a transcendent object which will make him one of the community of saints:

> I see thee blessed soule, I see,
> Walke in *Elisian* fieldes so free.
>   O happy herse,
> Might I once come to thee (O that I might)
>   O joyful verse.
>
> (179–82)

Spenser's is a Christian elegy, whose Elysian fields figure the heavenly bliss of blessed souls. *November's* Christian poetry is a revision of both Vergil's *Aeneid* and Spenser's Vergilian *Aprill*, of both pagan imperial epic and Anglican dynastic eclogue. Elisa upon her "grassie greene," an idealizing pastoral emblem of Elizabethan England, is succeeded by Dido in the *"Elisian* fieldes so free," a vision of the spiritual reality Elisa is claimed to prefigure. "Fayre *Eliza*, Queen of shepheardes all," reigns at the center of *Aprill*; "Christ, the very God of all shepheards," reigns at the center of *Maye*. In *November*, Dido "raignes a goddesse now emong the saintes, / That whilome was the saynt of shepheards light" (175–76).[14] The "forswonck and forswatt" *Aprill* celebrant no longer looks for patronage from one who is far above him in the social hierarchy but for a communion of transfigured souls. The great reversal upward that is the central strategy of Christian elegy—"Dido nis dead, but into heaven hent. / O happye herse" (169–70)—follows immediately upon the revelation that worldly ambition is the pursuit of an illusion. Colin's vision of Dido's apotheosis does not provide him with an image to be adored but rather with a model to be emulated. The strategy of the elegy is to transform the "earthlie mould" of a literal Dido into a symbolic vehicle of the poet's own aspiration. In his creation of the *November* elegy, Colin enacts "the perfecte paterne of a Poete" that Piers had advanced in *October*: "Then make thee winges of thine aspyring wit, / And, whence thou camst, flye backe to heaven apace." Colin now sings in a visionary, prophetic mode that leaves the courtships of Rosalind and Eliza behind.

The sequence of Colin's presences in the *Calender* explores the problematics of poetic vocation. These explorations constitute a progression that culminates in *November*'s revaluation of the whole enterprise in the light of eternity. *Januarye* sets out the framing biographical fiction of Colin's erotic frustration and the Pan/Syrinx and Pan/Apollo myths that inform his imaginative life. Colin attempts to deal with his Rosalind-problem by emulating Pan's metamorphosis of life into art; his failure suggests that Pan's resources and pastoral's range are inadequate effectively to manage complex human needs. Colin rejects his vocation as recreative pastoral poet by breaking his pipe. The song re-created in *Aprill* returns us to an earlier recreative state; Pan's powers had then been sufficient for Colin to enact symbolically a genealogical myth of metamorphosis *within* a pastoral world. At the outset of the *November* eclogue, Colin keeps to his *Januarye* vow: he will sing neither of Rosalind nor Pan. Through his power to enact symbolically a myth of sacrifice and apotheosis that *transcends* the pastoral world, he demonstrates his progression toward a higher kind of poetry and his emulation of a higher poetic genius.

In *November*, Colin spurns Pan's paradigm of metamorphosis:

> The sonne of all the world is dimme and darke:
> The earth now lacks her wonted light,
> And all we dwell in deadly night,
>   O heavie herse.
> Breake we our pypes, that shrild as lowde as Larke,
>   O carefull verse.
>
>   (68–72)

The poem's repetition of the breaking of the pipe re-emphasizes the inadequacy of Pan's myth of change and fixity. But the conditions of separation from the beloved object are more radical than before: the context is neither the lady's refusal nor her metamorphosis but her physical extinction. The poem is in the process of articulating a sacred mystery of death and rebirth that can guarantee not merely displacement and consolation but rejoicing and the expectation of a sanctified future union. In *Januarye*, Colin is symbolically associated with a declining Phoebus. In *November*, Colin builds his elegy by transfiguring solar myth into Christological symbol:

> She hath the bonds broke of eternall night,
> Her soule unbodied of the burdenous corpse.
> . . . .
> Dido nis head, but into heaven hent.
>   O happye herse,
> Cease now my Muse, now cease they sorrowes sourse,
>   O joyfull verse.
>
>   (165–66, 169–72)

In turning from Rosalind-Eliza to Dido, Colin turns from Pan to Apollo-Christ, a greater Pan. "O heavie herse . . . O carefull verse" is transformed into "O happye herse . . . O joyfull verse" at the point at which the poet's spirit is liberated from the lure of the mutable earthly things that have held it in its ceaseless cycle of desire and frustration. *November* is the antitype of *Januarye*; it records the authentic spiritual experience that the aesthetic paganism of *Januarye* merely adumbrates. Complaint becomes Recreation through an act of transfiguration, through the spiritual re-creation of subject, singer, and audience.

VI

E. K.'s hybrid "Recreative" category—"matter of love or commendation of special personages"—is an explicit acknowledgment of the analogy of sexual and social modes of literary courtship. Eliza and Rosalind are realizations of the dual aspect of the Petrarchan mistress: Eliza of her virtue and purity, which are the source of the lover's aspiration and the poet's inspiration but which, at the same time, put her beyond his reach; Rosalind, of her cruelty and pride, which frustrate the lover and inhibit the poet. Underlying the encomiastic song of *Aprill* is a tension between the poet's power to create and control an ideal image within his poem and his dependency upon the actual personage whom it perfects. This paradox of power and powerlessness characterizes Colin's plaintive state. Spenser is exploring the metaphorical transactions between the private poetry of love and the public poetry of praise, and he uses them in such a way as to reveal the rhetorical principles upon which personal and political relations are organized in courtly society.

In the fictional experience of Colin Clout, the political and the personal are superficially characterized as the pure and polluted forms of erotic relationship; each is more ambivalent than its conventionalized presentation implies. As lover, Colin is thrall to the cruel Rosalind, but he struggles to purge his plaintiveness by re-creating it as plaintive poetry. As courtier, Colin re-creates Elizabeth's ideal image within the forms of celebratory poetry but he remains wholly impotent to effect a re-creation of poetic vision as a social fact. The breakthrough that occurs in the *November* elegy is the verbal enactment of a rite of transition. The problematic carnal and political complexities of Rosalind and Eliza are separated out from the pure spirit of Dido through the sacramental symbolism of death and rebirth. The poet uses the lady as a sacrificial victim, to mediate between his present "trustlesse state of earthly things, and slipper hope" (153) and his desired future "in *Elisian* fields so free" (179).

In Petrarch's *Canzoniere*, as in Dante's *Vita Nuova*, the lady's death is the turning point in the poet-lover's life and in its poetic record. That death makes possible, or symbolizes, the resolution of a war between the antithetical inclinations of body and spirit that has wracked the lover during the lady's lifetime. The lady's sublimation into spirit brings about the lover's purification by obliterating the object of his earthly desires. Few Elizabethan sonnet cycles elaborate the spiritual aspect of the lady and in none does she die. But these elements of the Petrarchan experience are present in *The Shepheardes Calender*—which precedes the main wave of Elizabethan sonnets by over a decade—as aspects of the spiritual biography of Colin Clout. Colin yearns for the recovery of a mode of relationship which is truly recreative, which is based on love rather than on power, and is grounded in a spiritual model of creaturely communion rather than in a sociopolitical model of strict hierarchical statuses. Colin's elegy for Dido is a displacement of the Rosalind-Eliza problem in which Spenser attempts a radical solution by symbolic means: kill the lady, thus sending her spirit to heaven, where the lover's spirit might hope eventually to join her in a communion free from the accidents and constraints that characterize earthly life—life within the body and the body politic. The tensions and contradictions underlying the plaintive and moral impulses of the shepherds in Spenser's *Calender* are versions of an essential thematic antithesis that the Renaissance imagination habitually embodies in pastoral form. Dissatisfactions with the way things are can be assuaged by the artistic generation of pastoral counter-worlds. But the act of imaginative transformation is always suspect—potentially dangerous, escapist, or regressive. The "transcendence" achieved by Colin's *November* elegy is an ambiguous, melancholic, and symbolic remedy for actual problems. To make poetry a vehicle of transcendence is tacitly to acknowledge its ethical and political impotence.

Notes

1. The reading text of a paper based on an earlier version of this study has been published on microfiche in *Spenser at Kalamazoo: Proceedings from a Special Session at the Thirteenth Conference on Medieval Studies in Kalamazoo, Michigan, May 5-6, 1978,* ed., David A. Richardson (Cleveland, 1978), 254–266. I am grateful to those who have heard or read versions of this study and have improved it by their comments; above all, I thank Thomas K. Dunseath.

2. References are to the often reprinted one-volume *Oxford Standard Authors* edition of Spenser's *Poetical Works,* eds., J. C. Smith and E. De Selincourt. In quotations from this and other Elizabethan texts, I have modified obsolete typographical conventions.

3. The ambiguous mixture of progress and failure that characterizes Colin's life within the *Calender* has led to various critical perspectives. Readings which emphasize rigorous moral choices between fleshly and spiritual values rely upon a distinction between Colin's mutable, spiritually unfulfilled existence within the eclogues and the order, harmony, and plenitude of being figured in the encompassing calendrical form: See Robert Allen Durr, "Spenser's Calendar of Christian Time," *ELH,* 24 (1957), 269–295; S. K. Heninger, Jr., "The Implications of Form for *The Shepheardes Calender,*" *Studies in the Renaissance,* 9 (1962), 309–321; Isabel G. MacCaffrey, "Allegory and Pastoral in *The Shepheardes Calender,*" *ELH,* 36 (1969), 88–109; Michael Murrin, *The Veil of Allegory* (Chicago, 1969), 156–163. A. C. Hamilton's classic essay, "The Argument of Spenser's *Shepheardes Calender,*" *ELH,* 23 (1956), 171–183, emphasizes the ethics of Christian Humanism rather than theology and eschatology: Colin's appearances enact a rejection of the otiose pastoral life and the recreative values of pastoral poetry for the active, morally committed life in heroic poetry. In "Mode and Diction in *The Shepheardes Calender,*" *Modern Philology,* 67 (1969), 140–149, Harry Berger, Jr. revises Hamilton's argument by discriminating Colin's level of poetic and ethical achievement from Spenser's: Colin is "the fledgling imagination . . . disporting itself in the Muses' garden of conventions and reluctant to pass . . . into the world" (147); Spenser himself is in the process of forging a mature union of life and art. Patrick Cullen, *Spenser, Marvell, and Renaissance Pastoral* (Cambridge, Mass: Harvard University Press, 1970), 76–98, proposes that Colin fails within the pastoral world because he does not realize his vocation as its great poet; he fails through frailty rather than through sin. Paul Alpers, "The Eclogue Tradition and the Nature of Pastoral," *College English,* 34 (December, 1972), 365–366, rejects judgmental criticism: Colin's end is neither a failure nor a transcendence but a submission "to the nature of things"; he is an Everyman coming to terms with experiential reality. My own understanding of Colin and of his creator is most indebted to the work of Harry Berger, Jr., notably the seminal essay, "The Prospect of Imagination: Spenser and the Limits of Poetry," *Studies in English Literature, 1500–1900,* 1 (1961), 93–120.

4. See Lawrence Stone, *The Family, Sex and Marriage in England 1500–1800* (New York: Harper & Row, 1977), Pt. III, ch. 5; Keith Thomas, "Age and Authority in Early Modern England," *Proceedings of the British Academy,* LXII (1976), 205–248. The fullest generational study of the period is Anthony Egler, *The aspiring mind of the Elizabethan younger generation* (Durham, North Carolina: Duke University Press, 1966).

5. See Cullen, *Spenser, Marvell, and Renaissance Pastoral,* 29–76; and compare Michael F. Dixon, "Rhetorical Patterns and Methods of Advocacy in Spenser's *Shepheardes Calender,*" *English Literary Renaissance,* 7 (1977), 131–154.

6. Spenser's literary source for the myth is Ovid, *Metamorphoses,* I.698–712. Lucretius (*De rerum natura,* V) interprets the myth as an aetiology of song, which began among

primitive pastoralists whose poetry manifested their *otium*. George Sandys, *Ovid's Metamorphosis Englished, Mythologized, and Represented in Figures* (1632; ed., Karl K. Hulley and Stanley T. Vandersall, Lincoln, Nebraska: University of Nebraska Press, [1970]), quotes Lucretius and euhemerizes Pan as the first pastoral poet—a human shepherd who, for his invention of the pipes, "was esteemed a God, as others were for other inventions" (77).

7.   For other interpretations, see John W. Moore, Jr., "Colin Breaks His Pipe: A Reading of the 'January' Eclogue," *English Literary Renaissance*, 5 (1975), 3–24: Colin's rejection of Pan is "a renunciation of his quest to serve society as a divine pastoral poet" (22); and David R. Shore, "Colin and Rosalind: Love and Poetry in the *Shepheardes Calender*," *Studies in Philology*, 73 (1976), 176–188: Colin's "rejection of the pipe is a sign of sorrow and of loss, not . . . a sign that his love is in some way morally culpable" (180).

8.   This paragraph borrows from my "Celebration and Insinuation: Sir Philip Sidney and the Motives of Elizabethan Courtship," *Renaissance Drama*, N.S. 8 (1977), 3–4. On the theory and practise of encomium, see O. B. Hardison, Jr., *The Enduring Monument* (Chapel Hill: University of North Carolina, 1962), esp. 95–102; and Barbara Kiefer Lewalski, *Donne's Anniversaries and the Poetry of Praise* (Princeton, N.J.: Princeton University Press, 1973), 11–41. On the ideology of the Elizabeth cult and its iconography, see Frances A. Yates, *Astraea* (London: Routledge & Kegan Paul, 1975), 29–120; and Roy Strong, *The Cult of Elizabeth* (London: Thames & Hudson, 1977). Elkin Calhoun Wilson, *England's Eliza* (Cambridge, Mass.: Harvard University Press, 1939), usefully surveys the literary idealization of Elizabeth.

9.   Compare Cullen, *Spenser, Marvell, and Renaissance Pastoral*, 114; and Thomas H. Cain, "The Strategy of Praise in Spenser's *Aprill*," *Studies in English Literature 1500–1900*, 9 (1968), 45–58.

10.   Harvey quotes Cuddie's complaint (*October*, 7–18) from the "famous new Calender," in a letter "to my very friend *M. Immerito*." Harvey's context is the pursuit of personal ambitions through poetry: "Master *Colin Cloute* is not every body, and albeit his olde Companions, Master *Cuddy*, and Master *Hobbinoll* be as little beholding to their *Mistresse Poetrie*, as ever you wilt: yet he peradventure, by the meanes of hir special favour, and some personall priviledge, may . . . purchase great landes, and Lordshippes, with the money, which his *Calender* and *Dreames* have, and will affourde him" (*A Gallant familiar Letter*, etc. [1580], reprinted in Spenser, *Poetical Works*, 627–628). Harvey's tone is ironic, but Spenser's life and works suggest that his aspirations were permeated by the thoroughly materialistic concerns that he projected and censured in the figure of Cuddie. For a reading of the eclogue that embraces the perspective of Piers' moral idealism, see Richard F. Hardin, "The Resolved Debate of Spenser's 'October,'" *Modern Philology*, 73 (1976), 257–263.

11.   George Puttenham, *The Arte of English Poesie* (1589), eds., Gladys Doidge Willcock and Alice Walker (Cambridge, England: Cambridge University Press, 1936), 38. Puttenham is characterizing the eclogue, which he classes with satire, comedy, and tragedy as reprehensive "*drammatick* poems."

12.   Reprinted in *Elizabethan Critical Essays*, ed., G. Gregory Smith, 2 vols., (Oxford: Oxford University Press, 1904), I, 245, 264.

13.   See *The Works of Edmund Spenser: A Variorum Edition*, ed., Edwin Greenlaw, et al. (Baltimore: Johns Hopkins University Press, 1932–49). *The Minor Poems, Volume One*, 402–04; and Paul E. McLane, *Spenser's Shepheardes Calender: A Study in Elizabethan Allegory* (Notre Dame: University of Notre Dame Press, 1961), 47–60.

14.   Dido has a central place in Petrarch's "Triumph of Chastity," where she is celebrated as an example of honor, led to a virtuous suicide by faithful love for her husband rather than by despair and shame following Aeneas' desertion. Yates, *Astraea*, 112–119, explores the political use of the Triumph of Chastity in the iconography of Elizabeth. Dido is a negative antithesis to Troynovant's heroic virgin queen; Elizabeth is a female Aeneas. Yates identifies the vastly influential *Trionfi* as the source of the Elizabethan icon while ignoring the apparent contradiction between the censoriously moralized Elizabethan image of Dido and Petrarch's very sympathetic treatment. Spenser's Dido *triumphans*, presumably conceived in opposition to Vergil's Dido, is in fact close in spirit to Petrarch's.

The Mirror Stage of Colin Clout

HARRY BERGER, JR.

Commenting on Colin Clout's wintry analogizing in *Januarye*, Isabel MacCaffrey writes that "a sympathetic Nature offers ready emblems for the human psyche. It is the basic justification for pastoral, and as numerous Renaissance texts testify, the reciprocity of inner and outer worlds was based on something more solid than what Ruskin later termed the pathetic fallacy."[1] This way of putting it raises questions that place us directly before the chief problematical aspects of the eclogue. Why does MacCaffrey herself employ pathetic fallacy in personifying Nature? Is it to suggest the pastoral paradox that *nature* is really a synonym for *art*? Since she argues in her essay on the *Calender* that Spenser shows the inadequacy of Nature's ready emblems,[2] does she mean to imply that this "justification" and "reciprocity" may be characteristic of the naive versions of pastoral that Spenser criticizes? MacCaffrey does not confront these issues because the above passage is an aside that gives way immediately to a discussion of Britomart's employment of the ocean-passion analogy in *Faerie Queene* III.iv. But the questions implicit in her statement may profitably be submitted to the arbitration of the eclogues themselves; hence I use them to frame the doorway leading over the dedicatory lintel and into the eclogue named after Janus.

I

Since *nature* in the *Calender* means primarily a set of references to their environment by imaginary speakers, the semantic problem about the status of references to nature is inseparable from the rhetorical or dramatic problem about the ethical status of those speakers. For how can the aspects of nature they mention be any more "real," "three-dimensional," or (above all) autonomous and autotelic than the speakers themselves are? From the outset their status is placed in question by the coy manner in which Spenser adopts the mask of Immerito and then duplicates this act when he, or Immerito, gives way to Colin Clout.

From *Helios* 10 (1983): 139–60. Reprinted by permission of the editor.

The dedicatory poem that performs the first of these two conventional reductions is a parodic display of *sprezzatura*. Spenser flaunts his artful facility in striking artless poses and shows his mastery of the convention in which claims to worthlessness, anonymity, inadequacy, and so on, are stated to be discounted.[3] The modesty *topos* is deployed along two fronts at once, political and literary. He plays the humble suitor seeking Sidney's protection against the blatant beast of envy so as to imply that his book contains matter interesting enough to make him hide his identity (which only adds to the interest). At the same time he evokes and stands in the legitimizing shadow of the two poets he aspires to emulate and overgo, the two traditions—native and classical—he draws on and combines (Cain, 30). The opening words of the poem remind us of Chaucer and of the pastoral image of Virgil:

> *Goe little booke: thy selfe present,*
> *As child whose parent is unkent:*
> *To him that is the president*
> *Of noblesse and of chevalree,*
> *And if that Envie barke at thee,*
> *As sure it will, for succoure flee*
>   *Under the shadow of his wing,*
> *And asked, who thee forth did bring,*
> *A shepheards swaine saye did thee sing,*
> *All as his straying flocke he fedde:*
> *And when his honor has thee redde,*
> *Crave pardon for my hardyhedde.*
>   *But if that any aske thy name,*
> *Say thou wert base begot with blame:*
> *For thy thereof thou takest shame.*
> *And when thou art past jeopardee,*
> *Come tell me, what was sayd of mee:*
> *And I will send more after thee.*
>   *Immeritô.*

The tetrameters and triple rhymes lend an air of simplicity visually enhanced, in the first edition, by large, well-spaced italic print filling a page that faces the much smaller and more crowded roman print of E. K.'s pedantic epistle. The combination of triple rhyme and tetrameters itself makes the simplicity hyperbolic, and it is marked as pretense or caricature not only by subtly varied patterns of enjambment but also by the vigor and fluency of diction.

Spenser's *sprezzatura* thus extends to his easy control of prosody and beyond that to the wit and rhetoric that signal mastery of the tonal etiquette of courtiership. The puns on *unkent* ("unknown" and "unkempt") and *president* testify to this, as does the reference to envy, which is a boast thinly masked as apprehensiveness. Similarly the professions of low status are phrased so as to seem false—mere defenses against envy. The directions to his book, which are simultaneously performatives addressed to Sidney, are confidently voiced, revealing a knowledgeable worldliness that belies as another pretense the innocent's need "for succoure." Finally, the playful archness and aggressiveness of the concluding tercet belie the signature humbly prostrate at the bottom of the page. Louis Montrose, from whose essays on pastoral and courtiership I have greatly profited, notes that "this conjunction of humility and pride exemplifies the pastoral poet's capacity to strike ambivalent poses."[4] Montrose goes on to state that "Spenser articulates a tense relationship to literary and social patriarchy," and at least in the case of Immerito's little poem I would argue that the tenseness is mimed rather than dramatized. Spenser refers to the existence of envy as a predictable response to his work but scarcely seems anxious about it; he all but commands its appearance. The reference is witty and high-spirited, it has (as I suggested) the force of a disguised boast, and it is used with a certain *brio* to justify the necessity of adopting the conventional mask of humility.

When we turn from Immerito to Colin Clout we shall find that Spenser's handling of these two reductions differs, and the difference throws considerable light on the way he conceives the "mode of existence" of his pastoral speakers. Neither is an autonomous character to whom an interpreter may apply ethical criteria, but Immerito has even less fictional substance than Colin—as little, in fact, as that possessed by the subject of the following lines: "A shepheards swaine saye did thee sing, / All as his straying flocke he fedde." The lines glance toward a story, a setting, an implication of "nature," but "saye" aborts these possibilities. Immerito is a mere passing tone mediating the transition from Spenser to what Richard Helgerson has nicely called the "melodious self-pity" of Colin Clout.[5] Immerito, "the persona of the poet who has written the *Calender*" (Montrose, 36), is as transparent as the pastoral image he uses, and if all the *Calender*'s speakers were equally transparent the reader would be encouraged to be more energetic in his allegorical labors, diverting the references to sheep, shepherds, and song more quickly from the objects they name to secondary referents in the world not of the personae but of the poet.

II

Spenser begins *Januarye* by distancing and lowering Colin even as he establishes a link to him and uses phrases that recall Immerito:

A Shepeheards boye (no better doe him call)
When Winters wastful spight was almost spent,
All in a sunneshine day, as did befall,
Led forth his flock, that had bene long ypent.
So faynt they woxe, and feeble in the folde,
That now unnethes their feete could them uphold.

All as the Sheepe, such was the shepeheards looke,
For pale and wanne he was, (alas the while,)
May seeme he lovd, or els some care he tooke:
Well couth he tune his pipe, and frame his stile.
Tho to a hill his faynting flocke he ledde,
And thus him playnd, the while his shepe there fedde.

Immerito's pastoral image is echoed and amplified, and the parenthetical phrase in the opening line is an inelegant variation of *Immerito*. In the dedicatory poem it is not clear whether we are meant to distinguish between Immerito as "swaine" and Spenser as the shepherd (thus interposing another pastoral mask), but here the distinction is less casual, more marked, so that we assume Colin to be Spenser/Immerito's "boye." The connection between them is maintained in the second line: on the one hand the alliterative stressing and the incipient personification of winter anticipate Colin's standard procedure, but on the other hand "Winters," while capitalized, is not italicized, and unlike Colin his author minimizes winter's "spight," punctuating his optimism with a reference to the sunny day. This presages "the return of spring and the renewal of life," and by the same token prepares us to view as excessive Colin's feeling "that his spring once lost can never be recovered."[6]

The continuity binding Colin to Spenser/Immerito is also stressed by two putatively different speakers' sharing the same stanza form and the same penchant for alliteration. When Colin begins to speak, the effect of the change of voices is comparable to what would happen if an actor, after speaking in his own voice, spoke through an ancient theatrical mask equipped with a megaphonic amplifying device—a *prosōpon*, or better, a *persona* (etymologically linked by Boethius to *per-sonando*). Miming Colin, Spenser exaggerates the prosodic and pathetic features of his introductory stanzas so that while his pleasure in artifice merges with Colin's, he also lets us distinguish his pleasure in mimicry from Colin's pleasure in the arts of singing and savoring pain. Hence it is difficult to isolate Colin and view him as an autonomous or "round" character. Framing a style he identifies as his own, Spenser/Immerito hands it to the "boye" into which he "folds" himself. Colin becomes his fold and his pipe, a kind of pastoral and prosodic enclosure built "of lighter timber cotes" (*Dec.* 77) within whose narrow lines the poet pens his voice. Or perhaps we could liken Spenser-playing-Colin to the wolf in sheep's clothing.

After comparing Colin to his forlorn flock, Immerito marks his detachment from Colin's personal affairs with a conjecture ("May seeme he lovd, or els some care he tooke") the tone of which casually understates Colin's most pressing concerns, and he follows this with a more assured opinion in line 10, the verdict of a professional on a colleague's skill.[7] Though the second response seems unrelated to the first, the two are separated, or joined, by a colon rather than a full stop, and they converge two lines later in the phrase "thus him playnd," for we see *play* in *playnd* and feel the force of a conventional motif: the metamorphosis of pain into poetry, sorrow into song, with the implication that pain and sorrow are part of the *playing*. *Playning* combines *play* with *payne*, and the ethical dative ("*him* playnd") signifies that Colin is no less part of his own audience than the gods he invokes. Complaint is expected to give pleasure, and pain may therefore be cherished as well for the artfulness with which it can be amplified as for the art into which it is sure to be transformed. These introductory lines, then, enable us to infer Spenser/Immerito's view of some of the expectations generated by the pastoral paradigm. They are at most implied, not in any way evaluated, but they provide a backdrop against which Colin's performance may be judged. The expectations are more clearly focused when Colin in the next stanza singles out Pan for special attention, alluding to his encounter with Syrinx.

While locating the relevant thematic features of the many-sided Pan, such as allusion is not particularly reverent, and John Moore has remarked a "note of ambivalence" in Colin's invocation. Moore sees it as "both a petition for divine pity and a test of the gods' loving relationship to him," and he connects this mixed tone with a departure from convention:

Where the conventional amorous pastoral eclogue begins with a complaint to the reluctant mistress, "January" does not begin by imploring Rosalind for pity; it begins by appealing to the gods for pity. In the first stanza, the gods of love and Pan appear as the source of the comfort he seeks and, like the conventional mistress, they are presented as aloof and indifferent, withholding the perfect happiness he wishes them to share with him. By this revision of the conventions Spenser makes the gods the reluctant mistress of Colin's song and not Rosalind. (p. 9)

> Ye Gods of love, that pitie lovers payne,
> (If any gods the paine of lovers pitie:)
> Looke from above, where you in joyes remaine,
> And bowe your eares unto my dolefull dittie.
> And *Pan* thou shepheards God, that once didst love,
> Pitie the paines, that thou thy selfe didst prove.
> *(13–18)*

Moore inaccurately conflates "the gods of love and Pan" and soon ignores the former to concentrate on the latter, arguing that Colin serves the wrong god in serving "Pan, the amorous nature god," that he must choose "between divine love and erotic" and "seek his values not in the temporary and fragile beauty of nature's spring, but in the enduring beauty of heaven's eternal springtime" where he will find a "harvest free of mutability" (pp. 12, 22–23). Moore detects a glimmer of hope under Colin's bushel of January despair: "Colin's false values have revealed their inadequacy and prepared him for a possible spring-like birth of a better set of values" (p. 23). *Januarye* is the first step in a "spiritual odyssey" that takes him "from allegiance to Pan, the nature God, to the real Pan, the real All, Christ" (p. 22).

My own view is that if Colin makes an odyssey through the *Calender* it is not so much toward increasing spirituality as toward increasing petulance, which by *December* attains to heaven only in the sense that it assumes cosmic proportions. Moore's emphasis on the problematical and central significance of Pan nevertheless strikes me as an important insight, and to expropriate it from the high road of Christian wayfaring I shall return to consider Colin's January petulance at closer range. It makes its first appearance in the parenthetical second line of his invocation and is sharpened by the contrast to his own sad case implied in the next line—"where *you* in joyes remaine." Whoever these gods are—and that there are more than one rules out Christianity—their high altitude, joy, and success will probably keep them from appreciating the intense pain and failure reverberating from the "barrein ground" where a mere shepherd's boy makes rural music.[8] Hence Colin turns to address a god who dwells below, and with less deference he imposes a claim on Pan by reminding the goat-god of *his* past failure: "that once didst live" carries the implication that the Ovidian *amator* may have retired from the field in defeat and now, presumably, consoles himself with his (and his devotees') music. Colin rejects Pan's example: he will give up music and remain, defeated, in the field.

III

Lovelorn and lovelocked in the January frosts of unrequited love, his rural suit and "Shepheards devise" contemned by fair Rosalind, Colin Clout shivers through five stanzas while turning winter's "waste," the "barrein ground," the "naked trees," and his "feeble flocke" into reflections of his woe. The first two stanzas, and especially the two lines of fustian that introduce them, deserve close attention:

Thou barrein ground, whome winters wrath hath wasted,
Art made a myrrhour, to behold my plight:
Whilome thy fresh spring flowrd, and after hasted
Thy sommer prowde with Daffadillies dight.
And now is come thy wynters stormy state,
Thy mantle mard, wherein thou maskedst late.

Such rage as winters, reigneth in my heart,
My life bloud friesing with unkindly cold:
Such stormy stoures do breede my balefull smart,
As if my yeare were wast, and woxen old.
And yet alas, but now my spring begonne,
And yet alas, yt is already donne.

(19–30)

There is something comically redundant in the fervor with which Colin announces what the convention has already prepared us to take for granted. The pastoral semantics put into play by the eclogue context give the imitation of literature priority over that of nature, and this means we are encouraged to take Colin's utterances to refer to other utterances of the same kind and not merely to the objects his utterances designate. Since pastoral is a kind of literary metalanguage, the natural objects or processes signified by Colin's terms are themselves signifiers of the countless poems in which such references and images have characteristically appeared. The tree lovelier than any poem refers me more directly to Joyce Kilmer's poem than to God's tree.

At second glance, however, and in spite of their conventionality, these two lines yield considerable insight into the complicit relations between tradition and the individual talent: "Thou barrein ground, whome winters wrath hath wasted, / Art made a myrrhour, to behold my plight." This is either an evasive passive construction—"made" by whom, if not by Colin?—or else an active construction in which *Art* is a noun in agentive relation to *made*. Perhaps the necessities of the syntactical pun call for the sense of completed action ("Art already made you a mirror"; "you are already made a mirror") that strains against the apparent force of the complaint, since Colin seems to be making his mirror now. This sense makes us notice that the illocutionary force of the phrase ("with my art I now make a mirror") is suppressed and displaced to the literary precedents that have already prepared the ground ("Art *made*") for Colin to embroider on.

"To behold" is another focus of significant troping. If we take it in its familiar sense it feels like an ellipsis: "to enable me—or anyone else—to behold my plight." The infinitive shifts back and forth between "in order to behold" and "in which to behold"; the first stresses the speaker's own purposiveness in making the mirror while the second connects more easily with the past tense of literary preparation, implying that the mirrored plight already exists for Colin to imitate, in which case he himself becomes a mirror transmitting a reflected semblance of conventional despair. But *behold* also has more aggressive meanings—"keep hold of," "contain," "signify"—that reflect into the speaker's words a certain pride in achievement: his plight is preserved, amplified, rendered significant by being externalized and mirrored in the barren ground. This enables him not only to keep despair alive and publicize it but also to naturalize it, give it legitimacy by invoking the man-nature correspondence.

John Moore has sternly taken Colin to task for relying too much on "the book of nature, Pan's book," and as a result basing "his life on a set of inadequate and therefore false analogies" (pp. 15–16). But of course it literally *is* a book he relies on, a book written not by nature but by Colin in collaboration with his literary predecessors. It is convention rather than nature that supplies the false analogies. That Colin and convention mirror each other signifies his commitment to the literary and extra-literary norms embedded in the genre of the pastoral love lyric (with Petrarchan trimmings). Spenser's critique of Colin is thus one with his critique of the genre, and it is through his portrayal of Colin's response that he reanimates the ethico-psychological attitudes that give rise to the genre and sanction its continuing influence.

"Art made a myrrhour, to behold my plight": the line takes on Orphean implications resembling those explicitly indicated in the undersong of *Epithalamion*: "The woods shall to me answer and my Eccho ring." And as the presence of "Eccho" suggests, the artist's power to make nature his echo and mirror conflates Orpheus with Narcissus.[9] The two together preside as Ovidian proxies over the metamorphosis taking place. For even as *Colin* moves to naturalize his plight, *we* perceive his language to conventionalize it in distortions that denaturalize nature. Personification is merely the surface of this denaturalizing process, that is, the apostrophe to the ground, the attributes *wrath* and *prowde* assigned to winter and summer, and the image of the ground cloaking its barrenness in a flowery mantle. Less superficial is the "philosophy of nature" embedded in Colin's rhetoric: if "sommer prowde with Daffadillies dight" is a "mantle" worn in a masque,[10] then this artificial masking conceals the real or "natural" condition of the ground, which is barrenness. According to this logic the sweeter seasons inspire false pride and illusory hopes. It is as if the anti-erotic animus of such critics of youth as E. K., Thenot in *Februarye*, and Piers in *Maye* had displaced to nature the "follies fitte" for "love lads" who "masken in fresh aray" (*Maye* 17, 2). Nature is indeed at this very moment being "made a myrrhour" that serves the function of a scapegoat: it be-holds human folly so that the seasonal round may be blamed and man absolved for, say, falling in love.

Colin's image implies that behind the mask life's real face is the face of winter, "for ever the latter end of joy is woe." Like the rage of the spider in *Muiopotmos*, winter's destructive wrath is the spite of an embittered have-not—a seasonal counterpart to the "Envie" predicted by Immerito—who lies in wait to punish summer's pride and self-love by stripping it of its finery. This view of nature is thus the familiar sadbrow obverse and consequence of golden-age idyllicism. It makes interesting contact with the "spight" of old men, "Stoicke censours," and others who "ill judge of love, that cannot love, / Ne in their frosen hearts feele kindly flame" (*FQ* IV.Pr.2); as Patrick Cullen has noted, this resemblance suggests that Colin's premature senility—his "life bloud friesing with unkindly cold"—has already begun to have its effect.[11]

In the "barren ground" stanza, earlier commentators have noted one detail that adds to the sense of conspicuous artifice. Palgrave, for example, remarked sternly that "a poet who had his eye closely on natural fact" would not have assigned to summer the daffodils that, as Shakespeare knew, "come before the swallow dares, and take / The winds of March with beauty" (*Variorum, Minor Poems* 1:245). But whether intentional or not, the mistake works to enhance the fragility, and therefore the folly, of summer's pride—compare the "wandring wood" of *Faerie Queene*, Book I, "Whose loftie trees yclad with sommers pride, / Did spred so broad, that heavens light did hide" (i.7). Perhaps also the pride receives a peculiar inflection if "Daffadillies" is taken as a slant rustic allusion to Narcissus. It is an appropriate instance of the metamorphosis theme lurking in the previous reference to Pan and in the figurative arborealization of Colin that occurs two stanzas later, and it appears in the vicinity of Colin's reference to the mirror in which he beholds his plight.

Though E. K. does not get around to mentioning the metamorphosis of Syrinx until *Aprill* and the related tale of Argus and Io until *Julye* and *October*, this Ovidian network hovers over the *Calender* as a whole. A moment's reflection will suggest how relevant Ovidian metamorphosis is to any inquiry into the constitution of pastoral "nature." Ovid's is not the simple reforestation project Marvell wittily proclaimed it to be in "The Garden." His flora and fauna are simultaneously reminders of failure, danger, or loss, and figures expressing the magical wish-fulfilling escape from pain, which is dissolved in the loss of consciousness but memorialized by the transformation of natural forms to symbols. So Mercury tells Argus how Syrinx, weary of fleeing from satyrs, found peace and plaintive immortality among the watery reeds (*Metamorphoses* 1.705 ff.). And so, in the wonderful lines about Myrrha, Ovid speaking through Orpheus imagines her impatience as the tree rises to her neck:

> non tulit illa moram venientique obvia ligno
> subsedit mersitque suos in cortice vultus.
> quae quamquam amisit veteres cum corpore sensus,
> flet tamen, et tepidae manant ex arbore guttae.
> est honor et lacrimis, stillataque robore murra
> nomen erile tenet mulloque tacebitur aevo.
>
> (*10.497–502*)

but she could not endure the delay and, meeting the rising wood, she sank down and plunged her face in the bark. Though she has lost her old-time feelings with her body, still she weeps, and the warm drops trickle down from the tree. Even the tears have fame, and the myrrh which distils from the tree-trunk keeps the name of its mistress and will be remembered through all the ages.[12]

With its displaced populations haunting the wood, the *Metamorphoses* is a mythological *Origin of Species* not in nature but in the imagination, and whether we think of it as the projection of human affairs into nature or the expropriation of natural forms, the idea of metamorphosis interprets the process by which pastoral nature is created. It is hard to resist the reflection that the myrrh is a "myrrhour" of Myrrha.

The second of the two stanzas under discussion only makes clear what was already implicit in the first: Colin does not compare himself to nature; he compares nature to himself. Though he appears to complete the analogy by internalizing the wintry landscape, what he actually internalizes is a projected distortion of nature congruent with his self-pity.[13] He begins with commendable restraint to describe his relation to the barren ground as one merely of likeness, not identity: "Such rage *as* winters," "*As if* my year were wast, and woxen old." But in "*my* year . . . woxen old" and "*my* spring begonne" the natural terms take on metaphoric shading and press away from the recurrent annual cycle toward the unique life cycle. The finality of the last line, "And yet alas, yt is already donne," completes this shift. The figurative result is neither an analogy between the two cycles nor an identification of the man's "season" with the year's. Rather the two are conflated to produce a hyperbole of premature aging; the lifetime is contracted to a year, but by the same distortion the annual cycle assumes the irreversibility of the life cycle.

Nancy Jo Hoffman remarks the humanization of nature in this passage but ignores the possibility of an ironic relation between Spenser and Colin:

Nature loses its material referent, and becomes a language. . . . An analogy that does not make pictorial sense turns out to be a skillful and deliberate metaphor for the change and disorder that characterize Colin's love. Furthermore, meaning does not derive from what Colin sees but from what he thinks and feels *when* he sees. . . . Although winter's barren ground is called a "mirror," what Colin beholds is not a realistic image but an evaluative metaphor given meaning by the responsive poet's mind. . . .

. . . By the time Spenser returns to winter landscape with its marred mantle, he has entwined nature and human nature to such an extent that no truly visual quality or precise analogy remains.

(pp. 45–46)

Whose is the "skillful and deliberate metaphor"? And if it does not matter whether it is Spenser's or Colin's, does this mean that both evaluate Colin's "disorder" in the same way? If Colin is substantial enough to see, think, and feel, in what sense does he, or can he, behold "not a realistic image but an evaluative metaphor"? It would be more promising if Hoffman meant that what Colin sees as a realistic image we read as an evaluative metaphor given meaning, and so on. Then she would be in a better position to sort out what Colin sees, how he interprets it, and how we interpret his interpretation. As the final sentence shows, these distinctions are not entertained, and the consequence is that if we discern in the passage the Stoic censor's attitude toward nature, life, and love, we must ascribe this view to Colin's author as *his* sentiment.

IV

Continuing the project of naturalizing his plight in the following stanzas, Colin's bathos increases together with his increasingly grotesque metamorphosis—or better still, anamorphosis—of nature and man into distortions each of the other until he seems on the verge of ending his race in a tree:

> You naked trees, whose shady leaves are lost,
> Wherein the byrds were wont to build their bowre:
> And now are clothd with mosse and hoary frost,
> Instede of bloosmes, wherwith your buds did flowre:
> I see your teares, that from your boughes doe raine,
> Whose drops in drery ysicles remaine.
>
> All so lustfull leafe is drye and sere,
> My timely buds with wayling all are wasted:
> The blossome, which my braunch of youth did beare,
> With breathed sighes is blowne away, and blasted
> And from mine eyes the drizling teares descend,
> As on your boughes the ysicles depend.
>
> *(31–42)*

Like Orpheus, Colin is trying to "learne these woods, to wayle my woe, / And teache the trees, their trickling teares to shedde" (*June* 95–96). Tree-person analogies are so common in Ovidian and Petrarchan traditions that the first thing we recognize about these stanzas is their aggressive claim to the status of literary cliché. The primary message is not "my trouble is like a tree's" but "my plight is like a poet's." Such a message, conveyed by the poet's plethora of dainty devices, ought to control our reaction in a manner that makes his tree trope less intrepid by directing us to classify it as the intertextual trope of allusion rather than as a species of iconic similitude. But even while flashing this signal, Spenser neutralizes it by a pictorial emphasis that diverts us from literary to arboreal emulation.

The bathetic effect owes partly to Colin's insistence on spelling out the analogy in visual images that are merely redundant. In her account of the stanzas Hoffman tries to blink this insistence away (pp. 45–46), but "lustfull leafe," "timely buds," and "blossome" confuse a simple commonplace by forcing us to visualize (we ask, do they figure parts of the body?), and if this effect is momentarily mitigated by the metaphoric "braunch of youth" it is revived by the bizarre *enargeia* of the concluding eyes-boughs equation. And it is reinforced by Colin's emphasizing the exactness of the visual comparison—reading "all so" with the first three Quartos; the "Also" of the Folio and fourth and fifth Quartos weakens this emphasis but accentuates the impression of redundancy. The clear difference between descending tears and hanging icicles impels us to challenge the claim to exact resemblance; we note and resist the straining toward convergence conveyed by steady alliteration and the cluster of internal rhymes ("sighes," "eyes," and "ysicles").

These details move the passage into the realm of literary parody, and yet at the same time the complex implications of the theme of narcissistic metamorphosis resonate in the imagery, providing a critical analysis of the self-indulgent motives, the "melodious self-pity," that inform it. For the image of icicles, like the effect of redundancy, indicates the "frozenness" of the emotion locked within the poet and "beheld" by the frigid fire of his rhetoric. If Colin's "All so" ultimately prevails it is because we decide the real flow of his grief is not only congealed but also concealed in the icy glitter of his images. The image then turns on the imagist: visually the tree does not resemble the man, for it "weeps" but does not weep; figuratively the man may resemble the tree in "weeping" rather than weeping. In this connection it is interesting that line 41 reads like a free translation of the line describing Myrrha's tears (*Metamorphoses* 10.500) quoted above—Myrrha's *warm* tears turning into "tears" of myrrh.

V

Colin's final stanza of comparison extends the pattern of conspicuous redundancy from vegetable to animal life:

> Thou feeble flocke, whose fleece is rough and rent,
> Whose knees are weake through fast and evill fare:
> Mayst witnesse well by thy ill governement,
> Thy maysters mind is overcome with care.
> Thou weake, I wanne: thou leane, I quite forlorne:
> With mourning pyne I, you with pyning mourne.
>
> *(43–48)*

A confession of misgovernment by Colin! Enough to make any attacker or defender of his character prick up ears. R. A. Durr, who generally found Colin depraved, thought this proved he was bad; John Moore thought it showed him "being responsible in a difficult situation" and was therefore an earnest of superior virtue in the future; and Patrick Cullen—holding his Aristotelian fire for bigger game, the Tragic Flaw—argued against Durr that any delinquency caused by Rosalind's wintry effect on her lover bothers the shepherd as much as his sheep. Cullen cites the opening two stanzas of the eclogue to prove that it is "real winter" rather than "bad shepherding" that tatters the flock, and he responds to the gravamen like a private investigator reporting to the counselor for the defense: "There is no substantial evidence to indicate that Colin fails to discharge his obligation to his sheep."[14] But perhaps by this time in the eclogue we don't find bad weather any more troublesome to Colin than—comparing small things to great—it is to King Lear. Both appreciate its seminal power to legitimize self-pity and to supply the imagery of barrenness. The bad weather real to Colin is only as real to us as his suffering body. And since the voice and mind projected into a puppet by his ventriloquising author may be taken more seriously than his body ("his" body, therefore his "body"), our attention is diverted from the dummy's grief to his enjoyment of winter's fitness to serve as his mirror. To this the counselor for the defense may object, "That's what the sheep are for—to revive the reality of winter." But like the barren ground and naked trees, the ragged sheep seem to be the symbols rather than the objects of the shepherd's care. Cullen so much as says this when he suggests that the case against Colin can be dismissed on grounds of insignificance: "Colin's self-accusation here is less moral reprobation than it is a conventional pastoral assumption of correspondence between the mood of the master and the condition of the sheep" (p. 80).

The ethical debate must have taken place in an environment specially designed to cut down the noise of alliteration, which reaches a deafening level as assonantial contrast and variation are played off against the steady beat of echoing consonants. Colin's flock is less weatherproof than his rhetoric, which leads one to wonder how he found time to pay any more attention to their misery than did Herbert Rix, who uncovered an apostrophe, an anaphora, a double parison, and an antimetabole all within the space of six lines (*Variorum, Minor Poems* 1:246). There may well be sermons in sheep, but since by this time in the eclogue we have a fairly good idea of "the mood of the master" we are perhaps more impressed by the scrupulousness with which he summons every item in the pastoral inventory to witness that the master's mind is overcome with tropes, Colin's sheep are scarcely more durable than the poor lamb that follows Una across the plain in one line ("by her in a line a milke white lambe she lad") only to be analogically sacrificed to her in the next ("So pure an innocent, as that same lambe, / She was . . . ," *FQ* I.i.4–5).

VI

Colin's stanzas of apostrophe sacrifice the pastoral inventory to the despotism of an art that deprives "things" of their otherness and reduces them to expressions—however elegantly or inelegantly varied—of a single plaintive theme. But this gives rise to a question: does such redundancy manifest primarily an erotic or a poetic obsession? The question receives an equivocal answer in the concluding section of his complaint:

> A thousand sithes I curse that carefull hower,
> Wherein I longd the neighbour towne to see:
> And eke tenne thousand sithes I blesse the stoure,
> Wherein I sawe so fayre a sight, as shee.
> Yet all for naught: such sight hath bred my bane.
> Ah God, that love should breede both joy and payne.
> . . . .
>
> I love thilke lass, (alas why doe I love?)
> And am forlorne, (alas why am I lorne?)
> Shee deignes not my good will, but doth reprove,
> And of my rurall musick holdeth scorne.
> Shepheards devise she hateth as the snake,
> And laughes the songes, that *Colin Clout* doth make.
>
> Wherefore my pype, albee rude *Pan* thou please,
> Yet for thou pleasest not, where most I would:
> And thou unlucky Muse, that wontst to ease
> My musing mynd, yet canst not, when thou should:
> Both pype and Muse, shall sore the while abye.
> So broke his oaten pype, and downe dyd lye.
>
> $(49-72)$

The shepherd's "good will" and "love" are less evident than the sense of injured merit "beheld" by his rhetoric. What seems most to rankle him is that his pipe, the "Shepheards devise" (emblem, mask, and art) that all his country cousins praise, is not merely ineffective in moving Rosalind but is unappreciated as art. Rosalind's response is close enough to Nysa's in Virgil's eighth eclogue to suggest by allusion that "Shepheards devise" is of ancient pedigree: despising all men, Nysa hates Damon's pipe, goats, shaggy brows, and scraggly beard ("tibi est odio mea fistula, dumque capellae / hirsutumque supercilium promissaque barba," (33–34). Spenser significantly shifts the emphasis from Colin's person to his music.

   This combined emphasis on Colin's music and on the antiquity and conventionality of the situation focuses the poetic motive in a manner that makes it conflict with the erotic motive. As there is a difference between the two motives, so there is a difference between the respective audiences of lover and poet, that is, between the participant(s) primarily addressed by the poet as lover and the auditors or spectators addressed by the lover as poet. To which audience was Colin's "rurall musick" primarily directed? His response shows him to be stung by literary as well as erotic rejection. It is as if the conventional "myrrhour" of art that "beheld" and foreordained Colin's plight confused the fledgling poet-lover with its own demand for attention. Perhaps, to speculate idly, this confusion of literary and erotic motives informed the poetry addressed to Rosalind and affected her adverse reaction; perhaps she questioned the poet-lover's sincerity as well as his taste. Some evidence may be adduced from another quarter for this fantasy. The reaction Colin reports resembles that reported by the lover-poet in *Amoretti* 18 and 54:

> But when I pleade, she bids me play my part,
>   and when I weep, she sayes teares are but water:
>   and when I sigh, she sayes I know the art,
>   and when I waile she turnes hir selfe to laughter.
>
> Of this worlds Theatre in which we stay,
>   My love lyke the Spectator ydly sits
>   beholding me that all the pageants play,
>   disguysing diversly my troubled wits.
>
> Sometimes I joy when glad occasion fits,
>   and mask in myrth lyke to a Comedy:
>   soone after when my joy to sorrow flits,
>   I waile and make my woes a Tragedy.
>
> Yet she beholding me with constant eye,
>   delights not in my merth nor rues my smart:
>   but when I laugh she mocks, and when I cry
>   she laughes, and hardens evermore her hart.
>
> What then can move her? if nor merth nor mone,
>   she is no woman, but a sencelesse stone.

But of course her spectatorship seems appropriate to the theatrical pleasure his language betrays: playing all the pageants and disguising "diversly" in a one-man *tour de force*, he inflates his joy and sorrow into their formal dramatic equivalents. His delight in artifice, interfering with the more genuine impulses of love evident in other sonnets, reverses the Pygmalion story and turns his Galatea back into a statue. The obvious fitness of her response, however, testifies to the reflexive irony that animates the sonnet. We sense this irony in the reference to her "constant eye": unmoved, unwavering, she provides a contrast to his rapid and histrionic changes of mood; the constancy that makes him feel and play the fool is a promise of stability and steadfast devotion.[15] The same irony vibrates in the concluding couplet: the rhetorical question and the disparaging hyperbole manifest the very staginess he knows she scorns. Even as he blames her, he persists in humoring his penchant for striking the literary poses that maintain her in, and justify, the role of critical spectator.

In this manner the *Amoretti* poet knowingly persuades us to accredit and share his beloved's response and therefore to feel the interaction of two self-aware human persons behind the literary charade. Although this is precisely what Spenser denies us and Colin Clout in the *Calender*, he nevertheless depicts in flatter or more stenographic terms the same crossing of erotic and literary motives. E. K.'s delight in finding "a pretty Epanorthosis . . . and withall a Paronomasia" in line 61 directs our attention to it by its very pedantry. "I love thilke lass, (alas why doe I love?)": why love a lass rather than someone or something more tractable—for example, Hobbinol or the "refyned forme" of the woman as Idea—and more susceptible to the allure of Epanorthosis and Paronomasia? Yet if Colin is less a person than the *Amoretti* lovers, the response he models is not entirely predictable. He does not say he will stop loving, or even stop trying to persuade Rosalind; he says he will stop trying to do it with his pipe. He feels snubbed chiefly for serenading her with music that suited Pan's more countrified taste. I find it surprising that Colin hybristically passes Rosalind's contempt for him on to his god in the epithet *rude*. Something resembling a pastoral Peter Principle may be discernible here: a touch of restlessness on Colin's part with the limits of "Shepheards devise," a touch of ambition, a desire to promote himself beyond the level of his pastoral competence.

VII

Colin's reaction is emphasized, rendered more dramatic and sudden, by his failure to complete the penultimate stanza. Spenser/Immerito steps in with a direct and laconic stage direction. Although its rhythm enforces the sense of a predictable and unremarkable conclusion, the gesture it indicates is mannered; it is a comic hyperbole, amplified by conspicuous alliteration, assonantial in the first clause and consonantial in the second, with an alliteratively (and orthographically) induced trace of "dyd dye" behind "dyd lye." The poet flattens his puppet in a single line. Yet this is far from the whole story, for he picks him up again and sends him home with a certain sympathy:

> By that, the welked *Phoebus* gan availe,
> His weary waine, and now the frosty *Night*
> Her mantle black through heaven gan overhaile.
> Which seene, the pensife boy halfe in despight
> Arose, and homeward drove his sonned sheepe,
> Whose hanging heads did seeme his carefull case to weepe.

Hoffman, who stresses the conventional character of this ending, notes the continuity: "the mood of melancholy" is carried into "an emblematic nature" as Spenser takes over "Colin's now-familiar vocabulary of grief. . . . Independent of Colin, Spenser affirms the proportion between man and nature. The poem has defined a conventional pattern of experience and thought that is confirmed in the conventional pattern of nature just at the moment when Colin seems to have 'broken' pastoral possibility." She thinks the chronographic phrases "set us at a distance from Colin because, ultimately, the linear flow of human life is less capricious and more dependable than he is. Nature intrudes, not to end song, but to establish a ritual of order and poetic harmony" (p. 52). This perception of continuity between Spenser and Colin is important, but the terms of that continuity need some restatement to bring out the complexity of the relation.

It is Spenser, not Nature, who intrudes with imagery that scarcely betokens order or harmony; however conventional the *chronographia* is in itself, there is a touch of menace in the rhetoric through which the failing sun with its rustic "wain" is contrasted to the powerful epic gesture ("through heaven gan overhaile") of "frosty *Night*."[16] It is a hyperbole implying the correspondence of day's and season's end to life's end. And since "mantle black" echoes the earlier reference to the ground's "mantle mard," the figure may be felt to project Colin's mental state into the amplifying mirror of the cosmos. If so, the poet momentarily shares his mood. Setting the "boy" against this background makes him more rather than less sympathetic. He and his woe are diminished in scale, subdued by "pensife" and "*halfe* in despight," while his dependability is asserted in the word *sonned* as it was earlier in the reference to his feeding sheep (12). The extra foot of the hexameter accentuates the poet's commitment to at least the semblance of pathetic fallacy and thus withdraws from the onslaught of cosmic night to the more comforting pastoral enclosure.

Yet this return to pastoral only emphasizes by contrast the momentary transcendence centered in the word *heaven* (not *sky*) and in the energy of "gan overhaile." The menace carried by the vague and comprehensive economy of the phrase composes into a glancing allusion to powers and dangers beyond the pastoral confine. This is a device Spenser could have found in Virgil's *Georgics.*[17] Viewed with the hindsight afforded by knowledge of Spenser's other poetry, it takes on the character of an unspecified prolepsis into which we may read an emblematically mediated glimpse of real "despight" and "Envie," of "mighty Peres displeasure," of the "mishaps" of "death, or love, or fortunes wreck," of "idle hopes, which still doe fly away." Sharing Colin's mood, the poet carries its emblem beyond his enclosed mind. But *Anchora speme*: if one reads the night figure in this manner, then one also feels that Spenser anticipates the ulterior darkness only to exclude it from the present scene as the world he and Colin cannot yet, but must at some point, confront with their art. The concluding image reminds us that Colin's life is still proportioned, as E. K. might put it, to the care and feeding of sheep: "All Colin's skills cannot make him other than a shepherd. Fully to confront in poetry the problems he encounters in his progress through the *Calender*, problems of unrequited love and unredeemed time, he would have to deny his pastoral nature."[18]

This sympathetic closure, in which the poet joins with his puppet, nevertheless takes another turn in the final line, a turn reinstating the ambivalence of the relation between them. For "carefull case" may refer either to Colin's grief or to his art: the flock seemed to beweep either his woeful condition or the carefully constructed "case" he made for it, that is, the rhetorical grounds on which he rests his claim to nature's sympathy.[19] And the sheep only *seemed* to weep: the poet flags this as an interpretation with the same counterfactual quality as the teary icicles on Colin's naked trees. Perhaps Colin's tears are also no more than a semblance of tears: "May seeme he lovd, or els some care he tooke." The disjunctive phrase and its verb will now bear closer scrutiny: "or, if he didn't love, if he only seemed to love, he took some care"—not merely suffered or experienced some care ("some care *him* tooke"), but actively took it. At least some of his care went into tuning the pipe and framing the style with which he dresses the barren ground in flowery tropes to amplify his woe. Does he also take care in cherishing his care, drawing it out—like the poetic "honey Bee" in *December*—through the "formall rowmes" (*Dec.* 68) of verse so as to be-hold it in the Narcissan mirror?

The conclusion of the eclogue moves us to ask the questions about love and poetry that were gathering force through Colin's careful stanzas of complaint. How real—how genuine or authentic—are the love and grief that can be proportioned to the demands of poetry and displayed in the mirror of art? Can they be any more authentic than a "nature" so proportioned and so viewed? Isn't the disappearance of nature into art accompanied by a parallel disappearance of genuine love and grief? And is the love or grief that seems to be oriented toward another person, Rosalind, only a semblance of that which the poet-lover directs toward himself as he admires "the mirror of his owne thought" and "feeds his hungrie fantasy" with images whose "plenty makes me poore"?[20] On the other side of the equation, how authentic or adequate is an art that mirrors only the endless love and grief that fit conveniently (conventionally) into its "formall rowmes" and have their end, like Ovid's *amatores* and *nymphae*, in the poet-tree? Andrew Marvell's wry interpretation of these themes makes explicit the essence of Spenser's sympathetic critique:

> When we have run our Passions heat,
> Love hither makes his best retreat.
> The Gods, that mortal Beauty chase,
> Still in a Tree did end their race.

Apollo hunted Daphne so,
Only that She might Laurel grow.
And Pan did after Syrinx speed,
Not as a Nymph, but for a Reed.
("The Garden," 25–32)

Notes

1. *Spenser's Allegory: The Anatomy of Imagination* (Princeton: Princeton University Press, 1976), 292–93.

2. "Allegory and Pastoral in *The Shepheardes Calender*," *ELH* 36 (1969).

3. Cf. Thomas H. Cain, "Spenser and the Renaissance Orpheus," *University of Texas Quarterly* 41 (1971): 30; Spenser's use of the "inability-topos" makes it "a protestation of modesty and at the same time an advertisement."

4. "'The perfecte paterne of a Poete': The Poetics of Courtship in *The Shepheardes Calender*," *Texas Studies in Language and Literature* 21 (1979): 36.

5. "The New Poet Presents Himself: Spenser and the Idea of a Literary Career," *PMLA* 93 (1978): 899.

6. John W. Moore, Jr., "Colin Breaks His Pipe: A Reading of the 'January' Eclogue," *English Literary Renaissance* 5 (1975): 16. See Bruce R. Smith, "On Reading *The Shepheardes Calender*," in *Spenser Studies I*, ed. Patrick Cullen and Thomas Roche (Pittsburgh: University of Pittsburgh Press, 1980), 86–87.

7. Nancy Jo Hoffman thinks this line indicates that the narrator "is as much in the dark as we" about the source of Colin's woe, which would be odd if (as I believe) there is truth in her previous assertion that Spenser's "single characters are merely convenient vehicles for expressing emblematic human moods and circumstances" (*Spenser's Pastorals: "The Shepheardes Calender" and "Colin Clout"* [Baltimore: Johns Hopkins University Press, 1977], 44). This remark detracts from the novelty of Spenser's approach: they are indeed vehicles but at the same time they have enough autonomy to model attitudes from which the author at least partly dissociates himself. The understated conjecture has the effect of a stage direction suggesting that we not take too seriously what Colin is about to take terribly seriously: "he seemed troubled about something or other." Furthermore, "some care he tooke" conveys more willfulness than, e.g., "some care him tooke" (see below).

8. Colin's reaction to the gods will be echoed by another subject of Spenser's critical portraiture, Alcyon in *Daphnaida* (183 ff.), and Alcyon, whose plight is more drastic, is correspondingly more explicit in his negative view of the gods.

9. See Calvin R. Edwards's fine essay, "The Narcissus Myth in Spenser's Poetry," *Studies in Philology* 74 (1977): 63–88.

10. See below on these anomalous daffodils.

11. *Spenser, Marvell, and Renaissance Pastoral* (Cambridge: Harvard University Press, 1970), 82–83.

12. Trans. F. J. Miller, Loeb Classical Library (Cambridge: Harvard University Press, 1946), 2:99.

13. This projection can be seen by substituting first- for second-person pronouns in the first stanza: "my fresh spring," "my sommer prowde," etc.

14. R. A. Durr, "Spenser's Calendar of Christian Time," *ELH* 24 (1957): 271; Moore, 14; Cullen, 80–81.

15. He conveys the sense that she is patiently waiting him out—waiting for the nonsense to stop.

16.   Montrose, 39, stresses the conjunction of "rude *Pan*" and "welked *Phoebus*" and sees the transition from the first to the second as an "oblique allusion to the singing contest between Pan and Apollo," a reminder that "Colin's Apollonian aspirations are frustrated." But I fail to comprehend the logic of this reading. Phoebus, who defeated Pan, is here on the verge of being overhailed by Night. If Phoebus equals the god of poetry as well as the sun-god, then what is the "Night" that threatens it? Colin's frustration, at any rate, is explicitly Panic rather than Apollonian.

17.   Cf. my "Archaism, Vision, and Revision: Studies in Virgil, Plato, and Milton," *The Centennial Review* 11 (1967): 24–52.

18.   David R. Shore, "Colin and Rosalind: Love and Poetry in the *Shepheardes Calender*," *Studies in Philology* 73 (1976): 186.

19.   I owe this reading to my former student, D. S. Manning.

20.   *An Hymne in Honour of Beautie* 224; *An Hymne in Honour of Love* 198; *Amoretti* XXXV; cf. Edwards, 71 ff.

Colin to Hobbinol:
Spenser's Familiar Letters

JONATHAN GOLDBERG

The *Januarye* eclogue of Spenser's *Shepheardes Calender* is filled with Colin Clout's insistent complaint about the unresponsiveness of Rosalind. Not far from the close of this lament, the text exhibits an exorbitancy beyond its compulsive repetitiveness:

> It is not *Hobbinol*, wherefore I plaine,
> Albee my love he seeke with dayly suit:
> His clownish gifts and curtsies I disdaine,
> His kiddes, his cracknelles, and his early fruit.
> Ah foolish *Hobbinol*, thy gyfts bene vayne:
> *Colin* them gives to *Rosalind* againe.[1]

A gloss for the third of these lines, provided by the marginal figure of E. K., seeks to establish the propriety of the entrance of Hobbinol onto the scene of Colin's complaint: "His clownish gyfts . . . imitateth Virgils verse, Rusticus es Corydon, nec munera curat Alexis."[2] E. K. invites the reader to open Virgil's second eclogue to line fifty-six, in which the shepherd Corydon addresses himself and scores the folly of his suit: his gifts have not won Alexis. "Ah foolish *Hobbinol*": the line translates and transfers "rusticus es, Corydon" to Hobbinol, doubling the allusion, provoking exorbitant questions—not only the question of what Hobbinol's love for Colin Clout is doing in this text, with its monomaniacal lament for Rosalind, but also this one: if Colin is Alexis to Hobbinol's Corydon, is Colin thereby cast as Corydon in relationship to Rosalind's Alexis? How far does the allusion to Virgil's eclogue go? Where does the literary allusion place the erotics of Spenser's text?

The questions begin to answer themselves, but only insofar as they point to an excessive economy, literary and erotic at once, of translation and transference. "It is not *Hobbinol*, wherefore I plaine"; Colin is not Corydon complaining about Alexis—*his* Alexis is Rosalind. The allusion establishes the genre of the *Januarye* eclogue through its Virgilian antecedent, and

From *South Atlantic Quarterly* 88, no. 1 (Winter 1989): 107–26. Reprinted by permission of the author and Duke University Press.

Colin's complaint transfers Corydon's, rewriting Virgil in a series of reversals. The iciness of January replaces the scorching heat of Virgil's second eclogue. Corydon burns: "Formosum pastor Corydon ardebat Alexim."[3] Colin freezes: "Such rage as winters, reigneth in my heart, / My life bloud friesing with unkindly cold." Genre revision is also gender revision; Rosalind, the woman from "the neighbour towne" who scorns Colin's rustic music, takes the part of Alexis, the urbane favorite of his master who cannot be persuaded of the pleasures of the countryside. E. K. gratuitously suggests the translation in a further gloss: "Neighbour towne . . . the next towne: expressing the Latine Vicina,"[4] a note that refers to no original Latin "vicina"; it suggests the "vicinity" of the *Januarye* eclogue nonetheless, for Spenser's poem translates Virgil's eclogue back to its model, the eleventh idyll of Theocritus, Polyphemos's lament for Galatea. The reversals of genre and gender are true to a doubled source.

"Ah foolish *Hobbinol*, thy gyfts bene vayne: / *Colin* them gives to *Rosalind* againe." The analogical structure of this exchange of gifts (Hobbinol is to Colin as Colin is to Rosalind) repeats the generic transformation of the second eclogue, a doubling (giving again) that splits the same, rerouting Corydon's catalog of gifts for Alexis. The same gifts pass from Hobbinol to Colin and from Colin to Rosalind; the same "vayne" effect is achieved in each case—it passes through several hands and is yet refused. Although it is the same, it is no one's and never proper, a text circulating from hand to hand, always out of hand, never arriving. Yet this circulation within the same also opens difference, sexual difference most notably. For the circular structure further suggests that if Colin is Alexis to Hobbinol's Corydon, and Corydon to Rosalind's Alexis, he plays Rosalind to Hobbinol's frustrated suit. The homologies of this circulation place Colin at a split center, doubling himself; Janus-faced, he looks two ways.

Mirror tricks of genre and gender: true, again, to the source. Colin looks at the "barrein ground" and sees "a myrrhour"; Corydon looks at the sea and sees himself, in an ideal projection, as Daphnis, as the image does not deceive ("si numquam fallit imago"). Corydon offers Alexis the chestnuts that pleased Amaryllis when she was his beloved; Colin passes Hobbinol's gifts on to Rosalind. Duplicating images, the same becomes different. In Virgil's poem, Corydon has loved Amaryllis and now loves Alexis to his sorrow; he might better, he says, have borne the disdain of Amaryllis, or have accepted Menalcas, unattractive as he is. In Virgil's Rome, such alternatives were possible—the love of boys and the love of women were not opposing categories.[5] And in Elizabethan England? "A Shepheards boye (no better do him call)": so is Colin Clout introduced. Can this boy thus play the woman's part? Another Rosalind, Shakespeare's, playing the part of Ganymede in *As You Like It*, might reply, affirming the identification: "for every passion something and for no passion truly anything, as boys and women are for the most part cattle of this color."

Such a reading is policed from the margin in E. K.'s gloss on Hobbinol: "In thys place seemeth to be some savour of disorderly love, which the learned call pæderastice: but it is gathered beside his meaning."[6] E. K., whose earlier translation of neighborhood had granted proximity to vicinity, rules "disorderly love" out of "thys place" and "beside his meaning." Beside: extraneous or parallel? The question, once again, is of the economies of exchange, of genre and gender. For, even as E. K.'s citation of Virgil suggests, the *Januarye* eclogue operates through displacement and replacement. Its "place" is translation, the mirrored spacing of a proximity; "thys place" is always "beside his meaning." The exorbitancy of allusion guarantees such proximity. And thus E. K.'s gloss registers its refusal of "disorderly love" by ordering it through an act of learned translation; this love properly speaks Greek (pæderastice) even as the poem's "neighborhood" is translated Latin. What is "gathered beside" is an exorbitancy written within the economies of exchange, the circulation of the gift and text: "for every passion something and for no passion truly anything," as Shakespeare's Rosalind puts it, the exorbitancy—something and nothing at once—of literature.

Even as E. K. rules out a reading, he rules it into the textual economies of the *Shepheardes Calender;* E. K.'s gloss continues with classical citations of a *proper* pederasty, the example of Socrates, to arrive at this conclusion: "And so is pæderastice much to be præferred before gynerastice, that is the love whiche enflameth men with lust toward woman kind."[7] Does this classicism—from Virgil's second eclogue to a platonized and delibidinized Socrates—secure the literary propriety of the text? Consider Erasmus's account of the second eclogue in *De Ratione Studii,* where Virgil's poem is chosen to illustrate pedagogic method. The poem, Erasmus says, will allow the teacher to discourse on friendship: "'The essence of friendship,' the Master would begin, 'lies in similarity.'"[8] Pairs of friends like Castor and Pollux are to be adduced, and then the poem may be read: "Now it is as a parable of unstable friendship that the Master should treat this Eclogue. Alexis is of the town, Corydon a countryman; Corydon a shepherd; Alexis a man of society. Alexis cultivated, young, graceful; Corydon rude, crippled, his youth far behind him. Hence the impossibility of a true friendship."[9] For Erasmus, Virgil's poem savors of disorderly love, "unstable friendship," differences that refuse the homeostasis of "similarity," identifications within the self-same and proper. From an Erasmian perspective, E. K.'s glosses—the poet "imitateth Virgils verse," the learned disquisition on a proper pederasty—would be excessive; rather than placing Spenser's poem within the confines of classical purity, they overstep those limits.

Yet the "place" of that textual exorbitance, as we have remarked already, is within similitude, and even the Erasmian text offers a mirror. Among the exemplars of friendship adduced by Erasmus is "the beautiful myth of Narcissus." "What has more likeness to ourselves than our own reflection?" Erasmus goes on to ask. His text, too, succumbs to the mirror effects of the *Januarye* eclogue, displays the same logic as the marginal (and exorbitant) glosses of E. K. and their double-edged reflections that attempt to "place" the poem within its sexual and textual economies, a place that escapes those confines by passing through the mirror. The excessive logic of the mirror of Narcissus may overcome the moral economies in which Erasmus would place Virgil's second eclogue—or those that regulate a reading of the *Januarye* eclogue: "The Mirror Stage of Colin Clout."

Thus Harry Berger, Jr., titles his complaint against the *Januarye* eclogue for its "self-indulgent" displays of "narcissistic metamorphosis": "Perhaps, to speculate idly, this confusion of literary and erotic motives informed the poetry addressed to Rosalind and affected her adverse reactions: perhaps she questioned the poet-lover's sincerity as well as his taste."[10] Whether she did or not, Berger does. His "speculations" pass through the mirror as he assumes the place of Rosalind, disdaining Colin Clout's narcissistic literary love; or when he occupies the place in which he muses, "why love a lass rather than someone or something more tractable—e.g., Hobbinoll or the 'refyned forme' of the woman as Idea—and more susceptible to the allure of Epanorthosis and Paronomasia?" Berger reacts excessively to Colin's line "I love thilke lasse, (alas why doe I love?)" and to E. K.'s gloss, "a prety Epanorthosis in these two verses, and withall a Paronomasia or playing with the word." Mere rhetoric, Berger charges; rhetoric, E. K. defends. Berger "speculates" within the exorbitancy of identifications within the mirror—voicing, variously, vicariously, the positions of Rosalind, of Colin, of E. K., and Hobbinol. "How real—how genuine or authentic—are the love and grief that can be proportioned to the demands of poetry and displayed in the mirror of art?"[11] One answer suggests itself as the text places Berger's ethical stance, capturing it within the mirror. What, we may ask again, is the "place" of the *Januarye* eclogue within the "real"?

Alan Bray addresses the question, taking up the nineteenth-century misapprehension that the imitation of classical literature in the Renaissance functioned (as it did for the Victorians) as a sign "implying a tolerant attitude to homosexuality."[12] "Apparently homosexual themes in Renaissance literature need to be treated with extreme caution," Bray argues. Perhaps, he suggests, the extraordinary case of Christopher Marlowe (his supposed saying that St. John was "Our Saviour Christ's Alexis") does represent Marlowe's homosexual appropriation of Virgil's second eclogue, but more often classical imitations (as when Richard Barnfield writes to his Ganymede) are "literary exercises" and nothing more—except to those readers who wanted to find in such poems justifications for their sexual tastes.[13] They prove, Bray contends, nothing about their authors. Bray, then, would appear to agree with Berger; there is nothing real in the *Januarye* eclogue, it tells us nothing about Spenser himself, or his loves; it is all rhetorical play, exercises in a literariness at a remove from history.

What is shaky in Bray's argument is implicit in the title of the chapter in which he discusses these questions, "Society and the Individual," for those terms have already assumed an opposition that is, arguably, a post-Renaissance, post-Cartesian development, and whose use by Bray has the unfortunate effect of making an ideological argument by assuming as universal a quite particular historical (and liberal, bourgeois) construction of the "individual" subject.[14] This is something that Bray knows quite well since it helps him to explain the emergence of homosexual "individuals" in the early eighteenth century, and he cautions that the terms are not to be found in the Renaissance: "To talk of an individual in this period as being or not being 'a homosexual' is an anachronism and ruinously misleading"—misleading, as I have argued elsewhere, even in the case of Christopher Marlowe.[15]

When Bray decides that Barnfield's commonplace book, "never intended for publication and . . . both robustly pornographic and entirely heterosexual," offers the real truth about its author's sexual orientation, savoring of the "personal experience" lacking in his literary exercises addressed to Ganymede and other Arcadian shepherds, he anachronistically assumes the opposition of homosexual and heterosexual, and he assumes that Barnfield must have been one or the other. The characterization of those entries as "robustly pornographic" (as opposed to the "delicate sensibility" of the poems) as well as the categories of "entirely heterosexual" and "personal experience" needs to be scrutinized for what Eve Kosofsky Sedgwick might call their "inadvertent reification."[16] For Bray, the secret status of the commonplace book assures the truth of Barnfield's heterosexuality; but this, too, is anachronistic. It assumes a modern "deployment of sexuality" (in Foucault's term)[17] to be in place, in which one can be sure that the deepest secret of the self is its sexuality, especially if, as in the case of Barnfield, it assumes the excessive form that Bray calls pornographic. Yet to read the evidence about Barnfield this way rewrites him as a modern subject. It dismisses what might be called the "open secret" of Barnfield's published poems without asking how they assumed a "place" in the Elizabethan world.[18] For the answer to that question cannot be the one that Bray assumes: that its classical literariness necessarily assured that it would go unremarked (Erasmus suggests otherwise); nor that it could be read homosexually by those inclined in that direction. For, as Bray himself argues, one could not identify oneself as being so inclined. Or, to put the point—*Bray's point*—more radically, there were no homosexuals in Renaissance England.

Such, too, was the case in Virgil's Rome; if homosexuality is a term that signifies only in relationship to the binary opposition homosexual/heterosexual, then the second eclogue does not operate within that system. Within the Roman sexual system, as Veyne has argued (following Foucault), what mattered was not the gender of the love object but his/her class and age;

sexuality was congruent with power differences. So long as a man was the penetrator, he was a man; slave boys and women were the appropriate objects of his desire. Virgil's poem is not necessarily circumscribed by this system—Alexis is not a slave, but his master's favorite; Corydon, who may well be older, also appears to be of a lower class than Alexis, and his love seems to exceed the Roman norm of a passionless sexuality. Virgil's poem, translating the grotesquerie of Polyphemos's love for Galatea, opens itself toward the Erasmian dismissal of its disorderliness even as it uses that safeguard to extend the limits of acceptability, an extension that may also return his poem to the orbit of the erotic system of ancient Greece, which, although similar to the Roman system, had not viewed slave boys as the preferred sexual objects. Rather, as Foucault has claimed, the entire ethical system of Greek pederasty was directed at questions having to do with free-born boys.[19]

Bray argues that differentials of class and age in a number of institutional sites—the family, the school, the apprentice system—also operate to define sexual spheres in Renaissance England in which homosexual acts could and did take place. Such acts do not prove their actors homosexual; likewise, texts like the *Januarye* eclogue (or Barnfield's classical pastorals) will never tell us whether their authors slept with boys. But they may, in the very exorbitancy that I have been reading, tell us about the "place" of homosexuality in Renaissance England; not least if, as Bray contends, it had no place, was not a site of recognition of sexual identity. Bray posits a *disconnection* between the stigmatization of homosexual acts (within the larger category of sodomy) and their enactment in places in which they went unseen and seen. This is, in effect, to describe the place of homosexuality as an open secret. If sodomy is the term most proximate to homosexuality in the period, it functions neither solely to designate sex between men, nor is it only (perhaps not even primarily) a sexual term. Designating a range of interlinked social and religious transgressions, it also leaves untouched, Bray argues, the ordinary social channels that permitted homosexual acts to be disseminated through all the differentials of power that mark the hierarchies of Renaissance society. "The individual could simply avoid making the connection; he could keep at two opposite poles the social pressures bearing down on him and his own discordant sexual behavior, and avoid recognising it for what it was."[20] But what *was* it? Bray's sentences, brilliant in suggesting the dehiscence that opens the place of homosexuality, has already foreclosed it by assuming an identity for that "it" which, as his argument suggests, cannot succumb to the later scheme in which "homosexuality" is a recognized and recognizable category.

The reading of *Januarye* that I have been offering may appear to have been an exercise in deconstructive undecidability, merely rhetorical play. I would contend, however, that it offers a way to read the (no) place of homosexuality in Renaissance culture—that the mirror effects of *Januarye* secure a place for homosexuality through such tactics of resemblance. How to move from the text, and these textual effects, into the world are in fact suggested by the *Shepheardes Calender*, not least by E. K.'s tactics of reading. For his gloss, on the margins, also opens up a relationship between the text and the world, opens it and covers it over as does his gloss on "pæderastice." That double play has the structure of the open secret. Who is Colin Clout? "Under which name this Poete secretly shadoweth himself." Hobbinol?: "a fained country name, whereby, it being so commune and usuall, seemeth to be hidden the person of some his very speciall and most familiar freend, whom he entirely and extraordinarily beloved, as peradventure shall be more largely declared hereafter." "Rosalinde . . . is also a feigned name, which being wel ordered, wil bewray the very name of hys love and mistresse, whom by that name he coloureth."[21] E. K.'s directions for reading cannot be taken very straightforwardly (nor, for that matter, can "E. K.," whose initials remain to be deciphered). If Spenser "is" Colin Clout, for example, he is also figured as Immerito in the *Shepheardes Calender* and no "proper" name is ever delivered for the doubly named author of a yet anonymous text.[22] E. K.'s directions for reading Rosalind treat her name as an anagram—as if the name were itself disordered (or the name of disorderly love), and as if to find her would be the same as performing a play on the letter. In this teasing play between revelation and reveiling, the *Calender* dangles its secrets—the secret of an authorship maintained through a disappearing act in disseminative naming; of an Eros that may never pass beyond the letter, and which yet opens a way (within a certain psychoanalytic framework, *the* way).[23] The open secret of this text is not homosexuality, as might well be the case if this were a Victorian imitation of a classical poem. Instead, it has no name, "being so commune and usuall" and, at the same time, "very speciall and most familiar." Or, if it does have one, it could be called (following Sedgwick) homosociality. In this text, the name of the open secret is Hobbinol.

Spenser's name remains veiled in the *Calender*. E. K. and Rosalind have never been deciphered. But E. K.'s promise to declare hereafter the identity of Hobbinol is delivered in a gloss to *September*. "Colin cloute . . . Nowe I thinke no man doubteth but by Colin is ever meante the Authour selfe. Whose especiall good freend Hobbinoll sayth he is, or more rightly Mayster Gabriel Harvey: of whose speciall commendation, aswell in Poetrye as Rhetorike and other choyce learning, we have lately had a sufficient tryall in diverse his workes." That revelation is prepared for from the start. E. K.'s dedicatory epistle to the *Calender* is addressed to Harvey, introducing the new poet to someone who scarcely needs such an introduction, "his verie special and singular good frend," and that description is immediately applied to Hobbinol, as we have seen, in the gloss to *Januarye*: "his very speciall and most familiar freend."[24] Hobbinol, moreover, is a name that

Harvey takes for himself at the close of the third of the *Three Proper, and wittie, familiar Letters* that he exchanged with "Immerito" in a volume that appeared in 1580, a year after the publication of the *Calender*, another anonymous production in which Harvey's name is the open secret as soon as one gets past the title page and to the first letter addressed by Immerito to his "long approoved and singular good friende, Master *G. H.*" And, if there were any doubt about who "Maister G. H. Fellow of Trinitie Hall in Cambridge" is, as he is addressed in the first of the *Two Other very commendable Letters* that accompanied the first three, a poem of Immerito's enclosed in that letter twice names "Harvey" explicitly, puns on his angelic first name, Gabriel, and ends by bidding farewell to *"Mi amabilissime / Harveie, meo cordi, meorum omnium longè charissime"*: "My sweetest Harvey, to me of all my friends by far the dearest."[25]

Within the *Shepheardes Calender*, Hobbinol is the shepherd suffering from unrequited love for Colin, and that fiction is maintained from *Januarye* to *Aprill*, where, in response to Thenot's question about the causes of his sorrow—lambs stolen by wolves? bagpipe broken? abandoned by a "lasse"? weeping like the showers of April?—Hobbinol replies "Nor thys, nor that, so muche doeth make me mourne, / But for the ladde, whome long I lovd so deare"; to *June*, where Colin tells Hobbinol that his paradise is not for him; to *September*, and the line that E. K. glosses: "Colin he whilome my ioye." But in the gloss, and in the surrounding apparatus that extends from the poem to other texts and into the world, Hobbinol is Gabriel Harvey, and the poet's special friendship for him is repeatedly announced. Indeed, in the farewell poem to Harvey (written when Immerito plans to leave England on a voyage to the continent), Immerito's veil is almost dropped as well when he ventriloquizes Harvey's lament for his absent friend: "Would Heaven my Edmund were here. / He would have written me news, nor himself have been silent / Regarding his love, and often, in his heart and with words / Of the kindest, would bless me."[26] The relationship between Hobbinol, in the eclogues of the *Calender*, and Harvey, in the margins, functions like the reverse mirror of *Januarye*, identifying (Hobbinol is Harvey), doubling (Harvey is Hobbinol), and reversing (the rejected lover is the special friend) all at the same time. This mirror extends into the world, Harvey taking Hobbinol for his own name in a letter to Immerito. What the eclogues structure as denial and refusal, the surrounding context figures as the acceptance of a special friendship. How is this (non)relationship to be read?

One answer lies within the eclogues themselves, and Hobbinol's role within the pastoral fiction; there he secures a literariness associated with that transformative place, and Colin's refusal of his advances also signals his frustrated attempts to pass beyond pastoral. From the start, Colin has broken the pipes of Pan, moved toward the urban Rosalind, to his devastation; and as late as *Colin Clouts Come Home Again* (1595), his return to pastoral is a return to Hobbinol, as "The shepheards boy (best knowen by that name)" re-encounters the one who "lov'd this shepheard dearest in degree." As late as that poem or the sixth book of *The Faerie Queene*, Rosalind still names what cannot be had. And those returns to pastoral and to Hobbinol remain returns to a refusal of Hobbinol. Colin continues to look elsewhere. This is how Hobbinol explains his plight to Thenot in *Aprill:* "the ladde, whome long I lovd so deare / Now loves a lasse," and that love has made the writing of pastoral poetry impossible. "Lo *Colin*, here the place": so Hobbinol in *June* speaks to Colin, luring him to a "Paradise" that Colin rejects as no longer possible. Hobbinol, throughout the *Calender*, is associated with "the place"—the literary, erotic, and sociohistorical place—from which Colin affirms his displacement.

This refusal reads doubly, however; within a duplicity that can be found in the *Calender*, one can begin to move toward the world which it mirrors in reverse. For however much Colin denies, he is a figure in a pastoral poem; the place from which Colin affirms his displacement is the place in which he affirms it. The poet embraces what his figure refuses. The denials are productive. They produce the poems as that double place from which aspirations—toward Rosalind, toward kinds of poetry other than pastoral—can be launched and denied at the same time. Rosalind refuses Colin; in *June*, he reports that she has instead taken Menalcas, the dark young man whom Virgil's Corydon scorned. Even as the poems glance beyond the confines of pastoral, they are returned within its limits, still turning on Virgilian tropes. But it is also within the confines of Virgilian pastoral that it be exorbitant, that it establish relationships with the world; it establishes them by denying them, and Hobbinol is within the eclogues the figure for that denial.

It has become commonplace in certain critical practices that are called "new historicist" to argue that "love is not love" or that pastoral otium is really negotium.[27] This essay shares with such work the desire to read texts into the world. But in describing the trick mirror that the *Shepheardes Calender* holds up to the world, in pursuing the reversed identification of Hobbinol and Harvey, it seems to me important not to allegorize and thematize the text so entirely that its sole function is to read the world at the expense of the text, to decide beforehand that the world is real and that the only reality that a text might have would be its ability to translate the world in terms that need to be translated back into the social, historical, or political. The literary and erotic translations performed in the *Calender* extend into the world, as the Hobbinol-Harvey identification would seem to guarantee. But it cannot be read as a simple act of translation. The name "Hobbinol" is carried beyond the confines of the *Shepheardes Calender*, even as the name "Harvey" appears on its borders. And the double structure within pastoral also extends into the "real" world. We can see it as congruent with the dehiscence that Bray describes, articulating the site of a (non)relationship and a (non)recognition. We can see it, too, in the fact of double nomination, Harvey/Hobbinol, Immerito/Colin, and the space of (non)identification that it opens. These are structures of identification in a mirror, a productive site of replication.

If we look at the moment in *September* when the veil is dropped, and Harvey's name delivered, we find it in a gloss on Hobbinol's request that Diggon tell the tale of Roffynn; Hobbinol would hear the story since "Colin clout I wene be his selfe boye"—i.e., Colin is Roffynn's boye and not, as Hobbinol goes on to say, as he once was, his own: "(Ah for Colin he whilome my ioye)." *September* is a particularly dark eclogue, glancing in Roffynn's tale and elsewhere at matters of state and church, but this particular identification is not all that hard to decipher. We can find "Roffynn" on the flyleaf to Harvey's copy of Jerome Turler's *The Traveiler*, as he records it as a gift from Spenser: "ex dono Edmundi Spenserii, Episcopi Roffensis Secretarii. 1578."[28] Roffynn anglicizes the Latin name of John Young, Bishop of Rochester, whose secretary Spenser became in the spring of 1578. If, elsewhere in the *Calender*, and throughout Spenser's poems, Hobbinol appears as the rival for Rosalind, here he is in a similar position with Roffynn; as Colin moves beyond the pastoral world, Hobbinol stays behind, representing what must be refused in order to advance. But advancement also occurs through what is represented by Hobbinol: a mode of high literariness that gives one credentials within the world—in this instance, the classicizing pastoral of the *Calender*—within the exorbitancy of humanistic pedagogy. The secrets of the *Calender* are the open secrets of a secretariat, and of aspirations that must veil themselves in this humble form.

Harvey's role in this worldliness is insisted upon as E. K. continues his gloss, identifying Harvey in the *September* eclogue; he lists his recent publications "aswell in Poetrye as Rhetorike" and details Harvey's presentation of a copy of "his late Gratulationum Valdinensium" to Queen Elizabeth "at the worshipfull Maister Capells in Hertfordshire."[29] Harvey's attempts to use his rhetorico-literary skills to secure him a place in the world are perhaps the most spectacular examples of the failure of the promises of humanistic pedagogy in the Elizabethan period. Uncannily, Spenser uses Hobbinol/Harvey as the name that secures failure by denying the very tools by which success can be achieved. Yet Harvey, probably not more than a couple of years Spenser's senior but, more importantly, already a Fellow at Pembroke when Spenser entered as sizar, a poor boy, in 1569, also functions as mentor and guide. The intimacy with his special friend writes the aspirations within the rhetorico-literary even as the name Hobbinol insists that such aspirers know their place: boys, secretaries to the great and powerful.

The trick mirrors of *Januarye* negotiate the place of the literary within the sociopolitics and the homoerotics of a textual economy that extends into the world and writes the world as much as the world writes the text. The veils of the *Calender* can be drawn only when they open upon an acceptable version of aspiration within the homosocial sphere, aspiration, that is, that knows its place—"A Shepeheards boye (no better doe him call)." Immerito, the worthless one, attaches himself to his special friend Gabriel Harvey, hailing him as in his farewell poem as "a poet transcendent" ("egregium . . . Poetam") addressed by "the lowliest poet" ("malus . . . Poeta"). The point of homeostasis in this differentiated and hierarchized relationship with angel Gabriel is their friendship; to this friend, the first line of the farewell poem insists, he is not unfriendly ("non inimicus Amicum"); no disorderly love, it secures the status quo. Within this mirror relation, Harvey/Hobbinol functions as an alter ego, so much so that E. K. can close his dedicatory epistle by urging Harvey to imitate the new poet and publish: "Now I trust M. Harvey, that upon sight of your speciall frends and fellow Poets doings, or els for envie of so many unworthy Quidams, which catch at the garlond, which to you alone is dewe, you will be perswaded to pluck out of the hateful darknesse, those so many excellent English poemes of yours, which lye hid, and bring them forth to eternall light."[30] And the letters exchanged between Immerito and G. H. continue this theme, referring again and again to their secret poems, and urging each other to make them public. This is a structure of emulation recommended by Erasmus and his followers as necessary to pedagogic success; the title page of the *Three Proper, and wittie, familiar Letters* proclaims the writers as "*two Universitie men.*"

Yet in the poem of farewell to Harvey, Edmund urges him to venture even further, beyond such pedagogic, humanistic, pastoral economies, toward the love that Harvey despises, what G. H. designates in the last of the letters as Immerito's "womanly humor": "A magnanimous spirit, I know, spurs you up to the summits / Of honor and inspires your poems with emotions more solemn / Than lighthearted love."[31] For the point seems to be that Harvey' misogyny (displayed at length in the three letters, as when he paraphrases "Arte Amandi" as "Arte Meretricandi," or offers two accounts of earthquakes, one for women, another for men) is not requisite for their attachment, nor does the poet's desire for Rosalind mean the end of their extraordinary friendship. So, Immerito's final letter closes, urging Harvey to believe in "the eternall Memorie of our everlasting friendship, the inviolable Memorie of our unspotted friendshippe, the sacred Memorie of our vowed friendship. . . . Farewell most hartily, mine owne good *Master H.* and love me, as I love you, and thinke upon poore *Immerito*, as he thinketh uppon you."[32] This mirroring reciprocity defines a proper "unspotted" relationship between men, not the path of Harvey's aspirations (figured in the *Calender* as Hobbinol's rootedness), and one secured through the negations written as Rosalind's refusals and transferred from Colin to Hobbinol, from Immerito to G. H. Letters of farewell, again and again. Harvey/Hobbinol confined to the margins—where the "real" enters the poem—and Harvey, in life, never making his way, confined to *his* marginalia.

The love of women does not interrupt this love. Thus the *Shepheardes Calender* closes by dispatching Hobbinol as go-between to Rosalind: "Adieu good *Hobbinol*, that was so true, / Tell *Rosalind*, her *Colin* bids her adieu." These poems of farewell to Harvey/Hobbinol also write him into Colin/Immerito/Spenser's position, structures of denial that ramify out into the world. Here, as they establish a relationship of nonrelationship *between men*, they do so as Hobbinol is asked in *December* to voice the farewell to Rosalind that he has so often received from Colin. In these (un)productive circles, the woman is drawn into the circuit of letters passing between men (Rosalind's name is never realized beyond such anagrammatization); the woman is infolded as that furthering negation that opens a movement toward the real.

So, too, in response to Immerito's question in the first of the *Three Proper, and wittie, familiar Letters*, asking why G. H. had not responded to his beloved's letters, G. H. responds—as Hobbinol—promising to reply in letters that are worthy of her: "By your own Venus, she is another dear little Rosalind; and not another but the same Hobbinol (with your kind permission as before) loves her deeply. O my Mistress Immerito, my most beautiful Collina Clout, countless greetings to you and farewell."[33] The *same* Hobbinol/Harvey (one and two at once) writes to Mrs. Immerito (the beloved Immerito has married), who is *not* Rosalind, within the folds of this letter to Immerito. But it is also within the letter that Immerito tells G. H. to remember their special friendship and love—"Continue with usuall writings," although he wishes for "a Reciprocall farewell from your owne sweete mouthe." And G. H. hopes to comply, wishing that "I may personally performe your request, and bestowe the sweetest Farewell, upon your sweetmouthed Mastershippe."[34]

These *proper familiar* letters exchanged between friends openly declare their secrets of translation and transference from the start, beginning with a *literal* scene of translation in the very first letter from Immerito to G. H. Immerito offers samples of his skills in translation, his efforts (under the tutelage of G. H.) to classicize his English verses and make their meters Latin: "Seeme they comparable to those two," he asks, "which I translated you *ex tempore* in bed, the last time we lay togither in Westminster?"[35]

Spenser slept with Harvey, and it is no secret. Indeed this is the open secret of a *proper* and *familiar* scene, exhibiting the very structure E. K. read in the name of Hobbinol in *Januarye*, "so commune and usuall," "very speciall and most familiar," for men habitually shared beds in the Elizabethan age. A secret written elsewhere too, for there is nothing to hide. So Roger Ascham, pausing to memorialize his student John Whitney, now dead, and to bid him farewell, recalls, in his book on double translation, the scene of instruction: "John Whitney, a young gentlemen, was my bedfellow, who, willing by good nature and provoked by mine advice, began to learn the Latin tongue."[36] The text chosen for this double translation "out of Latin into English and out of English into Latin again" was "Tully *De amicitia.*" A proper choice. The scene fulfills the dictates of Erasmian pedagogy to the letter, as the teacher incites the pupil to learn—by loving imitation within the specular relationship of similarity and simulation. The child "must be beguiled and not driven to learning," Erasmus writes in *De Pueris Instituendis,* and he continues: "For a boy is often drawn to a subject first for his master's sake, and afterwards for its own. Learning, like many other things, wins our liking for the reason that it is offered to us by one we love."[37]

To that bedroom scene Harvey brings another. Judging some other efforts at translation, he recommends the use of models for imitation: "some *Gentlewooman,* I coulde name in England . . . might as well have brought forth all goodly faire children" [as a poet might produce excellent poems] "had they at the tyme of their *Conception,* had in sight, the amiable and gallant beautifull Pictures of *Adonis, Cupido, Ganymedes,* or the like, which no doubt would have wrought such deepe impression in their fantasies, and imaginations, as their children, and perhappes their Childrens children too, myght have thanked them."[38] "Nature has made the first years of our life prone to imitation," Erasmus writes; pedagogy is founded in simulation.[39] But for Harvey, all conception is specular, for men and women alike are produced in the mirror, after the images of desire—Adonis, Cupid, Ganymede.

This is not only Harvey's fantasy; it is one shared by his culture. Consider the lines that open Shakespeare's first and third sonnets in the 1609 edition: "From fairest creatures we desire increase / That thereby beauties *Rose* might never die"; "Looke in thy glasse and tell the face thou vewest, / Now is the time that face should forme an other." This is, indeed, the mirror stage, and not only of Colin Clout. For, as Lacan writes in his essay on the role of the mirror stage in the formation of the "I," that initiation into an alienated and split subjectivity has a biological support instanced, for example, by the necessity for the maturation of the gonad of the pigeon that it see another member of its species—of either sex—or even that it see itself in a mirror: "Facts which inscribe themselves into an order of homeomorphic identification which would fold within itself the question of the notion of beauty as formative and as erogenic."[40]

The homeomorphic structures identified in this essay ramify within an order that Lacan calls "orthopedic," the (non)support of an ideal projection—for which Lacan finds the "ancient term *imago*" apt, and Spenser, the Virgilian *imago*—in which subjectivity is founded. The Lacanian insistence on the prematurity of human arrival, and its destiny within an imaginary scene, has its Erasmian correspondent: "Man, lacking instinct, can do little or nothing of innate power; scarce can he eat, or walk, or speak, unless he be guided thereto"; "a man ignorant of Letters is no man at all."[41] Imitation of the letter founds the human within a pedagogic apparatus, the "virage du *je* spéculaire en *je* social," turning the specular I into the social I.[42] Such destiny, as Derrida argues, is a destinerrance, a straying within a letter whose arrival is never guaranteed.[43] Within that spacing, which, for Elizabethans like Spenser and Harvey, takes the historically specific situation of the apparatuses of a homosocial pedagogy, the Spenserian career—in life, in letters—is launched. In it, Hobbinol/Harvey serves—in life, in letters—as a marginal site, the "place" of the exorbitant *méconnaissance* that guarantees that institution.

Notes

1. All citations are from *The Poetical Works of Edmund Spenser*, ed. J. C. Smith and E. De Selincourt (London, 1912). Here and elsewhere, inconsistencies in spelling in my text mirror those in the texts cited.

2. Ibid., 422.

3. "A shepherd, Corydon, burned with love for handsome Alexis." Citations of Virgil are from *The Eclogues and Georgics of Virgil*, trans. C. Day Lewis (Garden City, N.Y., 1964).

4. Spenser, *Poetical Works*, 422.

5. See Paul Veyne, "Homosexuality in Ancient Rome," in *Western Sexuality*, ed. Philippe Ariès and André Béjin (Oxford, 1985), 26. For a brilliant historical survey, see David M. Halperin, "One Hundred Years of Homosexuality," *Diacritics* 16 (1986): 34–45.

6. Spenser, *Poetical Works*, 422–23.

7. Ibid., 423.

8. William Harrison Woodward, *Desiderius Erasmus Concerning the Aim and Method of Education* (New York, 1964), 174.

9. Ibid., 175.

10. Harry Berger, Jr., "The Mirror Stage of Colin Clout: A New Reading of Spenser's *Januarye* Eclogue," Helios 10 (1983): 151, 154.

11. Ibid., 156, 158.

12. Alan Bray, *Homosexuality in Renaissance England* (London, 1982), 59. Nothing in my critique of Bray is meant to devalue his book; the problem of literary evidence troubles many distinguished historians, and Bray remains the best guide to the question of homosexuality in Renaissance England.

13. Ibid., 65, 61.

14. My critique here follows Eve Kosofsky Sedgwick, *Between Men: English Literature and Male Homosocial Desire* (New York, 1985), 83–90.

15. Bray, *Homosexuality in Renaissance England*, 16; Jonathan Goldberg, "Sodomy and Society: The Case of Christopher Marlowe," *Southwest Review* 69 (1985): 371–78.

16. Bray, *Homosexuality in Renaissance England*, 61; see Sedgwick, *Between Men*, 86.

17. Michel Foucault, *The History of Sexuality*, trans, Robert Hurley (New York, 1980), pt. 4.

18. For the role of "open secrets" to secure the secret subjectivity of the modern subject, see D. A. Miller, "Secret Subjects, Open Secrets," in *The Novel and the Police* (Berkeley and Los Angeles, 1988), 192–220.

19. See Michel Foucault, *The Use of Pleasure*, trans. Robert Hurley (New York, 1986), 187ff. In Virgil's second eclogue, much depends on the final lines of the poem, whether Corydon continues to address himself or is being addressed—something that remains undecidable and thus keeps open the question of the perspective taken on his "dementia."

20. Bray, *Homosexuality in Renaissance England*, 67.

21. Spenser, *Poetical Works*, 422–23.

22. For further discussion of these issues, see my "Consuming Texts: Spenser and the Poet's Economy," in *Voice Terminal Echo: Postmodernism and English Renaissance Texts* (New York and London, 1986).

23. I have in mind the Lacanian framework, in which the refusal ever to embody Rosalind as a "real" woman would testify to the structure of desire shaped by an Other that is, by definition, inaccessible. This leads, within the Lacanian schema, to the postulate that there is no woman per se; and this leads, within an argument like Sedgwick's, to a realization of the homosocial structure between men that covers over the place of woman. Thus Berger's ethical complaint—that Colin is in love with a projected idea of woman—can be supported by the recognition of psychic and social structures that make the place of woman insupportable. Yet this structure obtains not only in the case of Rosalind, but also underwrites the place of Colin Clout—and that place writes itself into the real, although never in the same way for each gender.

24. Spenser, *Poetical Works*, 455, 415, 422.

25. Spenser, *Poetical Works*, 632, 611, 635, 638; translation of the Latin poem is included in *Spenser's Prose Works*, ed. Rudolf Gottfried (Baltimore, 1949), 258.

26. Spenser, *Prose Works*, 258; for the Latin text see Spenser, *Poetical Works*, 638.

27. The first phrase is Sidney's and is invoked by Arthur Marotti, "'Love is not love': Elizabethan Sonnet Sequences and the Social Order," *ELH* 49 (1982): 396–428, and is the guiding thesis as well in Marotti's *John Donne: Coterie Poet* (Madison, 1986). The translation of pastoral otium into negotium is the theme in a number of essays by Louis Montrose; see, for example, "Of Gentlemen and Shepherds: The Politics of Elizabethan Pastoral Form," *ELH* 50 (1983): 415–59. My argument attempts to modify the point made repeatedly in such work, that love must be translated into something "real"—ambition—or that pastoral functions as a cover for a place in the world and negotiates the desire for it.

28. Cited in Virginia Stern, *Gabriel Harvey: His Life, Marginalia, and Library* (Oxford, 1979), 237; for information on Spenser's secretaryship to Young, see 48–49. Harvey's parasitic relationship to texts, living in his marginalia, I take to describe a modus vivendi, an argument I make in part thanks to work in progress by Jennifer Summit.

29. Spenser, *Poetical Works*, 455.

30. Ibid., 419.

31. Spenser, *Poetical Works*, 641; Spenser, *Prose Works*, 256. For the Latin text, see Spenser, *Poetical Works*, 637.

32. Spenser, *Poetical Works*, 641, 638.

33. For the Latin text, see Spenser, *Poetical Works*, 632. My translation depends on the one offered in Frederic Ives Carpenter, *A Reference Guide to Edmund Spenser* (Chicago, 1923), 58.

34. Spenser, *Poetical Works*, 638, 636, 641.

35. Ibid., 611.

36. Roger Ascham, *The Schoolmaster*, ed. Lawrence V. Ryan (Ithaca, 1967), 80. The secret of the shared bed is more usually declared in patronage and servant-master relations where, as Bray argues in "Dreams, Fantasies, and Fears: Defining Sexuality in Elizabethan England" (a paper distributed at the International Scientific Conference on Gay and Lesbian Studies, Free University, Amsterdam, 15–18 December 1987), shared beds (or tables) suggest intimate power and influence. Thus Archbishop Laud recorded in his diary on 21 August 1625 a dream of sleeping with Buckingham. When these relations were politically suspect, such intimacies could fall under the shadow of sodomy. In another paper, "Pederasty in Elizabethan London," from the same conference, Robert M. Wren starts with the *Januarye* eclogue and extends Bray's argument to the theaters and schools—pointing as well to shared beds in such plays as Middleton's *Michaelmas Term*, Chapman's *Sir Giles Goosecap*, and Shakespeare's *Henry V* and *Othello*, suggesting too that medical manuals may have encouraged masturbation in a widespread and culturally countenanced pederasty.

37. Woodward, *Erasmus Concerning . . . Education*, 203.

38. Spenser, *Poetical Works*, 626.

39. Woodward, *Erasmus Concerning . . . Education*, 189.

40. Jacques Lacan, *Écrits I* (Paris, 1966), 92: "Faits qui s'inscrivent dans un ordre d'identification homéomorphique qu'envelopperait la question du sens de la beauté comme formative et comme érogène." In *Ecrits: A Selection*, trans. Alan Sheridan (New York, 1977), the passage reads: "Such facts are inscribed in an order of homeomorphic identification that would itself fall within the larger question of the meaning of beauty as both formative and erogenic" (3).

41. Woodward, *Erasmus Concerning . . . Education*, 184, 181.

42. See Lacan, *Écrits I*, 94, 90, 95.

43. See Jacques Derrida, *The Post Card from Socrates to Freud and Beyond*, trans. Alan Bass (Chicago, 1987).

The Faerie Queene

♦

Spenser's Poetics:
The Poem's Two Bodies

DAVID LEE MILLER

> How might I that fair wonder know
> That mocks desire with endless No?
> John Dowland, *Third Book of Airs*

On the fifteenth of January 1559, a sacred transformation was wrought in the person of Elizabeth Tudor. The ceremony of royal coronation had not technically been classed as a sacrament since the twelfth century, but in many ways it still bore the stamp of its ecclesiastical original, the ordination of a bishop; each smallest detail of word, gesture, and regalia was understood as "the outward and visible sign of an inward and spiritual grace" (Schramm 6–9; Churchill 20). At the heart of this inwardness, created and sustained by an impressive array of sacred objects and solemn actions, lay the arch-mystery that anchored all other: the investiture of a natural body with the *corpus mysticum* of the realm. Drawn by analogy from Western culture's central religious ceremonies, this "political sacrament" tended to deify both Elizabeth and the state she governed, converting what was essentially an allegorical personification into mystified or doctrinal form as a species of legal incarnation.[1]

From *PMLA* 101 no. 2 (March 1986): 170–85. © 1986 by the Modern Language Association of America. Reprinted by permission of the Modern Language Association of America.

This incarnation of empire is the central "figure" of Spenser's *Faerie Queene*—its founding trope as well as its title character.[2] Conceived and designed to abet the glorification of the body politic in Elizabeth, Spenser's epic reflects a distinctly imperial and theocentric poetics.[3] In his magisterial study of early Renaissance "political theology," Ernst Kantorowicz has written that "in 16th-century England, by the efforts of jurists to define effectively and accurately the King's Two Bodies, all the Christological problems of the early Church concerning the Two Natures once more were actualized and resuscitated in the early absolute monarchy" (17). In much the same way, certain contradictions embedded in Tudor "Royal Christology" reemerge in the aesthetic theology of *The Faerie Queene*, where an implicit doctrine of "the poem's two bodies" constitutes the literary self-image of Spenser's epic tribute to early absolute monarchy under Elizabeth.[4]

In centering his artistic vision on Elizabeth, whose various names point outward to the sixteenth century's far-reaching reinscription of the received "text" of English monarchy, Spenser opens his poesis to the forces of contemporary history. Elizabeth is Gloriana, and she in turn is the ideal form of the poem itself: the Fairy Queen is *The Faerie Queene*, a vision of perfection pursued along parallel lines by Arthur and the reader. We will return to the complexities of this conceit; for the moment it is enough to observe that it represents a prophetic wager on the historical fortunes of the house of Tudor, as well as a singular act of invention, compounding and overgoing such precedents as Vergil's Augustus, Dante's Beatrice, Petrarch's Laura, and Ariosto's house of Este. In this respect *The Faerie Queene* stands out even among Spenser's poems for its willingness to take up the burden of history.

Kantorowicz's remark suggests that the legal problematics of the king's two bodies must be understood as a special case of the body-soul dualism endemic to Christian and Platonic thought. This observation may also apply to key structural features in the broadly Platonized Christianity that informs the medieval tradition of allegorical and philosophical fiction. Beginning with the strange two-bodied monster we meet in constitutional theory, we will follow three motifs—perfect wholeness, secular perpetuity, and the doctrine of "assimilation"—from political into aesthetic theology, where they emerge as an implicit poetics of two bodies. . . .

Two aspects of the legal fiction known as the king's two bodies will help focus our inquiry into Spenserian poetics. First is the corporate metaphor, a figure of integral wholeness: like Christianity, Spenser's art fantasizes its own perfection as full access to a spiritual body replete with truth.[5] "*The Faerie Queene*," writes Leonard Barkan, "is a limitless landscape of the world, a vast number of men who are themselves multiple and subdivided, and finally a simple, perhaps perfect, human being who contains in body and spirit all the virtues of the heroes and all the struggles necessary to gain and keep those virtues" (6). This simple, perhaps perfect human being who figures the complex unity of Spenser's poem is figured in turn by the marriage of Arthur and Gloriana. "The Faerie Queene," writes Rosemond Tuve, "holds that role of shadowy but great importance, the Sovereignty itself, in a sense 'the realm'" (347). Separate quests begin and end at Gloriana's court because all adventures (as Tuve reminds us) belong to the sovereign, who grants them as favors to individual knights and who acts "through his fellowship as through an extended self" (348). Arthur meanwhile serves "as a combined figure for the dynasty, the all-inclusive virtue, the spouse-to-be of the personified realm, [and] the royal house through whom divine power flowed into country and people" (350). The mystical union of these two persons in one flesh perfects the image of sovereignty and constitutes the ideal body of Spenser's poem.

This ideal body is diffracted into many signatures, from the "pressed gras" Arthur finds in the wake of his dream, or the image graven on Guyon's shield, to the numerological patterns that mimic celestial symmetry, the "golden wall" that surrounds Cleopolis (2.10.72), the name "Telamond" at the head of book 4, the veiled shapes of Venus and Nature, or the sacramental embrace in which Scudamour and Amoret became one flesh in the first ending to book 3.[6] Ultimately perhaps all the words and things in the poem are synecdochic traces in quest of the wholeness they signify. Even Spenser's figure for his textual source, the "everlasting scryne" from which the Muse lays forth ancient scrolls telling of Arthur's quest, is a synecdoche for what we might call "the archive": it represents nothing less than the perpetuity and coherence of Western imperial culture. As synecdoche, it attributes a distinctly global unity to the scattered hoards of documents found, purchased, transported, translated, reread, and otherwise recovered during the late medieval and early modern explosion of *translatio studii* in Western Europe. Thus the gentleman Spenser seeks to fashion pursues an ego ideal that would integrate the private self with an encyclopedia of the culture's symbolic matrices, from literary genres to chronicle histories, from legal fictions to theological doctrines.[7] In Arthur's quest for Gloriana, Spenser recasts the Ur-narrative of his culture's search for this global unity—now in the millennial form of a Protestant world empire.

The second feature of Tudor political theology that is important for our understanding of Spenser's poetics is the relation between the bodies natural and politic. Although the body politic was denied a living soul and acknowledged as an artifact of human policy, it was nevertheless held to be perfect and imperishable, "utterly void of Infancy, and Old Age, and other natural Defects and Embicilities, which the body natural is subject to." Most important, this ideal fictive body was held to "assimilate to its own excellence" all defects and imbecilities in the monarch's natural body (Kantorowicz 7–12).[8]

. . . .

The amendment of Redcrosse [in the House of Holinesse] is a powerful version of the negative moment intrinsic to Spenser's poetics. It suggests that the poem's vision of its own risen or incorruptible body rests on a pervasively internalized principle of self-renunciation. What we find in the *The Faerie Queene* is, after all, romance—the genre of unconstrained fabulation—in love with didactic allegory. The fiction has introjected a powerful cultural demand for truth, a demand it can meet only by striving to differ internally from itself as fiction. In the effort to secure within itself a *decisive representation* of this difference, *The Faerie Queene* becomes allegory, or "otherwords," in the most radical sense—generating itself out of internal contradiction in forever divided form, at once the integral body of truth and its repressed or uncanny "other." . . . *The Faerie Queene* is able to summon its ideal form into representation only as a sublimated negative image of itself.

This is why in book 1, for instance, the Redcrosse Knight's betrothal to the whole body of Truth can never finally cast out the demons of duplicity and illusion. Superficially the contrast between Una and Duessa could not be clearer: the One, "Who, in her self-resemblance well beseene, / Did seeme, such as she was," versus the Other, declaring just as flatly, "I, that do seeme not I, Duessa ame" (1.12.8; 5.26). Yet Spenser can represent Una to us only in divided form. Initially she is set apart from us by a veil, recognizable in that she is hidden. But even when she stands revealed in canto 12, Spenser's language can express Una's integrity only as mediated relation, "self-resemblance." . . . Una emerges into representation only through a differential repetition that sets her apart from herself and so makes her dependent on what she is not—dividing Truth to assert its self-resemblance in a phrase that echoes, as it opposes, Duessa's counterepiphany. However deeply Spenser may desire to set his own poetic activity in opposition to Archimago's, structurally they are alike, for he can create Una only by doubling her.[9]

In a poem where Truth appears as a romance heroine, we should expect the structure of knowing to coincide with that of desire. The epistemological quandary that identity depends on repetition is venerable enough, and vexing enough in its implications, that it drove Plato to postulate seminal reasons. His doctrine of anamnesis makes all knowledge déjà vu, and every philosopher therefore a kind of sublime Narcissus, striving to resurrect the fragments of a lost self-knowledge into perfect correspondence with their imagined heavenly paradigm and origin. The Protestant doctrine of "inner light" works in much the same way: for this reason Fidelia and Heavenly Contemplation must represent at once a condition still to be achieved by the knight and a principle already latent within him. . . . [T]hey enable the subject's return to a divine source he already contains. Allegory is the literary method appropriate to a recognition theory of knowing because, as Rosemond Tuve remarked, allegorical fictions make us think about what we already know: they seek to awaken and charge with motive force a knowledge that remains latent, passive, or merely implicit in the reader (Roche 30). . . .

As a structure of desire, epistemological romance begins in the loss or denial of bodily presence. . . . We see an early example of this myth of bodily loss in the April eclogue to *The Shepheardes Calender*, where the Ovidian episode of Pan and Syrinx becomes in Spenser's hands a fable of the poem's two bodies. Ovid tells of a god in pursuit of carnal ecstasy, intent on ravishing a river nymph. The nymph cries out to Diana, and just at the liminal moment—at the edge of the river, as the god's embrace gathers her in and his sigh passes over her lips—she is transformed into water reeds, and the breath of violent passion yields a harmonic chord. For Ovid as for Spenser this is primarily a story not of feminine protest against rape but of masculine consolation, a story of loss made over into renunciation as it is replayed in a ludic register, where mastery and recuperation seem possible after all. "This union, at least, shall I have with thee," says Pan to the vanished Syrinx (Ovid 1.710); and he makes the reeds over into another "syrinx," a shepherd's pipes—reasserting his baffled will and recovering, in symbolic form, the lost feminine body. Spenser works this narrative into the self-referential symbolism of his pastoral debut, making "Elisa," queen of shepherds, the fruit of an immaculate union between Pan and Syrinx. At once pastoral mask for the queen of England and metafictional symbol for Colin's song,[10] "Elisa" names the sublimated body that comes to occupy the space of loss—the space opened up for Pan by his loss of Syrinx, for Colin by his failure to win Rosalind, and for Spenser, as for his culture generally, by the renunciation of the body as an object of desire.

Elisa is a prototype for Gloriana, who also represents both the English queen and the aesthetic body "assimilated" to her visionary form. Arthur desires the Fairy Queen first in an adolescent fantasy of sex (1.9.9–15) but wakes to find "her place devoyd, / And nought but pressed gras where she had lyen." Since then he has sought out her ideal, displaced form through synecdochic traces like the pressed grass beside him or the image on Sir Guyon's shield. Freud tells a story much like Arthur's in a celebrated passage from *Beyond the Pleasure Principle*. He has observed the game his grandson plays with a string and wooden reel:

> What he did was to hold the reel by the string and very skillfully throw it over the edge of his curtained cot, so that it disappeared into it, at the same time uttering his expressive "o-o-o-o." [Earlier Freud had remarked, "His mother and the writer of the present account were agreed in thinking this was not a mere interjection but represented the German word '*fort*' ('gone')."] He then pulled the reel out of the cot again by the string and hailed its reappearance with a joyful "*da*." This, then, was the complete game—disappearance and return.
>
> (33)

Freud may hesitate over the question this anecdote raises for his theory of the instincts, but he has little trouble in reconstructing the primary episode reenacted in the game of *fort-da:* it is the infant's constrained renunciation of his mother's immediate presence. *Da!* is the first in an open series of symbolic substitutions in which he will keep on seeking that lost original. *The Faerie Queene,* we might say, unfolds in the long interval between the *fort!* of Arthur's awakening from erotic revery into moral consciousness and the terminally postponed *da!* of his nuptial entry into the body of glory. Arthur bears the attendant loss of presence as a "secret wound" (1.9.7)—the melancholy that persists in the waking aftermath of his dream, signifying his painful renunciation of the carnal immediacy suffusing that fantasy.[11]

The emphasis in this poetics on the wounding renunciation of sexual desire makes it seem inevitable that Gloriana's alter ego should be *la belle dame sans merci* and her avatars: predatory succubae who enervate their victims. Redcrosse melting in Duessa's arms is only the first of many such images in the poem. The most remarkable, surely, is Verdant, preyed on by the witch Acrasia in the Bower of Bliss:

> And all that while, right over him she hong,
> With her false eyes fast fixed in his sight,
> As seeking medicine whence she was stong,
> Or greedily depasturing delight:
> And oft inclining downe, with kisses light,
> For feare of waking him, his lips bedewd,
> And through his humid eyes did sucke his spright,
> Quite molten into lust and pleasures lewd;
> Wherewith she sighed soft, as if his case she rewd.
> (2.12.73)

Many readers have testified to the fascination of this passage, with its eerie transfusion of erotic and sadistic frissons. Its special horror lies in its uncanny affinity with the epic's scene of conception, Arthur prostrate and dreaming of Gloriana. In the Bower of Bliss this dream has become a lurid tableau of predatory metaphysical fellatio. Verdant, like Adonis later in the poem, shares Arthur's "secret wound": his recumbent passivity, his expenses of spirit, and the erasure of his heraldic insignia (st. 80) all testify to his symbolic castration.[12] Meanwhile Acrasia, in a wicked parody of Venus's pietà sorrow over the fallen Adonis, mocks pity for her enervated victim even as she battens on his soul. She is truly Spenser's "faery quean," secret sharer of the principle by which the succuba of the superego feeds on bodily energy, summoning desire to ends beyond its knowing.[13]

This reading of Arthur's melancholy as the private wound of Spenserian poetics will seem like neo-Freudian critical fantasy only if we forget the mythic provenance of Arthurian romance. Behind Spenser's Arthur stands the Arthur of medieval romance, and behind him the shadowy image of the

Fisher King, whose identity with the realm he governs is powerfully expressed in the mysterious wound or sickness that dries up his organs of increase and renders the land barren. Rosemond Tuve argues persuasively that Arthur's role in *The Faerie Queene* "is directly in line with what a reader of earlier Arthurian romance expects" (345). There is, however, one major exception: "Spenser makes no important use of the motif of a land waste through a wound given the ruler, which is the form of a clear identification between king's and country's health most common in Arthurian romances" (351). True enough; Spenser had a different and far more sophisticated form of clear identification closer to hand in the constitutional theory of his age, an extensively rationalized version of the ancient myth. Crown law had evolved a doctrine of incorruptible perpetuity: sovereignty has neither defect nor mortality and assimilates the sovereign's nature to its own. Thus what was for Spenser the "authorized" version of the myth denies the burden of more archaic versions, precisely inverting their symbolism: instead of contaminating his realm, the king is purified by it. We have seen how radically this doctrine depends on a negative moment it can never finally recuperate. In this respect it has something in common with the Arthurian materials Tuve has studied, where the king's mysterious ailment is rationalized in all sorts of unconvincing ways. Beneath the explanations, writes Tuve, we glimpse "the more primitive conception of a *loss of sovereignty* or [an] unexpected decline of power that cannot be countered in natural ways" and also "some sense of deep human inadequacy which must be expiated even though it is not understood" (353–54; emphasis added). Looking to still older forms of the legend, we find this inadequacy expressed as impotence or castration—sent down by God, in one version, to punish the king's concupiscence (Weston 20–21).

This loss of sovereignty is just what the doctrine of the king's two bodies was calculated to economize. . . . Spenser follows legal theory in rejecting the tragic myth of Arthur's wound, but the wound returns to haunt his protagonist in the form of that nostalgia for lost pleasure on which culture is founded, as Freud argued in *Civilization and Its Discontents.* (No wonder the bedrock virtue of Spenser's knights is sheer persistence.[14] Certainly that is what it takes to read *The Faerie Queene.*) Leigh DeNeef, in a subtle reading of the role of Cupid in book 3, suggests quite accurately that all the poem's heroic lovers must learn to sublimate love's wound into a figurative pregnancy, so that love will inspire them to bring forth worthy deeds (173). Arthur, for instance, rescues Redcrosse "Nyne monethes" after his dream of Gloriana (1.9.15)—having gestated her image until it matures into an ethical ideal whose parturition is heroic action (cf. 1.5.1). One effect of this half-hidden metaphor is to make Arthur a sort of spiritual hermaphrodite; sexually ambiguous, he anticipates Spenser's grand icons of the marriage of opposites: Scudamour and Amoret, the statue of Venus, Dame Nature of the *Mutability Cantos.* Roche suggests that Scudamour's canceled fusion with Amoret alludes to Ephesians 5.25–32, where man and wife are said to be "one flesh" (133–36); we are similarly instructed at Galatians 3.27–28 that "there is neither male nor female" in the *corpus mysticum*, "for you are all one in Christ Jesus." The politico-religious symbolism of marriage that is so pervasive in our culture rests partly on these passages, and the projected union of Arthur and Gloriana is no exception. With these associations in mind we may see Arthur's metaphoric femininity as a typological anticipation of his union with Gloriana. The hermaphrodite that emerges from their marriage is Spenser's implicit figure for the perfected spiritual body of his poem.

. . . .

If it seems in the end that the ideal form into which Spenser recuperates castration can only be sexed as an epicene hermaphrodite—perhaps that should not come as a surprise. Indeed, how except by catachresis could one hope to name a body that transcends the mark of gender, without which never a body could come into being?[15] If with Leonard Barkan we follow the anthropocosmic metaphor back to Plato's *Timaeus*, here is what we find:

> . . . he made the world one whole, having every part entire, and being therefore perfect and not liable to old age and disease. And he gave to the world the figure which was suitable and also natural. Now to the animal which was to comprehend all animals, that figure was suitable which comprehends within itself all other figures. Wherefore he made the world in the form of a globe, round as from a lathe, having its extremes in every direction equidistant from the center, the most perfect and most like itself of all figures; for he considered that the like is infinitely fairer than the unlike. This he finished off, making the surface smooth all around for many reasons: in the first place, because the living being had no need of eyes when there was nothing remaining outside him to be seen, nor of ears when there was nothing to be heard: and there was no surrounding atmosphere to be breathed. . . .
>
> (Plato 15–16)

And so it goes. The cosmos appears to be a body extensively reformed "by way of retractation": eyeless, earless, noseless, mouthless, anusless, limbless, and sexless, "for there was nothing beside him" (16). And yet this spherical animal, sans organs, apertures, and appendages, is nevertheless *the* perfect figure, the plenum of animal forms, comprehending "within itself all other figures." It is also distinctly masculine, despite—or rather, by virtue of—its lack of appendages. As in the design of Alma's castle, the privileged signifier of masculinity is no longer the penis, but the circle, "immortall, perfect, masculine"—that crown of divine self-sufficiency from which the "imperfect, mortall, foeminine" body represents a falling away.

Barkan observes that Plato's figure is constructed according to a doctrine of likenesses and answers to the nature of its divine creator (9–14).

Yet however mimetic of transcendent reality it may claim to be, the erasure of all signs of its relational dependency on an ecosystem renders this creature a sheer anomaly in the world of nature. Perhaps, then, its real "figure" may be *catachresis*. This term bears two distinct meanings: it is the "forced," or unnatural, use of metaphor, and it is the "extensive" use. Here "extensive" denotes the transfer of a name from its right object to something otherwise nameless (Miller et al. 106–09). The difference between a meaningful "extensive" figure and a flurry of language signifying nothing is thus made to depend on whether a nameless referent does in fact wait patiently for its designation, preinscribed as the blank fourth corner of an analogy that was already in place. A difference of this kind will always be open to question, which is one reason Derrida, in his discussion of Aristotelian rhetoric, calls metaphor the "risk of mimesis" (*Margins* 241). Displacing names from their conventional referents, metaphor opens a space of figuration that it does not control; there is no telling what anomalies may be troped into being through the constitutive force of language. Arthur and Gloriana, comprehending within themselves all lesser knights and virtues and combining to form a transcendental hermaphrodite, type of the Christian apocalypse, may equally put mimesis at risk.

We saw earlier that the ideal totality sought by epistemological romance is called forth by an elaborate metaphoric system. Prosopopoeia, or personification, may be the most prominent trope in this system, but metalepsis and synecdoche also play important roles. . . .

Insofar as it tropes into being that superphenomenal totality which has been given so many names (the cosmos, the soul, the body politic, the *corpus mysticum*, Telamond, Arthur plus Gloriana), this metaphoric system may be seen as an elaborate catachresis, constituting anomalies under a mimetic alibi and offering them to us as images of the world. Arthur's quest for Gloriana depends on a curious splice in Spenser's genealogy of the English throne: the Tudors' mythic progenitor, Arthur, has been displaced from the "literal" body of history, Britomart ruling with Arthegall in his stead. This break in Spenser's mimesis of chronicle history creates the anomalous space in which his fiction can emerge. Thomas Roche has observed that

> by his elliptical treatment of Arthur, Spenser is able to imply a relationship between the historical Arthur and Elizabeth that he could not convey if either were present in the action as historical personages. The Arthur of *The Faerie Queene* exists only in his quest for Gloriana. Elizabeth exists only as a prophecy and in the archetype of her Glory, Gloriana. But at that point (unrealized) when Arthur finds Gloriana, England and Faeryland, Elizabeth and Gloriana, become one . . . all [are] subsumed in the triumph of the Tudor Apocalypse.
>
> (49)

The distance between Arthur and Gloriana is thus the purely negative space of resistance to the millennial advent, but this resistance is also the figural space in which the poem has its being, the distance between Elizabeth and Gloriana. In the terms developed in this essay, it is an interval of catachresis at the heart of the poem's constitutive metaphor, across which Spenser tropes conventional signs toward a beyond they artfully summon to the threshold of recognition.

Spenser tells us he chose the history of Arthur partly because it was "furthest from the daunger of envy, and suspition of present time" ("Letter to Raleigh," *Works* 136). Yet his fable departs from the historical present of Elizabethan England precisely in order to circle back, elevating romance quest into a typological summons to the Tudor apocalypse. In this respect the poem, for all its fictive remove from the present, has something in common with political rhetoric. If we look outward from Spenser's text to the history it both receives and reinscribes, we find the same rhetorical structures that organize the poem, working to shape history as the poem would also do. Consider the efforts in the lower house of successive Elizabethan parliaments to establish freedom of speech among the recognized "privileges of the house." Traditionally the prerogatives of the throne had included setting the agenda for parliamentary debate; when Sir Thomas More succeeded in getting Parliament's "freedom of speech" formally instituted, in 1523, it represented only the right of dutiful opposition to royal bills. In effect, what was then established was a rule of interpretation: all speeches delivered in Parliament were to be understood within the assumption of a loyal intentionality, so that no member's opposition to the crown on legislative matters could be taken as evidence of treason. Radical Protestant factions in subsequent parliaments seized on this "freedom of speech" as a precedent for insisting on the Commons' right to set its own legislative agenda, even though royal prerogative comprehended the power to forbid discussion of certain topics and even though Elizabeth continued trying to exercise this prerogative throughout her reign (Neale, *Elizabeth I* 1: 17–28). This creative use of precedent is a form of metalepsis, a revision of origins; under a shaky mimetic alibi (the claim to be correctly interpreting constitutional history) it did eventually trope into being the precedent it claimed merely to preserve.

The mimetic alibi says the use of verbal signs answers to their referents. Political rhetoric offers easy illustrations of the reverse—that the referent of a phrase like "free speech" or "the privileges of the house" can be altered by the way the words are used. Language is always to some extent "performative," generating authority out of misreading, just as community, or the body politic, is always to some extent a project rather than an artifact—forever in the making as particular, strategically motivated utterances compete for authority.[16] The transformation of Elizabeth Tudor into Elizabeth I is a striking example of authority re-creating itself through a massive display of signifiers—for as a contemporary witness of her coronation progress so blandly noted, "In pompous ceremonies a secret of government doth much consist" (Neale, *Queen Elizabeth* 59). The history of the English coronation, reflected in a series of *ordines*, or protocols, that goes back to the tenth century, may be read as an exemplary tale of the struggle for control over privileged signifiers. One fascinating episode involves an early twelfth-century cleric, the "Anonymous of York," who argued for the king's right to interfere in ecclesiastical affairs. What makes his case interesting is not that he anticipated events of the Reformation but that he offered a structural interpretation of the coronation ritual, comparing it point for point with the Church's episcopal confirmations. Initially of course the sacramental character of the royal coronation had served to strengthen the arguments of pope against crown: the ceremonial anointing of the monarch sanctified royal claims to authority at the same time as it helped annex the right of coronation to the pope and his delegates. But as our modern historian of the English coronation relates, the result was a structure of signifiers that could easily be reversed: "It was . . . possible to draw up out of the old *ordo* a sort of 'Bill of Rights' in favor of the encroachment of the king on the administration of the Church. If in the tenth century the clergy had thoroughly clericalized the coronation, the wheel had come full circle, and the argument of the Anonymous showed how the coronation service supplied the legal title for a regalization of the Church" (Schramm 35). Here again the act of interpreting authoritative precedent uses a mimetic alibi to trope its supposed origin into existence in the present, converting the form of ceremony into the force of persuasion.

There is no question that Elizabeth understood the instrumental (as opposed to mimetic or referential) value of language; the hallmark of her political style was its shrewd deployment of ambiguity. Time after time she sought compromise in obscure or even contradictory wording, as in the communion service and "Ornaments Rubric" that formed part of the Elizabethan settlement (Neale, *Elizabeth I* 1: 78–80). The pattern was established early, when she was confronted in the first year of her reign with the problem of formulating her royal title; should she revive the controversial wording "Supreme Head of the Church," abandoned by Mary? Elizabeth finessed the problem by adding an ambiguous "&c" ("etceterating" herself, as Neale puts it [46]). The strategic feel for language reflected in these and many other incidents is pointed up nicely in the note she sent to her fifteen-year-old godson, Harrington, along with a copy of her 1576 address to Parliament: "Boy Jack," she began, ". . . ponder [my words] in thy hours of leisure, and play with them till they enter thine understanding. So shalt thou hereafter, perchance, find some good fruits hereof . . ." (Neale, *Elizabeth I* 1:367–68).

Elizabeth contrived her verbal labyrinths with a shrewd eye to their deployment in the overdetermined contexts of action. Spenser too returns from his long detour through fairyland by way of the catachresis we have examined, exhorting his readers to see the Tudor apocalypse and become its imperial *figurae*. For modern readers such a response is historically impossible, not to mention ideologically unacceptable. Yet the poem still demands from us a catachrestic, and not just a mimetic, reading: as Spenser overgoes Ariosto, as Troynovant overgoes Rome, so we are asked to overgo the text we read in the direction of something as yet nameless.[17]

The traditional name for this something is apocalypse. Perhaps the biblical Apocalypse, an extended catachresis so authoritative it portends the destruction of nature, may be thought of as the negative moment of transcendence writ large. The impulse to self-renunciation we have been tracing in Spenser's text would then be seen as a continuous mini apocalypse that releases the revelatory energy of writing.[18] . . .

Notes

1. Its political importance had always meant that the coronation ritual's form, status, and significance were subject to revision and dispute. Religious controversy surrounding the coronations of Edward, Mary, and Elizabeth appears to have hastened the secularizing of the ceremony; Richard C. McCoy suggests that Elizabeth in particular relied far more on civic pageantry than on the less public rite of coronation to glorify herself as a figure of English sovereignty.

2. Nearly every critic who writes on *The Faerie Queene* speaks to the role of Elizabeth. Early work by Frances Yates on contemporary images of Elizabeth opened a rich vein of inquiry, brought to bear on the reading of Spenser's poem most recently by Robin Headlam Wells (whose useful study provided the epigraph for this essay [153]). The main focus of work since Yates has been on establishing the historical context of Spenser's celebration of his queen and on analyzing specific representations of her in the poem. My emphasis in the present essay on the role of sovereignty in the implicit poetics of *The Faerie Queene* owes a debt to recent studies by Goldberg and Greenblatt.

3. Traces of Christian empire are everywhere in the text. Andrew Fichter offers a clear account of the dynastic framework for Britomart's quest in *Poets Historical*, but it is worth stressing how pervasive imperial symbolism is in the poem. It informs not only the large narrative patterns and iconic images Fichter analyzes but details and episodes not obviously political. Goldberg's fine reading of the river marriage as imperial pageantry is a case in point; more recent commentaries by Quint (esp. 161) and Guillory on the ocean-river complex as an imperial image of "the source" have corroborated and extended his insight. The opening lines of book 1 are also imprinted with royal-imperial associations. The royal stole used in the coronation ceremony bears the ubiquitous red cross of Saint George, and another piece of coronation regalia, "St. George's Spurs," reminds us why we first see Redcrosse "pricking" across the plain: because his spurs, an emblem of imperial chivalry, end in a sharp point and not in a rowel (Churchill 37–39).

4. In *The Queene's Two Bodies*, Marie Axton demonstrates the importance of the Elizabethan succession controversy and Jacobean unification debates in popularizing Edmund Plowden's legal theory. She stresses that the notion of the king's two bodies "was never a *fact*, nor did it ever attain the status of orthodoxy; it remained a controversial idea" (x). In excellent discussions covering the Inns of Court revels, court entertainments, and popular drama of the period, she explores the development of a complex symbolic vocabulary for implicit exhortation, criticism, and praise of the queen and for veiled debate over the troubled question of the succession. Spenser tends to avoid the succession question in *The Faerie Queene*, but his

use of Gloriana to represent the sovereignty both draws on and lends support to the notion that Elizabeth "beareth two persons, the one of a most royall queene or empresse, the other of a most vertuous and beautiful Lady" ("Letter to Raleigh," *Works* 136).

5. As a general metaphor for things invisible to mortal sight (the coherence of a body of writing, the unity of a society), the body and its related terms are not only pervasive but inescapable, as was brought home to me by the anonymous reviewer who concluded that an earlier draft of the present essay "does not quite amount to the study of a subject . . . because it is stretching things fairly thin to say that 'meaning' is a 'body,' when all is said and done."

6. On the wall of gold as an emblem of the monarchy as protectorate, see Axton 103–05. Roche suggests that "Telamond" should be decoded "the perfect world," a reading he finds allegorically adumbrated in the tale of Agape's sons, Priamond, Diamond, and Triamond.

7. A useful survey of the textual history effaced in the figure of the Muses' scryne may be found in Reynolds and Wilson's *Scribes and Scholars*. On the human ego as itself derived from bodily wholeness and coordination, see Fisher and Cleveland, and for a brief but slightly more recent summary of body-ego theories, see Shontz 65–67.

8. Axton refers to instances of assimilation as "miracles" and stresses both skeptical resistance to the doctrine and possibilities for using it to criticize the queen. That it had other uses may be seen in Neale's observation that the body politic could even "assimilate to its own excellence" defective origins (a version of metalepsis): Elizabeth had been declared illegitimate by statute during her father's reign; Mary, in rehabilitating her own legitimacy, left this statute on the books, but when Elizabeth ascended to the throne "it remained unrepealed, on the constitutional ground that the crown covered all such flaws" (*Elizabeth I* 1:34). It was the sovereignty's legal capacity to absorb flaws that so complicated proceedings against that other Mary, who was at once queen of Scotland and the most dangerous traitor in England.

9. My argument comes very close here to that of Leigh DeNeef (esp. 95–96), who stresses the unsettling affinities between Spenser and Archimago. In general, DeNeef's chapter 6 offers an original and persuasive demonstration of Spenser's need for, and dependency on, "false" versions of his own activity. I would add that the pattern DeNeef observes is another version of Spenser's dependency on a negative moment; Spenser can assimilate his own image making to the spiritual body of truth only by negating, in such figures as Archimago, the instability inherent in representation.

10. On Spenser's use of the Pan-Syrinx myth in "Aprill," see Cullen 112–19, Cain 16–17, Montrose 40–43, and D. Miller, "Authorship" 230–32.

11. Lacan reads the *fort-da* passage as emblematic of the infant's "birth" at once into language and into "fully human" desire (ch 3; Muller and Richardson 9–12, ch. 3). The Lacanian argument that Spenser's poetics is grounded in the essential lack that constitutes human desire has been set forth by Goldberg in *Endlesse Worke* and by Guillory, especially in his provocative reading of the Acidalian vision as a Spenserian *mise en abŷme* (33–48).

12. My use of the term *castration* in this essay derives from Barthes's Lacanian extension of the Freudian concept (*S/Z*).

13. Cf. Guillory's remarks on the Bower of Bliss and on the relation of desire to "the approved concept of generation" (35–39).

14. Tuve reads Arthurian magnificence as *Fortitudo*, or perseverance (57–59, 134–40).

15. Paglia suggests that Spenser veils his hermaphroditic deities and that he canceled the 1590 ending to book 3 because although "thematically apposite" as "a rich metaphor of heterosexual union," such figures are "glaringly divergent in aesthetic mode" from the Hellenic sensibility that governs "an imagistic pattern universal in the poem" whereby "deformations of the human figure . . . are always monstrous" (62–63). Spenser's image of spontaneous generation at 1.1.21 supports this insight; there Errour's vomit is compared to Nile mud, which breeds "creatures, partly male / And partly femall." In *Milton's Spenser* Quilligan remarks that such details "image our subterranean terror at the slime of origin" (82–83). My point is that the

repressed figure of monstrosity can be traced in the poem's catachrestic efforts to project an image of its own risen body.

16.   Among Axton's most valuable revisions of Kantorowicz is her demonstration that the theory of the king's two bodies itself developed out of a strategically motivated misreading of legal precedent, used by Catholic jurists in the *Duchy of Lancaster Case* (1561) to "minimize the personal impact of the new sovereign" (16), and that the theory was first popularized by supporters of Mary Stuart for the succession (18–20).

17.   There can be no question of choosing *between* mimesis and catachresis as if they were alternative critical programs. Maureen Quilligan separates the two by labeling deconstructive criticism "allegoresis," which she then distinguishes from her own form of allegorical commentary according to a criterion of intentionality: allegoresis rests on "a huge and ahistorical freedom," she says, including the freedom to contradict "the text's manifest intentions," whereas "a reading of an allegory" proceeds "within the limits of the text's surface (generic) intentionality" (25–26). Such critical prophylaxis appears to me futile, resting on a failure to recognize the implications of Derrida's work in particular. The point is neither to read simply "*against* the text's manifest intentions" nor to read "within [their] limits" but to situate those intentions—to read *them.* To claim that one reads the text "in its own terms" simply begs the question. For an extended consideration of this issue in terms of the Derridean-Heideggerean metaphor of "framing," see Jay and Miller, "The Role of Theory in the Study of Literature?" in *After Strange Texts* (1–28).

18.   My work on this essay was supported by a fellowship to the School of Criticism and Theory at Northwestern University in the summer of 1982 and by a stipend from the University of Alabama (RGC Project 1216) in the summer of 1984. For comments on drafts of the essay I would like to thank Dwight Eddins, Jonathan Goldberg, Pat Hermann, William Ulmer, Elizabeth Meese, and especially Greg Jay.

Works Cited

Axton, Marie. *The Queen's Two Bodies: Drama and the Elizabethan Succession.* London: Royal Historical Soc., 1977.

Bahti, Timothy. "Auerbach's *Mimesis:* Figural Structure and Historical Narrative." Jay and Miller, 124–45.

Barkan, Leonard. *Nature's Work of Art: The Human Body as Image of the World.* New Haven: Yale UP, 1975.

Barthes, Roland. *S/Z: An Essay.* Trans. Richard Miller. New York: Hill, 1974.

Cain, Thomas H. *Praise in* The Faerie Queene. Lincoln: Nebraska UP, 1978.

Churchill, Randolph S. *The Story of the Coronation.* London: Derek Verschoyle, 1953.

Cullen, Patrick. *Spenser, Marvell, and Renaissance Pastoral.* Cambridge: Harvard UP, 1970.

DeNeef, A. Leigh. *Spenser and the Motives of Metaphor.* Durham: Duke UP, 1982.

Derrida, Jacques. *Of Grammatology.* Trans. Gayatri Chakravorty Spivak. Baltimore: Johns Hopkins UP, 1976.

———. *Margins of Philosophy.* Trans. Alan Bass. Chicago: U of Chicago P, 1982.

Douglas, Mary. *Purity and Danger: An Analysis of the Concepts of Purity and Taboo.* 2nd ed. London: Routledge, 1969.

Fichter, Andrew. *Poets Historical: Dynastic Epic in the Renaissance.* New Haven: Yale UP, 1982.

Fisher, S., and S. E. Cleveland. *Body Image and Personality.* Princeton: Van Nostrand, 1958.

Fletcher, Angus. *Allegory: The Theory of a Symbolic Mode*. Ithaca: Cornell UP, 1964.
———. *The Prophetic Moment: An Essay on Spenser*. Chicago: U of Chicago P, 1971.
Freud, Sigmund. *Beyond the Pleasure Principle*. Trans. James Strachey. New York: Bantam, 1959.
———. *Civilization and Its Discontents*. Trans. James Strachey. New York: Norton, 1961.
Goldberg, Jonathan. *Endlesse Worke: Spenser and the Structures of Discourse*. Baltimore: Johns Hopkins UP, 1981.
———. *James I and the Politics of Literature: Jonson, Shakespeare, Donne, and Their Contemporaries*. Baltimore: Johns Hopkins UP, 1983.
Greenblatt, Stephen J. *Renaissance Self-Fashioning from More to Shakespeare*. Chicago: U of Chicago P, 1980.
Guillory, John. *Poetic Authority: Spenser, Milton, and Literary History*. New York: Columbia UP, 1983.
Halio, Jay L. "The Metaphor of Conception and Elizabethan Theories of Imagination." *Neophilologus* 50 (1966): 454–61.
Hamilton, A. C., ed. *Spenser:* The Faerie Queene. London: Longman, 1977.
Jay, Gregory S., and David L. Miller. *After Strange Texts: The Role of Theory in the Study of Literature*. University: U of Alabama P, 1985.
Kantorowicz, Ernst. *The King's Two Bodies: A Study of Medieval Political Theology*. Princeton: Princeton UP, 1957.
Lacan, Jacques. *Ecrits: A Selection*. Trans. Alan Sheridan. New York: Norton, 1977.
McCoy, Richard C. "From Sacred Ritual to Secular Pageantry in Tudor Coronations." Work in progress.
———. "'Thou Idol Ceremony': Elizabeth I, the Henriad, and the Rites of the British Monarchy." *Urban Life in the Renaissance*. Ed. Susan Zimmerman and Ronald F. E. Weissman. Newark: U of Delaware P, 1989. 240–68.
Miller, David Lee. "Authorship, Anonymity, and *The Shepheardes Calender*." *Modern Language Quarterly* 40 (1979): 219–36.
———. "'The Pleasure of the Text,' Two Renaissance Versions." *New Orleans Review* 9 (1982): 50–55.
———. "Spenser's Vocation, Spenser's Career." *ELH* 50 (1983): 197–231.
Miller, Joseph M., Michael H. Prosser, and Thomas W. Benson, eds. *Readings in Medieval Rhetoric*. Bloomington: Indiana UP, 1973.
Montrose, Louis Adrian. "'The perfecte paterne of a Poete': The Poetics of Courtship in *The Shepheardes Calender*." *Texas Studies in Literature and Language* 21 (1979): 34–67.
Muller, John P., and William J. Richardson. *Lacan and Language: A Reader's Guide to* Ecrits. New York: International UP, 1982.
Neale, J. E. *Elizabeth I and Her Parliaments*. Vol. 1, 1559–81. Vol. 2, 1584–1601. London: Cape, 1953, 1957.
———. *Queen Elizabeth*. New York: Harcourt, 1931.
Nohrnberg, James. *The Analogy of* The Faerie Queene. Princeton: Princeton UP, 1976.
Ovid. *Metamorphoses*. Ed. and trans. Frank Justus Miller. 2nd ed. Cambridge: Harvard UP, 1921.

Paglia, Camille A. "The Apollonian Androgyne and the *Faerie Queene*." *English Literary Renaissance* 9 (1979): 42–63.

Plato. *Timaeus*. Trans. Benjamin Jowett. Indianapolis: Bobbs, 1949.

Quilligan, Maureen. *Milton's Spenser: The Politics of Reading*. Ithaca: Cornell UP, 1983.

Quint, David. *Origin and Originality in Renaissance Literature: Versions of the Source*. New Haven: Yale UP, 1983.

Reynolds, L. D., and N. G. Wilson. *Scribes and Scholars: A Guide to the Transmission of Greek and Latin Literature*. 2nd ed. Oxford: Clarendon, 1974.

Robertson, D. W., Jr. *A Preface to Chaucer: Studies in Medieval Perspectives*. Princeton: Princeton UP, 1953.

Roche, Thomas P., Jr. *The Kindly Flame: A Study of the Third and Fourth Books of Spenser's* Faerie Queene. Princeton: Princeton UP, 1964.

Schramm, Percy Ernst. *A History of the English Coronation*. Trans. Leopold G. Wickham Legg. Oxford: Clarendon, 1937.

Shontz, Franklin C. *Perceptual and Cognitive Aspects of Body Experience*. New York: Academic, 1969.

Spenser, Edmund. *The Complete Poetical Works of Spenser*. Ed. R. E. Neil Dodge. Cambridge: Riverside, 1908.

Tuve, Rosemond. *Allegorical Imagery: Some Medieval Books and Their Posterity*. Princeton: Princeton UP, 1966.

Wells, Robin Headlam. *Spenser's* Faerie Queene *and the Cult of Elizabeth*. Totowa: Barnes, 1983.

Weston, Jessie L. *From Ritual to Romance*. New York: Smith, 1920.

Yates, Frances A. "Queen Elizabeth as Astraea." *Journal of the Warburg and Courtauld Institutes* 10 (1947): 27–82. Rpt. in *Astraea: The Imperial Theme in the Sixteenth Century*. London: Routledge, 1975. 29–88.

Spenser's Chivalric Restoration:
From Bateman's *Travayled Pylgrime* to the Redcrosse Knight

Anne Lake Prescott

In recent years it has become clear that, whatever Spenser's love of pagan fictions and tales of romance, he inscribed into his epic and deflected onto his villains certain perhaps Protestant and iconoclastic anxieties concerning his own feigning magic, his own spell weaving, the images that distract us from the straight and narrow way.[1] Spenser the creator of dreamy picture galleries has long since given way to a sterner Protestant, and at times he seems almost ready to become a sullen and disappointed Puritan. It is instructive, therefore, to see what his legend of Holiness looks like if set not against Italian or medieval romance, not against classical epic, but against another Protestant allegory of knightly quest and dynastic celebration, one also troubled by the temptations of imagined sights and the risks of repose. Luckily there is precisely such a test; it has, for all its limitations, a curious resemblance to the poem Spenser might have written had he fully shared the distrust of romance, feigning, love stories, and marvels felt by many Protestants, Counter-Reformation Catholics, and sober Humanists (including his friend Gabriel Harvey).

It is *The Travayled Pylgrime* (1569), a chivalric pilgrimage allegory by Archbishop Matthew Parker's protégé and librarian, Stephen Bateman. I am not the first to see a connection with Spenser, for Kathrine Koller, in 1942, tried to link the *Pylgrime* to the Book of Temperance; it goes better with Book I.[2] But the intertextual (or interfluvial) situation is in fact complicated. Although Bateman does not say so, his book is a reworking of the Burgundian Olivier de La Marche's nostalgic 1483 allegory, *Le Chevalier délibéré*, by way of Hernando Acuña's 1553 Spanish version published in Antwerp.[3] Even the many pictures perform a translation of their own, from the Burgundian autumn that followed the death of Charles the Rash in 1477, to the Hapsburg Netherlands, to Protestant England. In his fine study of Burgundian culture and the Tudors, Gordon Kipling compares La Marche

From *Studies in Philology* 86, no. 2 (Spring 1989): 166–97. Reprinted by permission of the author and the University of North Carolina Press.

himself to Spenser, but without reference to Bateman.[4] He is right to find similarities between the two allegorists: both follow a pattern alternating moralized wandering with emblematic structures set in a landscape devoid of specified locality or time, a world in which knights encounter abstract nouns and personages inhabiting primarily mental space.[5] To be sure, this technique and atmosphere are also found in Deguileville, Lydgate and, later, Hawes: that is, in a tradition owing some of its vocabulary to Prudentius' *Psychomachia* and one possible narrative structure to St. Bernard's allegorization of the Prodigal Son as an Everyyouth riding his horse Desire through a world of personifications.[6] To this La Marche adds both his grieving loyalty in old age to a defunct line of dukes and his aching awareness of Time. This is the Book of Holiness narrated by a victim of Mutability. Bateman erases some of the nostalgia Acuña had already diminished and incorporates his own centrist Protestantism, mild anxiety about the dangers of repose and visual distractions, suspicion of history and glory, gratitude to the Tudors, and a tendency to interiorize and individualize forces that La Marche found out there in history, language, or the place abstract nouns come from.[7]

Bateman's poem is, I think, England's only significant nondramatic Protestant quest allegory before Spenser; it shows what this genre could look like after the Reformation redefined the tradition's terms but before the Christian knight dismounted to trudge as Bunyan's pedestrian.[8] . . . Like Spenser, [Bateman] associates knightly errancy and recovery with his nation's restoration of a truth once lost to those same deceitful powers that stalk the *miles Christi.* We are on the way to Spenser, for it is precisely Bateman's combination of chivalric metaphor, pilgrimage allegory, dynastic praise, and national redemption from specifically papist darkness that makes his *Pylgrime* so interesting a precedent for *The Faerie Queene.* All Bateman lacks is love interest, better monsters (his giant is too small and talkative to be frightening), a wiser choice of meter, more awareness of the Italians, and—I admit—a greater talent for poetry.

Let me now describe this seldom-read text so as to suggest the likeness that makes difference worth noting. My method is narrative, for that is the best way to reveal how these two journeys coincide and diverge. I am not attempting to deny that Vergil, Ariosto, and Tasso are Spenser's most significant subtexts (although they do seem less central to Book I). And theoretical discussions of language and allegory in Bateman and Spenser are best postponed until the latter's place in this line of late Medieval and Renaissance personification narrative has been restudied.[9] I myself believe that Spenser read Bateman or at least looked at the pictures; he might have done so while working for Bishop Young, a friend of Bateman's employer Archbishop Parker. Skeptics, though, could consider Pilgrim and Redcrosse cognates, prodigal cousins descended from the house of Prudentius and Bernard but one of them owing more to other ancestors.

Bateman's title, *The Travayled Pylgrime*, punningly recalls how error first brought travail in field or childbed and travel far from Eden. His opening lines, indeed, evoke Adam, the namer and governor now "exilde" from his "accursed" land (sig. B2)—the same "forwasted" realm from which Una's parents have been "expeld" (I.i.5). But, says Bateman, God sent a "newe Adam," showing us a love seen also in his rescue of the Israelites from Egypt. In other words, like St. George, whose name is more or less Greek for Adam, "earth," Bateman's pilgrim enters on a quest immediately associated with Biblical and, by extrapolation, national history. After all, St. George's name, says the Golden Legend, may also mean (among other things) "pilgrim." Bateman's pilgrim is armed, if not with Pauline armor then with moral virtue, and mounted on Will, a horse "whose force few youth may stay" (B4v). Like George's "angry steede . . . disdayning to the curb to yield" (i.1), Will was sired by Bernard's Desiderium (himself a descendant of Plato's pair in *The Phaedrus*), the steed who whirls his rider up allegorical hills and down moralized dales. Pilgrim, in this also like Redcrosse, has Reason with him at least intermittently; and sometimes he has a lady: Dame Memory. Inspired by Thought, he sets forth "couragious, some prowesse for to winne," a conventional aim: Redcrosse hopes "To winne him worship" and "prove his puissance" (1.3). His quest is to seek Atropos and war against Debility and Dolor, energies that La Marche reads as the entropy and chance that destroyed Burgundy but that Bateman partially interiorizes into the concupiscible and irascible faculties.

Pilgrim's adventures, like George's, are structured by the sequence Bernard had suggested: initial ignorance and folly, rashness in success, despair in adversity, and recovery and perfection in knowledge.[10] To this Bateman adds, besides the admonitions and visions he modeled on those by La Marche, his own ruminations on time and history; Spenser adds the wanderings of Una, the tale of Fradubio, some epic touches, Arthur, and a betrothal. The two authors thus differ in how they interrupt and divide the pattern, but both follow a knight from error to pride to despair to recuperative education and a final battle.

Armed and advised, Pilgrim soon comes to "A goodly greene . . . which worldly pleasure hight," a place which so "delighted me, my selfe I cleane forgat" (B4v). Redcrosse too, "led with delight" (i.10), wanders into serpentine greenery. What follows in Bateman and Spenser is quite similar if one looks beyond the different ways of organizing error into episodes and forgets, for the moment, that Bateman's animated nouns become, in Spenser, more imaginable figures, mobile emblems. After entering a green world that each author unsurprisingly calls a labyrinth (C2v; i.11), the knights meet figures that are at once divisive and deceitful; both are then misled into worldliness and pride. Spenser shows us a major struggle with Error, then the encounter with Archimago, then the deflection to the House of Pride; Bateman hints at error, moves at once to divisive delusion, and then, after his knight's apparently ineffective visit to the House of Reason and a temporarily sobering defeat by Age, focuses on the dynamics of wandering as a prelude to false relaxation in the World.

Spenser is structurally clearer as well as subtler, yet if one combines Bateman's two descriptions of error anticipations of *The Faerie Queene* I.i leap out: green, delightful, tangled, the way to error is "obscure" (Bateman, F3v) and "shadie" (Spenser, i.7). Getting lost is easy, for this "crooked waye" is "not seene till some be in" and its deceit "so steales upon a man, that scarce he can be ware," especially if, like Redcrosse relying on his own virtue, one "puts confidence, on such as seemeth just." Here, says Pilgrim, live illusion and "That subtile stingbraine Error" who "much amasde my minde" (so too Spenser's knight is "amazde" by Error's repellent offspring). Like George, the horse Will rashly presses on "without all dread or feare" and Pilgrim so forgets himself that "I knew not mine owne estate nor how myselfe to name" (F4), a separation from the self that Spenser places after Archimago's machinations and that Bernard had allegorized as the "regio dissimilitudinis," that realm of unlikeness into which prodigals pass when they have forgotten themselves and their origin. But just as Una says "Add faith unto your force" (i.19), Pilgrim reports that "not by force and might, / The shielde of faith did me defende"; it does so "in midst of stormy showre," perhaps a reference, like Spenser's own cloudburst, to the blows of Fortune that invite us to Error's refuge.

After his initial misstep, Pilgrim meets the giant Disagreement, a figure in function not unlike Redcrosse's next enemy, Archimago.[11] Archimago promotes "ire" (ii.5), and Disagreement rides a horse of that name, but this "ire" is no mere wrath. Like Spenser's master magician, Bateman's giant seeks to divide and multiply, "all fleshe to stroy and waste," to "rent and plucke as small as sand," for he "all would deflowre, from quiet peace and rest" (B4v).[12] He is an anti-Sabbath, and his restless destruction is a sort of mutability: as he fought, says the knight, "Time my state did shake" (C1). In ways neither Bateman nor Spenser spell out, division is both cause and effect of temporality's breakages and slippages in the postedenic and sequential world. When force seems useless, furthermore, Disagreement resorts to hypocritical delusion, appealing to the knight's folly and "fickle fantasie." Seemingly pacified, he gives the knight a magic cap that he says restores its owner like a "springing Well" and confounds all "fonde device" (C2). This is an ancient fairy-tale motif, but Bateman does not believe in fairy tales or even in good marvels; not for him Prince Arthur's supernatural shield or wondrous medicine. Like Redcrosse crediting Archimago's false dreams, Pilgrim cannot read the gift's true nature, and since Bateman is not sure we can either, the margin explains that the cap signifies "the craftie illusions of Sathan, by coloured imaginations seeking all meanes possible, to deceive if he might, even the very elect." . . .

Pilgrim and Will come to the "palace of disordered livers," not, unless Bateman is guilty of a brilliant pun, an anatomical allegory, but a place like Lucifera's House of Pride. Naming itself Love, it is really "the world both fresh and gaye" (F4v), suggestive evidence that Patrick Cullen is right in identifying Spenser's version of this palace as the "world" third of the infernal triad.[13] Self-mocking when recounted by the courtier La Marche, the episode in Bateman's hands fits comfortably into a tradition of anti-court satire. There is, however, nothing like Spenser's parodic maiden queen and her deadly entourage, the negative version of Gloriana's Cleopolis. Bateman stresses the world's moral threat to a private knight (if that is not an oxymoron), but he avoids any mention of the local authorities; Spenser, thinking more politically, shows his knight dismayed by a vision of "pollicie" and evil magnates (iv.12). Still, the two palaces are remarkably similar, even granted the expectedness of many details and the probable impact on Spenser's imagination of Cartigny's *Wandering Knight*.[14]

. . . .

Seeming to offer "joyous rest" and "ease" (Bateman, F4v), both palaces are false Sabbaths, tempting us from a weekday path on which we should be up and doing. Both knights know this in their elect hearts, for both find the inhabitants "no fit companions" (Bateman, G1) and "unfit" (Spenser, who, however, also stresses George's "knightly vew," iv.37,15).[15] Each, though, needs his memory jogged. Looking in a mirror, Pilgrim sees his own sins and the face of Age; Lucifera also has a mirror, but hers is the normally Venereal glass wrenched to the use of unmarried pride, not the "crystal glass of reformation" on which Bateman wrote a book published this same year. In Bateman's picture (figure 1) the mirror's holder looks like Reason, but the text identifies the reminder as Memory. Redcrosse, too, is taught by reason and memory, for his dwarf gives him a lesson in history resembling the one which Reason has fruitlessly given Pilgrim several episodes before the latter's deviation into folly. Needless to say, the prudent dwarf prefers effective and sober nonfiction, so unlike Lucifera's "chroniclers" who—like Spenser—record "Old loves, and warres for Ladies" (v.3), George's teacher shows him the more humanist "ensample" and "sight" of political disaster (v.45–52). Pilgrim's rescuers, however, bypass both doubtful amorous records and vivid moral example in order to present unmediated self-knowledge. Within the fiction, that is, they do not use history as a mirror but show the mirror itself, directly. It is true that Memory has *energia*, speaking with "words of lively force" (G2), so perhaps she uses "ensamples" like those her friend Reason had relied on earlier (D3v–E1). Still, here Bateman separates the image of the image-making mirror from the report of unspecified words on sin. For him the "sight" is of the self, even if behind that allegory may be another in which Memory's possibly more general lecture in some sense "is" the mirror.

The Author being caried by his horſe Will to the palace of diſor-
dered liuers, ſeeing then the abuſe of all vertues, and the maintenance of filthy luxuria, remembreth hispromiſe made to Age, loo-
keth in the glaſſe of reformation, ſtraight taketh his iorney, forſa-
king vtterly thoſe abuſes.

The Author ſeeing Abuſion of all ordered vertues, ſo deckt like a foole, ſuſpecteth
that all the reſt inhabiters, are no fit companions, concerning his promiſe
to Age, leaueth all and departeth with Memorie .   G.i.

Figure 1. [*The mirror-holder is identified as Memory, but resembles the
Reason or Understanding in earlier illustrations.*]

Figures 1, 2, 3 are reproduced by permission of the Huntington Library, San Marino, California,
from its copy designated RB 31250.

Spenser's fiction at this point contains an image of effective history-telling; Bateman's fiction contains an image not of history or fable but of the hero looking at himself and seeing the results of time on his own face. In any case, both knights make their furtive escape, Redcrosse fleeing by Pride's filthy "privie Posterne" (a witty anatomical allegory), though "Scarce could he footing find in that foule way" (v.53), and Pilgrim, who "scarce could finde [his] way" in the Palace (F4), instructing Memory to tell any sin who asks after him that she does not know his whereabouts. A clever move, if unheroic.

After pride comes despair. Spenser's arrangements are again more structurally interesting, his language generates more implications, some of them grimly funny, and he infolds more tradition, but the cousinship of the two narratives remains striking. . . .

Released by Arthur from Orgoglio's prison, Redcrosse nearly despairs. And just as Orgoglio's victim is "Disarmed, disgrast, and inwardly dismayde" (vii.11), a soon to be "dismaide" Pilgrim finds this land ruled by "Dispaire, Dispraise, Disdaine and Ire" (H2v,G3). Like Orgoglio's castle the place seems a "dungeon," but like Despair's home it is a "tenebrous" and thorny wasteland (G2v). There is a well, not enervating like the one Redcrosse drank from before meeting his giant double, but bitter and named Violation. Recognizing himself in this "vacant," malodorous, and trap-filled land, Pilgrim thinks some of the thoughts that Spenser puts in the mouth of Despair, no mere noun now but a powerful rhetorician. As so often, what is scenery and names in Bateman, in Spenser becomes a vocal emblematic personage. Despair is in many ways chthonic, sitting on the ground that generated Orgoglio and out of which God shaped Adam and George, although his cave is "a greedie grave" (ix.33), not a womb. But in another sense, too, he is landscape's child, symbol and creation of the desert in which he lives: crouching amid trees that like Bateman's have "nor fruit, nor leafe," he wears the thorns that grow in Bateman's scenery and his body is as withered and dishevelled as Pilgrim's surroundings.

What Pilgrim tells himself, Despair tells Redcrosse: he has sinned and should die. La Marche's stress had been on aged regret, but Bateman has imagined a scene closer to Bernard's sequence and so emphasizes that what his knight sees is the world without God. Divine wrath hangs over it, and Pilgrim quakes to recall that "the count is great, that I to Jove must make" (G3). Like Bateman's careless world that forgets Heaven and Hell, Despair's rhetoric slithers past what follows the sleep of death to which he invites his visitor; but he remembers a just God's payment for accumulated sins: "Is not the measure of thy sinfull hire / High heaped up with huge iniquitie, / Against the day of wrath, to burden thee?" (ix.46). Bateman thinks of "grace" (G3v) and Una recalls mercy, adding logic—as the elect pile up sins they must increase God's mercy—and denigrating mere rhetoric—"Ne let vaine words bewitch thy manly heart" (ix.53).

But Pilgrim still hates himself. Tired, lonely, and "despairing of my selfe," he rides "halfe dead" into a "hollow cave." Even Will starts to "reele" (H2v–H3). Like Redcrosse, Pilgrim would gladly die; and he too feels filthy. Despair had rightly accused his victim of dirtying himself with Duessa "in all abuse" and Pilgrim must remember that the porter of the Palace of Love was named Abusion. Now he wishes that a "hollow grave, with bloudie bones, of me should be defilde" and longs "not in such a Laberinth, of endlesse woes to wende." Among his griefs, however, is one Spenser spares Redcrosse. Pilgrim has begun to question glory itself in a world where "ech man himselfe doth love" and sudden death makes hope of fame problematic: "For while he strives to get renowme, the thred of life is cut" (G3; cf. Milton's "Lycidas"). Here and elsewhere Bateman sets limits on the chivalric pursuit of even good glory, limits Spenser doubtless considered but Despair does not mention. That Book I's "glory" may indicate divine glory does not alter the fact that within the fiction Redcrosse desires "worship," something the hermit Contemplation does not discourage despite his doubts about bloodshed and ladies' love. For Bateman, finally, the New Jerusalem and knightly fame cannot be reconciled, whatever the continued usefulness of chivalric discourse as metaphor.

Bateman's knight raises his grieving eyes and sees Dame Memory. When cheering Redcrosse, Una had also been Memory, in a way, recalling him to himself and his task. Bateman's Memory offers Pilgrim something rather different this time, not a mirror of reformation but the assurance that he "should not go alone" on his quest to find Atropos (figure 2). Her history is less for moral education than for companionship, and it is perhaps because of this that Pilgrim calls Memory's conversation "mery tales and stories true" (H3v). Her nonfiction fashions a good death, not a many-virtued gentleman enabled by twelve or twenty-four books of dark conceit to serve the crown.

Una now takes Redcrosse to the House of Holiness, a correctional institution closer to similar structures by Bernard and Cartigny than to anything in *The Travayled Pylgrime*. Dame Memory, too, will bring her knight to a house, one where Reason (no hermit or palmer but a theologically informed layman) prepares him for his last duel. But first she gives him a tour of what Spenser was to call the Ruins of Time. It is now that Bateman introduces, through explicit and visionary nonfiction (Memory at her best, he must have thought), with a personification or metaphor here and there, the national history that in Book I Spenser both veils and figures forth in an allegory never calling the Tudors by their names. Bateman does so, however, while showing that Truth's champions also unwillingly teach us about death. The Tudors, like their Burgundian counterparts, enter the lists heroically to fight and lose—good is the life ending faithfully. But their chivalry is personal. As warriors against Dolor and Debility they enact their courage in terms familiar from court pageantry and knightly combat, but as

The trauailed Pilgrime

Here the Author and Memory riding alone, Memorie comforteth
him to prouide and arme himſelfe againſt Thanatos.

*The Authr being ſomewhat moued by Memori:, paſſeth ouer the fielde of
worldly pleaſure, and Time alſo nere paſt, beginneth to faint,
yet for a time recouered by Reaſon.*

Figure 2.   *Memory guiding the knight.*

Protestant reformers they act like statesmen with no time for courtly fiction. As individuals they play knights and as kings they play kings, for the monarch's two bodies yield two discourses: the metaphoric and the historical. True, Memory finds Biblical names and analogies, together with images that anticipate Spenser's extended fictions: Edward defeats the Pope Goliath (a real giant, however, not a pagan fable) and Henry battles the Catholic Church with a bright shield of faith. On the whole, though, allegory ceases when Bateman describes the Reformation. Spenser's anti-papist triumphs are more consistently and elaborately feigned.

. . . .

While they travel, Pilgrim stares with fascination, but Memory soon becomes oddly scornful about what he sees, as if remembering deeper truths. That is, she perceives behind history, and thus in a sense beyond herself, a sort of abyss against which our records and recollections seem not so very different from fiction after all. Spenser may have shared some of her doubts, but Memory's reminders have a directness he himself avoids. Her lesson in skepticism comes when she notes that her pupil is inattentive and replies only "hum and ha" when she speaks to him. He has in fact been so enchanted by *seeing* that he forgets to *listen*. Distracted by "toyes, and fancies that I sawe" and "fancies newe and straunge" (L4), his mind has forsaken words for images, just as many Protestant reformers said Christians had been drawn from God's Word by Catholic glitter and idolatry. "Me thou doest not heere," scolds Memory. "I am ravisht with the sight," explains Pilgrim. Spenser knew this danger, calling one of his chief villains "Arch*imago*," but if only for self protection as an arch-image-maker himself he usually separates those who abuse sight—deceivers like the creator of Redcrosse's false dreams or the manufacturer of the snowy Florimel—from the granters of true insight like Contemplation or Colin atop Mt. Acidale. . . .

Eventually the two arrive at Memory's cemetery to inspect "the auncient showe and Funerals of mightie Conquerours past." These "Pyramides, and Monuments right hie" (M1) memorialize the fame that the Renaissance liked to imagine for the virtuous, yet Memory understands that to live in the mouths of men is not a reward or consolation, only a neutral fact: we know of the good, the bad, and the ugly because they have caught history's sometimes amoral attention. Memory had claimed for a moment to have forgotten the unworthy "bitter floure" Mary Tudor, but now she remembers Goliath, Herod, Nero, and (Bateman was a Euhemerist) Bacchus, pointing out the markers that "stande to their shame" (M1v). Pilgrim is impressed, but Memory rebukes him for his spiritually ignorant gawking at celebrity: "The sights not seene with Jove above, doth breede more joy and ease: / For these are things though faire, yet vaine, a time to please the eye, / The life to come doth far surpasse. . . ."

Doubtless Spenser would agree, as would Milton, but when Arthur reads the Britons Moniments in Book II he is given no such advice; like chivalry, history survives Spenser's doubts better than it does those of Archbishop Parker's librarian. Bateman's ambivalence remains curious; knowledge of a history more significant than chronicle and more trustworthy than national fantasies had acquired increased importance for many humanists and theologians, whether as political and moral instruction or as an aid to better informed if less imaginative scriptural exegesis. More than Spenser, much more than his Burgundian model, Bateman seems to have regarded even history as potential deviation from the path to God, at least when visualized. History, apparently, is not only more fictional, more constructed by the projecting sight, than the straightness of Memory's path had at first implied—it offers us, in addition to consolation and company, the danger of premature rest as we glut the inner eye. We must, says Memory to her charge, push on to those better sights above: "that journey let us hye."

The only way to those sights, in Bateman's mind, is death; his poem is less visionary than Spenser's in this regard too, for the work's chief religious spectacle comes early, when Reason shows Pilgrim a chamber full of virtues—very pretty, but not the New Jerusalem. Before his last liberating battle, it is true, Memory provides one more glorious image: Elizabeth (figure 3). Yet even her splendor is shadowed, for the enthroned figure in the picture is Thanatos, ruler of dynasties.

Memory reacts more like a subject than an abstract noun, unless she is here Pilgrim's personal recollection: the queen is "our supreme head" whose benefits "No tongue ne pen may well expresse" (M3). We need fear no enemy "if we eche other love" and obey one whose "splendent face and Christall eyen, hir comly corps and gate, / Is able sure a hart of stone, to cause relent and quake." Guiding "hir publike wealth" with "sage sobrietie," Elizabeth has no equal Memory can recall. And yet Memory also draws Pilgrim's attention to the "bony figure" who "endes the life of every degree." To say that queens die is not normally *scandalum magnatum*. Still, the mention of Elizabeth's human frailty gently moves the historical woman away from her mythology. The queen on this particular progress rides from her immortal rule as an image to the mortal event of her individual death.[16]

. . . .

No doubt Elizabeth is a great and pious queen, sailing "on seas of troublous time" with "Gods gospell" as captain and keeping such a sharp eye on her coastline that "Pope and Jewe" stand "in feare, of hir most splendant face" (M3v). To include the Jews, hardly a geopolitical threat to England, may imply that her care is as much religious as military: the supreme head bewares both popish superstition and "Judaic" legalism as found, perhaps, in Geneva. But Bateman intrudes touches that qualify the

The trauailed Pilgrime

The Author beholdeth the difcourfe of Dolor and Debilitie, Thanatos fitting and giueth iudgement, Attropos giuing place.

As they are at contention, the worthy Queene Elyzabeth paſſeth by, neyther Dolor nor Debilitie, as yet not able to reſiſt.

Figure 3. *Elizabeth on progress to death, accompanied by her Council and by Fame.*

splendor beyond the shadow already cast by Thanatos. The queen and her cabinet ride "Through worldly pleasures trapped way," and although she seeks "the life to come" and although her progress "goes forward on, not minding once to stay," her constant if virtuous activity ("so that she feares scarce time to have, such is hir godly zeale") leaves little space for Memory and Pilgrim. Those two remain observers, and neither seems to think that the knight owes further service or is indeed attached in any way beyond admiration to this mobile court. Even Memory's praise, under these narrative circumstances, remains internalized in Pilgrim (Bateman himself, of course, has gone public). The vision moves out of sight and beyond relevance as dynastic celebration and personal allegory part company: "Forth on we needes must take our way, for we two will alone / Debate of matters past and gon" (M4).

At Memory's words, Pilgrim's color changes and "grayer head did then appeere." The two pass through an increasingly barren countryside while Memory argues with remarkably good cheer that "nothing bides in one estate" (N1). The knight broods over this thought in language close to that Spenser uses when reflecting on Nature's crisp rejection of Mutabilitie's similar claim: "When I considered hir words, and weyde them well in minde," he begins (cf. VII.viii.1), although his mind then moves not to the pillars of eternity but to Memory's kindness in showing "the daungers great, which passed were and gone." Eventually the two come to the shining House of Hoped Time, where True Zeal puts Pilgrim to bed in a room called Pain. It is here that the knight at last finds, more briefly described, the enlightenment his equivalents are allowed earlier in their careers by La Marche, Cartigny, and Spenser. Reason sends Diligence, Patience, and the three theological virtues. He even suggests that Pilgrim can win fame, although after what Memory has said about history the knight should perhaps greet this with some skepticism. Comforted by these bedside nouns, rested and instructed, Pilgrim summons his strength, mounts Will, and rides forth to his inevitable defeat in this world. And yet the poem does not quite close. Spenser's refusal to conclude is more elaborate and allegorically necessary: Redcrosse cannot rest with Una while there is work to be done for God and Gloriana, and so long as there are lies and divisions in a world of time mankind cannot join Truth in marital bliss. Bateman's humbler nonconclusion is merely the admission that his is not a very good poem and that he hopes someone will write a better. Someone did. . . .

Spenser is more seriously engaged by the chivalric metaphor that Bateman also adopts, more moved by knightly loyalty, service, and sacrifice. Not surprisingly, then, Redcrosse has more context than Pilgrim: he has a foster father, one true love, an evil mistress, future in-laws, a friend, a dwarf, "merie England" to patronize one day, and a queen to serve. Pilgrim's company is found chiefly in the ranks of the dead; despite his early identification in one of the early illustrations as "Obedience," his only true liege is God; and when as an aged knight he sees Elizabeth he does not even offer to be her beadsman. Even more than our literature's most famous pilgrim, fleeing his city and family to find eternal life, Pilgrim makes a lonely journey; Bunyan's Christian at least has fellow travellers. Redcrosse's task is to restore a lost kingdom; Pilgrim's last effort is to die well, not to rescue others. La Marche's knight, to be sure, was similarly isolated, but he was made so by the death of his duke. It seems appropriate, then, that one of the few pictures Bateman or his printer added to those derived from the Spanish translation shows an elderly man walking through a desert wood, on foot. In his heart, I think, Bateman did not believe the chivalric mythology that he adopts, whatever its still very audible Christian resonance. Pilgrim looks like a knight and wears, finally, all the right metaphoric armor, but somewhere within himself he is this determined but lonely pedestrian, not so much a *miles Christi* as one of the Lord's civilians.

Redcrosse is in love. With a little ingenuity, Bateman could have added something of the sort, although the pictures would have made it a challenge. Protestants valued marriage, and indeed Bateman's employer had annoyed Elizabeth by marrying, but beyond a hint in Age's lecture to the knight that the latter is married, chivalry in this poem is, here too, a solo affair with little room for an accompanying, distracting, or inspiring "other"—Pilgrim has Memory, true, but she is not his beloved, only his teacher.[17] It is tempting to recall the stereotypical middle-class Protestant whose family is doubtless dear to him but who wrestles alone in his chamber without wifely or even priestly counsel. La Marche's knight had no wife but did have the clergy and the sacraments. Bateman disallows these, and while he may simply have thought it undignified for decent clergymen to appear veiled in fiction (in the wrong vestments, so to speak), it can also be said that his imagination is quite unsacramental. La Marche's "Aucteur" goes to mass, but Bateman's pilgrim receives moral instruction and does not even go to church. Although detesting the Whore of Babylon as much as the next Protestant, Spenser is happier with certain Catholic remnants and seems even to have worked into Redcrosse's betrothal scene elements of the Sarum Missal's baptismal rite.[18] As a knight, then, Redcrosse has intermediary and preliminary loyalties, and as a Christian he has a faith likewise mediated through, for instance, a hermit, the sight of Heaven, and open references to baptism.

Spenser admits the marvellous; Bateman minimizes it, and behind this rejection of something he may have considered papist and medieval lies an even deeper worry about fiction itself. Recent criticism has, as I have said, identified Spenser's own inner quarrels with the spectacular and imagined, but although Bateman liked pictures, it is also evident that much more than Spenser he feared what might slink out of the gates of ivory. Yet the gates of horn seem not quite to have pleased him either, for the "sights" of history are almost as dangerous to Pilgrim as the feigned magic of Disagreement and the disguised demons of Love's Palace. In Book I, anyway, Spenser is less in a hurry for a final "sight," perhaps precisely because he can see it in the distance while standing here—or can at least imagine that his hero sees it. Bateman has *heard* good news and wants to press on. He seems more radical than Spenser, impatient to see face to face, to get going; even the pleasures of learning about history appear to him like dallying on the grassy ground when one should be putting on the new man as fast as possible. And the history Bateman enjoys most is that of the Tudor Reformation and not, despite a somewhat credulous reference to the defeat of Gogmagog, the ancient sources of Britain. Translation of empire interests him little; nor does he say that he himself is translating, if also subverting, a late Medieval and Catholic work as adapted for the Hapsburgs.

In sum, while Spenser was more up to date than Bateman in looking at Italian romance and dynastic epic he was also more hospitable to older tones and affections, both more humanist and more medieval. He is chivalric beyond mere metaphoric trappings, for his hero serves, rescues, and loves others in a knightly fashion and for knightly motives of duty and glory. He is more impressed by what we can envisage and invent, more willing to linger a while in fictions thicker and more multi-valent (and multi-veiled) than the nouns that delay or push Bateman's knight on his way to disappear. Much of this difference derives from the nature of Bateman's tradition, but some comes from his deeper distrust of the eye, of digression, of the feigned—an ancient distrust almost certainly accentuated by the Reformation. That Bateman wrote allegory at all is a testament to the part of his mind that could not resist gods, illustrations, and encyclopedic learning. Whatever his own Sabbath longings and whatever his own fear of Archimago, Spenser was surer than this earlier Protestant allegorist that the artist may by indirections find directions out; and, in finding them, he was more willing to take his time.

Notes

1.   Our lying "devil" derives from double-speaking "diabolus," but as Isabel MacCaffrey says, "A forked tongue is the poet's stock in trade": *Spenser's Allegory: The Anatomy of Imagination* (Princeton: Princeton University Press, 1976), 55. For more on this increasingly noted ambivalence see, e.g., Kenneth Gross, *Spenserian Poetics: Idolatry, Iconoclasm, & Magic* (Ithaca: Cornell Univ. Press, 1985). Ernest B. Gilman's *Iconoclasm and Poetry in the English Reformation: Down Went Dagon* (Chicago: Univ. of Chicago Press, 1986), has a fine chapter on "Spenser's 'Painted Forgery.'" "Puritan" iconophobia did not, however, preclude imagery and stageplays; for a salutary reminder, see John King, *English Reformation Literature: The Tudor Origins of the Protestant Tradition* (Princeton: Princeton University Press, 1982). And for Spenser's positive uses of magic, especially as an allegory or analogue of poetry, see Patrick Cheney, "'Secret Powre Unseene': Good Magic in Spenser's Legend of Britomart," *SP* 85 (1988): 1–28.

2.   "*The Travayled Pylgrime* by Stephen Batman and Book Two of *The Faerie Queene*," *MLQ* 3 (1942); her comments on faculty psychology bring out an element I downplay here,

and she may be right to find a touch of Debilitie (who sports a skull and crossbones) in Spenser's Maleger. Patrick Cullen, *Infernal Triad: The Flesh, the World, and the Devil in Spenser and Milton* (Princeton: Princeton Univ. Press, 1974), finds Koller's evidence "slight."

3. The revised STC identifies Bateman's poem as a translation of La Marche, although with no mention of Acuña. I have used the unillustrated Paris 1842 edition, consulting "*Le Chevalier délibéré,*" the *Illustrations of the edition of Schiedam*, with a preface by F. Lippman (London: Chiswick Press, 1898). So far as I know there is no modern edition of Acuña. There can be no question that Bateman knew who wrote the allegory, and Acuña even retains the puns on "la marche." La Marche and Acuña call the pilgrim "Author" (and "Acteur," as it was spelled, also means "actor"); except for a few references to the "author," Bateman never names his own hero, so I call him Pilgrim.

4. *The Triumph of Honour: Burgundian Origins of the Elizabethan Renaissance* (Leiden: Leiden University Press, for the Sir Thomas Browne Institute, 1977), 154. Kipling cites, e.g., p.14, the role of La Marche in keeping the court of Edward IV informed about proper chivalry; Edward was brother-in-law to Charles the Rash, and Henry VII's mother's people, the Woodvilles, had Burgundian connections.

5. "Mental space" is Coleridge, quoted by Michael Murrin in *The Allegorical Epic: Essays in Its Rise and Decline* (Chicago: Univ. of Chicago Press, 1980), 131. Murrin says, "Images and personifications appear and disappear in a largely deserted landscape. This dreamy sense contrasts markedly with the Italian romance epic" (144). Bateman adds one scene that stands out precisely because the landscape is so crowded: Pilgrim finds a valley filled with foolish women like Dame Flingbraine and Mrs. Nice (sigs. G4v–H1), who seem to have wandered in from Vanity Fair.

6. For the importance of Bernard's *Parabola I, De pugna spirituali* see Dorothy Atkins Evans' introduction to her edition of an allegory by the Flemish Carmelite, Jean Cartigny: *Le Voyage du Chevalier Errant*, 1557, translated by William Goodyear as *The Wandering Knight*, 1581 (Seattle: Univ. of Washington Press, 1951); Bernard's sermon is quoted 126–130. In "*The Wandering Knight*, the Red Cross Knight and 'Miles Dei,'" *HLQ* 7 (1943/4): 101–34, Evans shows how Cartigny often anticipates Spenser; Cullen, p. 16, agrees. The issue is muddied by Cartigny's evident debt to La Marche and by the possibility that Bateman read Cartigny. See also Sigfried Wenzel's important article, "The Pilgrimage of Life as a Late Medieval Genre," *Mediaeval Studies* 35 (1973): 370–88; he mentions La Marche and Bateman but does not appear to notice their connection. Edgar Schell, *Strangers and Pilgrims: from "The Castle of Perseverance" to "King Lear"* (Chicago: Univ. of Chicago Press, 1983), argues well for Bernard's impact on the drama.

Personification allegory is not much admired in modern times; Rosamond Tuve curtly dismisses La Marche in her *Allegorical Imagery: Some Mediaeval Books and Their Posterity* (Princeton: Princeton Univ. Press, 1966), 17. What depth the mode can offer, however, receives thoughtful sounding in Carolynn Van Dyke, *The Fiction of Truth: Structures of Meaning in Narrative and Dramatic Allegory* (Ithaca: Cornell Univ. Press, 1985), ch. I.

7. Susie Speakman Sutch and Anne Lake Prescott, "Translation as Transformation: Olivier de la Marche's *Le Chevalier délibéré* and its Hapsburg and Elizabethan Permutations," *Comparative Literature Studies* 25.4 (1988), 281–317, traces the transformations by Acuña, Bateman, and Lewis Lewkenor, who in 1594 published an unillustrated prose translation quite faithful to Acuña except for the added Tudors.

8. See, however, Hendrick Niclas' familist *Terra Pacis* (STC 18564, c. 1575), a prose pilgrimage allegory (the splendid frontispiece shows the Lamb of God crushing the world, flesh, and devil). There are a few parallels with Spenser, who might have found its defense of "Similitudes, Figures, and Parables" intriguing depite the notorious author's risky and perhaps not very Protestant theology, but its chief kinship is with Bunyan, for Niclas is indifferent to the chivalric metaphor and ignores the Tudors.

9. Spenser's relation, especially in Book I, to older French, Burgundian, and native allegory needs a new look. Carol Kaske, "How Spenser Really Used Stephen Hawes in the

ANNE LAKE PRESCOTT ◆ 93

Legend of Holiness," in *Unfolded Tales: Essays on Renaissance Romance*, ed. G. M. Logan and Gordon Tesky, (Ithaca: Cornell Univ. Press, 1989) studies what Spenser might owe Hawes' *Example of Vertue* (1504?). It is also entertaining to compare his methods to those of Barnaby Googe's *Shippe of safegarde* (1569), a seagoing pilgrimage that sails past sins such as sky-piercing Presumption and dark Desperation (sig. E3). Like Bateman's, Googe's doubts about images go beyond Spenser's even as he, too, relishes them: when his sailors reach Heresy they find among other abominations a picture of Saint George killing a dragon (sig. D5v). M. S. and G. H. Blayney, "*The Faerie Queene* and an English Version of Chartier's *Traité de L'Esperance*," *SP* 55 (1958): 154–63 find some parallels between I.ix–x and an early 15th c. allegory, a copy of which was in Leicester's library.

10.　Evans implies on occasion that Bernard's suggested structure is tripartite, but he is clear that there are four stages: "Primo enim est egens et insipiens; postea, praeceps et temerarius in prosperis: diende, trepidus et pusillanimis in adversis; prostremo, providus, et eruditus et perfectus in regno charitatis" (Evans, 130).

11.　To my inexpert eye there seems little of allegorical interest in the minutiae of combat or dress in Bateman's battles (beyond the obvious and explicit), although it may be that La Marche himself gave such details chivalric or moral significance (and see his deliciously elegant arming of a lady in allegorical finery, the *Parement et triumphe des dames*). Here again Spenser is restorative; see Michael Leslie, *Spenser's "Fierce Warres and Faithfull Loves": Martial and Chivalric Symbolism in "The Faerie Queene"* (Cambridge, Eng.: Barnes and Noble, 1983).

12.　Compare Orgoglio, by whom Red Crosse is nearly "pouldred all, as thin as flowre" (vii.12). Error, too, is divisive, of course; Gordon Teskey remarks of Red Crosse's encounter with her that "Spenser generates his narrative by driving good and evil apart so that a variety of adventures will unfold in the space opened between them" ("From Allegory to Dialectic: Imagining Error in Spenser and Milton," *PMLA* 101 (1986): 13). Bateman's pun on postedenic travel and travail suggests the same dynamic. The pulverizing giant is curiously like Arthur and his shield: "Men into stones therewith he could transmew, / And stones to dust, and dust to nought at all" (vii.35). Gilman, p. 66, notes the blank shield's iconoclastic power; Disagreement's force, on the other hand, is backed by an ability to manipulate fraudulent mental imagery.

13.　Cullen, 40–43.

14.　Spenser seems to me closer in content, working, and tone to Bateman; it is typical, for example, that Cartigny's palace has tennis courts, very specified landscape, and a closely described indoors. Compare, too, Googe's description of the rock of worldly pride (sigs. B2v–B5, including the competition to be chic) and his palace of lust (C5v ff), where the eyes dazzle and a scornful queen tortures her prisoners by tearing their hearts in a sort of Petrarchan parody, like Spenser's Busirane. There was, in fact, a fashion for describing the beautiful but dangerous building, the "pseudo-amoenus" topos, we could call it. Reaching towers, gold, crystal, and dazzled eyes are *de rigueur*. Thus Gavin Douglas describes the "Palice of Honour" as "like the hevin imperiall" with silver, jewels, and gold that daze the sight even though the visitor eventually learns that "eirdlie gloir is nocht bot vanitie"; he too has a mirror, in his case a magic glass in which one sees not the face, as in Bateman and Spenser, but "The deidis and fatis of everie eirdlie wicht" (*Poetical Works*, ed. John Small, Edinburgh, 1874, I, 57–74).

15.　Knights, particularly free lances, need not admire courts; indeed, the chivalric romance is particularly adroit in exploring tensions between public and private life. Nonetheless, Red Crosse judges according to a standard that is feudal and aristocratic as well as moral, even if the "knightly vew" itself signifies some spiritual awareness.

16.　That there may be something a little uncomfortable about the image of Elizabeth and Thanatos is amusingly indicated by the printer who recycled the picture for Anthony Munday's *Fountaine of Fame* (1582), literally erasing Death from the celebratory scene and leaving an awkward blank; true, several other pictures Munday or his printer borrowed from Bateman are similarly de-shadowed by simply excising Death. I thank Ruth Luborsky for alerting me to Munday's use of these illustrations.

17.   Pilgrim has Memory, but although a necessary guide she would make a dangerous wife; so he must go it alone, directed toward Heaven but not to a divine marriage or self-completion through unity with the feminine. On such matters see the fascinating study by Benjamin G. Lockerd, Jr., *The Sacred Marriage: Psychic Integration in "The Faerie Queene"* (Lewisburg: Bucknell Univ. Press, 1987).

18.   Links between the Holy Saturday baptismal ceremony in the Sarum Missal and the betrothal scene at the end of Book I are noted by Harold Weatherby, "What Spenser Meant by Holinesse: Baptism in Book I of *The Faerie Queene*," *SP* 84 (1987): 286–307. Recently he has also argued for a connection between St. George, so scorned by humanists and so doubted by the Church of England, and the Eastern Orthodox liturgy; see "The True Saint George," *ELR* 17 (1987): 119–41. For more on Spenser and Sarum, see my "The Thirsty Deer and the Lord of Life: Some Contexts for *Amoretti* 67–70," *Spenser Studies* 6 (1985): 33–76.

To Fashion a Gentleman: Spenser and the Destruction of the Bower of Bliss

Stephen Greenblatt

The destruction of Acrasia's Bower tests in a remarkably searching way our attitudes toward pleasure, sexuality, the body; tests too our sense of the relation of physical pleasure to the pleasure of aesthetic images and the relation of both of these to what Guyon calls the "excellence" of man's creation. By "tests" I do not mean that the work examines us to see if we know the right answer—the poetry of the *Faerie Queene*, as Paul Alpers has demonstrated, continually invites us to trust our own experience of its rich surface[1]—rather, this experience tends to reveal or define important aspects of ourselves. Thus when C. S. Lewis, invoking the "exquisite health" of Spenser's imagination, characterizes the Bower as a picture of "the whole sexual nature in disease," of "male prurience and female provocation," indeed of "skeptophilia," the reader familiar with Lewis's work will recognize links to his criticism of erotic passages in *Hero and Leander* and *Venus and Adonis*, links to his conception of maturity and of mental and moral health. This is not to deny that Lewis's brilliant account describes disturbing qualities that any attentive reader may recognize in the Bower, but it may help us to understand why he writes that "the Bower of Bliss is not a place even of healthy animalism, or indeed of activity of any kind," whereas Spenser depicts Acrasia and her adolescent lover reposing "after long wanton joys" and even (following Tasso) pictures droplets of sweat trilling down Acrasia's snowy breast "through langor of her late sweet toil." What for Spenser is the place "Where Pleasure dwells in sensual delights" is for Lewis the realm only of frustration; all sexual activity is in this way reserved for the Garden of Adonis and hence tied securely to reproduction.[2]

At the other extreme, Yeats dismisses the moral judgments in the canto as "unconscious hypocrisy." Spenser, he tells us, "is a poet of the delighted senses, and his song becomes most beautiful when he writes of those islands of Phaedria and Acrasia."[3] And here again the reader familiar with Yeats will recognize certain perennial interests and values. The point would

From *Renaissance Self-fashioning from More to Shakespeare.* © 1980 by the University of Chicago. All rights reserved. Reprinted by permission of the author and the University of Chicago Press.

be too obvious to belabor, were it not for the fact that much Spenser commentary of the past several decades treats the Bower of Bliss and comparable passages in Spenser as if they were technical puzzles to be solved, as if one could determine their meaning quite apart from their effect upon the reader: "The main subject of the bower of Bliss is disorder in the human body, the general image or picture is of the cause of that disorder, the imagery used in painting this picture is all of disorder, and the laws of decorum are satisfied."[4] A sympathetic response like Hazlitt's to the canto's "voluptuous pathos, and languid brilliancy of fancy" or a residual uneasiness about the destruction are dismissed as absurd. Indeed the Romantic readers of the poem implicitly stand charged as either degenerates or moral incompetents. To be sure, criticism has convincingly shown that the intellectual tradition behind Guyon's act of moral violence included not only Puritanism (which must, in any case, be understood as far more than a hysterical rejection of the flesh) but a rich matrix of classical and medieval thought.[5] Moreover, it has demonstrated that the description of the Bower itself is not an isolated "beauty" that Spenser, in growing uneasiness and bad faith, decided to crush, but an episode embedded in a narrative that is shaped throughout by the poet's complex moral intelligence. The Romantic critics who have been discredited by this scholarship, however, had the virtue of fully acknowledging the Bower's intense erotic appeal. It is frequently said in reply that Spenser has given us a picture of healthy sexual enjoyment in the Garden of Adonis where "Franckly each paramor his leman knowes" (3.6.41); but the comparison fails to take into consideration the fact that the Garden of Adonis, that great "seminary" of living things, has almost no erotic appeal. The issue is not whether sexual consummation is desirable in Spenser, but why the particular erotic appeal of the Bower—more intense and sustained than any comparable passage in the poem—excites the hero's destructive violence.

We are told that after an initial attractiveness the Bower becomes stultifying, perverted, and frustrating or that the reader's task, like the hero's, is to interpret the images correctly, that is, to recognize the danger of "lewd loves, and wasteful luxury" embodied in the Bower. I believe that one easily perceives that danger from the beginning and that much of the power of the episode derives precisely from the fact that his perception has little or no effect on the Bower's continued sensual power:

> Upon a bed of roses she was layd,
> As faint through heat, or dight to pleasant sin,
> And was arayd, or rather disarayd,
> All in a vele of silke and silver thin,
> That hid no whit her alablaster skin,
> But rather shewd more white if more might bee.
> (2.12.77)

"Pleasant sin"—the moral judgment is not avoided or suspended but neither does it establish its dominion over the stanza; rather, for a moment it is absorbed into a world in which the normal conceptual boundaries are blurred: languor and energy, opacity and transparency, flesh and stone all merge. Similarly, the close of the famous rose song—"Gather the rose of love, whilest yet is time, / Whilest loving thou mayst loved be with equall crime"—invites us momentarily to transvalue the word "crime," reading it as the equivalent of "passion" or "intensity," even as we continue to know that "crime" cannot be so transvalued. We can master the iconography, read all the signs correctly, and still respond to the allure of the Bower. It is, as we shall see, the threat of this absorption that triggers Guyon's climactic violence. Temperance—the avoidance of extremes, the "sober government" of the body, the achievement of the Golden Mean—must be constituted paradoxically by a supreme act of destructive excess.

The Bower's dangerous attractiveness is in sharp contrast to the Cave of Mammon, where Guyon's experience, and ours, is remarkable for the complete absence of sympathetic response to the temptation. The hero's journey through the Cave, past the fabulous displays of riches, embodies one of the basic patterns in the life of a temperate man: to be constantly confronted with baits which are at once spectacular and curiously easy to resist. The consequences of succumbing to these temptations are horrible—nothing short of being torn to pieces—but the temperate man resists far less for fear of the evil consequences than out of genuine indifference. That is, Mammon's offers are only attractive to those who are going to fall—a tautology not at all alien to Spenser or to Protestant thought. Guyon faints not as an emblem of tension, the strain of resisting temptation, but from want of food and sleep.

In the Bower of Bliss, Guyon's "stubborne brest gan secret pleasaunce to embrace" (2.12.45), and he does not merely depart from the place of temptation but reduces it to ruins. To help us understand more fully why he must do so in order to play his part in Spenser's fashioning of a gentleman, we may invoke an observation made in *Civilization and Its Discontents:* "It is impossible," writes Freud, "to overlook the extent to which civilization is built up upon a renunciation of instinct, how much it presupposes precisely the nonsatisfaction (by suppression, repression, or some other means?) of powerful instincts. . . . Civilization behaves toward sexuality as a people or a stratum of its population does which has subjected another one to its exploitation."[6] Modern criticism would make the destruction of the Bower easy by labeling Acrasia's realm sick, stagnant, futile, and joyless, but Spenser, who participates with Freud in a venerable and profoundly significant intertwining of sexual and colonial discourse, accepts sexual colonialism only with a near-tragic sense of the cost. If he had wished, he could have unmasked Acrasia as a deformed hag, as he had exposed Duessa or as Ariosto had exposed (though more ambiguously) the enchantress Alcina, but instead Acrasia remains enticingly seductive to the end. She offers not simply sexual pleasure—"long wanton joys"—but self-abandonment, erotic aestheticism, the melting of the will, the end of all quests; and Spenser understands, at the deepest level of his being, the appeal of such an end. Again and again his knights reach out longingly for resolution, closure, or release only to have it snatched from them or deferred; the whole of *The Faerie Queene* is the expression of an intense craving for release, which is overmastered only by a still more intense fear of release.

The Bower of Bliss must be destroyed not because its gratifications are unreal but because they threaten "civility"—civilization—which for Spenser is achieved only through renunciation and the constant exercise of power. If this power inevitably entails loss, it is also richly, essentially creative; power is the guarantor of value, the shaper of all knowledge, the pledge of human redemption. Power may, as Bacon claimed, prohibit desire, but it is in its own way a version of the erotic: the violence directed against Acrasia's sensual paradise is both in itself an equivalent of erotic excess and a pledge of loving service to the royal mistress. Even when he most bitterly criticizes its abuses or records its brutalities, Spenser loves power and attempts to link his own art ever more closely with its symbolic and literal embodiment. *The Faerie Queene* is, as he insists again and again, wholly wedded to the autocratic ruler of the English state; the rich complexities of Spenser's art, its exquisite ethical discriminations in pursuit of the divine in man, are not achieved in spite of what is for us a repellent political ideology—the passionate worship of imperialism—but are inseparably linked to that ideology.

To say that Spenser worships power, that he is our originating and preeminent poet of empire, is not, in the heady manner of the late '60s, to condemn his work as shallow, craven, or timeserving. Rather, his work, like Freud's, bears witness to the deep complicity of our moral imagination even in its noblest and most hauntingly beautiful manifestations in the great Western celebration of power. Alongside Freud, we may invoke Virgil, whose profound faith in Aeneas's personal and world-historical mission and whose adoration of Augustus are tempered but never broken by a bitter sense of all that empire forces man to renounce, to flee from, to destroy. The example of Freud is useful, however, because it helps us to grasp the relation of our response to the Bower to our own contemporary preoccupations, to perceive as well those qualities in Renaissance culture which we are at this moment in our history uniquely situated to appreciate.

If all of civilization rests, as Freud argues, upon repression, nevertheless the particular civilization we produce and inhabit rests upon a complex technology of control whose origins we trace back to the Renaissance. We are no longer inclined to celebrate this period as the lifting of a veil of childish illusion, nor are we concerned to attack it in the name of a nostalgic vision of lost religious unity. The great syncretic structures of the Renaissance humanists no longer seem as intellectually compelling or as adequate to the period's major works of art as they once did, and even the imposition upon nature of an abstract mathematical logic, which Cassirer celebrates so eloquently as the birth of modern science, seems an equivocal achievement. We continue to see in the Renaissance the shaping of crucial aspects of our sense of self and society and the natural world, but we have become uneasy about our whole way of constituting reality. Above all, perhaps, we sense that the culture to which we are as profoundly attached as our face is to our skull is nonetheless a construct, a thing made, as temporary, time-conditioned, and contingent as those vast European empires from whose power Freud drew his image of repression. We sense too that we are situated at the close of the cultural movement initiated in the Renaissance and that the places in which our social and psychological world seems to be cracking apart are those structural joints visible when it was first constructed. In the midst of the anxieties and contradictions attendant upon the threatened collapse of this phase of our civilization, we respond with passionate curiosity and poignancy to the anxieties and contradictions attendant upon its rise. To experience Renaissance culture is to feel what it was like to form our own identity, and we are at once more rooted and more estranged by the experience.

If it is true that we are highly sensitive to those aspects of the Renaissance that mark the early, tentative, conflict-ridden fashioning of modern consciousness, then *The Faerie Queene* is of quite exceptional significance, for Spenser's stated intention is precisely "to fashion a gentleman or noble person in vertuous and gentle discipline." This mirroring—the conscious purpose of the work seeming to enact the larger cultural movement—may help to account for the reader's sense of encountering in Spenser's poem the process of self-fashioning itself. In the Bower of Bliss that process is depicted as involving a painful sexual renunciation: in Guyon's destructive act we are invited to experience the ontogeny of our culture's violent resistance to a sensuous release for which it nevertheless yearns with a new intensity. The resistance is necessary for Spenser because what is threatened is "our Selfe, whom though we do not see, / Yet each doth in him selfe it well perceiue to bee" (2.12.47). We can secure that self only through a restraint that involves the destruction of something intensely beautiful; to succumb to that beauty is to lose the shape of manhood and be transformed into a beast.[7]

The pleasure offered by Acrasia must be rejected with brutal decisiveness, but how exactly does one distinguish between inordinate or excessive sexual pleasure and temperate sexual pleasure? Spenser does not, after all, wish to reject pleasure entirely: if Guyon's destruction of the Bower of Bliss suggests "the extent to which civilization is build up upon a renunciation of instinct," Scudamour's seizure of Amoret in the Temple of Venus, recounted in book 4, canto 10, suggests the extent to which civilization is built upon the controlled satisfaction of instinct, upon the ability to direct and profit from the "kindly rage" of desire. Pleasure can even be celebrated, as in the nameless supplicant's hymn to Venus, provided that its legitimating function, its "end" both in the sense of purpose and termination, be properly understood: "So all things else, that nourish vitall blood, / Soone as with fury thou doest them inspire, / In generation seeke to quench their inward fire" (4.10.46). Spenser cannot deny pleasure, even the extreme pleasure suggested by "rage," "fury," and "fire," a legitimate function in sexuality. Quite apart from the poet's own experience and observation, it may have been extremely difficult even for figures far more suspicious of the body than Spenser to imagine an entirely pleasureless generation of children (though, as we shall see later, such a doctrine found occasional expression), for there seems to have been widespread medical belief in early modern Europe that for conception to take place, both the male and the female had to experience orgasm.[8] Virtually all of Spenser's representations of sexual fulfillment, including those he fully sanctions, seem close to excess and risk the breakdown of the carefully fashioned identity:

> Lightly he clipt her twixt his armes twaine,
> And streightly did embrace her body bright,
> Her body, late the prison of sad paine,
> Now the sweet lodge of loue and deare delight:
> But she faire Lady ouercommen quight
> Of huge affection, did in pleasure melt,
> And in sweete rauishment pourd out her spright:
> No word they spake, nor earthly thing they felt,
> But like two senceles stocks in long embracement dwelt.
>
> (3.12.45 [1590])

The distinction upon which self-definition rests at the close of book 2—between temperate pleasure and inordinate pleasure—can only be understood in terms of a further distinction between a pleasure that serves some useful purpose, some virtuous end, and a pleasure that does not. Thus the denizens of the Bower acknowledge time solely as an inducement to the eager satisfaction of desire here and now, before the body's decay, and not as the agency of purposeful direction. That direction—expressed in *The Faerie Queene* as a whole by the idea of the *quest*—is for sexuality found in the power of love to inspire virtuous action and ultimately, with the sanctification of marriage, in the generation of offspring. Generation restores the sense of linear progression to an experience that threatens to turn in upon itself, reveling in its own exquisite beauty. A pleasure that serves as its own end, that claims to be self-justifying rather than instrumental, purposeless rather than generative, is immoderate and must be destroyed, lest it undermine the power that Spenser worships.

But this way of distinguishing temperate and inordinate pleasure is less stable than it first appears, for desire may be "quenched" in generation but is not itself temperate. On the contrary, generation only takes place because all living beings—men and beasts—are "priuily pricked with" Venus's "lustfull powres" (4.10.45). All attempts to restrain these powers must be overcome for fruitful sexual union to occur: thus Scudamour must seize Amoret from the restraining and moderating figures—Womanhood, Shamefastness, Modesty, Silence, Obedience, and the like—who sit at the feet of Venus's image. The fashioning of a gentleman then depends upon the imposition of control over inescapably immoderate sexual impulses that, for the survival of the race, must constantly recur: the discriminations upon which a virtuous and gentle discipline is based are forever in danger of collapsing. Hence, I suggest, the paradox of the Knight of Temperance's seemingly intemperate attack upon the Bower of Bliss: Guyon destroys the Bower and ties Acrasia "in chaines of adamant"—"For nothing else might keepe her safe and sound"—in a violent attempt to secure that principle of difference necessary to fashion the self. "Excess" is defined not by some inherent imbalance or impropriety, but by the mechanism of control, the exercise of restraining power. And if excess is virtually invented by this power, so too, paradoxically, power is invented by excess: this is why Acrasia cannot be destroyed, why she and what she is made to represent must continue to exist, forever the object of the destructive quest. For were she not to exist as a constant threat, the power Guyon embodies would also cease to exist. After all, we can assume that the number of people who actually suffer in any period from *melt-down* as a result of sexual excess is quite small (comparable to the number of cases of that spontaneous combustion depicted by Dickens), small enough to raise questions about the motives behind the elaborate moral weaponry designed to combat the supposed danger. The perception of the threat of excess enables institutional power to have a legitimate "protective" and "healing" interest in sexuality, to exercise its constitutive control over the inner life of the individual.

Self-fashioning, the project of Spenser's poem and of the culture in which it participates, requires both an enabling institution, a source of power and communal values—in *The Faerie Queene*, the court of Gloriana— and a perception of the not-self, of all that lies outside, or resists, or threatens identity. The destruction of the Bower is the fulfillment of the knight's quest—the institution has been glorified, the demonic other at once identified and destroyed—but the inherent contradictions in the relations between temperance and pleasure, restraint and gratification have been deferred rather than resolved. What appears for a moment as decisive closure gives way to renewed efforts, other quests, which, as we have already glimpsed in Scudamour, attempt to compensate for the limitations, the sacrifice of essential values, implicit in the earlier resolution.

In a remarkable study of how societies make "tragic choices" in the allocation of scarce resources (e.g. kidney machines) or in the determination of high risks (e.g. the military draft), Guido Calabresi and Philip Bobbitt observe that by complex mixtures of approaches, societies attempt to avert "tragic results, that is, results which imply the rejection of values which are proclaimed to be fundamental": these approaches may succeed for a time, but it will eventually become apparent that some sacrifice of values has taken place, whereupon "fresh mixtures of methods will be tried, structured . . . by the shortcomings of the approaches they replace."[9] These too will in time give way to others in a "strategy of successive moves" that comprises an "intricate game," a game that reflects the simultaneous perception of a tragic choice and the determination to "forget" that perception in an illusory resolution. Driven by the will to deny its own perception of tragic conflict inherent in the fashioning of civility, *The Faerie Queene* resembles such an intricate game. Thus a particular "move," here the destruction of the Bower, represents in effect a brilliant solution, constructed out of the most conventional materials and yet unmistakably original, of the uneasy, aggressive, masculine court identity fashioned by Wyatt: male sexual aggression—the hunt, the loathing, the desire to master—is yoked to the service of ideal values embodied in a female ruler, and it is through this service that identity is achieved. The conception obviously depends upon Queen Elizabeth's own extraordinary manipulation of a secular mythology infused with displaced religious veneration, yet Spenser manages to suggest that the "vertuous and gentle discipline" he chronicles is not limited by its historical circumstances. Like Elizabeth herself, Spenser appeals to an image of female power—the benevolent and nurturing life force—that transcends a local habitation and a name. But this "solution" has its costs that Spenser, as we have seen, represents with extraordinary power and that drive him to further constructions.

Each heroic quest is at once a triumph and a fight, an escape from the disillusionment glimpsed for a brief moment on the Mount of Contemplation and again at the close of the Mutabilitie Cantos. Spenser's knights live in the profound conviction that there is a moral task set for themselves by virtue of the power of Gloriana, a demonic object out there to be encountered and defeated. Each triumphant act of virtuous violence confirms this conviction, defending it from all that would undermine the rightness of the moral mission, all that would question the possibility of achieving a just, coherent, stable identity anchored in the ardent worship of power. But the destruction of the Bower of Bliss suggests the extent to which each self-constituting act is haunted by inadequacy and loss.

The experience I have just described is, insofar as the work retains its power, common to us all, embedded in each of our personal histories, though a protective cultural amnesia may have led us to forget it until we reexperience it in art. We need, at this level, bring nothing to the text but ourselves. Fuller understanding, however, requires that we confront not only personal history but the history of peoples. We must, as Clifford Geertz suggests, incorporate the work of art into the texture of a particular pattern of life, a collective experience that transcends it and completes its meaning.[10] If Spenser told his readers a story, they listened, and listened with pleasure, because they themselves, in the shared life of their culture, were telling versions of that story again and again, recording the texts on themselves and on the world around them. In this sense, it is not adequate for a cultural poetics to describe the destruction of the Bower of Bliss or any literary text as a *reflection* of its circumambient culture; Spenser's poem is one manifestation of a symbolic language that is inscribed by history on the bodies of living beings as, in Kafka's great parable, the legal sentences are inscribed by the demonic penal machine on the bodies of the condemned.

It is not possible within the scope of this chapter to outline the dense network of analogies, repetitions, correspondences, and homologies within which even this one episode of Spenser's immense poem is embedded. But I can point briefly to three reiterations by the culture of important elements of the destruction of the Bower of Bliss: the European response to the native cultures of the New World, the English colonial struggle in Ireland, and the Reformation attack on images. The examples suggest the diversity of such reiterations—from the general culture of Europe, to the national policy of England, to the ideology of a small segment of the nation's population—while their shared elements seem to bear out Freud's master analogy: "Civilization behaves towards sexuality as a people or a stratum of its population does which has subjected another one to its exploitation."

In the texts written by early explorers of the New World, a long, arduous voyage, fraught with fabulous dangers and trials, brings the band of soldiers, sailors, and religious fathers—knight, boatman, and palmer—to a world of riches and menace. The adventurer's morality is the morality of the ship, where order, discipline, and constant labor are essential for survival, and they are further united by their explicit religious faith and by an unspoken but powerful male bond. The lands they encounter are often achingly beautiful: "I am completely persuaded in my own mind," writes Columbus in 1498, "that the Terrestrial Paradise is in the place I have described."[11] So Spenser likens the Bower of Bliss to Eden itself, "if ought with Eden mote compayre," and lingers over its landscape of wish fulfillment, a landscape at once lavish and moderate, rich in abundant vegetation and yet "steadfast," "attempred," and well "disposed." If these descriptive terms are shared in the Renaissance by literary romance and travelers' accounts, it is because the two modes of vision are mutually reinforcing: Spenser, like Tasso before him, makes frequent allusion to the New World—to "all that now America men call" (2.10.72)—while when Cortes and his men looked down upon the valley of Mexico, they thought, says a participant, of Amadis of Gaule.[12] The American landscape has to European eyes the mysterious intimations of a hidden art, as Ralegh's description of the Orinoco suggests: "On both sides of this river, we passed the most beautiful country that ever mine eyes beheld: and whereas all that we had seen before was nothing but woods, prickles, bushes, and thorns, here we beheld plains of twenty miles in length, the grass short and green, and in diverse parts groves of trees by themselves, as if they had been by all the art and labor in the world so made of purpose: and still as we rowed, the Deer came down feeding by the water's side, as if they had been used to a keeper's call."[13]

Spenser, to be sure, has no need of the "as if"—he credits art as well as nature with the making of the paradisal landscape— but this difference should not suggest too sharp a contrast between an "artless" world described by the early voyagers and the poet's "artificial" Bower. The Europeans again and again record their astonishment at the Indians' artistic brilliance: "Surely I marvel not at the gold and precious stones, but wonder with astonishment with what industry and laborious art the curious workmanship exceedeth the matter and substance. I beheld a thousand shapes, and a thousand forms, which I cannot express in writing; so that in my judgment I never saw anything which might more allure the eyes of men with the beauty thereof."[14]

But all of this seductive beauty harbors danger, danger not only in the works of art which are obviously idolatrous but in the Edenic landscape itself. The voyagers to the New World are treated, like Guyon and the Palmer, to mild air that "breathed forth sweet spirit and holesom smell" (2.12.51), and they react with mingled wonder and resistance: "Smooth and pleasing words might be spoken of the sweet odors, and perfumes of these countries," writes Peter Martyr, "which we purposely omit, because they make rather for the effeminating of men's minds, than for the maintenance of good behavior."[15] Similarly, if the New World could be portrayed as a place "In which all pleasures plenteously abownd, / And none does others happiness envye" (2.10.58), a Golden World, it could also serve—often in the same text and by virtue of the same set of perceptions—as a screen onto which Europeans projected their darkest and yet most compelling fantasies: "These folk live like beasts without any reasonableness, and the women be also as common. And the men hath conversation with the women who that they been or who they first meet, is she his sister, his mother, his daughter, or any other kindred. And the women be very hot and disposed to lecherdness. And they eat also one another. The man eateth his wife, his children. . . . And that land is right full of folk, for they live commonly 300 year and more as with sickness they die not."[16] In 1582 Richard Madox, in Sierra Leone with Edward Fenton's expedition, heard from a Portuguese trader comparable stories of African customs: "He reported that near the mountains of the moon there is a queen, an empress of all these Amazons, a witch and a cannibal who daily feeds on the flesh of boys. She ever remains unmarried, but she has intercourse with a great number of men by whom she begets offspring. The kingdom, however, remains hereditary to the daughters, not to the sons."[17]

Virtually all the essential elements of the travel narratives recur in Spenser's episode: the sea voyage, the strange, menacing creatures, the paradisal landscape with its invisible art, the gold and silver carved with "curious imagery," the threat of effeminacy checked by the male bond, the generosity and wantonness of the inhabitants, the arousal of a longing at once to enter and to destroy. Even cannibalism and incest which are the extreme manifestations of the disordered and licentious life attributed to the Indians are both subtly suggested in the picture of Acrasia hanging over her adolescent lover:

> And oft inclining downe with kisses light,
> For fear of waking him, his lips bedewd,
> And through his humid eyes did sucke his spright,
> Quite molten into lust and pleasure lewd.
> (2.12.73)

In book 6 of *The Faerie Queene* Spenser offers a more explicit version of these dark imaginings;[18] here in book 2 the violation of the taboos is carefully displaced, so that the major threat is not pollution but the very attractiveness of the vision. Sexual excess has caused in Verdant a melting of the soul,[19] and this internal pathology is matched by an external disgrace:

> His warlike armes, the idle instruments
> Of sleeping praise, were hong vpon a tree,
> And his braue shield, full of old moniments,
> Was fowly ra'st, that none the signes might see.
> (2.12.80)

The entire fulfillment of desire leads to the effacement of signs and hence to the loss both of memory, depicted in canto 10 and of the capacity for heroic effort, depicted in the figure of the boatman who ferries Guyon and the Palmer to the Bower:

> Forward they passe, and strongly he them rowes,
> Vntill they nigh vnto that gulfe arryve,
> Where streame more violent and greedy growes:
> Then he with all his puisaunce doth stryve
> To strike his oares, and mightily doth dryve
> The hollow vessell through the threatfull wave,
> Which, gaping wide, to swallow them alyve
> In th'huge abysse of his engulfing grave,
> Doth rore at them in vaine, and with great terrour rave.
> (2.12.5)

The threat of being engulfed that is successfully resisted here is encountered again at the heart of the Bower in the form not of cannibalistic violence but of erotic absorption. Verdant, his head in Acrasia's lap, has sunk into a narcotic slumber: all "manly" energy, all purposeful direction, all sense of difference upon which "civil" order is founded have been erased. This slumber corresponds to what the Europeans perceived as the *pointlessness* of native cultures. It was as if millions of souls had become unmoored, just as their ancestors had, it was thought, somehow lost their way and wandered out of sight of the civilized world. Absorbed into a vast wilderness, they lost all memory of the true history of their race and of the one God and sank into a spiritual and physical lethargy. It is difficult to recover the immense force which this charge of idleness carried; some sense may be gauged perhaps from the extraordinary harshness with which vagabonds were treated.[20]

That the Indians were idle, that they lacked all work discipline, was proved, to the satisfaction of the Europeans, by the demonstrable fact that they made wretched slaves, dying after a few weeks or even days of hard labor. And if they were freed from servitude, they merely slid back into their old customs: "For being idle and slothful, they wander up and down, and return to their old rites and ceremonies and foul and mischievous acts."[21] That the European voyagers of the sixteenth century, surely among the world's most restless and uprooted generations, should accuse the Indians of "wandering up and down" is bitterly ironic, but the accusation served as a kind of rudder, an assurance of stability and direction. And this assurance is confirmed by the vast projects undertaken to fix and enclose the native populations in the mines, in encomiendas, in fortified hamlets, and ultimately, in mass graves. A whole civilization was caught in a net and, like Acrasia, bound in chains of adamant; their gods were melted down, their palaces and temples razed, their groves felled. "And of the fairest late, now made the fowlest place."[22]

Guyon, it will be recalled, makes no attempt to destroy the Cave of Mammon; he simply declines its evil invitations which leave him exhausted but otherwise unmoved. But the Bower of Bliss he destroys with a rigor rendered the more pitiless by the fact that his stubborn breast, we are told, embraced "secret pleasance." In just this way, Europeans destroyed Indian culture not despite those aspects of it that attracted them but in part at least because of them. The violence of the destruction was regenerative; they found in it a sense of identity, discipline, and holy faith.[23] In tearing down what both appealed to them and sickened them, they strengthened their power to resist their dangerous longings, to repress antisocial impulses, to conquer the powerful desire for release. And the conquest of desire had the more power because it contained within itself a version of that which it destroyed: the power of Acrasia's sensuality to erase signs and upset temperate order is simultaneously attacked and imitated in Guyon's destruction of the exquisite Bower, while European "civility" and Christianity were never more ferociously assaulted than in the colonial destruction of a culture that was accused of mounting just such an assault.

One measure of European complicity in what they destroyed is the occurrence of apostacy or at least fantasies of apostacy. Bernal Diaz del Castillo tells one such story about a common seaman named Gonzalo Guerrero who had survived a shipwreck in the Yucatan and refused to rejoin his compatriots when, eight years later, Cortes managed to send word to him: "I am married and have three children, and they look on me as a *Cacique* here, and a captain in time of war. Go, and God's blessing be with you. But my face is tattooed and my ears are pierced. What would the Spaniards say if they saw me like this? And look how handsome these children of mine are!"[24] The emissary reminded him that he was a Christian and "should not destroy his soul for the sake of an Indian woman," but Guerrero clearly regarded his situation as an improvement in his lot. Indeed Cortes learned that it was at Guerrero's instigation that the Indians had, three years before, attacked an earlier Spanish expedition to the Yucatan.

We have, in the tattooed Spanish seaman, encountered an analogue to those disfigured beasts who try to defend the Bower against Guyon and, in particular, to Gryll, who, having been metamorphosed by Acrasia into a hog, "repyned greatly" at his restoration. Such creatures give a local habitation and a name to those vague feelings of longing and complicity that permeate accounts of a sensuous life that must be rejected and destroyed. And if the Yucatan seems too remote from Spenser's world, we need only turn to our second frame of reference, Elizabethan rule in Ireland, to encounter similar stories. In Spenser's own *View of the Present State of Ireland*, probably written in 1596, Eudoxius asks, "is it possible that an Englishman brought up naturally in such sweet civility as England affords could find such liking in that barbarous rudeness that he should forget his own nature and forgo his own nation? . . . Is it possible that any should so far grow out of frame that they should in so short space quite forget their country and their own names? . . . Could they ever conceive any such devilish dislike of their own natural country as that they would be ashamed of her name, and bite off her dug from which they sucked life?"[25] In reply, Spenser's spokesman, Irenius, speaks bitterly of those Englishmen who are "degenerated and grown almost mere Irish, yea and more malicious to the English than the very Irish themselves" (48); these metamorphosed wretches even prefer to speak Irish, although, as Eudoxius observes, "they should (methinks) rather take scorn to acquaint their tongues thereto, for it hath been ever the use of the conqueror to despise the language of the conquered, and to force him by all means to learn his."[26] Irenius locates the source of this unnatural linguistic betrayal, this effacement of signs, in the subversive power of Irish women. The rebel Englishmen will "bite off her dug from which they sucked life" because another breast has intervened:

"the child that sucketh the milk of the nurse must of necessity learn his first speech of her, the which being the first that is enured to his tongue is ever after most pleasing unto him," and "the speech being Irish, the heart must needs be Irish."[27] The evil metamorphosis caused by Irish wetnurses is completed by miscegenation: "the child taketh most of his nature of the mother . . . for by them they are first framed and fashioned" (68). As the fashioning of a gentleman is threatened in book 2 of *The Faerie Queene* by Acrasia, so it is threatened in Ireland by the native women.

It is often remarked that the *View*, which Spenser wrote after his completion of *The Faerie Queene*, expresses a hardening of attitude, a harsh and bitter note brought on by years of tension and frustration. It may well reflect such a change in tone, but its colonial policies are consistent with those with which Spenser had been associated from his arrival in Ireland as Lord Grey's secretary in 1580, that is, from the time in which *The Faerie Queene* was in the early stages of its composition. When Spenser "wrote of Ireland," Yeats comments, "he wrote as an official, and out of thoughts and emotions that had been organized by the State."[28] It was not only in his capacity as an official that Spenser did so: in art and in life, his conception of identity, as we have seen, is wedded to his conception of power, and after 1580, of colonial power. For all Spenser's claims of relation to the noble Spencers of Wormleighton and Althorp, he remains a "poor boy," as he is designated in the Merchant Taylor's School and at Cambridge, until Ireland. It is there that he is fashioned a gentleman, there that he is transformed from the former denizen of East Smithfield to the "undertaker"—the grim pun unintended but profoundly appropriate—of 3,028 acres of Munster land. From his first acquisition in 1582, this land is at once the assurance of his status—the "Gent." next to his name—and of his insecurity: ruined abbeys, friaries expropriated by the crown, plow lands rendered vacant by famine and execution, property forfeited by those whom Spenser's superiors declared traitors.

For what services, we ask, was Spenser being rewarded? And we answer, blandly, for being a colonial administrator. But the answer, which implies pushing papers in a Dublin office through endless days of tedium, is an evasion. Spenser's own account presses in upon us the fact that he was involved intimately, on an almost daily basis, throughout the island, in the destruction of Hiberno-Norman civilization, the exercise of a brutal force that had few if any of the romantic trappings with which Elizabeth contrived to soften it at home.[29] Here, on the periphery, Spenser was an agent of and an apologist for massacre, the burning of mean hovels and of crops with the deliberate intention of starving the inhabitants, forced relocation of peoples, the manipulation of treason charges so as to facilitate the seizure of lands, the endless repetition of acts of military "justice" calculated to intimidate and break the spirit. We may wish to tell ourselves that a man of Spenser's sensitivity and gifts may have mitigated the extreme policies of ruthless men, but it appears that he did not recoil in the slightest from this horror, did not even feel himself, like his colleague Geoffrey Fenton, in mild opposition to it.[30] Ireland is not only in book 5 of *The Faerie Queene;* it pervades the poem. Civility is won through the exercise of violence over what is deemed barbarous and evil, and the passages of love and leisure are not moments set apart from this process but its rewards.

"Every detail of the huge resettlement project" in Munster, writes Spenser's biographer Judson, "was known to him as it unfolded, including its intricate legal aspects, and hence his final acquisition of thousands of acres of forfeited lands was entirely natural."[31] Natural perhaps, but equally natural that his imagination is haunted by the nightmares of savage attack—the "outrageous dreadfull yelling cry" of Maleger, "His body leane and meagre as a rake" and yet seemingly impossible to kill[32]—and of absorption. The latter fear may strike us as less compelling than the former—there is much talk, after all, of the "savage brutishness and loathly filthiness" of native customs—but the Elizabethans were well aware, as we have already seen, that many of their most dangerous enemies were Englishmen who had been metamorphosed into "mere Irish." Spenser's own career is marked by conflicting desires to turn his back on Ireland forever and to plant himself ever more firmly in Munster;[33] if the latter course scarcely represented an abandonment of English civility, it may nonetheless have felt like the beginning of the threatened transformation. I do not propose that Spenser feared such a metamorphosis on his own behalf—he may, for all we know, have been obscurely attracted to some of the very things he worked to destroy, though of this attraction our only record is his poetry's fascination with the excess against which it struggles—only that he was haunted by the fact that it had occurred over generations to so many of his countrymen. The enemy for Spenser then is as much a tenacious and surprisingly seductive way of life as it is a military force, and thus alongside a ruthless policy of mass starvation and massacre, he advocates the destruction of native Irish identity.

Spenser is one of the first English writers to have what we may call a field theory of culture, that is, the conception of a nation not simply as an institutional structure or a common race, but as a complex network of beliefs, folk customs, forms of dress, kinship relations, religious mythology, aesthetic norms, and specialized modes of production. Therefore, to *reform* a people one must not simply conquer it—though conquest is an absolute necessity—but eradicate the native culture: in the case of Ireland, eliminate (by force, wherever needed) the carrows, horseboys, jesters, and other "idlers"; transform the mass of the rural population from cowherds with their dangerous freedom of movement to husbandmen; break up the clans or sects; prohibit public meetings, councils, and assemblies; transform Irish art, prohibiting the subversive epics of the bards; make schoolchildren ashamed of their parents' backwardness; discourage English settlers from speaking Irish; prohibit traditional Irish dress; eliminate elections of chiefs, divisible inheritance, and the payment of fines to avoid capital punishment. And always in this immense undertaking, there is the need for constant vigilance and unrelenting pressure, exercised not only upon the wild Irish but upon the civilizing English themselves. "So much," writes Spenser, "can liberty and ill example do" (63) that the threat of seduction is always present, and the first inroad of this seduction is misguided compassion: "Therefore, by all means it must be foreseen and assured that after once entering into this course of reformation, there be afterwards no remorse or drawing back" (110). Pitiless destruction is here not a stain but a virtue; after all, the English themselves had to be brought from barbarism to civility by a similar conquest centuries before, a conquest that must be ever renewed lest the craving for "liberty and natural freedom" (12) erupt again. The colonial violence inflicted upon the Irish is at the same time the force that fashions the identity of the English.

We have returned then to the principle of regenerative violence and thus to the destruction of the Bower of Bliss. The act of tearing down is the act of fashioning; the promise of the opening stanza of canto 12—"Now gins this goodly frame of Temperance / Fairely to rise"—is fulfilled at the close in the inventory of violence:

> But all those pleasant bowres and Pallace braue,
> *Guyon* broke downe, with rigour pittilesse;
> Ne ought their goodly workmanship might saue
> Them from the tempest of his wrathfulnesse,
> But that their blisse he turn'd to balefulnesse;
> Their groues he feld, their gardins did deface,
> Their arbers spoyle, their Cabinets suppresse,
> Their banket houses burne, their buildings race,
> And of the fairest late, now made the fowlest place.
> (2.12.83)

If the totality of the destruction, the calculated absence of "remorse or drawing back," links this episode to the colonial policy of Lord Grey which Spenser undertook to defend, the language of the stanza recalls yet another government policy, our third "restoration" of the narrative: the destruction of Catholic Church furnishings. In the *Inventarium monumentorum superstitionis* of 1566, for example, we may hear repeated echoes of Guyon's acts:

Imprimis one rood with Mary and John and the rest of the painted pictures—burnt. . . .

Item our rood loft—pulled down, sold and defaced. . . .

Item our mass books with the rest of such feigned fables and peltering popish books—burnt. . . .

Item 3 altar stones—broken in pieces. . . .[34]

In 1572 Spenser, a student at Pembroke, could have witnessed a similar scene at nearby Gonville and Caius where the authorities licensed the destruction of "much popish trumpery." Books and vestments, holy water stoops and images were "mangled, torn to pieces, and mutilated"—*discerpta dissecta et lacerata*—before being consigned to the bonfire.[35]

There is about the Bower of Bliss the taint of a graven image designed to appeal to the sensual as opposed to the spiritual nature, to turn the wonder and admiration of men away from the mystery of divine love. In the Bower the love survives only in the uncanny parody of the Pietà suggested by Verdant cradled in Acrasia's arms. It is not surprising then to find a close parallel between the evils of the Bower and the evils attributed to the misuse of religious images. Devotion to the representations of the Madonna and saints deflected men from the vigorous pursuit of the good, enticed them into idleness and effeminacy. With their destruction, as Hugh Latimer writes, men could turn "from ladyness to Godliness."[36] Statues of the virgin were dismembered by unruly crowds, frescoes were whitewashed over and carvings in "Lady Chapels" were smashed, in order to free men from thralldom to what an Elizabethan lawyer calls, in describing the pope, "the witch of the world."[37]

But the art destroyed by Guyon does not pretend to image holy things; it is designed to grace its surroundings, to delight its viewers with its exquisite workmanship. Against such art there could be no charge of idolatry, no invocation of the Deuteronomic injunctions against graven images, unless art itself were idolatrous. And it is precisely this possibility that is suggested by Guyon's iconoclasm, for Acrasia's realm is lavishly described in just those terms which the defenders of poetry in the Renaissance reserved for imagination's noblest achievements. The Bower's art imitates nature, but is privileged to choose only those aspects of nature that correspond to man's ideal visions; its music is so perfectly melodious and "attempred" that it blends with all of nature in one harmony, so that the whole world seems transformed into a musical "consort"; above all, the calculation and effort that lie behind the manifestation of such perfect beauty are entirely concealed: "And that which all faire workes doth most aggrace, / The art, which all that wrought, appeared in no place." "Aggrace" has virtually a technical significance here; Castiglione had suggested in *The Courtier* that the elusive quality of "grace" could be acquired through the practice of *sprezzatura*, "so as to conceal all art and make whatever is done or said appear to be without effort and almost without any thought about it."[38]

Spenser deeply distrusts this aesthetic, even as he seems to pay homage to its central tenets; indeed the concealment of art, its imposition upon an unsuspecting observer, is one of the great recurring evils in *The Faerie Queene*. Acrasia as demonic artist and whore combines the attributes of those other masters of disguise, Archimago and Duessa.[39] Their evil depends upon the ability to mask and forge, to conceal their satanic artistry;

their defeat depends upon the power to unmask, the strength to turn from magic to strenuous virtue. Keith Thomas notes that in the sixteenth and seventeenth centuries the Protestant "emphasis upon the virtues of hard work and application . . . both reflected and helped to create a frame of mind which spurned the cheap solutions offered by magic, not just because they were wicked, but because they were too easy."[40] *Sprezzatura*, which sets out to efface all signs of "hard work and application," is a cult of the "too easy," a kind of aesthetic magic.

But what can Spenser offer in place of this discredited aesthetic? The answer lies in an art that constantly calls attention to its own processes, that includes within itself framing devices and signs of its own createdness. Far from hiding its traces, *The Faerie Queene* announces its status as art object at every turn, in the archaic diction, the use of set pieces, the elaborate sound effects, the very characters and plots of romance. For the allegorical romance is a mode that virtually by definition abjures all concealment; the artist who wishes to hide the fact that he is making a fiction would be ill-advised to write about the Faerie Queene.

If you fear that images may make a blasphemous claim to reality, that they may become idols that you will be compelled to worship, you may smash all images or you may create images that announce themselves at every moment as things made. Thus did the sixteenth-century kabbalists of Safed circumvent the Hebraic injunction against images of the Godhead;[41] their visions are punctuated by reminders that these are merely metaphors, not to be confused with divine reality itself. So too did the more moderate Protestant Reformers retain a version of the Communion, reminding the participants that the ceremony was a symbol and not a celebration of the real presence of God's body. And so does Spenser, in the face of deep anxiety about the impure claims of art, save art for himself and his readers by making its createdness explicit. Images, to be sure, retain their power, as the sensuous description of the Bower of Bliss attests, and Spenser can respond to the charge that his "famous antique history" is merely "th'aboundance of an idle braine . . . and painted forgery" by reminding his readers of the recent discoveries, of "The Indian *Peru*," "The *Amazons* huge riuer," and "fruitfullest *Virginia*":

> Yet all these were, when no man did them know;
> Yet haue from wisest ages hidden beene:
> And later times things more vnknowne shall show.
> When then should witlesse man so much misweene
> That nothing is, but that which he hath seene?
> What if within the Moones faire shining spheare?
> What if in euery other starre vnseene
> Of other worldes he happily should heare?
> He wonder would much more: yet such to some appeare.
> (2 Proem 3)

For a moment the work hovers on the brink of asserting its status as a newfound land, but Spenser immediately shatters such an assertion by invoking the gaze of royal power:

> And thou, O fairest Princesse vnder sky,
> In this faire mirrhour maist behold thy face,
> And thine owne realmes in lond of Faery,
> And in this antique Image thy great auncestry.
>
> (2 Proem 4)

In an instant the "other world" has been transformed into a mirror; the queen turns her gaze upon a shining sphere hitherto hidden from view and sees her own face, her own realms, her own ancestry. That which threatens to exist independent of religious and secular ideology, that is, of what we believe—"Yet all these were, when no man did them know"—is revealed to be the ideal image of that ideology. And hence it need not be feared or destroyed: iconoclasm gives way to appropriation, violence to colonization. J. H. Elliott remarks that the most significant aspect of the impact of the new world upon the old is its insignificance: men looked at things unseen before, things alien to their own culture, and saw only themselves.[42] Spenser asserts that Faerie Land is a new world, another Peru or Virginia, only so that he may colonize it in the very moment of its discovery. The "other world" becomes mirror becomes aesthetic image, and this transformation of the poem from a thing discovered to a thing made, from existence to the representation of existence is completed with the poet's turn from "vaunt" to apology:

> The which O pardon me thus to enfold
> In couert vele, and wrap in shadowes light,
> That feeble eyes your glory may behold,
> Which else could not endure those beames bright,
> But would be dazled with exceeding light.
>
> (2 Proem 5)

The queen is deified precisely in the act of denying art's claim to ontological dignity, to the possession or embodiment of reality.

Such embodiment is the characteristic achievement of great drama, of Marlowe and supremely of Shakespeare, whose constant allusions to the fictionality of his creations only serve paradoxically to question the status of everything outside themselves. By contrast, Spenser's profoundly *undramatic* art, in the same movement by which it wards off idolatry, wards off this radical questioning of everything that exists. That is, if art like Shakespeare's realizes the power we glimpsed in Wyatt, the power in Althusser's words, to "make us 'perceive' . . . from *the inside*, by an *internal distance*, the very ideology" in which it is held, Spenserean allegory may be understood as a countermeasure: it opens up an internal distance within art itself by continually referring the reader out to a fixed authority beyond the poem. Spenser's art does not lead us to perceive ideology critically,, but rather affirms the existence and inescapable moral power of ideology as that principle of truth toward which art forever yearns. It is art whose status is questioned in Spenser, not ideology; indeed, art is questioned precisely to spare ideology that internal distantiation it undergoes in the work of Shakespeare or Marlowe. In *The Faerie Queene* reality as given by ideology always lies safely outside the bounds of art, in a different realm, distant, infinitely powerful, perfectly good. "The hallmark of Spenserean narration," Paul Alpers acutely observes, "is confidence in locutions which are at the same time understood to be provisional."[43] Both the confidence and the provisionality stem from the externality of true value, order, meaning. For Spenser this is the final colonialism, the colonialism of language, yoked to the service of a reality forever outside itself, dedicated to "the Most High, Mightie, and Magnificent Empresse . . . Elizabeth by the Grace of God Queene of England Fraunce and Ireland and of Virginia, Defendour of the Faith."

Notes

1. Paul J. Alpers, *The Poetry of "The Faerie Queene"* (Princeton: Princeton University Press, 1967), and "How to Read *The Faerie Queene*," in *Essays in Criticism* 18 (1968), pp. 429–43.

2. C. S. Lewis, *The Allegory of Love* (New York: Oxford University Press [first published 1936]), p. 332. Lewis's description of the Bower has been discussed by Graham Hough, *A Preface to "The Faerie Queene"* (New York: Norton, 1963).

3. *Essays and Introductions* (London: Macmillan & Co., 1961), p. 370.

4. N. S. Brooke, "C. S. Lewis and Spenser: Nature, Art and the Bower of Bliss," in *Essential Articles for the Study of Edmund Spenser*, ed. A. C. Hamilton (Hamden, Conn.: Archon Books, 1972), p. 28. Typical of much recent criticism is the observation by M. Pauline Parker that the Bower's "painted golden ivy is used where the real plant could have grown and should have grown," indeed the ivy is "alive only with the horrible energy of corruption" (*The Allegory of "The Faerie Queene"* [Oxford: Clarendon, 1960], pp. 42, 152).

5. See especially Merritt Y. Hughes, "Spenser's Acrasia and the Circe of the Renaissance," *Journal of the History of Ideas* 4 (1943), pp. 381–99; Robert M. Durling, "The Bower of Bliss and Armida's Palace," *Comparative Literature* 6 (1954), pp. 335–47; James Nohrnberg, *The Analogy of "The Faerie Queene"* (Princeton: Princeton University Press, 1976), pp. 490–513.

6. Sigmund Freud, *Civilization and Its Discontents*, trans. James Strachey (New York: Norton, 1962), pp. 44, 51.

7. For modern versions, see Samuel Z. Klausner, "A Collocation of Concepts of Self-Control," in *The Quest for Self-Control: Classical Philosophies and Scientific Research*, ed. Klausner (New York: Free Press, 1965), pp. 9–48.

8. Natalie Zemon Davis, "'Women's History' in Transition: The European Case," *Feminist Studies* 3 (1976), p. 89 and the refs. in note 31.

9. Guido Calabresi and Philip Bobbitt, *Tragic Choices* (New York: Norton, 1978), p. 195.

10. Clifford Geertz, "Art as a Cultural System," *Modern Language Notes* 91 (1976), pp. 1473–99.

11. Christopher Columbus, *Journals and Other Documents on the Life and Voyages of Christopher Columbus*, trans. and ed. Samuel Eliot Morison (New York: Heritage Press, 1963), p. 287.

12. Tasso, *Gerusalemme Liberata* (book 15, stanzas 28ff.), relates the quest for the realm of Armida to Columbus's voyages. Spenser's Maleger carries arrows "Such as the *Indians* in their quiuers hide" (2.11.21). Bernal Diaz del Castillo recalls the first reaction to the sight of the Aztec capital in *The Conquest of New Spain*, trans. J. M. Cohen (Baltimore: Penguin, 1963), p. 214. On Spenser and the New World, see Roy Harvey Pearce, "Primitivistic Ideas in the *Faerie Queene*," *Journal of English and Germanic Philology* 45 (1945), pp. 139–51; A. Bartlett Giamatti, "Primitivism and the Process of Civility in Spenser's *Faerie Queene*," in *First Images of America: The Impact of the New World on the Old*, ed. Fredi Chiappelli, 2 vols. (Berkeley: University of California Press, 1976), 1:71–82.

13. Ralegh, *The Discovery of Guiana*, ed. V. T. Harlow (London: Argonaut Press, 1928), p. 42.

14. Peter Martyr, *The Decades of the New World*, trans. Michael Lok, in *A Selection of Curious, Rare, and Early Voyages and Histories of Interesting Discoveries chiefly published by Hakluyt . . .* (London: R. H. Evans and R. Priestly, 1812), p. 539.

15. Ibid., p. 530.

16. *Of the newe landes*, in *The First Three English Books on America*, ed. Edward Arber (Birmingham: Turnbull and Spears, 1885), p. xxvii; cf. Wilberforce Eames, "Description of a Wood Engraving Illustrating the South American Indians (1505)," *Bulletin of the New York Public Library* 26 (1922), pp. 755–60.

17. Elizabeth Story Donno, ed., *An Elizabethan in 1582: The Diary of Richard Madox, Fellow of All Souls*, Hakluyt Society, Second Series, No. 147 (London: Hakluyt Society, 1977), p. 183. The editor notes that "in the older maps the mountains of the moon figure as a range extending across the continent from Abyssinia to the Gulf of Guinea."

18. At 6.8.43, the cannibals who capture Serena consider raping her, but they are stopped by their priests.

19. Compare Redcrosse who, when he dallies with Duessa, is described as "Pourd out in loosnesse on the grassy grownd, / Both carelesse of his health, and of his fame" (1.7.7).

20. On vagabonds, see Frank Aydelotte, *Elizabethan Rogues and Vagabonds* (London: Frank Cass & Co., 1913).

21. Martyr, *Decades*, p. 628. On charges of idleness, see Edmund S. Morgan, *American Slavery, American Freedom: The Ordeal of Colonial Virginia* (New York: Norton, 1975).

22. Cortes "had ordered that all houses should be pulled down and burnt and the bridged channels filled up; and what he gained each day was thus consolidated. He sent an order to Pedro de Alvarado to be sure that we never crossed a bridge or gap in the causeway without first blocking it up, and to pull down and burn every house" (Bernal Diaz, *Conquest*, p. 369).

23. I am indebted here to Richard Slotkin, *Regeneration through Violence: The Mythology of the American Frontier, 1600—1860* (Middletown, Conn.: Wesleyan University Press, 1973).

24. Bernal Diaz, *Conquest*, p. 60.

25. *A View of the Present State of Ireland*, ed. W. L. Renwick (Oxford: Clarendon, 1970), pp. 48, 64, 65. Our primary purpose is to explore aspects of Elizabethan policy in Ireland as a reiteration of a characteristic cultural pattern rather than to detail the direct influence of Ireland upon *The Faerie Queene;* for the latter, see M. M. Gray, "The Influence of Spenser's Irish Experiences on *The Faerie Queene*," *Review of English Studies* 6 (1930), pp. 413–28; Pauline Henley, *Spenser in Ireland* (Folcroft, Pa.: Folcroft Press, 1920).

26. Ibid., p. 67. Cf. Louis-Jean Calvet, *Linguistique et colonialisme: Petit traité de glottophagie* (Paris: Payot, 1974) and Stephen J. Greenblatt, "Learning to Curse: Aspects of Linguistic Colonialism in the Sixteenth Century," in *First Images of America* 2:561–80.

27. *View*, pp. 67–68. Children "draweth into themselves together with their suck, even the nature and disposition of their nurses, for the mind followeth much the temperature of the body; and also the words are the image of the mind, so as they proceeding from the mind, the mind must be needs effected with the words" (p. 68).

28. Yeats, *Essays and Introductions*, p. 372.

29. R. Dudley Edwards, *Ireland in the Age of the Tudors: The Destruction of Hiberno-Norman Civilization* (London: Croom Helm, 1977); Nicholas P. Canny, *The Elizabethan Conquest of Ireland: A Pattern Established, 1565–76* (Hassocks, Sussex: Harvester Press, 1976); David Beers Quinn, *The Elizabethans and the Irish* (Ithaca: Cornell University Press, 1966). For an apologetic account of Spenser's involvement, see Pauline Henley, *Spenser in Ireland;* for an enigmatic indication of Spenser's personal profit from the Smerwick massacre, see Anna Maria Crinò, "La Relazione Barducci-Ubaldini sull'Impresa d'Irlanda (1579–1581)," *English Miscellany* 19 (1968), pp. 339–67.

30. Alexander C. Judson, *The Life of Edmund Spenser* (Baltimore: Johns Hopkins University Press, 1945), pp. 107–8.

31. Ibid., p. 116. The reference to the "fennes of Allan" in 2.9.16 indicates that it was written after Spenser acquired New Abbey, a ruined Franciscan friary in County Kildare, in 1582 (see Josephine Waters Bennett, *The Evolution of "The Faerie Queene"* [Chicago: University of Chicago Press, 1942], p. 131n.).

32. It has been frequently noted that Maleger and his band resemble accounts in Spenser's *View* and in other reports on Ireland of Irish kerns.

33. We should perhaps note in this connection that Guyon leaves the Bower immediately after its destruction: "But let vs hence depart," says the Palmer, "whilest wether serues and wind" (2.12.87).

34. Quoted in Philip Hughes, *The Reformation in England*, 3 vols. (New York: Macmillan, 1954) 3:408.

35. John Venn, *John Caius* (Cambridge: Cambridge University Press, 1910), p. 37. In a letter of the vice-chancellor, Dr. Byng, to the chancellor, Lord Burghley, dated 14 December 1572, the "trumpery" is catalogued: "vestments, albes, tunicles, stoles, manicles, corporas clothes, with the pix and sindon, and canopie, besides holy water stoppes, with sprinkles, pax, sensars, superaltaries, tables of idolles, masse bookes, portuises, and grailles, with other such stuffe as might have furnished divers massers at one instant." The Latin account is from John Caius, *The Annals of Gonville and Caius College*, ed. John Venn, Cambridge Antiquarian Society Octavo Series no. 40 (Cambridge, 1904), p. 185. Caius adds that iconoclasts used hammers to smash certain objects.

36. Quoted in John Phillips. *The Reformation of Images: Destruction of Art in England, 1535–1660* (Berkeley: University of California Press, 1973), p. 80.

37. Keith Thomas, *Religion and the Decline of Magic* (London: Weidenfeld and Nicolson, 1971), p. 69.

38. *The Book of the Courtier*, trans. Singleton, p. 43. On *sprezzatura*, see Wayne A. Rebhorn, *Courtly Performances: Masking and Festivity in Castiglione's "Book of the Courtier"* (Detroit: Wayne State University Press, 1978), pp. 33–40.

39. On demonic artists, see A. Bartlett Giamatti, *Play of Double Senses: Spenser's Faerie Queene* (Englewood Cliffs, N.J.: Prentice-Hall, 1975), pp. 106–33. We may observe that Spenser seems on occasion to invoke positive versions of self-concealing art:

> Then came the Bride, the louely *Medua* came,
> Clad in a vesture of vnknowen geare,
> And vncouth fashion, yet her well became;
> That seem'd like siluer, sprinckled here and theare
> With glittering spangs, that did like starres appeare,
> And wau'd vpon, like water Chamelot,
> To hide the metall, which yet euery where
> Bewrayd it selfe, to let men plainely wot,
> It was no mortall worke, that seem'd and yet was not.
>
> (4.11.45)

Spenser's suspicions of aesthetic concealment can be allayed by its use in a virtuous context, but we might also note that in this instance the device both hides and does not hide its own artifice. The art is designed to seem natural and yet at the same time to let men plainly know, through a kind of "self-betrayal," that it is not natural. For conflicting arguments on the status of artifice in Spenser, see C. S. Lewis, *The Allegory of Love*, pp. 326–33, and Hans P. Guth, "Allegorical Implications of Artifice in Spenser's *Faerie Queene*," *Publication of the Modern Language Association* 76 (1961), pp. 474–79.

40. Keith Thomas, *Religion and the Decline of Magic*, p. 275.

41. See Gershom Scholem, *Sabbatai Sevi* (Princeton: Princeton University Press, 1973).

42. J. H. Elliott, *The Old World and the New, 1492–1650* (Cambridge: Cambridge University Press, 1970).

43. Paul Alpers, "Narration in *The Faerie Queene*," *English Literary History* 44 (1977), p. 27.

Suspended Instruments: Lyric and Power in the Bower of Bliss

Patricia Parker

In the midst of the Bower of Bliss, the culminating episode of Guyon's quest in Book II of *The Faerie Queene*, the Elfin knight and his Palmer guide gain a sight of the Bower's reigning Enchantress and Verdant, her male victim:

> His warlike armes, the idle instruments
>   Of sleeping praise, were hong upon a tree,
>   And his brave shield, full of old moniments,
>   Was fowly ra'st, that none the signes might see;
>   Ne for them, ne for honour cared hee,
>   Ne ought, that did to his advauncement tend,
>   But in lewd loves, and wastfull luxuree,
>   His dayes, his goods, his bodie he did spend:
> O horrible enchantment, that him so did blend.
>   (II.xii.80)[1]

The immediate resonance of these "idle instruments / Of sleeping praise," suspended or "hong" upon a tree, is the iconography of Venus and Mars—with Verdant lying like the disarmed warrior in the lap of his paramour before Vulcan, the formerly impotent voyeur husband, rushes in upon them with his crafty "net." The suspension or hanging of these instruments reiterates the suspensions of the Bower itself, and the hovering of Acrasia as she cannibalistically "pastures" her eyes upon her powerless subject. But the instruments hung upon a tree also recall a very different and specifically lyric context—one that will lead us toward the various strains of lyricism that cross in this crucial Spenserian scene. This context is the suspended song and suspended lyric instruments of the haunting Psalm 137:

> By the rivers of Babel we sate, and there we wept, when we remembered Zion.
> We hanged our harpes upon the willowes in the middes thereof.

When thei that led us captives required of us songs and mirth, when we
    had hanged up our harpes, saying, Sing us one of the songs of Zion.
How shall we sing, said we, a song of the Lord in a strange land?
If I forget thee, O Jerusalem, may my right hand forget to play.
If I do not remember thee, let my tongue cleve to the rofe of my
    mouth. . . .
O daughter of Babel, worthie to be destroied, blessed shal he be [who]
    rewardeth thee, as thou hast served us.
Blessed shal be he that taketh and dasheth thy children against the
    stones.[2]

That this biblical lyric of lament should sound in the midst of the otherwise euphonious and *carpe diem* lyricism of the Bower of Bliss—filled with songs and lyric traditions of its own—should not, on reflection, be surprising. The psalm sings of abandoned instruments in Babylonian exile and captivity: Verdant's instruments are suspended on the tree of a "Witch" only too easily assimilated to Babylon and its famous Whore. Calvin, in his gloss on the psalm, speaks of its Babylon as a *locus amoenus* very much like the Bower of Bliss—as a "fair and fertile" place "with charms which could corrupt effeminate minds" and "tempt them to forget their native inheritance." Augustine speaks of its "Babylon" as the pleasures of this world and of the "willows" on which its lyric instruments are hung as ultimately barren rather than fruitful trees—an emblem of barrenness in the midst of apparent fertility that repeats the biblical dynamic of Spenser's principal subtext, the Garden of Armida in Tasso which stands upon a Dead Sea.[3] The invocation of the psalm not to forget—or to be punished with speechlessness and forcibly suspended song as a result—thus joins the Homeric, lotus-eating resonances of this Spenserian scene, and both figure the necessity of the withheld and vigilant mind, the reversal of Verdant's suspended instruments, which themselves provide a sign not of song refused but, more ominously, of song as in some other sense suspended.

    The psalm behind Verdant's suspended instruments, however, also imports into this private and enclosed erotic scene the powerful political dimension this psalm has always had for singers conscious of the wider context of their singing, a resonance that might make it a powerful subtext for lyric poets in the era of Spenser, subject to a queen who very much demanded their voices. Hanging up one's instrument stands here as a sign of resistance, a refusal to hire out one's voice on the part of a people who otherwise sure can sing and dance. The specifically political force of this psalm continues in a contemporary reggae version of the impossibility of singing in Babylon, a version that chillingly suppresses the psalm's own violent ending—"Blessed shal be he that taketh and dasheth thy children against the stones"—and ambiguously substitutes for it another very different psalm text, "May the words of our mouths and the meditations of our hearts be *acceptable* in thy sight" (my emphasis).

The echo of this psalm's suspended instruments introduces if only elliptically into Spenser's scene the threat of the silencing, controlling, or compromising of song, one that is biblical in its immediate reference but also, in Acrasia's leafy retreat, inevitably evokes a particularly pastoral lyric tension between power and song—that tension that opens Virgil's *Eclogues* with an allusion to the "god" who has given the singer his "ease." Indeed, the other lyric context recalled in the stanza of Verdant's suspended instruments is this specifically pastoral one, hanging up one's instruments being not just the gesture of a Mars-like warrior abandoning the instruments of war, the hanging up of trophies as signs of victory, or the lament of a Dido-like abandoned lover (as in Spenser's "Willow worne or forlorne Paramours" or "Hang my harp on a weeping willow tree"), but also the suspending of instruments on trees in pastoral lyric, a suspension of song that may reflect the suspension Paul Alpers and others find characteristic of pastoral lyric itself.[4] In Sannazaro's *Arcadia*, one of the principal subtexts for Spenser's *Shepheardes Calender*, the hanging of the instrument of Pan upon a tree generates an entire history of pastoral lyric from Theocritus to Virgil and, by implication, to the poet-persona of the *Arcadia* itself.[5] The suspending of Pan's instrument there—in a way suggestive for a Spenserian episode that signals its debts to multiple predecessors—is an emblem of the interval before a new poet takes up these temporarily "idle instruments" and turns them into the instruments of his own potency.

Within this specifically pastoral lyric tradition, Verdant's suspended instruments summon up a Spenserian echo as well, and one intimately bound up with the tensions within Spenser's lyric vocation. Readers of *The Shepheardes Calender* will remember that it opens with Colin Clout, Spenser's own pastoral persona, not just suspending but breaking his pastoral instrument. And it ends with Colin hanging his pipe upon a tree, in a gesture that more than one commentator has linked with a sense of the impotence of song, or the necessary compromising of lyric voice in a political context which would make only too appropriate a conflation of a recall of Psalm 137 with a reminder of Colin's own suspended instrument.[6] *Otium*, or idleness, is traditionally the attraction of pastoral, as it is also of the fatal Bower of Bliss; but the "idleness" of the suspended instruments of Verdant suggests in their echo of Colin's gesture the potential impotence of poetry itself in a state in which it was scorned as a form of effeminacy, of idle "toye," in contrast to more active, imperial pursuits.[7] In this context it was highly problematic whether there was any alternative to the opposed temptations of the idle Phaedria and the industrious Mammon of Book II—an opposition that Blake might later ridicule as a "cloven fiction," but one that continued to dominate a whole post-Spenserian tradition of the potential impotence or irrelevance of the poetic vocation. The Romantics' Aeolian harp, we may remember, is one of the lyric descendants of this suspended instrument.

There is, however, yet another aspect of Verdant's suspended instruments that needs to be explored and, though it will emerge only after a brief excursus, another specifically lyric dimension of this episode and the defeat of its reigning queen. The pervasive phallic symbolism of Guyon's Odyssean journey to the Bower of Bliss makes it impossible to miss the fact that these suspended "instruments" are also clearly *male* instruments and that the impotence their suspension betokens is an impotence that is sexual as well as martial or lyric.[8] A link between the instruments of war and the instruments of virility is, of course, part of the visual cliché of the iconography of Mars and Venus: we think of Botticelli's painting with its wreathed phallic lance, clearly no longer ready for immediate use as an instrument of war, though still serviceable as an instrument of a different kind.

The sense not just of lyric but of sexual contest within the stanza of Verdant's suspended instruments evokes a recall not only of Mars and Venus but of a whole series of subject males and dominating female figures, from Hercules and Omphale to Samson reclining in the lap of that Delilah who deprives him of his strength, a figure of the man dedicated to higher things who cannot, however, ultimately escape the power of women. The link between the latter emblem and Spenser's pair is made even stronger by the fact that Samson in sixteenth-century depictions was also represented as laying aside his warlike instruments. Spenser's scene manages to evoke the iconography of both Virgin Mother with her sleeping infant and the more sinister Pietà, a dead Adonis in the lap of a powerful maternal Venus. The emblem of Samson made impotent in Delilah's lap shares with the tableau of Verdant and Acrasia anxieties of a particularly oral kind, the reduction of the male subject to an infant, or *infans*. Acrasia, like Delilah throughout much of her pictorial history, is not just a temptress but an overpowering mother; and it is in this respect worth citing at least one Renaissance representation of that overpowering. Madlyn Millner Kahr, in *Feminism and Art History*, cites a late sixteenth-century drawing entitled "Allegory of the Power of Woman," which shows in the foreground a woman nursing an infant in one arm, holding a royal scepter and golden chain in the other, and standing on the broken instruments—shield and sword—of male power; in the background are the women who tempted Solomon to idolatry (and hence, ultimately, into Babylon) and Delilah cutting off the hair, and strength, of Samson in her lap.[9]

The underlying threat of the story of Samson's abandoned instruments is, of course, the threat of castration. The hair mentioned in the case of Verdant is the just-beginning hair on his boyish face: if Acrasia is a Delilah, she has only a symbolic need for scissors. But the sense of castration pervades the entire scene, and the unavoidably phallic overtones of Verdant's removed and now useless "instruments" bring to the scene an echo of the severed instruments of yet another boy—Attis, who after transgressing the demand of the Great Mother Cybele that he remain forever a boy, in a frenzy castrates himself, thus becoming not just an impotent Adonis to Cybele's Venus but also the prototype of the *Magna Mater*'s Galli or eunuch servants. Attis is traditionally represented as an effeminate youth, wearing the distinctive Phrygian cap whose droop, as Neil Hertz has recently reminded us,[10] conveys an equivocal sense of both the possession and the lack of phallic power, as indeed the effeminately dressed porter of the Bower of Bliss wields his "staff" for "more [we may hear 'mere'] formalitee" (II.xii.48.9), and reminds us of the Attis-like Aeneas at the court of Dido, another powerful female, his forgetfulness of outside world and higher task the Virgilian counterpart of the dangers of oblivion in Babylon.

The evocation of these pairs of dominant female and subject, even castrated, male in the episode of Verdant's suspended instruments works with other elements of the description to establish the Bower as a predominantly female space—whose enclosures suggest the *hortus conclusus* of the female body—and a place that might excite the knight to forget his own higher purpose, an act of submission that would suspend his "instruments." But the motif of male subjection within at least some of the plots suggested here—the case of Hercules, for example—is one in which the moment of male subjection is only one moment in a larger narrative progression. Though Guyon, unlike his prototype Odysseus, does not use his sword to overcome the Bower's witch, the culminating or phallic narrative "point" (1.7) of his Odyssean journey substitutes, for homecoming to Penelope, the overpowering of a threatening Circe through the potent "vertue" (41.9) of the Palmer's simultaneously phallic and Mosaic staff. Like the staff of Mercury to which it is kin, the staff is able both to recall souls from the symbolic Hades of subjection to female power and also to "rule the *Furyes*, when they most do rage" (41.8), a hint perhaps of the relation between the establishment of civilization and the taming of the female from the story of yet another dangerously powerful queen.

But the echo of Cybele in particular give a further dimension to this episode's suspended—and (in the case of Guyon) potentially suspended—instruments, both lyric and virile, one that involves not just the episode's narrative progression but a specific form of lyric tradition adumbrated within it. Cybele, the *Magna Mater* of imperial Rome, is one of *The Faerie Queene*'s most ubiquitous figures for the presiding patroness of "Troynovaunt" and hence for Elizabeth, the poem's allegorically shadowed queen, who was repeatedly represented (and self-represented) as the great "Mother," and even nursing mother, of her subjects. Virgil's Roman version of the *Magna Mater* carefully removes the more oriental and threatening female aspects of her cult—including the castration of Attis and her subject males. But Spenser's allusions to Cybele include this more ambivalent complex, Cybele's "franticke rites" (I.vi.15) as well as her maternal embodiment of order and civilization.[11] The Cybele-Attis iconography of the Isis Church episode of Book V of *The Faerie Queene*, with its Galli-like priests who "on their mother Earths deare lap did lie" (V.vii.9), links the pair of Great Mother and castrated boy emblematically with the posture of the mother-queen of the Bower of Bliss and the reclining youth who has surrendered his "instruments." But, interestingly enough, the vision at Isis Church also comes within the larger story of the powerful Amazon Radigund's subjection of Artegall, who comes under her control by abandoning his sword (V.v.17), which she then breaks, causing his "warlike armes" to be "hang'd on high," suspended so that they "mote his shame bewray," and forcing him to dress in "womans weedes" (20–2). The echoes of the Verdant-Acrasia scene in Artegall's humiliating subjection to a woman also, however, include a stanza that makes explicit reference to Spenser's ruling queen, the exceptional powerful female dominant over her male subjects.

> Such is the crueltie of womenkynd,
>   When they have shaken off the shamefast band,
>   With which wise Nature did them strongly bynd,
>   T'obay the heasts of mans well ruling hand,
>   That then all rule and reason they withstand,
>   To purchase a licentious libertie.
>   But vertuous women wisely understand,
>   That they were borne to base humilitie,
> Unlesse the heavens them lift to lawful soveraintie.
>   (V.v.25)

Elizabeth here is so belatedly made an exception to the rule—indeed only in a single concluding alexandrine—that what emerges in the picture of the monstrosity of the subjection of male to female power makes one wonder whether, reading back from this episode to the hints of Attis's severed instruments in the Bower of Bliss, Elizabeth herself is not also "shadowed" in the scene of suspended instruments, evocative both of male "vertue" and of instruments of a more lyric kind.[12]

Recent Spenser criticism has increasingly drawn attention to the relation between the combination of eroticized Virgin and dominating mother in the figure of Acrasia and the typical self-presentation of Spenser's ruling queen.[13] Certainly, the *otium* and debased lyric "toyes" of Acrasia's Bower echo the debased social situation of which Cuddie complains in lamenting the impotence of his own lyric instruments in the "October" eclogue, implying that, at least in part, the predicament of the poet in the age of Elizabeth—his potentially impotent, or suspended, instrument—is that he is subject to powers that necessarily compromise his song. Cuddie's complaint resembles the lyric lament of the Muses themselves in another Spenserian intertext for Verdant's suspended instruments, *The Teares of the Muses*, whose complaint of internal exile (341) and of the "idlenes" and brute sloth (99, 335) of the contemporary English context recall at once the language of the Bower of Bliss and the lament of suspended song in Psalm

124 ◆ PATRICIA PARKER

137, which might indeed provide its most appropriate lyric epigraph. The episode of Guyon in the Bower has long been interpreted, following Milton, as the drama of an individual trial. But the affinities of its language with a lament published only a year later imports into the Bower itself a suggestion of that contemporary "Babylon" in which the Muses' "sweete instruments" (20) can no longer be heard and are finally broken, replaced instead by vain idle "toyes" (325), a place where it is difficult to distinguish between "Poets" and "Sycophants" (471–2), or to save one's own lyric instruments from a subject's use.[14] Once again, in this lament, Elizabeth is made explicitly an exception, but in a fashion reserved until the end, and in a praise so exceptional that it too seems a second thought (571 ff.)

The iconography of subject male and dominant female in the scene of Verdant's suspended instruments brings us, then, to the last of the lyric traditions figured in this scene—not just the suspended lyricism of Psalm 137 or the pastoral topos of pipes hung on trees, but also the polarized structure of Petrarchan lyric, itself dependent on the polarity of male subject and elevated female figure, a polarity of which the suspended dyad of the subjected Verdant and dominant Acrasia offers an almost parodic visual emblem. This context for these suspended instruments necessarily returns us to our first—the suspension of song in an alien political context—for in both, as so much of recent Spenser criticism suggests, the relationship of lyric to society, in the terms of Adorno's famous essay, is one that cannot be overlooked.

It has long been recognized that the vogue for Petrarchan lyric in the era of Elizabeth was inseparable from the structure of a politics in which political and erotic codes interpenetrated to a remarkable degree, in which Elizabeth's courtiers related to their queen as Petrarchs to an often cruel mistress, and in which the male poet was "subject" in both the political and in the Petrarchan lyric sense. Petrarchism was not just a lyric but also a dominant cultural form, a politicized lyric structure inscribed within the complex sexual politics of the exceptional rule of a woman in an otherwise overwhelmingly patriarchal culture. Stephen Greenblatt and others have noted the antagonism—or implicit contest of wills—always present within this Petrarchan politics of courtier-lover and tantalizing, dominant, and even cruel mistress.[15] Greenblatt cites the example of Ralegh's playing a frenzied Orlando to Elizabeth's disdainful beloved; and Elizabeth figured as Ariosto's already highly Petrarchanized Angelica, who drives her courtier-knights mad, might also easily be shadowed as a dominating Acrasia artfully orchestrating both her own rival romance and her own Petrarchan poetics. The Bower of Bliss is a threatening female space not just because of its enervating *carmina* and etymologically related "charms" but also in part because, while it arouses hopes of gratification, it does not clearly fulfill them or fulfills them only in an illusory or compromising way; in the stanza of Verdant's suspended instruments, the knight's slumber seems post-coital, but it is not at all clear from the syntax what his share has been in these delights ("There she had him now layd a slombering, / In secret shade, after long wanton joyes"; 72.5–6). Bacon, for one, could easily assimilate Elizabeth's Petrarchan politics to the arts of "the Queen in the blessed islands . . . who allows of amorous admiration but prohibits desire."[16]

The antagonism within this politicized lyric structure, however, also left the way open for a male remastering of its dominant Petrarchan mistress. As Sir John Harington observed, the queen's male, Petrarch-like subjects could and would themselves make "matter" out of their *Magna Mater*. Her subjects (both in the political and in the erotic sense) could make the queen in turn the "subject" of their verse,[17] just as in the emblem of suspended pastoral instruments which Spenser echoes from Sannazaro, the origin of those instruments is in the death of Syrinx, in the transformed body of that female figure who becomes literally the enabling instrument of pastoral song.

The dynamics of this threatening female dominance and male remastery—the narrative dynamism of the overpowering of the Bower's Queen—is, however, already part of the sexual politics of Petrarchan lyric itself. Nancy Vickers, in *Writing and Sexual Difference*, describes the threat of dissolution or dismemberment that haunts the subject-object structure of the Petrarchan poetry of praise, in which the male subject is always potentially an Actaeon, torn apart after his vision of an unattainable Diana.[18] The canto of the Bower of Bliss bears a hint of this potential dismemberment as well as the castration of the male poet-lover in its reference both to Ida (II.xii.52)—sacred to Cybele and her Phrygian rites—and to Rhodope, where Orpheus, the male lyric poet par excellence, not only sang but was undone by women. Its suspended instruments obliquely recall the lyric contests not just between shepherd-singers hanging their pipes upon a tree or between sacred and secular lyric traditions (as is suggested in the echo of Psalm 137 in the midst of the Bower's very different lyricism) but also between male poet and female object of desire in Petrarchan lyric, a relationship of power translatable into both psychological and sociopolitical terms.

The vulnerable, subject status of the male lover within this Petrarchan lyric structure is countered by the mastery of the poet. In Petrarch himself, as Vickers suggests, the poet reverses the dangers of subjection and dismemberment by scattering the body of his mistress across his own *rime sparse* or scattered rhymes. In Spenser, the same stanza as evokes Ida and Rhodope in the Bower of Bliss makes reference to "Thessalian *Tempe*, where of yore / Faire *Daphne Phoebus* hart with love did gore" (4–5). The reference is to the first, or lover, moment of the myth— the victimage of the male subject before a cruel and unattainable mistress. But it inevitably provokes consciousness of its second moment—the transformation of the body of Daphne into a laurel, the triumphant sign of Phoebus' poetic power, the *lauro* that in Petrarchan lyric punningly assimilates the body of *Laura* just as Syrinx becomes in her death (an event that, though it means a loss for her lover, also removes her threat) the instrument of Pan.

The Diana-Actaeon structure of Petrarchan lyric and its underlying dyadic antagonism were clearly part of the Petrarchan politics of a reign in which the Ovidian story had already been assimilated to relationships of power through a play on the Latin words *cervus/servus* ("stag" and "slave") and a comparison of the fate of Actaeon to the perils of life at court.[19] Like the myth of Attis' permanently suspended instruments, the threat of the Actaeon persona of the Petrarchan lyric poet is, once again, castration—a threat that Spenser recalls in the "Some would have gelt him" (VII.vi.50.3) of the story of the Actaeon-like Faunus in the *Cantos of Mutabilitie*. The same threat enters euphemistically into the Bower of Bliss when Guyon's quaintly named "courage cold" (II.xii.68) begins to rise up at the sight of the naked bathing nymphs. The Actaeon-Diana story has been thought to be one of the many myths relating to the incest prohibition, the consequence of a forbidden view of the body of the mother; and certainly Guyon and the Palmer creep somewhat pruriently through the female brush ("couert groues, and thickets close"; 76) to gaze upon the simultaneously erotic and maternal "Witch" of this scene before they destroy it. The infant posture of the sleeping Verdant, together with the echo of the silencing of song from Psalm 137, reflects as well the threat of speechlessness in this Petrarchan structure, as in the Circean metamorphosis of her male victims. Petrarch, the threatened poetic Actaeon of his own canzone 23, can utter his lyrics only because he has an Orpheus-like respite between a forbidden seeing and dismemberment, and through his respite is able to silence rather than be silenced, to scatter the body of Laura rather than be dismembered himself. In Spenser's episode, Verdant's suspended instruments—signs of his status as what Mariann Sanders Regan suggestively calls "Lover infans"[20]—may figure a threat in which the potentially suspended instrument is poetic voice itself.

The split within the male subject of lyric that Regan represents as the split between Lover and Poet is matched in the episode of the Bower of Bliss by the splitting of the male figures of the scene between the subjected and symbolically castrated Verdant—his instruments hung like a sign of victory on Acrasia's tree—and the mastering Guyon, who by implication releases them. Ralegh presented the whole of *The Faerie Queene* not as the more usually cited outdoing of the narrative Ariosto but as an overgoing of the lyric Petrarch, written by a subject of a queen greater than Laura. But to become merely a Petrarch-like lyricist in praise of Elizabeth would be in some sense to become an imitative subject of the queen herself, held within a structure already appropriated as an instrument of power and presented elsewhere in *The Faerie Queene* as both paralyzed and paralyzing. In overgoing Petrarch in a poem that seems to repeat the Petrarchan lyric structure at a higher level, Spenser may also be subtly reversing the relation dictated by his own subject status. A gentleman by education only, himself dependent on the patronage system manipulated by the queen, might well conflate a visual icon reminiscent of a Petrarchan cruel mistress and her paralyzed male subject with echoes of the psalm of suspended instruments and potentially captive as well as captivating song. But, like Petrarch, the poet subject to his mistress is also capable of creating—or decreating—her, and Spenser at the end of Book II gives us an episode whose pervasive echoes of Aeneas at the court of Dido already evoke a text in which this moment of potential suspension is left behind by the narrative itself, and a female ruler is both surpassed and overruled.

Elizabeth was already identified by name with Dido or "Elissa." In the same legend which culminates in the overpowering of Acrasia, the Belphoebe who shadows Spenser's queen in her aspect as unattainable virgin or Petrarchan cruel mistress is introduced in a compound simile (II.iii.31). Its first part ("Such as *Diana* by the sandie shore / Of swift Eurotas . . .") makes her a reminiscence of Dido as she first appeared to the Aeneas she temporarily effeminated and forestalled. Its conclusion, however, compares her to "that famous Queene / Of *Amazons* whom *Pyrrhus* did destroye," an allusion which not only anticipates the Amazonian Radigund who suspends the warlike instruments of Artegall but manages, as Louis Montrose reminds us,[21] to suggest at once an exceptional female power and its destruction or remastery. The destruction of the Bower of Bliss is as violent as the prophesied ending of Psalm 137, with its captive and suspended instruments. Paradoxically, as Stephen Greenblatt and others have observed,[22] the final act of the Knight of Temperance is an act of intemperate violence, destruction of the Bower as a place of dangerous female dominance as well as of a suspect and secuctive lyricism. Though the Cave of Mammon in this book is left standing and Verdant is let go with a mere lecture, Acrasia herself is led away in triumph. As with the dyadic antagonism of Petrarchan lyric, there seems to be here, ironically, no temperate middle way, no alternative to the polarity of subject or be subjected.

The lyric appeal of the Bower of Bliss is the isolated moment of its *carpe diem* song and its suspended cynosure. Regan, in *Love Words*, offers a psychologized theory of amorous or Petrarchan lyric in which the "charm" or "spell" that holds the lover resembles the Lacanian Imaginary or Melanie Klein's primal dyad of mother and child. We do not need object-relations theory or Lacanian psychoanalysis to catch the spellbound or oral fix of Verdant in the arms of a maternal Acrasia: indeed, the attempt to apply such contemporary theories to Renaissance texts often simply reveals the bluntness of our own instruments. And yet the simultaneous use and critique of Lacan in a famous essay by Laura Mulvey on the male gaze (in cinema)[23] might provide a suggestive supplement for students of this particular Spenserian episode, undergraduates and overgraduates alike. Mulvey describes the mediatory function of the female—and the threat of castration she represents—in the movement from the mother-child dyad, which Lacan terms the Imaginary, to the realm of the Symbolic, the name of the Father and the Law. The narrative of the overpowering and surpassing of Acrasia uncannily resembles the narrative progression of this Lacanian family romance. The raised and potent Mosaic "staffe" of the Palmer (which makes possible a detour out of this enclosure) evokes both the Law and the Father at once and rescues Guyon as potential second Verdant or arrested boy from the fate of the latter's suspended instruments, from the posture of the speechless *infans* caught within a spellbinding female space.[24] What Mulvey goes on to say of the voyeuristic *scopophilia* of the male gaze recalls much of the striking voyeurism of the visitants who come to destroy the Bower of Bliss, and her description of the two ways of overcoming the threat of castration figured by the female has intriguing resonances both for the defeat of Acrasia and for the representation of Elizabeth, Spenser's Petrarchan mistress-queen. The first way, writes Mulvey, involves turning the danger-ous female figure into an image entirely outside the narrative—as, for example, in the cult of the female star, a strategy that might shed light on the cult of Elizabeth as Astraea, or quite literally a "star," transcendent embodiment of all the idealized Stella figures of Petrarchan lyric. This virgin star reigns outside the sublunar system as Gloriana is figured as outside *The Faerie Queene* or Elizabeth presented repeatedly as transcendent exception to the threatening dominant females within it.

The other means of escape from female power and the anxiety of castration, however, is a specifically narrative one, an overcoming through narrative of the "extradiegetic tendencies" of woman as spectacle, whose "visual presence tends to . . . freeze the flow of action in moments of erotic contemplation"—a visual freeze that resembles the moments of paralysis, astonishment, or stonification in Petrarchan lyric as well as the potentially suspending moments of centripetal gaze that A. Bartlett Giamatti and others have described within *The Faerie Queene*.[25] It is, in Mulvey's description, the active male protagonist, the gazer rather than the gazed upon, who neutral-izes this dangerous suspension by specifically narrative means, by a reen-actment that repeats both the original trauma of the castrating female and the process of her overcoming. The sense of resolute narrative movement and of reenactment as a form of control is conveyed in the canto of Acrasia by the resolutely "forward" movement (II.xii.76.5) of Guyon's quest and by the aura of repetition and even *déjà vu* in its imitation of earlier literary scenes, which suggests that the victory over its threatening female is in a sense already won: Guyon's almost ritual reenactment of Odysseus' resis-tance to the Sirens suggests that they are by no means as threatening the second time around.[26] In Mulvey's account, in a way reminiscent of Guyon's destruction of the Bower, this narrative process of overcoming is not only voyeuristic but sadistic, its violence a sign simultaneously of the form of the threat and of the imperative of asserting control. In Spenser, the "suspended instruments" of Acrasia's male captives are recovered as the Bower itself is overcome, and as Guyon and his Mosaic guide move forward to the narrative "point" or end of a Book of the Governor in which both a threatening female ruler and her suspect lyricism are finally mastered and surpassed.

Perhaps because of the notorious difficulty of defining it, lyric is frequently described in oppositional terms, by its relation or tension with something else—lyric cynosure as distinct from centrifugal movement, lyric as opposed to epic or narrative, and so on. *The Faerie Queene* seems to be exploring the implications of this opposition in its very form—narrative in its forward, linear quest and yet composed out of lyric stanzas that, like the enchantresses within it, potentially suspend or retard. It would be crude simply to transcode genre into gender here, though much of the history of lyric associates it with the female or the effeminate, and though Spenser's episode contains that confrontation which Horkheimer and Adorno saw as part of a revealing "dialectic of enlightenment" between a questing Odysseus and Sirens evocative of both lyric and threatening female "charm." But Guyon's defeat of Acrasia seems to involve something more than one of the poem's many narrative defeats of a potentially suspended, centripetal, "lyric" space, to be not just, as Greenblatt suggests, a repression of pleasure for the sake of an empire ruled by Elizabeth (who in this reading would be simply *opposed* to Acrasia) but more compexly an overgoing of the potentially paralyzing suspensions—unpleasure as well as pleasure—of a lyric form adapted to the domination of a woman.

Spenser's monarch was ultimately subject not only to the higher patriarchal authority of her God but to the allegorical fashioning of the poet who scattered her dread image into "mirrours more then one" (III. Proem.5.6). The allusive structures and staging of the Bower of Bliss suggest repeatedly that what is at stake within it is a complex hierarchy—the defeat of the Sirens by female Muses who are in turn subject to the authority of Apollo; the subordination, in Renaissance lyric theory, of secular lyric and its motivations to the higher lyricism and higher epideictic object of the Psalms; the surpassing, in Virgilian epic, both of the lesser pastoral genre of the Petrarchan *Shepheardes Calender* and of the power of eros and female rule. Its reticulation of these hierarchies suggests not simply the imperial politics inherited from Virgil and conveyed through the episode's unmistakeable echoes of contemporary colonial enterprise but the subtle gender politics inscribed within the contradictory structure of rule by a Queen whose name recalled not Aeneas but Elissa.

The Palmer's power to defeat all "charmes" gives to this episode a sense, ultimately, of something suspect about all *carmina*, something Protestant as well as male about its anxieties, though the defeat of Acrasia's "subtile web" (77) by the Vulcan-like Palmer's "subtile net" (81) suggests a strategy more complex than simple straightforward "enlightenment," a sense, as Keats put it, that only the poet's fine "spell of words" can rescue from a "dumb" and paralyzing "charm" and, perhaps, from an enchantress. A poem, finally, as dedicated as Spenser's to the polysemous perverse could easily encompass the psychological dynamic of the overpowering of a potentially castrating female, the covert political allegory of the overgoing of a lyricism associated with Elizabeth, and a simultaneously aesthetic and moral uneasiness about the seductiveness of lyric "charm," even if that charm is an inseparable part of the attraction of his own poetry, its own tantalizingly suspending instrument.

This essay is a revised version of the English Institute essay of the same title, published in Marjorie Garber (ed.), *Cannibals, Witches, and Divorce: Estranging the Renaissance* (Baltimore, 1987). I am grateful for the readings given it by Mary Nyquist, in preparation for its original presentation at the English Institute in 1984, and by Maureen Quilligan and Richard Strier.

Notes

1. The edition used for this and all subsequent quotations from Spenser is *Poetical Works*, ed. J. C. Smith and E. de Selincourt (London, 1912).

2. Geneva Bible (1560) version. I am indebted to John Hollander's valuable discussion of the different versions and pervasive poetic influence of this psalm in *The Oxford Anthology of English Literature*, ed. Frank Kermode *et al.* (New York, 1973), vol. 1. pp. 534–42. For the influence of the psalms themselves on Renaissance lyric and lyric theory, see, *inter alia*, O. B. Hardison, Jr, *The Enduring Monument: A Study of the Idea of Praise in Renaissance Literary Theory and Practice* (Chapel Hill, NC, 1962), pp. 95–102, and Barbara Kiefer Lewalski, *Donne's Anniversaries and the Poetry of Praise* (Princeton, NJ, 1973), pp. 11–41.

3. See Calvin, *Commentaries on the Book of Psalms*, trans. James Anderson, 5 vols (Grand Rapids, Mich., 1949), pp. 189–90, and Augustine, *Expositions on the Book of Psalms*, trans. J. Tweed *et al.*, 6 vols (Oxford, 1847–57), p. 163. Armida's garden appears in Tasso's *Gerusalemme liberata*, 16. Calvin's commentary doubles "hanged our harpes" with singers themselves held "in suspense," and this paralleling of the suspended instruments with a more properly psychological or spiritual "suspension" in the singer is continued in the versions of Thomas Campion, Thomas Carew, and Sir John Denham cited by Hollander in *The Oxford Anthology*.

4. See, for example, the analyses in Paul Alpers, *The Singer of the "Eclogues": A Study of Virgilian Pastoral* (Berkeley and Los Angeles, 1979), pp. 97 ff., 102, 134.

5. Jacopo Sannazaro, *Arcadia*, ch. 10, prose.

6. See, for example, the discussion in Richard Helgerson, *Self-Crowned Laureates* (Berkeley and Los Angeles, 1983), pp. 65–82; and Louis Adrian Montrose, "'The perfecte paterne of a Poete': The Poetics of Courtship in *The Shepheardes Calender*," *Texas Studies in Language and Literature*, 21 (1979), pp. 34–67.

7. The Bower of Bliss episode twice uses "toyes" for "trifles" or "trifling." Thomas Watson, *Hekatompathia or Passionate Centurie of Love*, ed. S. K. Heninger, Jr (Gainesville, Fla., 1964), p. 5, speaks of poems themselves as "idle toyes proceeding from a youngling [i.e. prodigal, errant] frenzy." Sir John Harington, Elizabeth's godson and translator of Ariosto, feared that, in becoming "a translator of Italian toys," he was wasting his education and later bade farewell to his "sweet wanton Muse." See Ludovico Ariosto, *Orlando furioso*, ed. Robert McNulty, trans. Sir John Harington (Oxford, 1972), pp. 14–15; Sir John Harington, *Nugae Antiquae*, ed. Henry Harington (London, 1804), vol. I, p. 333; and Helgerson's seminal

discussion of these and other texts in relation to the profession of poetry in *Self-Crowned Laureates*.

8. The crossing of phallic with lyric instruments is of course not an exclusively Spenserian one, "instruments" being itself a fertile source of sexual double entendre. Cloten in *Cymbeline* (II.iii.13–14), setting up with his musicians to woo Imogen, arranges his lyric entertainment in the hope that it will "penetrate" ("Come on, tune: if you can penetrate her with your fingering, so: we'll try with tongue too").

9. See Madlyn Millner Kahr, "Delilah," in Norma Broude and Mary D. Garrard (eds), *Feminism and Art History* (New York, 1982), p. 137, an essay first brought to my attention by Mary Nyquist. That the evocation of Samson and Delilah would not be inappropriate within a Renaissance *locus amoenus* such as the Bower of Bliss is suggested as well by Kahr's citation of the reclining Samson in the *Small Garden of Love*. Kahr's entire discussion of the oral and maternal aspects of this iconography is useful in juxtaposition with Spenser's scene. In one representation (*c.* 1508) by the great Dutch graphic artist Lucas van Leyden, Samson has laid his shield and halberd on the ground beside him, stressing his defenselessness as he sleeps in Delilah's lap; in another by the same artist (*c.* 1517–18), the abandoned weapon is a spiked club, perhaps a reference to the club of Hercules.

10. See Neil Hertz, "Medusa's Head: Male Hysteria under Political Pressure," *Representations* 1, 4 (1983), pp. 40–50.

11. See Peter Hawkins, "From Mythography to Myth-Making: Spenser and the *Magna Mater* Cybele," *Sixteenth Century Journal*, 12, 3 (1981), pp. 51–64. Hawkins reminds us that Isabel Rathborne long ago conjectured that Cybele was one of the literary ancestors of Gloriana: see her *Meaning of Spenser's Fairyland* (New York, 1937), p. 35. I am indebted to Hawkins's discussion of Cybele for the more general sense here of a link with *The Faerie Queene*, II.xii.

12. The episode in Book V also makes clearer the role of Britomart in this regard. She is the "martial maid" who defeats Radigund, but who, after the battle, softens from the counterpart of a warlike Amazon (V.v.29) into a waiting "Penolope" (39) who then, as reigning "Princess," the "liberty of women did repeale, / Which they had long usurpt; and them restoring / To Mens subiection, did true Iustice deale" (42.3–7). More detailed examination of the Britomart-Radigund pairing in relation to the Acrasia canto would suggest the tissue of contradictions at work in the reign of a Queen so clearly an exception to the patriarchal norm and under whom the situation of other women remained unchanged. The monstrosity of the rule of women is attested to, among other documents, by John Knox's attack on female rulers in his *First Blast of the Trumpet against the Monstrous regiment of women* (1558) and, after Elizabeth's accession as a female ruler sympathetic to Protestantism, his condition conveyed in a letter to her minister William Cecil that he would do "reverence" to the "miraculouse worke of God's comforting his afflicted by an infirme vessell," but only if the Queen would acknowledge "that the extraordinary dispensation of Godes great mercy maketh that lawfull unto her, which both nature and Godes law denye" to other women. See James E. Phillips, "The Background of Spenser's Attitude Toward Women Rulers," *Huntington Library Quarterly*, 5 (October 1941–July 1942), pp. 19–20.

13. See Maureen Quilligan, *Milton's Spenser: The Politics of Reading* (Ithaca, NY, 1983), pp. 67 ff.; and Louis Adrian Montrose, "'Shaping Fantasies': Figurations of Gender and Power in Elizabethan Culture," *Representations*, 1, 2 (1983), pp. 61–94.

14. The Muses' lament indicts the English nobility in phrases that directly recall the Bower of Bliss from the first installment of *The Faerie Queene* ("loathly idleness" (p. 335); "base slothfulnesse" (p. 99); "men depriv'd of sense and minde" (p. 156); together with an image of navigation that parallels that of the journey of Guyon and his Palmer guide: "But he that is of reasons skill bereft, / And wants the staffe of wisdome him to say, / Is like a ship in the midst of tempest left / Withouten helme or Pilot her to sway" (pp. 139 ff.)).

15. See the influential discussion of the Bower of Bliss in Stephen Greenblatt, *Renaissance Self-Fashioning* (Chicago, 1980), pp. 165 ff.

16. See Francis Bacon, "On the Fortunate Memory of Elizabeth Queen of England," trans. James Spedding, in *The Works of Francis Bacon*, ed. James Spedding and Robert Ellis (London, 1857–74), vol. VI, p. 317; and Greenblatt, *Renaissance Self-Fashioning*, pp. 166–7. Elizabeth was also both a forbidding Virgin and, in the words of Thomas Wenden, a yeoman subject, an "arrant whore." See Peter Stallybrass, "Patriarchal Territories: The Body Enclosed," in Margaret W. Ferguson *et al.* (eds), *Rewriting the Renaissance* (Chicago, 1986), p. 132.

17. See Sir John Harington's "Remembrauncer," *Nugae Antiquae* (1779; repr. Hildesheim, 1968), vol. II, p. 211, cited in Louis Adrian Montrose, "The Elizabethan Subject and the Spenserian Text," in Patricia Parker and David Quint (eds), *Literary Theory/Renaissance Texts* (Baltimore, 1986), p. 326, and Montrose's larger discussion there of the dynamic of subjection and remastery, esp. pp. 317–26.

18. Nancy Vickers, "Diana Described: Scattered Woman and Scattered Rhyme," in Elizabeth Abel (ed.), *Writing and Sexual Difference* (Chicago, 1982), pp. 265–79. I am indebted to Vickers's suggestive discussion of the "scattering" of Laura and of the Orpheus-like respite between seeing and dismemberment.

19. Leonard Barkan, "Diana and Actaeon: The Myth as Synthesis," *English Literary Renaissance*, 10, 3 (1980), p. 328, notes the Latin pun and George Sandys's explication of the myth as illustrating "how dangerous a curiosity it is to search into the secrets of Princes." See Sandys, *Ovid's "Metamorphosis" Englished, Mythologiz'd and Represented in Figures* (Oxford, 1632), pp. 151–2.

20. See Mariann Sanders Regan, *Love Words: The Self and the Text in Medieval and Renaissance Poetry* (Ithaca, NY, 1982), pp. 50–82.

21. See Montrose, "'Shaping Fantasies,'" p. 77. For a different discussion of the link between Elizabeth and Dido or Elissa, see Stephen Orgel, "Shakespeare and the Cannibals," in Marjorie Garber (ed.), *Cannibals, Witches, and Divorce: Estranging The Renaissance* (Baltimore, 1987), pp. 60 ff.

22. See, for example, Greenblatt, *Renaissance Self-Fashioning*, p. 177.

23. Laura Mulvey, "Visual Pleasure and Narrative Cinema," *Screen*, 16, 3 (1978), pp. 6–18.

24. Helgerson, in *Self-Crowned Laureates*, pp. 86–7, suggests as well a link between Verdant, "the green youth," and Spenser.

25. See Mulvey, "Visual Pleasure," pp. 12 ff.; and A. Bartlett Giamatti, "Spenser: From Magic to Miracle," in Herschel Baker (ed.), *Four Essays on Romance* (Cambridge, Mass., 1971).

26. Greenblatt, *Renaissance Self-Fashioning*, p. 177, also notes this sense of implicit repetition or reenactment, remarking on "why Acrasia cannot be destroyed, why she and what she is made to represent must continue to exist, forever the object of the destructive quest. For were she not to exist as a constant threat, the power Guyon embodies would also cease to exist." My analysis would also invoke this sense of reencounter, but it would shift the emphasis more clearly to the specifically sexual politics of this episode.

The Gender of the Reader and the Problem of Sexuality [in Books 3 and 4]

Maureen Quilligan

Book III and the Gender of the Reader

Titled "The Legend of Chastity," Book III directly addresses the problem of the queen's politically powerful virginity and the dynamics of its erotic allure. More importantly, it addresses these questions to overtly inscribed female readers. But before we can go on to see the immediacy and specificity of Spenser's appeal to a female reader, it is necessary to consider for a moment the possible differences between male and female responses to Book III. I take it that it is useful and legitimate to say that, in the main, men and women find the "other" sexually attractive, and that, unlike men, women (with some notable exceptions) bear children. Beyond that it may not be safe to go, neither is it necessary for the purposes of the present argument. The Renaissance had, of course, another much more elaborate set of terms for defining the differences: Ruth Kelso has massively and meticulously documented the entire doctrine for the lady of the Renaissance as it was written down in theory. The major component of the doctrine is not surprisingly the concept of chastity, which Kelso takes in the main to be a sexual continence of a sort not important for men.[1] Spenser's treatment of chastity in Book III of *The Faerie Queene* suggests that it is, however, something more than a mere physical negative. Milton's appropriation of the theme in *Comus* insists upon the potential there is to see in Spenser's treatment of it, a shaping of the self—an embracing of personal destiny that includes on Britomart's part an active confrontation of the misshaping power of the labyrinth in which she wanders.

If any of Spenser's books is organized with a gender-specific set of responses in mind, evidence is doubtless clearest in Book III. What can we say about the reader inscribed by its rhetoric? First, the homology between reading and action, whereby the reader is made to take on the perspective of the protagonist/reader of the landscape, establishes a

From *Milton's Spenser: The Politics of Reading.* © 1983 by Cornell University Press. Used by permission of the publisher.

133

female vantage point. Spenser further insists on Britomart's own responses as gender-specific. The troublesome beginning to the book makes absolute sense if and when we realize that with it Spenser is asking the reader to notice its female perspective. The opening scene, when Britomart un-horses Guyon, sets up the female's greater power: this opposition between Temperance and Chastity not only ranks their respective virtues, it also ranks, at least for the moment, female and male sexual values in a hierarchy. The second movement of the narrative establishes this perspective even more narrowly. When Florimell flies across the landscape, Spenser proceeds to bracket out the male experience of the labyrinth. As a damsel in distress, Florimell is notable for two characteristics: first, her extreme, cosmic beauty, and second, her fear, the latter easily understood because Spenser shows us a grisly forester riding after her in a manner most impressive in its phallic goal orientation. The three male knights who have been accompanying Britomart immediately take off after Florimell and her pursuer, in a way that the narrator describes as "full of great enuie and fell gealosie." This statement has given readers pause, especially because it seems to invite condemnatory moral judgments of the heroes Arthur, Guyon, and Timias. Thomas Roche first suggested that the mad rush after Florimell is there merely to insist that Britomart is female. Unlike the male knights, "she would not so lightly follow beauties chace / Ne reckt of Ladies loue." Roche remarks: "With the disappearance of the others, the point of view changes. We cannot suppose that Spenser intends the reader to think ill of Arthur and Guyon. . . . The motivation attributed to Britomart is one way of emphasizing the fact that she is a woman, which is the subject Spenser is about to undertake."[2] This is eminently sensible and a much better way to read Spenser's text than to translate the action into "allegorical" labels—which is always to end in a tangle in midspace, above the text. Thus, if we are meant to see that Magnificence and Temperance must attempt to save Beauty from Lust, why then doesn't Chastity also come to the aid of Beauty—surely a much more practical solution to the problem? A much better way of reading Spenser's text, attentive to its carefully constructed surface, is to take seriously the pun on *chase* here, which is not a bad one, or even merely witty, but a profound structuring principle at work throughout the book.[3] Thus Florimell remains "chaste" even though she is "chased" by every character she meets—save for Britomart. The pun coordinates Florimell's flight with the nature of two virgin hunts of singular importance in Book III—Diana's and Belphoebe's—and with another hunt that does not take place because it is written out of the myth of Adonis by Spenser's peculiar topography of the garden in canto vi. When the narrative proceeds to follow Britomart not on her "chace," but in her measured pace through the parlous place, we have no choice but to proceed in a manner distinctly different from the hot-footed race of the male knights.

A similar differentiation of male and female points of view may be said to occur as well at the opening of Book II; a brief glance at that episode will make Spenser's procedures clearer. At the beginning of his quest, Guyon witnesses a grisly scene: the death of two parents, Mordant and Amavia, the latter a suicide. As a result, he becomes responsible for the care of their baby boy, Ruddymane—so named because his hands are stained with his dying mother's blood. Finding he cannot wash the baby's hands, Guyon takes him to Medina and leaves him with her. We might read this extremely tricky episode (having to do with the original sin we all inherit at our physical engendering and birth) by suggesting from our gender-oriented stance that Guyon assumes the burden of articulating principles of order from which the idea of female nurturance (such as that which revives the Redcrosse Knight in the House of Holinesse) has been distinctly bracketed out—just as the male point of view is bracketed out of the narrative at the beginning of Book III by the precipitous departure of the three male knights. So Phaedria's appropriation of scriptural terms for peace are threatening to Guyon's laborious, pedestrian progress (terms themselves not threatening but reassuring when voiced by Cambina in Book IV), and his experience in the Bower of Bliss is a distinctly male version of the pornographic lure of the labyrinth's leisure.

Spenser's direct addresses to female readers are far more numerous in Book III than elsewhere throughout the poem. Here, too, he addresses the queen directly within the body of the narrative rather more often than in other books, because Britomart is presented as the founder of Elizabeth's line, the one in whom she is to see the warlike puissance of antique women, while, Spenser tells her directly, "of all wisdome be thou precedent." When it finds expression, the male perspective on the experiences of Book III's narrative is radically censured; such, for instance, is Spenser's judgment of that view in the opening stanzas to canto ii:

> Here haue I cause, in men iust blame to find,
>   That in their proper prayse too partiall bee,
>   And not indifferent to woman kind,
>   To whom no share in armes and cheualrie
>   They do impart, ne maken memorie
>   Of their braue gestes and prowesse martiall;
>   Scarce do they spare to one or two or three,
>   Rowme in their writs; yet the same writing small
> Does all their deeds deface, and dims their glories all.
>
> But by the record of antique times I find,
>   That women wont in warres to beare most sway,
>   And to all great exploits them selues inclind:
>   Of which they still the girlond bore away,
>   Till enuious Men fearing their rules decay,

> Gan coyne streight lawes to curb their liberty;
> Yet sith they warlike armes haue layd away:
> They haue exceld in artes and pollicy,
> That now we foolish men that prayse gin eke t'enuy.
>
> [III.ii.1–2]

The candor in the collapse of rhetorical distance between the narrator and one segment of his (double-gendered) audience is striking: that Spenser goes on to criticize at the same time he celebrates Elizabeth in a later canto reveals how real his confessed "envy" is.

In canto v, in one of his most extended direct addresses to his women readers, he praises Belphoebe's chastity. Using terms drawn out of the *Roman de la rose*, Spenser rewrites that text of deflowered virginity into a paean for Elizabeth's chastity—with, however, an undercutting twist at its end. In justifying Belphoebe's denial of the "soueraigne salve, in secret store," she might have granted to Timias, Spenser sings, "That dainty Rose, the daughter of her Morne, / More dear than life she tendered" (III.v.51), and traces the flower of chastity to God who implanted it in flesh as an example, which Spenser exhorts his women readers to copy:

> Faire ympes of beautie, whose bright shining beames
> Adorne the world with like to heauenly light,
> And to your willes both royalties and Realmes
> Subdew, through conquest of your wondrous might,
> With this faire flowre your goodly girlonds dight,
>
> . . . .
>
> To youre faire selues a faire ensample frame,
> Of this faire virgin, this *Belphoebe* faire,
> To whom in perfect loue, and spotlesse fame
> Of chastitie, none liuing may compaire:
> Ne poysnous Enuy iustly can empaire
> The prayse of her flesh flowring Maidenhead;
> For thy she standeth on the highest staire
> Of th'honorable stage of womanhead,
> That Ladies all may follow her ensample dead.
>
> [III.v.53–54]

The OED gives a 1561 citation of "dead" meaning "utmost." Here, then, Spenser is praising Belphoebe's utmost example of absolute virginity. But he is also saying that it is dead. Isabel MacCaffrey argues that "she is dead only in the sense that she was visible in Fairy Land, far away and long ago."[4] It is true that Spenser often distinguishes the degeneracy of his time from the purity of the ancient past, but Belphoebe is, in the sense announced in the Letter, Elizabeth herself; to preserve the compliment to Elizabeth—dead meaning "perfect"—is also to see the simultaneous criticism of such perfection.

In the next canto Spenser neglects to fulfill the narrative expectations he arouses by turning from the dead example of Belphoebe's chastity to the life-breeding forces of the place where her twin sister, Amoret, is reared.

The canto in which the Garden of Adonis is described is addressed at its outset to women readers, as if to answer a question such readers might have about the breeding of Belphoebe:

> Well may I weene, faire Ladies, all this while
> Ye wonder, how this noble Damozell
> So great perfections did in her compile,
> Sith that in saluage forests she did dwell,
> So farre from court and royall Citadell.
>
> [III.vi.1]

While we hear of Belphoebe's birth, we do not hear of her training, save that she is taken off by Diana while Amoret is taken off by Venus. The story of the birth of the twins, given to explain the genesis of the elder Belphoebe's character, swerves to emphasize instead twin Amoret's nature. The birth itself is one of "strange accident"—it is a wondrous virgin birth:

> For not as other wemens commune brood,
> They were enwombed in the sacred throne
> Of her chaste bodie, nor with commune food,
> As other wemens babes, they sucked vitall blood.
>
> [III.vi.5]

Belphoebe is born free of the loathly crime "that is ingenerate in fleshly slime." In correcting a specifically male reader—"him that reads / So straunge ensample of conception"—Spenser takes care to explain that the birth is reasonable: for it is like the process whereby, after the Nile's flood, "Infinite shapes of creatures men do fynd, / Informed in the mud, on which the Sunne hath shynd" (III.vi.8). By this correction of a specifically male vision of the action, Spenser rewrites his own first use of the spontaneous generation of the flooding Nile, which in Book I he had used to demonstrate the extreme sliminess of Errour's progeny (who are in themselves hermaphroditic, controlled moreover by an archetype of the devouring mother). In Book III he places this same image in the service of innocent, virginal impregnation and birth, as if the only slime (that from which Belphoebe escapes) were a mortal, human fatherhood (as "father of generation," the sun shares his celestial operations with his "fair sister" who "for creation ministreth matter fit" [III.vi.9]).

Our entry into the garden proper, by way of Venus's trespass on Diana's territory, provides another instrument for fine-tuning the perspective from which we are to view events in the garden; if I am correct, it is the subtlest of Spenser's bracketing procedures. When Venus finds Diana, the virgin goddess of the hunt has just taken off her clothes from the heat of the chase: she is at her bath. . . . [Spenser explicitly rewrote] the Actaeon myth in the *Mutability Cantos.* Spenser does not explicitly call up the same myth in this passage, yet it would doubtless have been a rare reader of Renaissance literature who would not have remembered Actaeon's tragic dismemberment as punishment for his vision of Diana at her bath.

> she found the Goddesse with her crew,
> After late chace of their embrewed game,
> Sitting beside a fountaine in a rew,
> Some of them washing with the liquid dew
> From off their dainty limbes the dustie sweat,
> And soyle which did deforme their liuely hew;
> Others lay shaded from the scorching heat;
> The rest vpon her person gaue attendance great.
>
> She hauing hong vpon a bough on high
> Her bow and painted quiuer, had vnlaste
> Her siluer buskins from her nimble thigh,
> And her lancke loynes vngirt, and brests unbraste,
> After her heat the breathing cold to taste;
> Her golden lockes, that late in tresses bright
> Embreaded were for hindring of her haste,
> Now loose about her shoulders hong vndight,
> And were with sweet *Ambrosia* all besprinkeld light.
>
> [III.vi.17–18]

In Ovid's version Diana cannot reach her quiver to shoot Actaeon, so she sprinkles water on him, and from these cursed drops the metamorphosis begins. The clustering movement of the nymphs who try to shield Diana in Spenser's rendition is similar to the movement in Ovid; yet Spenser's Diana is only half wroth:

> Soone her garments loose
> Vpgath'ring, in her bosome she comprized,
> Well as she might, and to the Goddesse rose,
> Wiles all her Nymphes did like a girlond her enclose.
>
> [III.vi.19]

The great difference, of course, is that "Goodly she gan faire Cytherea greet" (III.vi.20); this is not a mortal male's trespass on the sacred ground of the virgin goddess, but rather a meeting between two goddesses who share between them (and between their foster daughters) the definition of womanhood. The garden remains a completely female place.[5]

Here the potential male viewpoint, the point from which a male might view these events—"Look!" as Ovid tells his readers—is quietly elided; it is a viewpoint that needs first correction and then silent elision, as being a perspective not so much dangerous to, but potentially endangered by, the vision about to ensue. (An analogue is the way Calidore's trespass on Colin's vision in Book VI causes the evanescence of the vision of the Graces and the "hundred naked maidens lily white / All raunged in a ring, and dauncing in delight"; it is something which Calidore finally admits, "I mote not see.") Likewise, Chrysogone's mollifying bath, prefatory to her impregnation, takes place "In a fresh fountaine, farre from all mens vew" (III.vi.6)[6]

The unmentioned Actaeon myth subtly insinuates a warning that the safest vantage point for viewing the cycles of death and creation, and of the cosmic act of sexual intercourse played out in the landscape of the garden, is that of Venus herself—that is, the female perspective. From such a position there is no discomfort in acknowledging Venus's awesome power over Adonis, by which she makes safe his perpetual fatherhood. The vision of the garden's landscape is a vision of the female body, focused specifically on the "somewhat" that, in the *Mutability Cantos*, Faunus had seen and sniggered at. Here the image of the Mount of Venus is offered not merely to be translated into female genitalia—rather the genitalia are features within the garden's landscape to metonymize the power in which they participate—cosmic regeneration. Shakespeare's *Venus and Adonis* may offer an instructive contrast to Spenser's use of the anatomical landscape. In Shakespeare's version Venus herself offers the garden as metaphor for her own body:

> "Fondling," she said, "since I have hemm'd thee here
> Within the circuit of this ivory pale,
> I'll be a park, and thou shalt be my deer:
> Feed where thou wilt, on mountain or in dale;
>   Graze on my lips; and if those hills be dry,
>   Stray lower, where the pleasant fountains lie.
> "Within this limit is relief enough
> Sweet bottom-grass and high delightful plain,
> Round rising hillocks, brakes obscure and rough,
> To shelter thee from tempest and from rain;[7]

The salacious allure of this innuendo is posed by its invitation to translate different elements of the landscape into specific parts of the female body. Conversely, Spenser's landscape resists immediate one-for-one paraphrase:

> Right in the middest of that Paradise,
>   There stood a stately Mount, on whose round top
>   A gloomy groue of mirtle trees did rise,
>   Whose shadie boughes sharpe steele did neuer lop,

> Nor wicked beasts their tender buds did crop,
> But like a girlond compassed the hight,
> And from their fruitfull sides sweet gum did drop,
> That all the ground with precious deaw bedight,
> Threw forth most dainty odours, and most sweet delight.
>
> [III.vi.43]

As Isabel MacCaffrey notes, "this stanza is among other things a description of the Mount of Venus; but the erotic anatomical suggestion is undergirded by still deeper instincts and impulses." These impulses are served by Spenser's organizing the bower so that we do not have a sensation of "moving *up*" but "of coming into a small, protected, intimately enclosed space"; this movement, MacCaffrey explains, "probably satisfies an atavistic urge in all of us."[8]

> There wont faire *Venus* often to enjoy
> Her dear *Adonis* ioyous company,
> To reape sweet pleasure of the wanton boy;
> There yet, some say, in secret he does ly,
> Lapped in flowres and pretious spycery,
> By her hid from the world, and from the skill
> Of *Stygian* Gods, which doe her loue enuy;
> But she her selfe, when euer that she will,
> Possesseth him, and of his sweetnesse takes her fill.
>
> [III.vi.46]

The deepest and most atavistic urges satisfied by this landscape have, doubtless, to do with the desires involved in Venus's immense power, here essentially female—for her protection of Adonis is effected specifically by her power over the deepest point of this landscape, almost as if the cave beneath the mount were yet another image of the secret recess where Adonis lies "lapped" in spicery.[9] Venus provides Adonis his illogical subjection to mortality—while yet being "eterne in mutabilitie"—by means of her entrapment of the boar within the cave:

> There now he liueth in eternall blis,
> Ioying his goddesse, and of her enioyed:
> Ne feareth he henceforth that foe of his,
> Which with his cruell tuske him deadly cloyd:
> For that wild Bore, the which him once annoyd,
> She firmely hath emprisoned for ay,
> That her sweet loue his malice mote auoyd,
> In a strong rocky Caue, which is they say,
> Hewen vnderneath that Mount, that none him losen may.
>
> There now he liues in euerlasting ioy . . .
>
> [III.vi.48–49]

The location of the cave, along with confusions over who is everlastingly happy where (confusions caused by the ambiguous pronouns of the transition between stanzas), suggest that the anatomical allegory plays out in the landscape a female control over everlasting sexual communion. Of course, the boar "is" death: but, as MacCaffrey puts it, "the meekness and health of Adonis turn aside the wrath of fallen bestiality."[10] The boar therefore is a metonymy for fallen bestiality, which by its very name—"bore"—suggests the power of the male phallus. The boar's position within the landscape, functioning now as if it were a synecdoche, connects it to the threatened dismemberment of Actaeon, passed over in the erasure of that myth's presence from the text. Again, the most comfortable and unthreatened viewpoint for reading the events of the garden is female. Thus the garden's eroticism should not be read as dismemberment, but as the mythic displacement of desire and as a vision of male sexuality brought safely and creatively under the control of an awesome female power. (In a sense, Adonis's position is merely Verdant's passivity seen from a different perspective—one that insists on the cosmic legitimacy of the female Eros's triumph over a male Thanatos.)

We should remember, too, that the forester who had threatened Florimell at the outset of Book III was threatening precisely because he wielded a "bore speare":

> Lo where a griesly Foster forth did rush
> Breathing out beastly lust her to defile:
> His tyreling iade he fiercely forth did push,
> Through thicke and thin, both ouer banke and bush
> In hope her to attaine by hooke or crooke,
> That from his gories sides the bloud did gush:
> Large were his limbes, and terrible his looke,
> And in his clownish hand *a sharp bore speare he shooke.*
> [III.i.17; emphasis added]

In the center of the book, this threatening force is controlled by being contained, not destroyed. Out of its containment come the creations of chaste love, of the perpetual successions imaged by Adonis's fatherhood in his rewritten myth, and of the generations who, Merlin prophesies, will rise from Britomart's womb.[11] The end of this prophecy is, of course, the birth of the royal virgin Elizabeth, whose chastity Book III praises. That the female power the book does finally celebrate in the garden is a female power in conjunction with male sexuality (however disconnected from its social role of dominance) suggests not only the compelling importance of sexuality itself in Spenser's mythology, but the need to reintegrate female sexual power into a structure that includes male potency. Spenser may counsel his female readers to follow Belphoebe's example of virginity, but the chastity he truly extols is Amoret's: it is the chastity not of a virgin queen, but of a wedded wife.

If the allegorical core to Book III, the Garden of Adonis, is a look at female power from a peculiarly female perspective, the scene of Britomart's rescue of Amoret is a scrutiny of female sexual fear, seen again from a female vantage point. Spenser hints at the exchange of power for vulnerability when he says of Amoret at the end of the Garden of Adonis canto that she was so well brought up there that many a man found "His feeble hart wide launched with love's cruell wound." It is, of course, not a male knight's but Amoret's own heart that suffers the widely gaping, hideously sadistic wound in Busyrane's masque in canto xii. In listing the dramatis personae of this masque Spenser includes a signal remark:

> There were full many moe like maladies,
>> Whose names and natures I note readen well;
>> So many moe, as there be phantasies
>> In wauering wemens wit, that none can tell,
>> Or paines in loue, or punishments in hell;
> All which disguized marcht in masking wise,
> About the chamber with that Damozell,
>> [III.xii.26]

The "fantasies" that Spenser does not read for us doubtless derive from the figure of Danger in the *Roman de la rose*—a resource for most of the rest of the masque—and image therefore a legitimate female fear of sexuality, of the sort less easily dismissed in the first vision of Florimell pursued by the forester. The sadomasochism of the masque is troublesome because it is so relentless; if the twelfth canto of Book II images a male pornographic fantasy (and response to that fantasy), then canto xii of Book III may well be Spenser's version of a female pornographic fantasy—such, at least, is suggested by the line about "wavering wemens wit." But Britomart's response to this fantasy is not destruction, such as Guyon wreaks on Acrasia's bower at the end of Book III. Instead we see a typical response by female power to male violence very similar to that given in the Garden of Adonis: containment. Busyrane's instrument of torture is his lyric *pen*, and a profoundly reverberating pun on this word insists on the sterile, prisonlike effect of his art. Thus when Scudamour wails, "Why then is *Busirane* with wicked hand / Suffered, these seuen monethes day in secret den / My lady and my loue so cruelly to *pen*" (III.xi.10), we see that the sadistic sonneteer has written Amoret into an art that halts the flow of time, inscribing it within an ecphrastic paralysis, an ever-dying, but never really dead, death. In great part Spenser manages to correct this (male) art by viewing it from the opposite perspective of the lady, who usually merely peruses the lines of the poem. In the end, Britomart makes Busyrane reverse his verses; but, restrained by Amoret, she does not destroy him. Like the containment of the boar within the cave beneath Venus's mount, Britomart's forcing Busyrane to rewrite his verses reveals female control over the phallic power punningly metonymized by these instruments of male aggression. But here control is not, as it is at the close of Book II, pitiless obliteration. Amoret's wound is healed when Busyrane is made to chant his backward spells:

> The cruell steele, which thrild her dying hart,
>   Fell softly forth, as of his owne accord,
>   And the wyde wound, which lately did dispart
>   Her bleeding brest, and riuen bowels gor'd,
>   Was closed vp, as it had not bene *bor'd*,
>   And euery part to safety full sound,
>   As she were neuer hurt, was soone restor'd:
>   Tho when she felt her selfe to be vnbound,
> And perfect *hole*, prostrate she fell vnto the ground.
>   [III.xii.38; emphasis added]

As Jonathan Goldberg points out, the problematic pun insists on the "full ambiguity of being rendered 'perfect hole.'"[12] The wound is healed but remains still the wound of desire—which Britomart shares with Amoret in her own double-wounding, first by Gardante and then by Busyrane. A final pun in the 1590 version of the close of Book III makes the paradox of the wound of love clearer. Britomart regards Amoret's and Scudamour's final embrace:

> Had ye them seene, ye would haue surely thought,
>   That they had beene that faire *Hermaphrodite*,
>   Which that rich *Romane* of white marble wrought,
>   And in his costly Bath caused to bee site:
>   So seemd those two, as growne together quite,
>   That *Britomart* halfe enuying their *blesse*,
>   Was much empassioned in her gentle sprite,
>   And to her selfe oft wisht like happinesse,
> In vaine she wisht, that fate n'ould let her yet possesse.
>   [III.xii.46a]

Blesser, in French, is to wound; such wounding, a real anatomical event in sexual consummation, is bliss.

BOOK IV AND THE FAILURE OF ORPHEUS

This vision of ultimate sexual consummation ending Book III—addressed in the plural "ye" to an audience fashioned in gentle discipline by having empathetically shared in the sexual experience of the "other"—stood for six years, only to be canceled by the appearance of the 1596 installment of *The Faerie Queene*. The necessity for this had doubtless many causes—the sheer need to generate more story one of them. The cancellation witnesses allegory's generic tendency toward constant revision of threshold texts and pretexts.[13] But because dropping the vision of the hermaphrodite embrace is one of the most radical revising in the poem, we would do well to question Spenser's rationale for so complete an excision. Surely one reason for the cancellation has something to do with the response the poem had received during the six years between publication of the first and second installments. And it is the negative reaction of certain readers that Spenser specifically addresses in the proem to Book IV. There we see something odd occur: a change in Spenser's own stated view of his audience. The proem to Book IV turns into Spenser's statement about his fit audience though few:

> The rugged forhead that with graue foresight
>> Welds kingdomes causes, and affaires of state,
>> My looser rimes (I wote) doth sharply wite,
>> For praising loue, as I haue done of late,
>> And magnifying louers deare debate.
>>> [IV.Proem.1]

This critical statesman is almost assuredly Burleigh, as many have suggested;[14] the character painted here accords well with the nature of the man Spenser had addressed in his dedicatory sonnet to Burleigh appended to the 1590 *Faerie Queene* (where "graue" also predominates). Even then Spenser was worrying about Burleigh's "censure graue" and offering as protection against it the traditional defense of allegory:

> Yet if their deeper sence be inly wayd,
>> And the dim vele, with which from commune vew
>> Their fairer parts are hid, aside be layd.
>> Perhaps not vaine they may appeare to you.

But the reader whom Spenser censures in the proem to IV is not one who has failed to understand the nature of the allegory—it is one who is incapable of feeling love: "Such ones ill iudge of loue, that cannot loue, / Ne in their frosen hearts feele kindly flame." Perhaps more significantly, the censured reader is a traditionalist who appears to have argued that love is not a fit subject for an imperial epic:

> Which who so list looke backe to former ages,
>> And call to count the things that then were donne,
>> Shall find, that all the workes of those wise sages,
>> And braue exploits which great Heroes wonne,
>> In loue were either ended or begonne.
>>> [IV.Proem.3]

Defiantly, Spenser dismisses this censuring reader and chooses another:

To such therefore I do not sing at all,
　But to that sacred Saint my soueraigne Queene,
. . . .

To her I singe of loue, that loueth best,
　And best is lou'd of all aliue I weene:
　To her this song most fitly is addrest,
The Queene of loue, and Prince of peace from heauen blest.
[IV.Proem.4]

In fact, what Spenser does in this proem is to dismiss a male reader, select
a paradigmatic female one, and then reconstitute the canceled full-gendered
readership (as imaged in the closing embrace of Amoret and Scudamour)
within the "androgynous" queen—who is both queen of love and prince of
peace.[15] The argument of the proem suggests that Book III was the cause
of the negative response that the first installment received; only there is
lovers' dear debate magnified.[16] Spenser's censure of a male reader's reading
of Book III suggests the real risk he took in writing for his female reader
as he had in Book III. The only solution available to him appears to be to
privilege that readership again, explicitly.

However, the position of the queen in this proem is radically altered
from her place in the first three proems of the first installment. There she
functions much as a muse inspiring the poet (Book I), or as a poetic subject
(Book II), or as sovereign queen (Book III). In all these proems, moreover,
the queen is addressed directly in the second person. Strikingly, in the
proem to Book IV she has been moved back into the third person; the poet
tells another reader that he sings to the queen. Elizabeth now is uniquely
a reader, not a muse or poetic subject, and the poet's request for inspiration
is not that he may sing her praises (so far beyond his afflicted style); instead,
he prays to Cupid to make her an inspired reader:

Which that she may the better deigne to heare,
　Do thou dred infant, *Venus* dearling doue,
　From her high spirit chase imperious feare,
　And vse of awfull Maiestie remoue:
　In sted thereof with drops of melting loue,
　Deawd with ambrosiall kisses, by thee gotten
　From thy sweete smyling mother from aboue,
　Sprinckle her heart, and haughtie courage soften,
That she may hearke to loue, and reade this lesson often.
[IV.Proem.5]

There could be no better indication of how important the reader's inspiration is in reading an allegory than this prayer to Cupid not to inspire the
poet to write, but to inspire the queen to read. Doubtless the historical cause
of the abyss we see opened here between the poet and his patroness has

something to do with Ralegh—Spenser's presenter at court in 1590, himself a poet who shares the honors of the proem to Book III, and the shadow behind the Timias-Belphoebe misunderstandings played out in cantos vii and viii of Book IV (where a turtledove—like Venus's darling dove of the proem—effects a reconciliation). But whatever the causes, we see Spenser's later verse (especially *Colin Clouts Come Home Againe*, written in 1591 and dedicated to Ralegh, but not published until 1595) marked by increasing criticism of the mystifications of court mythology.

The virtues under scrutiny in the last three books of *The Faerie Queene* are not the "private" ones of the first installment but "public." And in the fifth book in particular we see Spenser's critical appraisal of contemporary English politics, more explicitly present in the poem than they have been before. This distinction between "private" and "public" virtues is Spenser's own, of course, part of his plan from the first, as described in the "Letter To Ralegh" (though the public virtues were to have been a separate twelve-book epic unto themselves). But the publicness of the second installment may be not so much an anticipation of the original plan as a result of the poem's own recent publicness, that is, its publication—the intrapsychic dynamics of the first installment's narrative become overtly political, as Spenser responds to the response the poem received.

We have just seen the subtle shift in the way the poem locates itself in relationship to its first reader—the queen—now insistently divorced from (but thereby placed within) an explicit political context (the realm of he who wields "affairs of state"). The "Letter to Ralegh" was canceled. And the cancellation of the hermaphrodite image would also suggest that the gynandromorphic flexibility that Spenser had asked of his readers in Book III would be canceled as well. The methods of the allegory in IV–VI are very different: the density of wordplay, so important to Spenser's accretion of meaning, thins out in the later installments (though it is, to be sure, still present). Indeed, Spenser's entire allegorical program suffers a subtle sea-change. This should not, however, be surprising. A poem aimed so directly at its readers would need to change its rhetoric had the desired response not been forthcoming—as the tone of the proem to IV so strongly insists did in fact happen.

We may sense the nature of the revisionary gestures of Book IV by noticing that Amoret's story begins, in Book III, in a rewritten text of Orpheus's, for it is Orpheus who sings the story of Venus and Adonis in the *Metamorphoses*. Rewriting Orpheus's story to his own purposes, Spenser denies the metamorphosis of Adonis (just as he denies Actaeon's transformation in the *Mutability Cantos*). . . . Spenser began his epic with a subtle indication that he hoped to be a different kind of poet from Orpheus, one who would successfully lead his reader out of the hellish wood of Errour. The process would not be simple, but given the grace of revelation, it would succeed. By canto x of Book IV, however, we find Spenser's narrative suffering a failure like Orpheus's. There Scudamour tells of his own capture of Amoret, prior to Busyrane's kidnapping of her on their wedding day. (This was new information, lacking during the six years between the two installments.) The knight ends his story of conquest by making a very dubious comparison—dubious because it tends to throw his whole discourse into doubt.

> No less did *Daunger* threaten me with dread,
>> When as he saw me, maugre all his powre,
>> That glorious spoyle of beautie with me lead,
>> Then *Cerberus*, when *Orpheus* did recoure
>> His Leman from the Stygian Princes boure.
>> But euermore my shield did me defend,
>> Against the storme of euery dreadfull stoure:
>> Thus safely with my loue I thence did wend.
> So ended he his tale, where I this Canto end.
>> [IV.x.58]

Here in the one perfect, closed ending to a canto among the otherwise loose and open-ended closings of all (save one) of the other cantos in the book, Spenser appears to conflate his own voice with Scudamour's; yet if Scudamour is unaware of the irony of this reference to Orpheus, Spenser is not. The irony seems designed to deflate Scudamour's claim about being a good husband—and serves to remind us of his former incapacity to penetrate the flames surrounding Busyrane's palace (Orpheus's failure had been read as an excess of passion). Wishing to disarm the irony of the reference to Orpheus, MacCaffrey argues that in Book IV, Orpheus is "connected with another range of meanings, the power of Concord and her human instruments"; therefore, the reference to Orpheus notwithstanding, Scudamour's triumph at the Temple takes its place alongside the unions of Britomart and Artegall, Belphoebe and Timias, Florimell and Marinell, and the wedding of the Thames and Medway.[17] The problem with this equation is that we do in fact see the other unions brought to successful (if, in the case of Florimell and Marinell, belated) conclusions; the union of Scudamour and Amoret would indeed be like these were we allowed to forget Scudamour's loss of her. But we are not. Scudamour's comparison of Orpheus's lack of dread to his own insists upon that loss most particularly, for Cerberus is not mentioned in the *Metamorphoses* until after Orpheus has already lost Eurydice.

> The double death
> Stunned Orpheus, like the man who turned to stone
> At sight of Cerberus, or the couple of rock,
> Oleonos and Letheaea, hearts so joined
> One shared the other's guilt, and Ida's mountain,
> Where rivers run, still holds them, both together.[18]

Spenser himself has just lost Amoret moments before Scudamour begins his narration in one of the more frustrating narrative dissolves in the whole poem. Thus at stanza 17 of canto ix, Prince Arthur has Amoret well in hand—"safe as in a Sanctuary" (ix.19); yet at stanza 36 when he composes the strife among Britomart, Scudamour, and four attacking knights, Amoret has unaccountably disappeared: Scudamour and Britomart vie in lamenting her loss (38). Amoret's story has been rewritten in Book IV to mark an absolute loss. From having begun her story by rewriting Orpheus's story of Venus and Adonis in Book III, Spenser ends it by confessing a shared failure with the pagan poet. Amoret will always be lost, never brought out from the peculiar hells of sexual desire, from which at the end of Book III she had been momentarily extricated. If, in fact, Spenser did intend the tree catalogue in the Wood of Errour in Book I to be a challenge to Orphic poetry, then we must see how far short of the mark he judges himself to have come. Orpheus may indeed share with David and Menenius Agrippa the "godlike" powers of taming passion (IV.ii.2). Yet in rewriting his own text of the canceled hermaphrodite (reconstituted yet again in the narrative as the statue of Venus in canto ix), Spenser resubjects Amoret to loss.[19] His voice, insofar as it elides into Scudamour's (and Orpheus's) cannot save her. Spenser cannot sing "With other notes than to the Orphean lyre."

Because Orpheus is a poet of such marked interest . . . for Spenser, it will be useful to consider for a moment the particular sexual dynamic that the mythic poet's career embodies. . . . His story figures the female threat to male poetic inspiration. After having lost Eurydice in a second death, Orpheus, Ovid tells us, turns to the love of boys; he then sings and summons the trees. The content of that singing is given in the tales of the rest of Book X of the *Metamorphoses:* Cyparissus, Ganymede, Apollo and Hyacinth, Pygmalion, Cinyras and Myrrha, and Venus and Adonis—in the middle of which is interpolated the story of Atalanta, told by Venus. Book XI then opens with the story of Orpheus's murder by the crazed maenads whose clamor drowns out the sounds of his magical, metamorphosing music. The maenads then dismember him. Finally Bacchus punishes these Thracian women by transforming them into rooted trees.

In the context of his entire career as recounted in the *Metamorphoses,* Orpheus becomes less the poet of concord—that power he demonstrates by swaying all the underworld to grant his request of Eurydice—than of husbandly love poetry, bizarrely at odds with the forces within ecstatic female worship. In this, he is as germane . . . to Spenser. In the tension between husbandly love and its implicit antagonism to women (as played out in Ovid's text), we can see a conflict present in the context of Scudamour's narration. Moments before Scudamour launches into his story of conquest, Arthur lectures the assembled knights on the chivalric franchise granted to women "that of their loues choice they might freedome clame / And in that right should by all knights be shielded" (IV.xi.37). Yet Scudamour tells his tale to assert his own right: "Certes her losse ought me to sorrow most / Whose right she is, where euer she be straide" (IV.xi.38). Freedom's rights are in conflict:

> She often prayd, and often me besought,
>> Sometimes with tender teares to let her goe,
>> Sometimes with witching smyles: but yet for nought,
>> That euer she to me could say or doe,
>> Could she her wished freedome fro me wooe;
>
> [IV.x.57]

There is much to be said in explication of Amoret's coy, reluctant, amorous delay here; it is proper and fitting virginal behavior; neither, doubtless, is Scudamour's exertion of gentle power wrong. What seems to be at issue is the conflict within the terms of chivalric love—those pronounced by Arthur about ladies' undeniable rights, and those rights granted by conquest. (They have persistently dogged the comedy of Amoret's travels with the disguised Britomart.) In this we may be being asked to consider how well Scudamour has understood the first part of the text he reads so carefully at the outset of his adventure in the Temple of Venus: *"Blessed the man that well can vse his blis: / Whose euer be the shield, faire Amoret be his"* [IV.x.8]. There is something more to love than the lady's faithful chastity (of which Scudamour finally has no doubts). Love fails and Amoret is lost in a fatal misuse of bliss.[20]

What we are left with is a desire for the canceled text of the 1590 ending, a desire that Spenser satisfies with illusory substitutions. The narrative unfolds as before with massive inventiveness but with less and less faith that conclusions can be reached. Like the cancellation of the happy ending to Amoret's story, the cancellation of the "Letter to Ralegh" suggests an entire reorientation of Spenser's initial program in the face of hard political realities. (The hardest being, no doubt, that Spenser did not win the privileged place at court to which he aspired.) The way the second installment incorporates these political realities into its texts demonstrates Spenser's abiding interest in his audience. The response of that audience becomes, in fact, part of the poem's subject, not merely in the proem to Book IV but at certain key moments throughout the narrative. One thinks of the position of the poet at Mercilla's palace, with his tongue nailed to a post. A more subtle moment is Calidore's trespass on Colin's vision of the graces on Mount Acidale in Book VI. As I have argued elsewhere, allegory more than most genres needs to posit its ideal readers; in the scene staging the poet's vision of his own inspiration, Spenser anatomizes the processes of bad reading, and of the political forces that cause it. Calidore finally admits that the vision of the Graces is something "I mote not see"—and in his misvision, he participates in the invidious detractions that will become forces so powerful, Spenser fears they will rend his own poem. The position of the queen, so closely tied to the position of the reader in the canceled "Letter," is to be displaced even further from her location at the center—removed explicitly in Colin's praise of his own country lass. So displaced is she that Thomas Cain argues that Spenser has nearly executed "an about-face" toward her as an encomiastic subject, turning praise of Elizabeth into blame.[21] If Cain is right in associating the figure of Orpheus in particular with the program of encomium which Spenser undertook in the poem, he is surely right to insist on the remarkable "self mutilation" of the last lines of the poem, where Spenser counsels his epic merely to please, no more to attempt to fashion his reader. In a sense, Spenser had already mutilated *The Faerie Queene* by rewriting the ending of Book III. Spenser as Orpheus fails, however, not because he could not lead his Eurydice out of hell, but because some of his readers would not leave the Wood of Errour.

Notes

1. Ruth Kelso, *Doctrine for the Lady of the Renaissance* (Urbana: University of Illinois Press, 1956), pp. 24–25.

2. Thomas P. Roche, *Kindly Flame: A Study of the Third and Fourth Books of Spenser's Faerie Queene* (Princeton: Princeton University Press, 1964), p. 14.

3. Angus Fletcher, *Prophetic Moment: An Essay on Spenser* (Chicago: University of Chicago Press, 1971), pp. 99–101, argues for the significance of such "bad" puns.

4. Isabel G. MacCaffrey, *Spenser's Allegory: The Anatomy of Imagination* (Princeton: Princeton University Press, 1976), p. 275.

5. The femaleness of the process of generation and culture imaged here finds an analogue in Titania's view of maternal generation in *Midsummer Night's Dream*, in which, as Louis Adrian Montrose describes it: "a biological genitor and social father play no role in the making of a child" ("*A Midsummer Night's Dream* and the Shaping Fantasies of Elizabethan Culture: Gender, Power, Form," in *Rewriting the Renaissance: The Discourses of Sexual Difference in Early Modern Europe*, ed. Margaret W. Ferguson, Maureen Quilligan, and Nancy J. Vickers [Chicago: University of Chicago Press, 1986], p. 75). See Edgar Wind, *Pagan Mysteries in the Renaissance* (1958; rpt. Harmondsworth, Middlesex: Penguin Books, 1967), pp. 77–78, for a discussion of the cult of the virgin Elizabeth as a "cult of Venus in disguise."

6. While the phrase "farre from all mens vew" is, of course, formulaic, the distinctly feminine context of the goddesses' meeting and the garden itself make the phrase function as if gender-specific. Childbirth was not, in any event, something males witnessed in the sixteenth century. In *Midwives and Medical Men* (New York: Schocken Books, 1977), Jean Dennison describes the ruses men-midwives had to resort to in order to enter the lying-in room undetected (men-midwives became recognized in the early seventeenth century); Percival Willughby crawled into the room on all fours in order to assist his daughter-midwife in a problem delivery (p. 11).

7. *The Complete Plays and Poems of Shakespeare*, ed. William A. Nelson and Charles J. Hill (Boston: Houghton Mifflin, 1942), "Venus and Adonis," 229–40; p. 136.

8. MacCaffrey, *Spenser's Allegory*, pp. 261–62.

9. Lauren Silberman describes the cave directly as the "vagina dentata, ultimate expression of Venus' fearsome power," in "Singing Unsung Heroines: Androgynous Discourse in Book III of *The Faerie Queene*" (*Rewriting the Renaissance*, pp. 259–71).

10. Stephen Greenblatt, *Renaissance Self-Fashioning from More to Shakespeare* (Chicago: University of Chicago Press, 1980), p. 171, notes that the Garden of Adonis "has almost no erotic appeal." MacCaffrey also notes the greater "sensual" excitement of the Bower of Bliss episode—with its "mindless somatic responses"—over the garden's appeal (*Spenser's Allegory*, p. 258).

11. For further discussion of the close connection between Britomart's sexuality and the garden's, see my "Words and Sex: The Language of Allegory in the *De Planctu naturae, Le Roman de la Rose*, and Book III of *The Faerie Queene*," *Allegorica* 1 (1977), pp. 208–9.

12. Jonathan Goldberg, *Endlesse Worke: Spenser and the Structures of Discourse* (Baltimore: Johns Hopkins University Press, 1981), p. 78.

13. See my *Language of Allegory: Defining the Genre* (Ithaca: Cornell University Press, 1979), pp. 45–47, 81–85.

14. See Paul J. Alpers, *The Poetry of The Faerie Queene* (Princeton: Princeton University Press, 1967), pp. 281–82; Thomas H. Cain, *Praise in The Faerie Queene* (Lincoln: University of Nebraska Press, 1978), p. 104.

15. I am indebted to Barbara Roche Rico for first suggesting this point to me.

16. Cain notes, p. 104, that many assumed Burleigh took the hermaphrodite image to be pornographic. Cain interestingly argues for a political rather than sexual objection (if the two are to be distinguished in Elizabethan diplomacy). Thus the Busyrane episode shadows and criticizes the Alençon match, which Burleigh had supported. That the fracas over the Alençon match was a good ten years old by the time Book III was published may not detract from this thesis entirely, especially in view of our ignorance of Spenser's chronology of composition.

17. MacCaffrey, *Spenser's Allegory*, pp. 327–28.

18. Ovid, *Metamorphoses*, trans. Rolfe Humphries (Bloomington: Indiana University Press, 1955), p. 236.

19. For another discussion of the differences between III and IV and the refiguring of the loss of Amoret, see Goldberg, *Endlesse Worke*, p. 79: "The crucial difference is the removal of the concept of singularity which seemed central to III. . . . Otherness is, with book IV, before us."

20. Alice S. Miskimin, *The Renaissance Chaucer* (New Haven: Yale University Press, 1975), p. 153, discusses Boethius's use of the Orpheus myth as an investigation into the "antithetical necessity" of love's power for cosmic harmony: "the devouring passion and self-destroying power latent in creation itself."

21. Cain, *Praise*, p. 185.

The Hermaphrodite and the Metamorphosis of Spenserian Allegory

LAUREN SILBERMAN

I

The second installment of Spenser's *Faerie Queene* begins with a spirited counterattack against critics of the poet's previous work. In the proem to Book IV of *The Faerie Queene*, Spenser sees fit to castigate "The rugged forhead that with graue foresight / Welds kingdomes causes, and affaires of state" (IV.P.1) for his reproof of the poet's "looser rimes" praising love. Spenser's frozen-hearted critic is usually identified as William Cecil, Lord Burleigh, and there is a certain tradition that Burleigh's displeasure was aroused by the "shocking" image of the Hermaphrodite at the conclusion of the 1590 edition of *The Faerie Queene*, which was excised from the later version in 1596.[1]

Whatever the merit of that tradition and however much Spenser's unnamed critic may have objected to the poet's choice of sexual love as an epic subject, the Hermaphrodite figures not only as the concluding image of Spenser's anatomy of love in Book III, but as the source of an allusion "in middest" of the Legend of Holiness as well.[2] When at the center of Book I the Redcrosse Knight couples with Duessa after drinking from an enchanted well, Spenser's etiological description of the fountain closely follows Ovid's description of the fountain of Salmacis (*F.Q.*I.vii.4–5; *Met.*4.297–315) and the subsequent appearance of Orgoglio rebukes the Redcrosse Knight's loss of potency in a complex revision of Ovid's sexual myth.[3]

I should like to suggest that the image of the Hermaphrodite in the original conclusion of Book III figures forth a set of concerns present from the beginning of Book I and that the displacement of the Hermaphrodite from the middest of Book I to the conclusion of Book III ratifies a larger structural and thematic shift from Book I to Book III. In Book I the allusion to Ovid's Hermaphrodite occurs in the determinate center of a Providential structure. Book III makes allusion to that figure in a conclusion that puts in question the very possibility of closure.[4] The Redcrosse Knight's liaison with

Reprinted with permission from *English Literary Renaissance* 17, no. 2 (Spring 1987): 207–23.

152

Duessa and his encounter with Orgoglio is a turning point, a fortunate fall, the first Pyrrhic defeat in a series of Pyrrhic victories over projections of his own faithlessness and joylessness. The pun error-*errare* that underlies the narrative of Book I as the hero's epic wanderings proceed from his initial mistake in doubting Una's truth becomes subsumed by the pattern of sin and redemption, which climaxes in the apocalyptic fight between St. George and the dragon.[5] The hermaphroditic embrace of Scudamour and Amoret, which concludes the 1590 *Faerie Queene*, only reminds the heroine, "halfe enuying their blesse," that her own quest is unfulfilled and her own love unrealized.

Although the coupling of Duessa and the Redcrosse Knight lies at the center of Book I, by the end, Duessa's testimony about the coupling fails to prevent the knight's betrothal to Una. By the conclusion of Book I troth—faith and loyalty (*OED*, s.v. "troth" I.1)—has come to overshadow its etymological cognate, truth—the conformity with fact (*OED*, s.v. "truth" II.5). Indeed, throughout Book I, psychosexual issues seem to be raised only to be deferred beyond the conclusion of that book. For example, as Mark Rose points out, the initial flight of Redcrosse and Una into the Wandering Wood to seek refuge from Jove's rainstorm suggests avoidance of sexuality and a childlike misreading of the loving father as an angry father.[6] Granted that, what else are Una and the Redcrosse Knight to do but get out of the rain? The allegory raises the issue of sexuality and sexual repression in such a way that the allegorical significance of the episode cannot determine the action of the figures. In general, Una and the Redcrosse Knight accord less with our notion of character than Britomart does and, as many critics have noted, Book I seems cast on a higher level of abstraction than Book III.[7] Although, at the conclusion of Book I, Redcrosse is described "swimming in that sea of blisful ioy" (I.xii.41), Una is left to mourn while her betrothed completes six years' service to the Faerie Queene. Marriage of Holiness to Truth must await the completion of human history.[8] Book I achieves its typological vision of spiritual oneness by transcending the sensual world and deferring the problem of actually coping with earthly experience.

In order to accommodate rather than transcend fallen experience, Spenser shifts the basis of his allegory and uses the figure of the Hermaphrodite to substantiate that shift. In Book I the word of the text is grounded typologically in the Word of God.[9] The hero learns to see through the apparent otherness of both Divine truth and his own sensuality as he overcomes the dual illusions of self-sufficiency and objectivity. The heroic reader receives an analogous education in reading typologically as he or she learns to negotiate the complexities of Book I and to understand the spiritual truth that underlies the hero's epic wandering.[10] Through the otherness of its female hero Book III focuses on what was peripheral to the typological vision of Book I and brings to center stage the problems of making sense of, rather than transcending, sensual experience and of fashioning rather than rediscovering a self. Book III reasserts the role of the reader in making meaning and emphasizes the uncertainty that results when allegory is conceived equally as a way of reading and a way of writing, as an enterprise shared by poet and reader.[11] Instead of training the reader to discover pre-determined truth, Spenser emphasizes how precariously meaning is created out of uncertainty and ignorance in the fallen world. Book I attests to the absolute authority of divine truth and shows how that truth is given to faith alone. When in Book III Spenser turns to the question of making sense of the fallen world, he grounds his allegory on an epistemology of learned ignorance, rather than one of authoritarian certitude, since truth is infinite and human understanding limited. Thus Spenser rejects Platonic, authoritarian epistemology, which considers who is the best judge and what is the origin of authority, for a proto-scientific epistemology in the tradition of Cusanus, Erasmus, and Montaigne, which treats knowledge as an evolutionary process and focuses on how a given judgment can be tested.[12]

Spenser's allusions to Ovid's myth of the Hermaphrodite (*Met.* 4. 285–388), in the middest of Book I and at the conclusion of Book III, define the shift from the typological allegory of Book I to the creative moralizing of Book III. The Ovidian myth befits the task since it addresses the specific issue of making sense of sensual experience deferred from Book I to Book III. Ovid tells the story of the naive youth Hermaphroditus, child of Hermes and Aphrodite, who rejects the advances of the nymph Salmacis. Salmacis pursues him into the pool of which she is tutelary spirit and, with the aid of divine intervention, is united to the recalcitrant young man. Hermaphroditus sees himself transformed into half a man [semimarem] and curses the fountain, so that anyone drinking from its waters will likewise become effeminate.

Ovid offers a myth of sexual identity in which the formal definition of manhood is set in paradoxical opposition to the active experience of it. Ovid's story presents a hermeneutical gap between a character's understanding of his own experience and what the narration of that experience conveys to the reader. Ostensibly, the myth of the Hermaphrodite defines the boundaries of manhood negatively, by Hermaphroditus' loss of shape and by the otherness of the female figure with whom he merges. At the same time, however, the sequence of events composing Hermaphroditus' loss of masculine shape presents an unmistakable, if parodic, representation of sexual intercourse. The potential double meaning of words such as "perstat" [stands firm], "mollita" [soft], and "mollescat" [become soft or effeminate] point up the gap between understanding of his experience and what his story can signify. Ovid describes Hermaphroditus' vision of his transformation, "fecisse videt mollitaque in illis / membra" (4.381–82), which can be rendered "and he saw that his members had become soft there" (Lewis-Short, s.v. "mollio" I.II; "membrum" I) or, following Miller's translation, "that his limbs had become enfeebled there."[13] Although Hermaphroditus gives an implicitly moral interpretation to his physical transformation—he has become weak and effeminate—the physical suggestions of post coital flaccidity indicate a physiological interpretation of his experience. Ovid reveals the nature of the duplicity when he finally summarizes the hidden cause of the fountain's reputation, the cause that the myth was proffered to explain, "motus uterque parens nati rata verba biformis / fecit et incesto fontem medicamine tinxit" (4.387–88). [His parents heard the prayer of their two-formed son and charged the waters with uncanny power.] Ovid plays "uterque parens . . . rata verba . . . fecit," which can be rendered "each of his parents fulfilled his wish" or, literally, "each of his parents made his words xed" (Lewis-Short, s.v."reor" II.B.2) against "nati biformis" [of their two-formed son].[14] On the one hand, words have the power to determine Hermaphroditus' form. Insofar as they ratify and make permanent limitations of understanding, words reify the hero's sexual inexperience and thereby create a monster: the Hermaphrodite. On the other, Hermaphroditus is more truly biform than he realizes. He is both an emblem of emasculation and an image of male sexuality; Hermaphroditus understands his transformed shape wholly as a sign of emasculation because he naively considers his body solely as a physical form and not at all as an instrument of sense experience. He presupposes that he can see himself objectively as he emphasizes the powers of the one parent—Hermes, god of language—over the other—Aphrodite, goddess of love. From our wider perspective, we can see the Hermaphrodite as a biform sign in which arbitrary semiological difference plays against sexual difference. The "he-she" hermaphrodite is neither genuinely androgynous nor genuinely a boundary figure: it is arbitrarily classed with "she." As far as Hermaphroditus is concerned, the critical difference is not he or she, but he or not-he; not male versus female, but male versus not-male. In so drawing the boundaries, Hermaphroditus excludes his own sexuality and effectively castrates himself.[15]

The Hermaphrodite is caught between the poles of language and desire. The myth suppresses Hermaphroditus' own desire by assigning it arbitrarily to the female. Hermaphroditus' sexual performance is presented as the object of Salmacis' desire rather than as an attribute of his own. The apparent formal unity of the Hermaphrodite's story excludes the sexual content of his experience. His concluding curse of the waters seems completely to fulfill the opening promise of an etiological explanation for the fountain. When, at Hermaphroditus' prayer, his parents invest the pool with the power to change any man who enters it into half-man, the narrator's initial pledge to tell the hidden cause of the fountain's enfeebling powers seems fully satisfied. Nevertheless, by slighting the questions raised during the course of the Hermaphrodite's story, Ovid diverts our attention from the interpretation of the protagonist's experience and from the protagonist's failure to make sense of the lineaments of gratified desire. The final curse, that anyone who enters the pool of Salmacis should emerge half-man, calls for the repetition of the protagonist's emasculation rather than inviting the retrospective understanding of his experience.

II

Ovid's myth reflects ironically on the powers of language. Naming things in ignorance multiplies entities needlessly and creates monsters. By misnaming his own desire, the Hermaphrodite seems to transform the universality of puberty into the anomaly of metamorphosis. Although the more sophisticated reader can see both aspects of his story, they remain unreconciled. On the one hand, Hermaphroditus' identity was not a riddle the hero could have guessed to save his manhood; he is doomed by the perverse twists of Ovid's story. On the other, in coupling with Salmacis, whatever divine assistance he receives and whatever interpretation he places on the experience, the Hermaphrodite raises the question of whether it might be possible to outperform one's own language.

As Spenser adapts Ovid's myth to accompany the shift in his allegory, he focuses on the relation of self to other by means of which Ovid defines Hermaphroditus' failure to make sense of experience. In the typological universe of Book I, where Truth is given, but not to the senses, otherness is seen as an illusion. In Book III, which treats what is accessible to the senses but is not absolutely certain, otherness is part of what it means to be human.

At the center of Book I, Spenser revises Ovid's myth of the Hermaphrodite in order to emphasize the moral component of the Redcrosse Knight's experience over the merely physical and to define the hero's identity as his moral self. For this reason, although Duessa is seductive, she is neither primarily responsible for the knight's fall nor the immediate agent of retribution. The knight is deceived by the witch because he fails to understand his own sensual nature and he is punished by the giant Orgoglio, who is both an earthquake, sign of divine anger, and an ambulatory erection, image of the hero's own sensuality.[16]

Spenser separates the Ovidian paradox—that what Hermaphroditus experiences as the loss of manhood can also be regarded as male sexual performance—into moral and physical components. The cause of the enfeebling property of the fountain from which Redcrosse drinks is distinguished from its effect on the knight. Ovid's "causa latet, vis est, notissima fontis" (4.287) [The cause is hidden; but the enfeebling powers of the fountain is well known] becomes:

The cause was this: One day when *Phoebe* fayre
With all her band was following the chace,
This Nymph, quite tyr'd with heat of scorching ayre
Sat downe to rest in middest of the race:
The goddesse wroth gan fowly her disgrace,
And bad the waters, which from her did flow,
Be such as she her selfe was then in place
Thenceforth her waters waxed dull and slow,
And all that drunke thereof, did faint and feeble grow.
(I.vii.5)

Ovid's erotic myth of the Hermaphrodite purports to reveal the hidden cause. The cause that Spenser here provides derives from a mythographic tradition that interprets the nymph Salmacis as an emblem of moral laziness.[17] No reference to the erotic aspect of the myth occurs until Redcrosse actually drinks from the stream; his reaction recalls, in part, another mythographic tradition, which holds that the fountain of Salmacis is aphrodisiac, promoting impotence through sexual overindulgence.[18] The Redcrosse Knight is surprised by sexuality, but his sin is the moral loss he brings from the House of Pride.

In Ovid's myth of the Hermaphrodite the false closure of the promise of an etiological explanation at the opening, and the explanatory curse at the conclusion, suppresses the punning sexual content of the protagonist's experience. In Spenser's revision repressed desire returns with a vengeance, as Orgoglio. Throughout his errancy the Redcrosse Knight has been naively confident in himself and in the evidence of his senses and inattentive to his surroundings in their relationship to himself: he understands neither how his feelings cloud his perception nor how external nature gives back projections of his own human nature. In return for his heedlessness, he is assaulted by a sense experience. Nonetheless, he survives his Pyrrhic defeat by Orgoglio because his fall is grounded typologically in Christ's redemption of fallen man. Prince Arthur rescues the Redcrosse Knight by violently demystifying Orgoglio: "That huge great body, which the Gyaunt bore, / Was vanisht quite, and of that monstrous mas / Was nothing left, but like an emptie bladder was" (I.viii.24). The monstrous allegorical figure disappears, leaving nothing behind but a simile. But Redcrosse remains, wasting away, "the chearelesse man" (I.viii.43) in both appearance and feeling (*OED*, s.v. "cheer" 1, 2, 3, 4). Orgoglio's defeat is an Ovidian joke that plays unstable language against insecure sexuality: as a purely rhetorical figure, Orgoglio has no more independent physical existence than an erection *post coitum*. But the Redcrosse Knight's manhood is not exhausted by the disappearance of Orgoglio. As a man, he is the pattern for physiological tropes as well as the image of something greater than his mere physical being. Orgoglio's destruction educates the Redcrosse Knight morally because it figures the emptiness of pride. Redcrosse experiences the loss that his physical and spiritual sins bring about, and is redeemed through that experience of loss.

III

The identity of St. George, the ploughman knight and destined dragonslayer, is grounded in Providential history. The presence of the Briton princess in Faerieland, dressed in armor appropriated from the Saxon queen Angela, is more of an impromptu self-creation.[19] When, at the opening of Book III, the narrator gleefully reveals that the knight who has just unhorsed Guyon is, contrary to appearance, really a girl, he sets out the principal ways in which differences—sexual difference and the difference between self and other—characterize Britomart's identity:

> Euen the famous *Britomart* it was,
>> Whom staunge aduenture did from *Britaine* fet,
>> To seeke her louer (loue farre sought alas,)
> Whose image she had seene in *Venus* looking glas.
>> (III.i.8)

Britomart seeks both lover and love; she seeks both a person and an emotion. The physical space marked out by Britomart's quest is given significance by the desire which animates her, just as her erotic pursuit is shaped by the physical absence of its object: she seeks a full presence that is not strictly Platonic. In pursuing her quest, Britomart is fetched far, "far fet" being Puttenham's term for metalepsis, or the substitution by metonymy of one figurative sense for another.[20] For Britomart, the self is based on figuration; her identity is the product both of self-fashioning and bodily determination. In Book III identity is put at risk by the assertion of sexual difference and the re-inclusion of sexuality. Britomart's quest for Artegall involves braving the hermeneutic gap between self and other; Book III defines reading as an act of courage, with both moral and sexual connotations of the word "courage" relevant to the hermeneutic enterprise.

While Britomart's enchanted spear lends symbolic (and practical) potency to her quest, the Martial Maid's courage is not simply the product of one phallic symbol. Rather, her chastity itself is the female equivalent of the Hermaphrodite's manhood. In fashioning a female hero, one who dons armor in pursuit of love, Spenser moralizes and transforms Ovid's paradox that the triumph of Hermaphroditus' manhood is also its loss into the paradoxical giving and withholding of the self that defines chastity in Book III. The translation of Ovidian manhood to Spenserian chastity is playful but not wholly capricious. Spenser's rendition reasserts the sexual difference that Ovid's myth slights in favor of arbitrary semiological difference. The Hermaphrodite loses his manhood in the irreconcilable gap between the givens of his existence and what he is able to understand. By naming desire in ignorance, he creates with his language an icon of his own want of experience. In contrast, Britomart fashions herself as a woman and a hero by braving the unknown. She undertakes a quest, in pursuit of a man she has never met, who she cannot be sure actually exists, and thereby transforms herself from a love-sick girl into an active heroine.

The risk Britomart faces as she fashions herself as the knight of chastity appears as Narcissism. In flashback we learn that Gardante's arrow betokens the purely visual source of Britomart's love for Artegall, whose image she has seen in Venus' looking glass. From the first, her love is beset by the danger of self-delusion: Britomart does not know whether she has fallen in love with a man, or, Narcissus-like, with the image of her own fantasy. It is appropriate that Britomart overcome the specter of Narcissism as she ventures out to realize an identity, since Ovid's myth ironically opposes security and self-knowledge. Tiresias prophesies that the boy will prosper, "si se non noverit" (3.348), if he doesn't know himself. Ovid exploits the paradox that although Narcissus' ultimate recognition of himself in the beloved reflection destroys him with the despair of unrequitable love, he initially fell victim to that deadly passion because he did not know himself when he encountered his own image. For Narcissus, self-knowledge and self-ignorance are both inescapably deadly. Tiresias' cryptic warning, in fact, conceals the curse of the rejected Echo.[21]

In the traditional interpretations of Narcissus that Spenser would have inherited, the Ovidian paradox of self-knowledge and self-ignorance is disentangled into two separate problems of being and of perception. Either Narcissus is treated as an icon of moral failure, of self-love, and of materialism, or he is considered the hapless victim of a mistake.[22]

Britomart overcomes the danger of Narcissism and fashions herself into a moralized version of the Hermaphrodite as she resists the tempting security of *a priori* certainty to risk performing as a Martial Maid.[23] When Britomart and her nurse Glauce debate the nature of Britomart's infatuation, the terms of their debate reunite the moral and epistemological aspects of the Narcissus tradition and suggest the movement from Narcissus to Hermaphrodite in Britomart's self-fashioning. Glauce offers a classic list of sexual monsters by way of contrast to Britomart's healthy passion. Britomart counters that, worse than any in Glauce's catalogue, she is a decadent version of Narcissus: at least Myrrha, Biblis, and Pasiphae satisfied their desire, however monstrous; she vainly loves a shadow.

The two women argue from opposite traditions of interpreting the Narcissus myth. Britomart interprets Narcissus' fault to be that he mistakingly loves a shadow, Glauce that he ignobly loves himself. Nonetheless, they achieve common ground between moral and epistemological interpretation because both parties concede genuinely radical moral value to reality. In her high-minded outrage, Britomart asserts that sodomy is better than nothing. In quelling Britomart's worry, Glauce urges the girl to strive for satisfaction and avows, "To compasse thy desire, and find that loved knight" (III.ii.46). Glauce's attitude toward Britomart's distress combines a cheerful faith in objective reality—"No shadow, but a bodie hath in powre" (III.ii.45)—with a strong concern for Britomart's psychological well-being. Her initial response, "why make ye such Monster of your mind?" (III.ii.40), implies both that Britomart's troubles are largely the product of her imagination and that, in condemning her love, Britomart wrongs her own mind, making it out to be a monster. Unlike Hermaphroditus, who multiplies entities and truncates a self in making a monster out of his mind, Britomart fashions herself through loving another.

IV

The Martial Maid's victory over the Narcissistic Marinell confirms the movement from infamous Narcissus to moralized Hermaphrodite. Marinell's life story is a Spenserian revision of Ovid's myth of Narcissus.[24] Tiresias' prophecy that Narcissus will prosper if he does not know himself becomes Proteus' prophecy that "of a woman he should haue much ill, / A virgin strange and stout him should dismay, or kill" (III.iv.25). While Tiresias' warning, apparently contingent on circumstances, conceals Narcissus' inescapable fate, Proteus' prophecy of seemingly inevitable misfortune is transformed by the play of double senses into the needless defeat and ensuing salvation of Marinell. The false closure of the prophecy plays against the self-fulfilling nature of the sexual fears it secretly embodies: a man who gives himself over to fear of women has little to lose to them. Marinell's response to the prophecy, to avoid danger from women by waiving his manhood and refraining from all contact with women, is precisely what makes him vulnerable to Britomart. The narrator's comment "This was that woman, this that deadly wound" (III.iv.28) makes it seem that Marinell's doom is both final and inevitable. Yet on the one hand, he has quite a future ahead of him, and, on the other, Marinell is dismayed by Britomart's spear precisely because of his virginal refusal to be dismayed in a less bellicose sense.[25] The apparent closure of Marinell's life story, whereby Britomart's attack fulfills Proteus' prophecy, is subverted by the possibility of multiple interpretation. As in Ovid's myth of the Hermaphrodite, the appearance of closure is achieved by the exclusion of desire, and that excluded desire becomes property of the female. Marinell's mother chooses the interpretation of Proteus' prophecy according to her own self-interested desire to keep her son boy eternal. Her fear—"Least his too haughtie hardines might reare / Some hard mishap, in hazard of his life" (III.iv.24)—seems at least as much a dread of having her son reach sexual maturity as it is worry about his health and safety. The bad faith of a castrating mother, who wants to reduce her son to the "Deare image of [her] selfe" (III.iv.36), determines Cymoent's interpretation of Proteus' words, which, in turn, affects the fulfillment of his prophecy: "So weening to haue armed him, she did quite disarme" (III.iv.27). His mother has induced him to secure the integrity of his being by fleeing from love, only to discover too late that "they that loue do liue" (III.iv.37). Marinell is nearly destroyed by Proteus' prophecy because he fails to understand it as a call to courage, both in reading his fate and living his life.

V

Book III presents the unavoidable battle for interpretation. Britomart's final adventure of Book III is to rescue Amoret from the art of Busirane. She proves herself as the knight of chastity through a subtle combination of martial prowess and exegetical skill. Her response to the enigmatic inscription *Be bold* epitomizes the way in which Britomart fashions herself through heroic reading. Although Britomart is unable to explicate the inscription, undiscouraged she obeys the command; she makes sense of the words *Be bold* by being bold and entering the doorway over which the words are written. In her response Britomart both figures and finds meaning; she resolves the Hermaphrodite's dilemma by reconciling modes of expression with modes of understanding, and by spontaneous performance into accord with linguistic givens. When Britomart boldly passes into the next room, she gives the inscription a particular meaning it did not have before her particular act. She obeys the command to be bold, yet in so obeying, she asserts her own resoluteness.

Busirane's art is the antithesis of Spenser's poetics in Book III. Instead of fashioning readers Busirane abuses them by trying to write the act of interpretation out of the story: the reader sees representations of Cupid decorating the House of Busirane and is tempted to accept the figure uncritically, without realizing that to represent desire as Cupid is to impose an interpretation on desire. As Busirane's artworks become increasingly three-dimensional and life-like—from the tapestries and the idol, to the relief figures and the broken swords and spears of mighty conquerors, to the Masque of Cupid—they become not more perfect imitations of reality, but more perfect spoils.[26] The art of Busirane reifies desire by naming it "Cupid" and reduces the human body to an arbitrary sign of Cupid's power.

The final battle of Book III pits Britomart, the champion of chastity, against Busirane, the perpetrator of abuse. At issue in Britomart's rescue of Amoret from the power of Cupid is how meaning is to be determined. By imprisoning Amoret in the Masque of Cupid, Busirane attempts to be supreme arbiter of meaning.[27] By thwarting his attempt, Britomart reaffirms the view of allegory as a shared enterprise figured by the Hermaphroditic embrace of the lovers at the conclusion of the 1590 *Faerie Queene*.

Busirane seemingly violates Amoret's physical integrity as he attempts to usurp the steadfast love that is her chastity. But as Britomart discovers, Amoret's wound is an illusion. The version of love named Cupid denies sexual difference in making both men and women Cupid's spoil. Like Hermaphroditus, Amoret suffers spoliation because desire is misnamed. Both are disfigured by a system of signs that repudiates bodily integrity. The Hermaphrodite emasculates himself by misreading his metamorphosed body; in distinguishing male from not-male, he denies physical sexuality and consigns desire to the female other. Amoret is assaulted by the art of Busirane, who attempts to redefine her chastity in order to violate it. Amoret's torment, her heart drawn forth from the orifice riven in her breast, transfixed with a deadly dart, evokes both the literalized alienation of her affections and the graphic penetration of her body. By misrepresenting Amoret's chastity in reductively physical terms, Busirane seeks to deny her desire. In this case, however, desire is not mistakenly assigned to the female in an inadvertent self-castration, but deliberately suppressed by Busirane in an attempt to violate both Amoret and the audience. He fails, however, in his attempt to impose meaning covertly on his unresisting victim. "The cruell steel, which thrild [Amoret's] dying hart" (III.xii.38) thrills her heart in the sense of "to pierce" (*OED*, s.v. "thrill" I.1.), but her heart is thrilled with desire (*OED*, s.v. "thrill" II.4) only when she is reunited with Scudamour.

Britomart thwarts Busirane's design when she discovers his authorship of the masque and reveals the enchanter "Figuring straunge characters of his art" (III.xii.31). Although the pageant seems intended for Britomart in that she is the only spectator, Britomart is also clearly destined to be Busirane's most violent critic. For Britomart, the Masque of Cupid is not just a spectacle but the scene of battle in her quest to liberate Amoret from Amor and define her own chastity.[28]

VI

At the conclusion of the 1590 *Faerie Queene*, both Britomart and Spenser's reader are onlookers. Both Britomart and the epic reader bear witness to the union of Amoret and Scudamour as part of their own self-fashioning in virtuous and gentle discipline. Both are challenged to be chaste readers, to make right use of poetry as of sexuality, to undertake humanist not hedonist imitation:

> Had ye them seene, ye would haue surely thought,
>   That they had beene that faire *Hermaphrodite*,
>   Which that rich *Romane* of white marble wrought,
>   And in his costly Bath caused to bee site:
>   So seemd those two, as growne together quite,

> That *Britomart* halfe enuying their blesse,
> Was much empassioned in her gentle sprite,
> And to her selfe oft wisht like happinesse
> In vaine she wisht, that fate n'ould let her yet possesse.
>
> (III.cancelled stanza.iv)

Half envying their bliss, Britomart is moved by what she sees to pursue her own love. The reader is challenged to imitate Britomart in fashioning a self in virtuous and gentle discipline rather than emulating the nameless Roman in trivializing art as a mere erotic fetish. The complex reference to the Hermaphrodite alludes to Ovid's text at the same time that it subtly calls attention to an absence. The image is not a direct reference to a Hermaphrodite, nor to a statue of the Hermaphrodite, nor is it even a simple metaphor likening the embracing Amoret and Scudamour to a Hermaphrodite. Spenser refers to a specific statue that is not present in the scene he is describing: the reader, were he or she observing the scene directly and not reading about it, would have mistaken the fictional characters for the statue. So alerted, we are not likely to overlook the fictiveness of the final embrace and to treat the conclusion as mere romantic wish-fulfillment. The statue of the Hermaphrodite, set as it is in the Roman's bath, forms a strange domestic tableau of the Ovidian myth. If the statue represents the metamorphosed Hermaphroditus, the bath itself must evoke the infamous fountain of Salmacis whose waters caused men to become effeminate. The reader is challenged to moralize art, to engage the text in a process of sense-making, rather than to reify art, to repeat the Hermaphrodite's act and fulfill his curse by avoiding the role of interpreter.

The picture of chaste love presented for our education is not the traditional image of two becoming one but the two lovers becoming a new entity. Amoret and Scudamour are not the Hermaphrodite because their embrace does not depend upon the effacement of sexual difference and the disfigurement of bodily form:

> Lightly he clipt her twixt his armes twaine,
> And streightly did embrace her body bright,
> Her body, late the prison of sad paine,
> Now the sweet lodge of loue and deare delight:
> But she faire Lady ouercommen quight
> Of huge affection, did in pleasure melt,
> And in sweete rauishment pourd out her spright:
> No word they spake, nor earthly thing they felt,
> But like two senceles stocks in long embracement dwelt.
>
> (III.cancelled stanza.iii)

Amoret's body is first a prison, then a lodge, then both lovers dwell in mutually defined embracement. Her body is metamorphosed, not to the monstrous form of the Hermaphrodite, but to an instrument of mutual pleasure. Considered solely as a dividing barrier, the body is a prison, painfully imprisoning experience. The prison is transformed into a lodge as the body is considered an instrument of sense experience. The lovers' union is a mutually defined relationship—not a monster—which accounts for sexual difference and sexual desire.

Replacing Hermaphroditic denial of sexual difference is an androgynous reversal of roles. In an inversion of traditional, Petrarchan imagery, Scudamour is compared to a deer "that greedily embayes / In the cool soile, after long thirstinesse" (III.cancelled stanza.ii). Amoret "in sweete rauishment pourd out her spright," a transformed allusion to the Redcrosse Knight "pourd out in loosnesse on the grassy grownd" (I.vii.7) with Duessa. This ravishment is not the violation offered by Busirane, but physical and emotional transport, which Spenser has rendered with great circumspection. The simile "like two senceles stocks" suggests both that the lovers have gone beyond earthly things and that the onlooker is not privy to their experience: seen from without, the embracing couple appears like two senseless stocks, whether through earthly transcendence or mere senselessness the observer is perhaps left to ponder. Saved from the spoils of Cupid, the lovers "Each other of loues bitter fruit despoile" (III.cancelled stanza.v), while the reader, like Britomart, is left with the quest of making sense unfinished.

Notes

1. All quotations from Spenser taken from *The Poetical Works of Edmund Spenser* (Oxford, 1909), ed. J. C. Smith. In *Endlesse Worke: Spenser and the Structures of Discourse* (Baltimore, Md., 1981), pp. 124–26, Jonathan Goldberg raises provocative questions about whether one can assign a real historical name to these lines at all. On the identification with Burleigh, see Thomas H. Cain, *Praise in "The Faerie Queene"* (Lincoln, Neb., 1978), pp. 164–65; *The Faerie Queene* (London, 1977), ed. A. C. Hamilton, p. 426n; and Anne K. Tuell, "The Original End of *Faerie Queene*, Book III," *Modern Language Notes*, 36 (1921), 309–11. On the Hermaphrodite, see C. S. Lewis, *The Allegory of Love: A Study in Medieval Tradition* (London, 1936), p. 344; Thomas P. Roche, *The Kindly Flame: A Study of the Third and Fourth Books of Spenser's "Faerie Queene"* (Princeton, N.J., 1964), pp. 133–36; Donald Cheney, "Spenser's Hermaphrodite and the 1590 *Faerie Queene*," *PMLA*, 87 (1972), 192–200; and A. R. Cirillo, "The Fair Hermaphrodite: Love-Union in the Poetry of Donne and Spenser," *Studies in English Literature*, 9 (1969), 81–95.

2. In "Placement 'In the Middest' in *The Faerie Queene*," *Papers on Language and Literature*, 5 (1969), 227–34, Michael Baybak, Paul Delany, and A. Kent Hieatt demonstrate the importance of the phrase "in the middest" and the significance of midpoints in Books I, II, and III of *The Faerie Queene*. One might, in this regard, note the contrast between the *mons veneris* in middest Book III and the phallus in Book I.

3. For a discussion of the sexual allegory of the Orgoglio episode, including the allusion to Ovid, see John W. Schroeder, "Spenser's Erotic Drama: The Orgoglio Episode," *ELH*, 29 (1962), 140–59.

4. See Goldberg, *passim*.

5. For a subtle treatment of the motif error-*errare*, see Patricia A. Parker, *Inescapable Romance: Studies in the Poetics of a Mode* (Princeton, N.J., 1979), pp. 54–77.

6. Mark Rose, *Spenser's Art: A Companion to Book I of "The Faerie Queene"* (Cambridge, Mass., 1975), p. 5.

7. Paul J. Alpers, *The Poetry of "The Faerie Queene"* (Princeton, 1967), pp. 370–71; Judith H. Anderson, *The Growth of a Personal Voice: "Piers Plowman" and "The Faerie Queene"* (New Haven, Conn., 1976), pp. 98–113; and Isabel MacCaffrey, *Spenser's Allegory: The Anatomy of Imagination* (Princeton, N.J., 1976), pp. 133–52.

8. Hamilton annotates Una's father's injunction to the Redcrosse Knight "Soone as the terme of those six yeares shall cease, / Ye then shall hither backe returne againe, / The marriage to accomplish vowd betwixt you twain" (I.xii.19) with the Geneva gloss to Rev. 19.7, "God made Christ the bridgrome of his Church at the beginning, and at the last day it shalbe fully accomplished when we shall be joyned with our head" and notes with regard to "accomplish" the distinction between "wedlock which is contracted or performed . . . and completed, i.e. consummated," p. 158.

9. Maureen Quilligan, *The Language of Allegory: Defining the Genre* (Ithaca, N.Y., 1979), pp. 97–155.

10. On the education of the reader, see Maureen Quilligan, *Milton's Spenser: the Politics of Reading* (Ithaca, N.Y., 1983), pp. 19–78; MacCaffrey, pp. 81–103; and Rose, *passim.*

11. On the separate allegorical traditions of reading and writing, see Joseph Anthony Mazzeo, *Varieties of Interpretation* (Notre Dame, Ind., 1978), pp. 47–69. Spenser announces a revisionary approach to the two traditions with the first stanza of *The Faerie Queene*. The word "moralize" subtly disrupts the first Alexandrine, "Fierce warres and faithfull loues shall moralize my song" (Proeme.i). The surprise of discovering that "fierce warres and faithfull loues" are the subject of the verb "moralize" rather than the object of the epic verb "I sing" leads the reader to recognize that "moralize" is used in a novel way. In this context, "moralize" cannot refer primarily to an act of interpretation—the standard idiomatic use of the word before Spenser put it into his epic invocation—but seems to signify "providing subject matter for moral interpretation." Spenser's opening subverts the distinction to be made between the act of writing and the act of interpretation and the distinction to be made between a given subject matter and the treatment of that subject matter by both writer and reader. Moralizing—making meaning—entails the mutual interaction of writer and reader.

12. Sir Karl Popper, in *Conjectures and Refutations: The Growth of Scientific Knowledge* (1965; New York, 1968), pp. 15–17, identifies an epistemological tradition of learned ignorance, originating with Xenophanes, Democritus, and Socrates (of the *Apology* rather than the *Meno*) and revived by Nicolas of Cusa, Erasmus, and Montaigne. For a discussion of Cusa's doctrine of learned ignorance and its implications for Renaissance notions of conjecture and creativity, see Ronald Levao, *Renaissance Minds and Their Fictions: Cusanus, Sidney, Shakespeare* (Berkeley, Cal., 1985), pp. 3–96.

13. All quotations from Ovid are taken from the Loeb edition, as are other translations unless otherwise indicated.

14. Ovid also plays "uterque parens" [each of his parents—my trans.] against "neutrumque et utrumque videntur" [They seemed neither, and yet both] (4.379). The parents' oneness contrasts with their son's sense of noneness, of being neutered. One might consider, in this regard, James Nohrnberg's observations in *The Analogy of "The Faerie Queene"* (Princeton, N.J., 1976), pp. 606–07, about the hermaphroditism of Spenser's couples: Scudamoret, Britomartegall, Osirisis, Paridellenore, Thamedway, and Claribellamour.

15. As Thomas Laqueur points out, in "Orgasm, Generation, and the Politics of Reproductive Biology," *Representations*, No. 14 (Spring 1986), 1–41, from classical antiquity to the eighteenth century, it was a medical commonplace that female reproductive organs were homologous with the male organs, differing hierarchically in perfection rather than absolutely in kind. On Renaissance medical theory of biological hermaphrodites, see Stephen Greenblatt,

"Fiction and Friction," in *Reconstructing Individualism: Autonomy, Individuality, and the Self in Western Thought*, ed. Thomas C. Heller, Morton Sosna, and David Wellbery (Stanford, 1986), pp. 30–52.

16. See S. K. Heninger, "The Orgoglio Episode in *The Faerie Queene*," *ELH*, 26 (1959), 171–87; Rose, pp. 91–92; and Schroeder, pp. 140–59.

17. Specifically, Arnolph d'Orleans (3.13); Ovide moralisé (4.2284–2311); Thomas Peend (B2v). See *Arnolfo d'Orleans: Un Cultore di Ovidio nel secolo xii*, ed. Fausto Ghisalberti, Memorie del R. Istituto Lombardo di scienze e lettere: Classe di lettere, scienze morale e storiche, 3rd ser. 15 (Milan, 1932); Cornelius de Boer, ed. *"Ovide moralisé:" poème du commencement quatorzième siècle*. Verhandelingen der koninklijke Akademie van Wetenschapen to Amsterdam Afdeeling Letterkunde 15, 21. (Amsterdam, 1915, 1920); and Thomas Peend, *The Pleasant Fable of Hermaphroditus and Salmacis with moral* (1565).

18. Specifically, Vitruvius, *De Architectura*, (2.100.8.12); Sextus Pompeius Festus, *De Verborum Significatione*, ed. Wallace M. Lindsay (Leipzig, 1913), p. 439; and Giraldi, *De Deiis Gentium*, in *Opera omnia* (Leyden, 1696), p. 181 D & E.

19. Compare Glauce's assurance to her charge that "Ne aught ye want, but skill, which practize small / Will bring, and shortly make you a mayd Martiall" (III.iii.53) to the upbringing of Britomart's literary predecessors, Camilla and Clorinda, who were suckled by tigresses and trained in arms from early childhood. One might note in this connection Popper's observation that, in an epistemology of learned ignorance, questions of validating knowledge take precedence over questions of the origin of human knowledge. He associates the quest for the origins of knowledge with a Platonic authoritarianism, whereby one tends to ask who is the best judge and what is the source of his authority, rather than how can a given judgment be tested, pp. 3–30. Significantly, in the proem to Book II Spenser seems to defend his fiction against the charge that it is the painted forgery of an idle brain rather than matter of just recollection, not, as John Guillory suggests in *Poetic Authority: Spenser, Milton, and Literary History* (New York, 1983), p. 37, by associating allegory with *anamnesis*, but by shifting grounds away from the Platonic theory of recollection. Spenser defends his allegory by asserting the growth of knowledge as the corollary of human ignorance and cites two areas in which Elizabethan knowledge had grown spectacularly: geographic exploration and astronomy. Spenser asks rhetorically, "Who euer heard of th'Indian *Peru?*" (II.P.ii) and "What if in euery other starre vnseene / Of other worldes he [Spenser's judge] happily should heare?" (II.P.iii).

20. George Puttenham, *The Arte of English Poesie*, gen. ed. Hilton Landry (rpt. Kent, O., 1970), p. 193.

21. John Brenkman, "Narcissus in the Text," *Georgia Review*, 30 (1976), 293–327.

22. Among commentators who consider Narcissus as an icon of moral failure are Arnolphe d'Orleans (3.5–6); John of Garland *Integumenta* (2.165), ed. Fausto Ghisalberti (Messina, 1933); Giovanni del Virgilio (3.6), ed. Ghisalberti (Florence, 1933); the author of the *Ovide moralisé*, (3, 1904–1964); and Giovanni Boccaccio, *Genealogie Deorum Gentilium Libri* (7.59), ed. Vincenzo Romano (Bari, 1951). Commentaries that interpret Narcissus as the victim of a mistake include that attributed to Lactantius Placidus (3.5.44–45), ed. Augustus van Staveren (Leyden, 1742); and those of the first two Vatican mythographers (I: 185.11.21–22; II: 180.11.19–20), ed. G. H. Bode (Belli, 1834).

23. There is precedent for this association of Narcissus with the Hermaphrodite. As Nohrnberg points out, in his discussion of the associations between Narcissus and the Hermaphrodite in Book III, the two stories in Ovid show much similarity (p. 474). Poets before Spenser have exploited the potential analogy. In *Reson and Sensuallyte*, ed. Ernst Sieper (The Early English Text Society, Extra Series 84 [1901], rpt. New York [1965]), John Lydgate compares the well of Narcissus to the well of the Hermaphrodite, which is "more perilouse a thousand foled" (3803–3896). The sixteenth-century French poet Pontus de Tyard writes poems about Narcissus and the Hermaphrodite to be illustrated by companion-piece paintings. See de Tyard, *Oeuvres Complètes*, ed. John Lapp (Paris: Didier, 1966).

24. See Nohrnberg, pp. 431–32, 645–46.

25. For a discussion of the pun on "dismay," see Schroeder, p. 149.

26. For specific references to spoils and despoiling, see *F.Q.* III.xi.45; III.xi.52; III.xii.20; III.xii.22; and III.xii.cancelled 5.

27. C. S. Lewis first identified the masque of Cupid with courtly love in *The Allegory of Love*, pp. 340–44. Since then, the nature of Busirane's abuse has been the subject of much critical debate. A useful summary of the main positions is given by Hugh Maclean in *Edmund Spenser's Poetry* (2nd ed.; New York, 1982), pp. 670–85.

28. For a different view, see A. Leigh De Neef, *Spenser and the Motives of Metaphor* (Durham, N.C., 1982), pp. 157–73.

"In liuing colours and right hew": The Queen of Spenser's Central Books

JUDITH H. ANDERSON

Even in the 1590 *Faerie Queene*, Spenser's reverence for Queen Elizabeth is accompanied by a cautionary awareness of the temptations and dangers of queenly power and by a complementary awareness of the cost—the denial or exclusion of human possibilities—an ennobling Idea exacts of its bearer. The one is evident in the House of Pride and Cave of Mammon, and the other in the treatment of Belphoebe. The attainments of Una, the "goodly maiden Queene," are threatened demonically by their perversion in Lucifera, the "mayden Queene" of Pride, and parodied again in Book II by the verbally reiterative image of Philotime.[1] Belphoebe, beautiful, inspiring, and goddesslike, is momentarily locked in comic encounter with Braggadocchio in Book II, an encounter which, though it leaves the worth of her ideal essentially untarnished, resembles another famous encounter between honor and instinct: between Hotspur's extravagant idealism, his "easy leap, / To pluck bright honor from the pale-fac'd moon," and Falstaff's unenlightened but earthy sense: "Can honor set to a leg?"[2] Specifically aligned with Queen Elizabeth in the Letter to Ralegh and in the proem to Book III, the chaste Belphoebe is in human terms both an aspiration and an extreme, paradoxically both more and less nearly complete than ordinary mortals.

In the 1596 *Faerie Queene*, while still persuaded of the value of the queenly ideal, Spenser is more disillusioned—or at least less illusioned—with the real Queen and her court. In the notorious proem to Book IV, he complains openly of misconceived criticisms of *The Faerie Queene* emanating from Elizabeth's court and goes so far as to summon help from Eros for "that sacred Saint my soueraigne Queene." He urges " *Venus* dearling doue," a benign Cupid, to "Sprinckle" the Queen's "heart, and haughtie courage soften, / That she may hearke to loue, and read this lesson often." Thus introduced by hope for improvement in queenly attitudes and by implied criticism of her present ones, Books IV to VI are bedeviled by recurrent images of revilement and public infamy: Ate, Slander, Malfont, Envy,

From *Poetic Traditions of the English Renaissance*, edited by Maynard Mack and George deForest Lord, © 1982 by Yale University. All rights reserved. Reprinted by permission of Yale University Press.

Detraction, the Blatant Beast. Most of these glance at the Queen, the Queen's court, or events impossible to dissociate from the Queen without transforming her into a mythic ideal isolated from history—at best a hope or an unrealized promise but no longer, by any stretch of the epic imagination, a present reality. In the proem to Book VI—the beginning of *The Faerie Queene's* end—this is the route Spenser attempts, but with a trail of hesitation, bitterness, and painful reassessment still fresh behind him.

Despite recognition of the poet's cautionary awareness in Books I to III and despite his more open disappointment in Books IV to VI, we have been reluctant to admit their persistence and strength, especially as they touch the Queen. We rightly note the danger to a mere poet of criticizing his sovereign and the real power the cult of the Virgin Queen exerted over men's imaginations. Nothing in this paper denies these realities, but my argument considers them large designs in the poem's fabric rather than its whole cloth.

Reluctance to see the extent to which Spenser criticizes the Queen does him a particular disservice in Books III and IV. Here it obscures the relation of ideal or antique image to the present age, a relation of which the Queen is the measure throughout the poem, and thus it obscures the developing relation of Faerie to history and of fiction to life. Still more serious, to my mind, this reluctance leads us to pretend that the poet did not really mean certain lines or hear certain verbal ambiguities and, in short, was not fully sensitive to his own words or alert to their surrounding contexts.[3] My present undertaking is to examine several passages in Books III and IV that involve verbal cruxes, the Queen, and the relation of present age to antique image. These passages indicate that Spenser's depiction of the Queen's bright image is more complexly shaded in Book III than is generally acknowledged and is in Book IV more critical, perhaps shockingly so. In Book IV, something of the nightmare image of the slanderous Beast who bites "without regard of person or of time" at the end of Book VI is already present and implicates the Queen.

I

In the proem to Book III, the poet observes a distinction between present and past and between truth and Faerie image that is absent from the proems to Books I and II, and without them, its significance could easily pass unnoticed. In the first of these proems, the living Queen, "Great Lady of the greatest Isle," is a "Mirrour of grace and Maiestie diuine," and the poem is a reflection, in effect itself a mirror, of "that true glorious type" of the Queen. In the proem to Book II, despite poetic play about the location of Faerie, the Queen is the living reflection of the "antique Image," and so the poem, or Faerie image, is a "faire mirrhour" of her "face" and "realmes." The first two proems present one continuous, unbroken reflection: the Queen reflects Divinity; like the Queen herself, the poem reflects the glorious origins, person, and reign of the living Queen.

Referring to the Queen's face, realms, and ancestry, the final stanza of Proem II offers an apology for the antique Faerie image that is in fact a confident justification of it:

> The which O pardon me thus to enfold
> In couert vele, and wrap in shadowes light,
> That feeble eyes your glory may behold,
> Which else could not endure those beames bright,
> But would be dazled with exceeding light.

The dazzling brightness of the living Queen is enfolded in shadow to enlighten feeble eyes, enabling them to behold true glory. This veil reveals a single truth instead of obscuring it, and these shadows, unlike those in the second three books, do not splinter truth or transform its character. They do not make true glory truly fictive.

In the proem to Book III, the poem continues to be the Queen's mirror, and although she is now invited to view herself "In mirrours more then one"—that is, in Gloriana or in Belphoebe—both glasses are essentially virtuous and can be seen primarily as an outfolding of the good Queen rather than as a dispersion of her unity. But as I have noted elsewhere, in this proem the present embodiment also begins to vie with the antique image, living Queen with Antiquity, and, indeed, to challenge it.[4] Uneasy nuances (not quite tensions) cluster around the word "living." In order to perceive the fairest virtue, chastity in this case, one "Need but behold the pourtraict of her [the Queen's] hart, / If pourtrayed it might be by any liuing art." The poet continues, "But liuing art may not least part expresse, / Nor life-resembling pencill it can paint . . . Ne Poets wit, that passeth Painter farre." Then comes a plea for pardon that recalls the one in the second proem:

> But O dred Soueraine
> Thus farre forth pardon, sith that choicest wit
> Cannot your glorious pourtraict figure plaine
> That I in coloured showes may shadow it,
> And antique praises vnto present persons fit.

More opaque than the "shadowes light" of Proem II, these shadows testify to the poet's "want of words" and wit more than they serve the purpose of revelation. The poem here becomes a slightly compromised "coloured show" that can only shadow the Queen's "glorious pourtraict" and tailor antique praises to present persons, a "fit" that sounds neither so natural nor so close as the continuity of bright reflections in Proems I and II. The poem becomes the glass through which the living sovereign's true portrait is somewhat obscurely seen.

The difference in tone and emphasis between Proems II and III might, I suppose, be attributed to an unusually severe onset of the modesty topos or, that failing, to one of Spenser's regrettable catnaps, this time right on the threshold of Book III. But if these dismissals of particular significance were adequate, the lines that directly follow Spenser's apology for "coloured showes" and "antique praises" would positively resonate with his shameful snoring. They refer to the depiction of Queen Elizabeth in Sir Walter Ralegh's *Cynthia*: "But if in liuing colours, and right hew, / Your selfe you couet to see pictured, / Who can it doe more liuely, or more trew . . . ?" When Spenser thus sets the "liuing colours" and "right hew" of his sovereign, Queen Elizabeth, against his own "colourd showes" and "antique praises," he introduces into the poem a far-reaching distinction between life and antiquity, historical present and mythic past, current truth and Faerie image. Spenser himself glosses and simultaneously reinforces the startling phrases "liuing colours" and "right hew" two lines later: *living* colors are "liuely" or lifelike, and the *right* hue is true-to-life or, more simply, "trew."

Referring a true and lively picture of the Queen to Ralegh's *Cynthia*, Spenser is unlikely to have meant a picture that is merely realistic or unembellished by art. Ralegh's fragmentary *Ocean to Cynthia*, much of which relates to Ralegh's imprisonment in 1592, a disgrace subsequent to publication of Book III, is the best indication of *Cynthia*'s nature we have, and while Ralegh's voice in it is distinct, individual, and passionate, such highly artificial modes as the Petrarchan ("Such heat in Ize, such fier in frost") and the pastoral ("Vnfolde thy flockes and leue them to the feilds") are also much in evidence.[5] The nostalgic—indeed, the bereaved—employment of pastoral in *Ocean to Cynthia* suggests that the Shepherd of the Ocean's earlier versions of *Cynthia*, written in less desperate straits, might have been more conventional than less so.[6] When Spenser writes of the living colors and right hue of *Cynthia*, he implies a portrayal that is less hieratic and allegorical but more contemporary and personal than his own. Such a portrayal as Ralegh's might be less universal and more ephemeral, but it belongs more truly to time.

Spenser's reference to Ralegh certainly does not discredit the Faerie image but does limit its authority unless that image itself can be expanded to embrace life more closely. The third proem provides a particularly apt introduction to a book in which time and eternity or present age and ideal image are not so smoothly continuous. Nothing quite like the "heauenly noise / Heard sound through all the Pallace pleasantly" at the betrothal of Una—a noise like the voices of angels "Singing before th'eternall maiesty, / In their trinall triplicities on hye"—reverberates through Book III, and no one quite like the brilliantly winged angel who succors Guyon materializes to rescue its heroes. In fact, the closest we get to an angel in this book is

Timias' illusion that Belphoebe is one when he wakens from his swoon to find her ministering to his wounds: "Mercy deare Lord . . . what grace is this," he asks, "To send thine Angell from her bowre of blis, / To comfort me in my distressed plight?" (v. 35). And even he adds on second thought, "Angell, or Goddesse do I call thee right?" thereby echoing Virgil's famous lines from Aeneas' meeting with Venus in the guise of Diana's maiden and avouching his perception that this angelic illusion originates in a more worldly pantheon than Una's "trinall triplicities."[7]

A blushing Belphoebe disclaims the angelic or godly status Timias imputes to her and declares herself simply a maid and "mortall wight" (36). Unfortunately her declaration is exactly what Timias might have longed, but should never have been allowed, to hear, for he falls irrevocably and irremediably in love with her. Belphoebe not only denies him a reciprocal love but also fails to comprehend or even to recognize the nature of his response to her. More than once the poet criticizes her failure as a "Madnesse" that saves "a part, and lose(s) the whole" (43, cf. 42).

While Timias languishes in love's torments, Belphoebe spares no pains to ease him, but still not comprehending his malady, "that sweet Cordiall, which can restore / A loue-sick hart, she did to him enuy," or refuse to give. Few readers or rereaders of these lines are prepared for those that follow, in which "that sweet Cordiall . . . that soueraigne salue" is suddenly transformed to "That dainty Rose, the daughter of her Morne," whose flower, lapped in "her silken leaues" she shelters from midday sun and northern wind: "But soone as calmed was the Christall aire, / She did it faire dispred, and let to florish faire" (51). As Donald Cheney has suggested, precise equivalents for these lines do not exist. "For her," he adds, "the rose is a rose, not a euphemism."[8]

But surely not just a rose, either. Belphoebe's dainty blossom soon opens into a flower strongly redolent of myth: "Eternall God," we learn, "In Paradize whilome did plant this flowre" and thence fetched it to implant in "earthly flesh." Soon we recognize the flower as the ur-rose that flourishes "In gentle Ladies brest, and bounteous race / Of woman kind" and "beareth fruit of honour and all chast desire" (52). A truly marvelous hybrid, this is none other than the *rosa moralis universalis*. It is hardly surprising that one of Spenser's eighteenth-century editors compared the rose to Milton's "Immortal Amarant" in the third book of *Paradise Lost*, "a flow'r which once / In Paradise, fast by the Tree of Life, / Began to bloom."[9]

In Belphoebe's transformation from uncomprehending nurse to vestal votaress of the rose, to antique origin and a fructifying virtue undifferentiated by time, person, or place, Timias is forgotten. Her specific relation to him will not align with the general moral statement into which it is transformed. Honor and chaste desire, the fruit of the flower, are indeed virtuous, but Timias' love is honorable in Book III, and his desire, if not virginal, is decent and pure and, in these senses, chaste. The general moral statement not only transcends the particular case but wholly misses it. Timias is one person these antique praises of the flower do not fit, and when we consider that Belphoebe's use of tobacco (v. 32) to heal Timias' wounds signals an obvious allusion to Ralegh, we might also think one "present person."

Having glorified the rose, the poet appears in no hurry to return from antique ideal to the person of Belphoebe. He directly addresses the "Faire ympes of beautie" and urges them to emulate their origin by adorning their garlands with "this faire flowre . . . Of chastity and vertue virginall." These "ympes" (shoots, scions) of beauty are preeminently the "Ladies in the Court," to judge both from the poet's present address and its resemblance to the final dedicatory sonnet of *The Faerie Queen*.[10] Timias aside, the poet opts for the general application of the antique ideal to his present world of readers. But with the poet's final promise that the flower will not only embellish the ladies' beauty but also crown them "with heauenly coronall, / Such as the Angels weare before Gods tribunall," we might feel for a moment that we have somehow traveled beyond even Timias' first flush of illusion to a still simpler, purer, less earthly vision (53).

The poet's address to the ladies continues in the next stanza, where he now commends to their attention not the beatifying rose, upon which he has spent the mythmaking of the previous stanzas, but Belphoebe herself as true exemplar of its virtue. In effect he returns the rose, but now in its glorified form, to her person. Of particular note in the present stanza are the initial occurrences of the word "faire" and the phrases "none liuing" and "ensample dead," curious phrases whether taken alone, together, or with the "liuing colours and right hew" of the third proem:

> To youre faire selues a faire ensample frame,
> Of this faire virgin, this *Belphoebe* faire,
> To whom in perfect loue, and spotlesse fame
> Of chastitie, none liuing may compaire:
> Ne poysnous Enuy iustly can empaire
> The prayse of her fresh flowring Maidenhead;
> For thy she standeth on the highest staire
> Of th'honorable stage of womanhead,
> That Ladies all may follow her ensample dead.

The repetition of "faire" is insistent, even anxiously so, but it enforces a link between present persons and Belphoebe. This link, if only a matter of rhetoric and fair appearance, suggests a series of steps from the ladies' "faire selues," surely many of whom were bound to marry; to a generalized "ensample" of purity, to its more exclusive, or higher, form, virginity; and finally to the individual fulfillment of virginity in fair Belphoebe herself, who is found on the "highest staire . . . of womanhead."[11] The poet's conception of a series of steps—that is, a "staire"—becomes additionally significant once we have looked closely at the other verbal oddities in the stanza.[12]

The first of these, the phrase "none liuing," presumably means "none of you ladies" or "no one living," since the poet here addresses his present audience, "youre faire selues," and compares them to Belphoebe, the exemplar of ideal chastity, to which "none liuing" has yet attained. Alternatively, if we take the word "liuing" to be applicable to Belphoebe, the phrase could mean "no other living lady" except Belphoebe herself. This is the meaning of a remarkably similar claim about chaste Florimell earlier in the same canto where her dwarf declares of her, "Liues none this day, that may with her compare / In stedfast chastitie" (v. 8).[13] But there are also significant differences between a claim made by a distraught dwarf within the narrative context of Faerie and one made by the poet himself and addressed to an audience outside the poem. We readily see that the loyal dwarf speaks loosely or hyperbolically. He really means no *other* living lady in all the realm of Faerie is chaster than Florimell or simply that she is the chastest lady imaginable. The word "liuing," however, is not so readily defused in relation to Belphoebe, who mirrors the chastity of the living Queen, especially when it occurs in a direct address to the poet's living audience. If in this context we were to consider Belphoebe "liuing," then she seems actually to become the Queen, a development at variance with statements in the proem to Book III and downright embarrassing when we reach "her ensample dead" in the alexandrine of this stanza. Such a radical dissolution of the fictional character of Belphoebe is entirely unexpected and would probably be largely wasted or, worse, misunderstood.

The natural reading of the phrase "none liuing" is, as suggested, the obvious one, "no one living" or simply "no living lady." While this reading does not refer specifically or directly to the Queen, it increases the distance between Belphoebe as a mythic ideal and any living referent, including the Queen, and thus the distance between antiquity and present age. The increased distance reflects the strains between ideal exemplar and human response in the story of Belphoebe and Timias and helps to bring their story to an appropriate conclusion in 1590.

But if the obvious reading of "none liuing" is also the right one, it is designed to give us another, longer pause for thought when we reread the alexandrine that succeeds it: Belphoebe "standeth on the highest staire . . . of womanhead, / That Ladies all may follow her ensample dead." If Belphoebe is a mythic ideal who has moved farther away from a living referent, what has she to do with death? First she seems to be mythic in this stanza and now to belong to history. The obvious reading of "none liuing" and the alexandrine clearly do not as yet accord.

The phrase "ensample dead," when glossed at all, is taken to be an ellipsis of the clause "when she is dead,"[14] and it can be referred to the occurrence of a parallel construction in Merlin's prophecy to Britomart of the child or "Image" Artegall will leave with her when he is dead (III.iii.29):

With thee yet shall he leaue for memory
Of his late puissaunce, his Image dead,
That liuing him in all actiuity
To thee shall represent.

But the phrase "ensample dead" could just as well mean "her dead, or lifeless, example." At first glance, before we are startled into reassessment, this is exactly what it seems to mean, and if this were in fact all it meant, it would serve as a chilling comment on the ideal Belphoebe embodies and, although at a distinctly greater remove than before, on that of the Queen as well. This alternative meaning of "ensample dead" also finds a relevant parallel in an alexandrine of Book III. It occurs when the witch creates false Florimell, that parody of coldly sterile, lifeless Petrarchism: "and in the stead / Of life, she put a Spright to rule the carkasse dead" (viii.7). Death is this carcass' present condition (dead carcass), not its future one (when dead).

The occurrence in a single stanza of two verbal cruxes as immediately and obviously related as life ("none liuing") and death ("ensample dead") is unlikely to be adventitious. The reading "dead example"—the more obvious reading of "ensample dead"—accords better with the more obvious reading of "none liuing," since it does not require, as does the alternative "when she is dead," an abrupt and irrational shift from mythic to historical reference and, to put it bluntly, from an ageless Belphoebe to an aging Elizabeth. There is no way for us to cancel the obvious reading of "ensample dead," but perhaps we need not stop with its dispiriting message. In the context of Timias' highly Petrarchan adoration and idealization of Belphoebe, the alternative reading, "ensample [when she is] dead," need not refer to death as an exclusively physical event. It can also be taken in a way that makes sense of the mythic Belphoebe's connection with death and offers the positive reflection on her ideal that balances, though it cannot wholly offset, the negative one.

In its Petrarchan context, the reading "when she is dead" points to the resolution of the conflict between body and spirit that comes with the lady's physical death and spiritual transcendence. The phrase "ensample dead" therefore implies the ideal, the life-in-death, that the deadly carcass, the death-in-life, of false Florimell parodies. This reading of the phrase balances the cold reality of human loss—death, denial, lifeless example—with high praise of Belphoebe and of the Queen whose chastity, if only dimly, she still mirrors. At the same time, it continues Belphoebe's movement away from an earthly reality and suggests the only possible solution of Timias' dilemma—and seemingly the destined conclusion of Ralegh's—to be the symbolic or actual transfiguration of Belphoebe into pure spirit.[15]

Looking back at the same stanza with our Petrarchan reading in mind, we might be struck anew by the phrases "perfect loue" and "spotlesse fame." It suddenly makes more sense that "none liuing" should be perfect or spotless in Book III, where the possibility of a living Una has receded like a setting sun, and that the "highest staire . . . of womanhead" should be reached with the lady's transformation through death into spirit. Presumably this is also the "staire" on which worthy emulators of the true rose are crowned "with heauenly coronall . . . before Gods tribunall."

It is even tempting to see a relation between the Petrarchan praise of fair Belphoebe in Book III and the first of Ralegh's commendatory sonnets to accompany *The Faerie Queene:*

> Me thought I saw the graue, where *Laura* lay
> Within that Temple, where the vestall flame
> Was wont to burne, and passing by that way,
> To see that buried dust of liuing fame,
> Whose tombe faire loue, and fairer vertue kept,
> All suddenly I saw the Faery Queene:
> At whose approch the soule of *Petrarke* wept,
> And from thenceforth those graces were not seene.
> For they this Queene attended, in whose steed
> Obliuion laid him downe on *Lauras* herse.

But there is also a significant distance between this vision of Laura's living successor and Spenser's fully idealized Belphoebe, whose rose opens fully only in death. Perhaps because farther removed from it personally, Spenser saw more clearly the temporal, human cost—to Belphoebe and Timias both—of the fully realized Petrarchan vision. By the writing of Book III, he certainly knew that in time Laura's tomb could only be replaced by another's "ensample dead."[16]

II

When Belphoebe is last seen in Book III, response to her is poised between timeless and temporal truth, rather than being torn apart by their conflict. In Book IV, Belphoebe's next and also her last appearance, this duality of response to her remains, but with a difference. Her estrangement from Timias intersects with his relation to Amoret, Belphoebe's twin sister; and Belphoebe's reconciliation with Timias clashes conspicuously with the abandonment and slander of Amoret. With Timias' reconciliation and Amoret's revilement, duality of judgment and of truth can no longer be contained in a single phrase or image or even in a single character or event. Belphoebe herself—or what she was in Book III, an ideal maintaining some relation to worldly reality—is fractured. The alternatives of love and loss, of timeless and temporal truth, are no longer grasped together, no longer simultaneous and complementary dimensions of awareness, as they were in the phrase "ensample dead." They have become sharply distinct and are in danger of becoming mutually exclusive. The distance between ideal image and present age, antique praises and living colors, is widening rapidly.

The story of Belphoebe and Timias is inseparable from the last stages of Amoret's story in Book IV. Wounded and then tended by Timias, Amoret becomes the unwitting cause of Belphoebe's estrangement from him. She is part of their story, and when she is simply abandoned by them in the middle of it, she becomes, both narratively and morally, a loose end waiting to be woven into the larger design. Amoret's ties with the story of Belphoebe and Timias are also symbolic and thematic. The ruby that helps to bring Belphoebe back to Timias is "Shap'd like a heart, yet bleeding of the wound, / And with a little golden chaine about it bound" (viii.6). A jeweler's replica of Amoret's heart in the Masque of Cupid, this lapidarian heart that Belphoebe once gave Timias alludes to Amoret's real one, suggesting contrast with, as well as resemblance to, it. The twin birth of Belphoebe and Amoret, the complementary maids of Diana and Venus, provides a richly allegorical backdrop to their aborted reunion, and although Amoret is much more complexly human than an abstract conception of Love or Amor, the latter is one kind of meaning she carries when she is wounded, then abandoned, and later reviled. The most provocative imitation of Amoret's thematic congruence with Belphoebe comes when the poet interrupts his narrative during Slander's revilement of Amoret to recall an Edenic age when the "glorious flowre" of beauty flourished, a time when ". . . antique age yet in the infancie / Of time, did liue then like an innocent, / In simple truth and blamelesse chastitie" (IV.viii.30). Antiquity, ideal image, mythic flower, even chastity—the poet associates them all now with Amoret or, more accurately, with her revilement.

In addition to the connections between the stories of Amoret and of Belphoebe and Timias sketched above, there are pointed contrasts. The reconciliation of Belphoebe and Timias is extremely artificial, effected through the agency of a sympathetic turtle dove and a lapidary's heart and totally removed from temporal reality. When he is reconciled, Timias' condition anticipates Melibee's self-enclosed vulnerability: he is "Fearlesse of fortunes chaunge or enuies dread, / And eke all mindlesse of his owne deare Lord" (viii.18). Still more noticeable, even while the estrangement of Belphoebe from Timias alludes unmistakably to Ralegh's fall from queenly favor, their reconciliation in Book IV conflicts with the real state of Ralegh's affairs in 1596.[17] After Ralegh's secret marriage to Elizabeth Throckmorton, one of the Queen's maids of honor, and the consequent imprisonment of them both in 1592, he was, although released fairly quickly from prison, not in fact reconciled to the Queen until 1597. His wife, left to languish in prison longer than he, never returned to favor with the Queen. In the reconciliation of Timias and Belphoebe, artificial thus means twice unreal—unreal at once in manner and in reference.

The abandonment of Amoret contrasts sharply with the artifice of reconciliation. When Arthur finds her in the forest, she is "almost dead and desperate," ingloriously wounded and unromantically in need. In his effort to shelter Amoret (and her less vulnerable companion, Aemylia), Arthur unwittingly takes her to the House of Slander, a foul old woman "stuft with rancour and despight / Vp to the throat" (24). Once they are within her house, an indignant and somewhat bitter poet intrudes at length in the narrative to connect Slander to the present age ("Sith now of dayes") and to oppose this age to the ideal or antique image. Slander's railings therefore have a general historicity or timeliness pointedly attributed to them for which Amoret's own adventures—apart from the topicality of her relation to Timias' estrangement from Belphoebe—fail to account. In short, what befalls Amoret in the two cantos she shares with Belphoebe and Timias looks very much like the other half of their story, the half muted in Belphoebe's withdrawal from Timias and suppressed in her return to him. What befalls Amoret unfolds the "inburning wrath" of Belphoebe (viii.17) and gives tongue to the revilement and infamy that Ralegh's secret marriage incurred.

Writing presumably in 1592 from the Tower, Ralegh contrasted the Queen's formerly gracious favor to him with his present state:

> Thos streames seeme standinge puddells which, before,
> Wee saw our bewties in, so weare they cleere.
> Bellphebes course is now obserude no more,
> That faire resemblance weareth out of date.
> Our Ocean seas are but tempestius waves
> And all things base that blessed wear of late.
>
> [ll. 269–74]

If we remember Spenser's final vision of Belphoebe in 1590, with its series of "faire" steps from living audience to the highest ideal, these words from *Ocean to Cynthia* have an added edge. But even without this refinement, they afford a commentary on the distance we have seen opening between living Queen and ideal image, in this case, Belphoebe: as the imprisoned Ralegh again observes of this distance, "A Queen shee was to mee, no more Belphebe, / A Lion then, no more a milke white Dove" (ll. 327–28). The extreme artificiality of the reconciliation of Belphoebe and Timias in Book IV bears a similar testimony. As the distance widens, as an ideal Belphoebe becomes further detached from living reference, other kinds of references to the present age build up and push intrusively into Faerie. Their violence and their ugliness, unparalleled by the more controlled images of evil in Books I, II, and even III, do not just threaten the Faerie vision but actually violate it.

The old hag who reviles Amoret, her companion, and her would-be rescuer is nothing short of hideous, as extreme in her violent ugliness as conciliatory dove and ruby-heart are in their artificiality. The poet seems almost unable to put a stop to his description of her. "A foule and loathly creature" with "filthy lockes," she sits in her house "Gnawing her nayles for felnesse and for yre, / And there out sucking venime to her parts entyre" (23–24). The description continues for another two stanzas with a reiterative emphasis and expansiveness that partial quotation hardly conveys. She abuses all goodness, frames causeless crimes, steals away good names. Nothing can be done so well "aliue"—that is, in life—without her depriving it of "due praise." As the poet continues, castigating the verbal poison Slander spues forth from her hellish inner parts, she becomes an unmistakable precursor first of Detraction and then of that poet's nightmare, the Blatant Beast, "For like the strings of Aspes, that kill with smart, / Her spightfull words did pricke, and wound the inner part."[18]

"Such was that Hag," the poet concludes, "vnmeet to host such guests, / Whom greatest Princes court would welcome fayne" (27). Then, just before the poet in his own voice breaks into the narrative for five stanzas to decry the distance between antique age and present corruption, he praises the patience of Slander's "guests," who endure every insult she can offer, "And vnto rest themselues all onely lent, / Regardlesse of that queane so base and vilde, / To be vniustly blamd, and bitterly reuilde" (IV.viii.28). *Quean*, meaning "harlot," "hussy," or in Spenser's case, "hag," is not the same word as *queen*, and it should be obvious from the poet's virulent description of Slander that she is not an image of the Virgin Queen.[19] But the word "queane" in this context is not disposed of so easily, nor is the possibility that for one awful moment the image of the bitter old woman glances at the living Queen.

Philologists have been reluctant to recognize the likelihood of the homonymic pun on *quean/queen* in Renaissance English that exists in modern English. Kökeritz notes that contemporary philological evidence proves the possibility of such a pun in colloquial speech but doubts that polite speakers would have found the pun readily accessible. Dobson likewise notes the distinction in pronunciation of the two vowels in educated southern speech but allows for vulgar or dialectical variations in which the pun would exist.[20] The pun is therefore possible but unlikely or inappropriate in a polite context, an argument that might, indeed, recommend it on grounds of aesthetic decorum—not to say political prudence—for the impassioned description of an impolite hag. The historical imagination is hard pressed to picture a courtier who would be likely to explain such a pun to the Queen or even willing to admit recognition of its presence.

Admitting the pun in Spenser's use of *quean*, we might regard it as one of the many signs in Book IV that the poem is becoming more private and personal, but we can do so without having to argue that the pun or at the very least the possibility of wordplay would not have been recognized by a number of Spenser's readers. Wordplay on the combination *quean/ quean* has a long history, in part because of its alliterative potential, as, for example, in Langland's lines, "At churche in the charnel cheorles aren vuel to knowe, / Other a knyght fro a knaue, other a queyne fro a queene."[21] In passing, I should also note that in an age of printing like the Renaissance the spelling of *quean*—"queen" and "queyn" in Thynne's Chaucer—was a visual invitation to wordplay, which philology would be inclined to discount.[22] Whatever its causes, the pun on *quean/quean* almost certainly exists in Shakespeare's *Antony and Cleopatra* when Enobarbus quips that Apollodorus has carried "A certaine Queene to *Caesar* in a Matris" (II.vi.72).[23] The same pun also occurs in Middleton's *A Trick to Catch the Old One* when Witt-Good disclaims youth's follies, including "sinful Riotts, / Queanes Evills, Doctors diets" (V.ii.185–86). The evils of queans are venereal, but highly qualified readers agree that the pun on *quean/quean* and the consequent play on *king's evil* (scrofula) is present here.[24] Contemporary dramatic use of a pun argues its accessibility to auditors, and a play on diseases dependent on the pun urges this fact.

To my mind, the most illuminating information about Spenser's calling Slander a "queane" is that this is his sole use of the word. Occasion, Duessa, Impatience, Impotence, the witch who creates false Florimell—not a one of these hags wears this common Renaissance label, and we might almost suppose that Spenser was deliberately avoiding it. That he should suddenly have used the word "queane" accidentally or innocently in a context inseparable from Belphoebe, Timias, and the relation of Faerie ideal to present age defies credibility, and does so much more, in view of Spenser's verbal sensitivity, than does the possibility that he alludes momentarily to the Queen.

As with Belphoebe's rose in Book III, there are now no precise or steady equivalents for the figures gathered in Slander's House: Amoret does not equal Elizabeth Throckmorton, Arthur does not equal Ralegh, Aemylia does not equal anybody, and Slander certainly does not equal the Queen.[25] In the moments and ways I have suggested, however, what happens to Amoret reflects on one level the scandal, wrath, and disgrace Ralegh's marriage unleashed, and briefly the poet holds up to his sovereign the kind of distorted reflection found in a hideous cartoon. The figures of Lucifera, Philotime, and false Florimell bear witness that such a distorted image— such parody—is not entirely alien to the poet's techniques in earlier books, but it recurs here with a difference. Lucifera is not a missing side of Una or of the Queen but a denial of what they truly are. Where she is a possible threat, Slander is a present reality.[26] Complex yet still balanced and grasped together in Book III, contrasting violently and centrifugally in Book IV, opposite words, opposite meanings, and opposite realities figure crucially in the troubled process of reassessing the relation of the Faerie vision to the living Queen.

Notes

1. *The Faerie Queene* I.xxi.8, 23; iv.8, II.vii.44–45. All Spenserian references are to *Works: A Variorum Edition*, ed. Edwin A. Greenlaw et al., 11 vols. (Baltimore: Johns Hopkins University Press, 1932–57), cited hereafter as *Var.*

2. *Henry IV* I.iii.201–02, V.i.131, ed. Herschel Baker, in *The Riverside Shakespeare* (Boston: Houghton Mifflin, 1974).

3. Long since, in an illuminating and liberating article, Louis Martz showed that Spenser was not unaware of comic nuances in his sonnets: "The *Amoretti:* 'Most Goodly Temperature,'" in *Form and Convention in the Poetry of Edmund Spenser*, ed. William Nelson (New York: Columbia University Press, 1961), pp. 146–68. We continue to make progress regarding the poet's control of his meaning elsewhere, but slowly sometimes.

4. This paragraph borrows from my "What comes after Chaucer's *BUT:* Adversative Constructions in Spenser," in *Acts of Interpretation: The Text in Its Context*, ed. Mary J. Carruthers and Elizabeth D. Kirk (Norman Okla.: Pilgrim Books, 1982), n. 6.

5. "The 11th: and last booke of the Ocean to Scinthia," ll. 69, 497 ff., cf. 29–30, *The Poems of Sir Walter Ralegh*, ed. Agnes M. C. Latham (London: Routledge & Kegan Paul, 1951). All references to *Ocean to Cynthia* are to this edition. On the dating of *Cynthia*, see Latham's introduction, pp. xxxvi–xl; and Stephen J. Greenblatt, *Sir Walter Ralegh: The Renaissance Man and His Roles* (New Haven: Yale University Press, 1973), pp. 12–13.

6. In "Colin Clovts Come Home Againe," Spenser calls Ralegh "shepheard of the Ocean" (l. 66); see also ll. 164, 174–75 in connection with the dating of *Cynthia*. On possible earlier versions of *Cynthia*, see Agnes M. C. Latham, ed., *Sir Walter Raleigh: Selected Prose and Poetry* (London: Athlone Press, 1965), p. 25, and on the style of *Cynthia*, pp. 210–11. Greenblatt's discussion of *Cynthia* is invaluable (pp. 77–98); his remarks on pastoral are especially pertinent (pp. 80, 84–85).

7. See *Var.*, 3:245–46 (xxvii ff.), but also 3:247 (xxxv). The Virgilian text is available in *Var.*, 2:219 (xxxii.6–xxxiii.4): "O—quam te memorem, virgo? Namque haud tibi vultus / Mortalis, nec vox hominem sonat; O, dea, certe." Given Spenser's earlier association of this passage with Belphoebe (II.iii.33), its bearing on Timias' lines is unmistakable.

8. *Spenser's Image of Nature: Wild Man and Shepherd in "The Faerie Queene"* (New Haven: Yale University Press, 1966), p. 102.

9. *Var.*, 3:248 (lii). The reference is to Ralph Church's edition, 1758.

10. *Var.*, 3:198. The full title of the final sonnet is "To all the gratious and beautifull Ladies in the Court."

11. Cf. *Faerie Queene* III.v.53: "Of chastity and vertue virginall." Chastity and virginity are not identical in this line.

12. *OED*, s.v. *Stair sb*, 1: "An ascending series . . . of steps"; 2: "One of a succession of steps"; 2d. *fig:* "A step of degree in a (metaphorical) ascent or in a scale of dignity"; 2e: "A high position."

13. A. C. Hamilton, ed., *The Faerie Queene* (London: Longman, 1977), p. 354, aligns this claim about Florimell with that about Belphoebe.

14. Hamilton, ed., *The Faerie Queene*, p. 354. Hamilton's sensitivity to the need of a gloss is notable.

15. Cf. Louis Adrian Montrose's highly provocative analysis of Petrarchan sublimation in "'The perfecte paterne of a Poete': The Poetics of Courtship in *The Shepheardes Calender*," *TSLL* 21 (1979), 34–67, esp. p. 54 (November Eclogue: Dido/Elissa).

16. In *Mirror and Veil: The Historical Dimension of Spenser's "Faerie Queene"* (Chapel Hill: University of North Carolina Press, 1977), pp. 113–14, Michael O'Connell rightly locates a "sense of paradox" in the final stanza of III.v, the result especially of the word "Nathlesse." Although I do not agree with all of O'Connell's views on p. 114, this sense of paradox follows naturally from my own reading of the penultimate stanza ("ensample dead") and fittingly concludes the canto.

17. See O'Connell, *Mirror and Veil*, p. 116; and A. L. Rowse, *Ralegh and the Throckmortons* (London: Macmillan, 1962), pp. 164, 204–06.

18. Cf. *Faerie Queene* V.xii.36, VI.vi.1.

19. *OED*, s.v. *Quean*, 1; s.v. *Queen* (etymology): *quean* and *queen* have an ablaut-relationship. Thomas P. Roche, Jr., ed., *The Faerie Queene* (Harmondsworth, Middlesex: Penguin, 1978), p. 1176, glosses *quean* as *hag*. This meaning seems obvious from several examples in the *OED* and is the most appropriate one for Spenser's context.

20. Helge Kökeritz, *Shakespeare's Pronunciation* (New Haven: Yale University Press, 1960), p. 88; E. J. Dobson, *English Pronunciation 1500–1700* (Oxford: Oxford University Press, Clarendon Press, 1968), 2:640, 612, n. 2.

21. *The Vision of William concerning Piers the Plowman in Three Parallel Texts*, ed. Walter W. Skeat (London: Oxford University Press, 1886), C.IX.45–46 (my punctuation). For a concise discussion of Langland's "punning" on quean/queen and its basis in Old English, see Mary Carruthers, *The Search for St. Truth: A Study of Meaning in "Piers Plowman"* (Evanston: Northwestern University Press, 1973), pp. 60–61, n. 19. Carruthers discusses a second instance of wordplay in Langland's line "*here* nis no quen queynt*ere hat* quyk is o lyue" (A.II.14: George Kane, ed.).

22. Chaucer, *Works 1532*, supplemented by material from the editions of 1542, 1561, 1598, and 1602 (London: Scolar Press, 1969), fol. 104, verso, Manciples Prologue, l. 34; fol. 165, verso, column a, l. 19.

23. From the Norton facsimile of the First Folio.

24. Quotation from Middleton is from Charles Barber's edition (Berkeley: University of California Press, 1968); Barber considers the play on *king's evil* "doubtless." For the same view, see James T. Henke, *Renaissance Dramatic Bawdy (Exclusive of Shakespeare): An Annotated Glossary and Critical Essays, Jacobean Drama Studies*, 39 (Salzburg: Institut für Englische und Literatur Universität Salzburg, 1974), 2:249.

25. On the presence of Aemylia and other levels of meaning in IV.viii, see my "Whatever Happened to Amoret? The Poet's Role in Book IV of *The Faerie Queene*," *Criticism* 13 (1971), 180–200, esp. 181–85.

26. Near the end of the poet's praise of antiquity and denunciation of the present, he first appears to compliment the Queen but does not in fact do so. Instead he speaks with an evasive ambiguity that is to become increasingly characteristic of his compliments to her and, it would appear, of his disillusionment with her. In xxxii.8, "her glorious flowre" is beauty's (l. 1). In xxxiii.5, the word "her," while ambiguous, logically refers to beauty's glorious flower in l. 6 (chastity, to judge from Book III); from this flower proceed the "drops" or dew or nectar of virtue. The near, but failed, reference of the pronouns in these stanzas to the living Queen is further testimony of the distance between her and the ideal image.

Scapegoating Radigund

Mihoko Suzuki

In the 1596 *Faerie Queene*, Spenser diverges from his earlier mode of allegory by introducing in Book 5 the Amazon queen Radigund, with whom Britomart shares her androgyny as a "martiall Mayd" (3.4.18). Britomart's distinction from the Amazon queen becomes of necessity more problematic than in the previous instances, where her knightly armor and prowess distinguished her quite clearly from more conventionally feminine figures such as Hellenore and Florimell. At the same time, Spenser diverges from his use of the Virgilian model: Artegall displaces Britomart as "Aeneas" in this episode, thus making Radigund a Dido figure and Britomart, surprisingly, a Lavinia. Both the difficulty of maintaining distinctions between Radigund and Britomart and the displacement of Britomart as an epic hero announce Spenser's departure from his earlier poetry of praise.

This subversion of Britomart, I suggest, expresses Spenser's disillusionment with the Elizabethan order. Several recent critics have observed this disillusionment in the latter part of Spenser's poetic career. For example, Richard Helgerson locates this disillusionment in the split between heroic action and love that marks Books 5 and 6: "The optimistic faith that had animated the early books, the faith that history was going the right way, seems to have left Spenser in the 1590s. Heroic poetry requires, as Cuddie argued in the October eclogue, an heroic age. By the time he wrote Books V and VI, that age seemed to have passed."[1] David L. Miller also sees in Spenser's late work signs of withdrawal from "his engagement *as a poet* with the cultural and political institutions of late sixteenth-century England," manifested in his questioning of the humanist faith in literature as a mode of persuasion.[2] Recent social historians of this period also see the closing years of Elizabeth's reign as a time of economic crisis, political disintegration, and burgeoning corruption, an age in which things turned horribly sour.[3] Since Spenser's praise of Elizabeth's order in Book 3 focused on her special status as a woman ruler, which allowed him to represent her as both the object of desire, on the one hand, and the ruler and patron to be praised on the other, it is not surprising that Spenser's later expression of ambivalence

From *Metamorphoses of Helen: Authority, Difference, and the Epic.* © 1989 by Cornell University. Used by permission of the publisher, Cornell University Press.

centers also upon the gender of his sovereign, especially in Book 5's Radigund episode.[4]

The confrontation between Britomart and Radigund has traditionally been read as Spenser's heroine's triumph over "the masculine, violent, inequitable aspect of her own Amazonian nature."[5] Simply put, Radigund, according to this interpretation, represents the "bad Amazon," over whom Britomart, the "good Amazon," will inevitably prevail.[6] Critics have also argued that from this episode can be deduced Spenser's so-called "moderate Puritan position" regarding women in power: that women in general (including Mary Tudor and Mary Stuart) are not equipped to exercise political authority, but God sometimes sees fit to endow certain exceptional women (such as Elizabeth) with the necessary qualifications.[7] According to this reading, then, Radigund functions as a convenient scapegoat for Spenser and his heroine Britomart: Radigund's destruction allows Spenser to dissociate Britomart from anxiety-producing qualities traditionally associated with Amazons and to assert her prerogative to found the Tudor line.

Yet Spenser complicates this apparently simple allegorical conflict, and his artistic choice expresses ambivalence toward Elizabeth's rule. Spenser forgoes his control over Radigund's meaning by quite deliberately swerving from his representation of her as an allegorical figure signifying belligerence and tyranny.[8] At the heart of Book 5, which has been noted for its conspicuous political and historical allegory, Spenser develops and complicates Radigund beyond a personified abstraction into something closer to a dramatic or novelistic character, thereby creating tensions in his chosen allegorical mode which result in its eventual breakdown. Spenser's departure from allegory in representing Radigund as a complex character who appeals to the reader's sympathy recapitulates Virgil's depiction of Dido not simply as an obstacle for Aeneas' epic mission but as a tragic heroine in her own right.

Spenser need not motivate the Amazon Radigund's animosity toward men, but he nevertheless explains it as resulting from anger and humiliation arising from unrequited love. Having been rejected by Bellodant (a characteristically allegorical name meaning "wargiver"), Radigund "turn'd her love to hatred manifold" (5.4.30). Radigund's conception of love, like Malecasta's, does not respect the integrity and difference of the Other: in her failure to possess Bellodant, to "w[i]nne [him] unto her will" (5.4.30), her love turns to angry spite. She reacts to this disappointment by dressing men in "womens weedes" (5.4.31) and compelling them to perform domestic chores. Like Virgil, Spenser dramatizes his anxiety concerning what is perceived as the necessary correlation between female ascendancy and male humiliation; here Radigund follows the hallowed tradition of domineering and emasculating queens such as Omphale, who bought Hercules as a slave and put him to woman's work. But at the same time, by explaining Radigund's motives for her actions, Spenser already departs from his treatment of previous allegorical figures such as Lucifera in Book 1 and Malecasta in Book 3, whose motivations were irrelevant and thus never explained. Moreover, unlike Bellodant's transparently allegorical name, Radigund's name, derived from St. Radegunde—who was known for piety, meekness, virginity, and special charity to prisoners—stands in tension with the character Spenser gives her;[9] through this ironic discrepancy between Radigund and her name, Spenser again signals his divergence from allegory.

Spenser complicates Radigund further by having her fall in love with Artegall, whom she has vanquished. Initially, she persists in speaking of her love as bondage, revealing yet again her conception of love only in terms of domination and submission: "It is so hapned, that the heavens unjust, / Spighting my happie freedome, have agreed, / To thrall my looser life, or my last bale to breed" (5.5.29).[10] Yet her love allows her to see herself and her relationship with Artegall in a new perspective. Her transformation by the "kindly flame" (4.Pr.2) is made evident in her new-found humility: she admits that it was not her "valour" but Artegall's "owne brave mind" that led to his subjection, and she voices remorse over her unjust treatment of him although he had saved her life (5.5.32). She also appears to abandon her conception of love as possession; she no longer is satisfied to have Artegall under "bondage" but instead desires his "free goodwill" (5.5.32). Radigund's self-consciousness arising from her love for Artegall recalls Britomart's similar awakening when she saw his image in her father's mirror. Unlike Virgil, who makes Dido less sympathetic after she falls in love with Aeneas, Spenser makes evident his intention to win the reader's sympathy for Radigund by transposing Radigund's duplicity, manifested during her combat with Artegall, to her handmaid Clarinda (a confidante like Virgil's Anna), who deceives her mistress in order to further her own love toward Artegall.[11]

As well as displaying affinities with Britomart, Radigund's development from cruelty to humility parallels Artegall's similar transformation in this episode. The moment that encapsulates the old and new Artegall occurs when he spares Radigund's life upon unvizarding her.[12]

> But when as he discovered had her face,
>> He saw his senses straunge astonishment,
>> A miracle of natures goodly grace,
>> In her faire visage voide of ornament.
>>> . . .
>
> At sight thereof his cruell minded hart
>> Empierced was with pittifull regard,
>> That his sharpe sword he threw from him apart,
>> Cursing his hand that had that visage mard:
>> No hand so cruell, nor no hart so hard,
>> But ruth of beautie will it mollifie.
>>> [5.5.12,13]

Artegall's pity for Radigund is clearly the cause of his later woes, but his pity, which was absent from his justice up to this point, is also a "ruth of beautie." The erotic overtone of this moment is underlined not only by the reference to Achilles' falling in love with Amazon Penthesilea as he was about to slay her but also by the close verbal echo of Artegall's earlier unvizarding of Britomart—a repetition that again serves to link the two women.[13]

> With that her angels face, unseene afore,
> Like to the ruddie morne appeard in sight,
>
>   . . .
>
> His powrelesse arme benumbd with secret feare
> From his revengefull purpose shronke abacke,
> And cruell sword out of his fingers slacke
> Fell downe to ground, as if the steele had sence,
> And felt some ruth, or sence his hand did lacke.
>   [4.6.19,21]

Although some may criticize Artegall for sparing the Amazon (or for abandoning his "sharpe sword"), if he were to destroy Radigund at this point, he would be no different from the ruthless and inflexible Talus. More difficult and perhaps even more crucial than maintaining the distinction between Artegall and Talus is telling apart Britomart and Radigund. For Artegall, and even for the reader, the similarity between the two moments of unvizarding prefigures the conflation of Britomart and Radigund and the consequent breakdown of allegory in this episode.

   Just as Artegall's attraction to Britomart was predicated on their resemblance to one another—Artegall, after all, is Britomart's mirror image—so his attraction to Radigund bespeaks his resemblance to the Amazon queen. In Book 3, Spenser signaled Britomart's imaginative affinity with her British progeny and Trojan forebears by stating that her heart was "empierst" with pity by the story of their misfortunes (3.9.39). Artegall's similar figurative wound, therefore, links him to Radigund, for it is his "cruell hart" that is "empierst" by the sight of Radigund's face. Spenser had figured Artegall's cruelty in his companion Talus, "that great yron groome, his gard and government" (5.4.3). Moreover, at the end of canto 3, which immediately precedes Radigund's introduction to the poem, Guyon restrained Artegall's "choler" from exacting excessive punishment on Braggadocchio (5.3.36). Finally, at Isis Church, where Britomart arrives while Artegall is imprisoned by Radigund, the priest interprets Britomart's dream thus:

> For the same Crocodile doth represent
> The righteous Knight, that is thy faithfull lover,
> Like to *Osyris* in all just endever.
> For that same Crocodile *Osyris* is,

> That under *Isis* feete doth sleepe for ever:
> To shew that clemence oft in things amis,
> Restraines those sterne behests, and cruell doomes of his.
>
> [5.7.22]

Artegall is susceptible to Radigund precisely because he shares with her the propensity toward "cruell doomes." In a simile comparing Artegall's subjugation by Radigund to Hercules' choice of pleasure with Iole (5.5.24), Spenser highlights the willfulness of Artegall's choice and his attraction for Radigund.[14] As Kathleen Williams shrewdly notes, Artegall's tyrannous and ruthless character paradoxically implies a "capacity for submission," what we might less charitably call a sado-masochistic tendency that he shares with Hercules.[15] But once vanquished, Artegall diverges from the Herculean model. Unlike Hercules who "with his mistresse toyed" (5.5.24), Artegall deflects the advances of both Radigund and Clarinda. In addition, he accepts the consequences of his "choice" with a humility uncharacteristic of him up to this point. Through his subjection by Radigund and his consequent taking on of "feminine" roles, Artegall seems to learn to incorporate those characteristics necessary to temper his excessively "masculine" justice. Just as Britomart's heroism is predicated upon her combination of both traditionally feminine and masculine characteristics, so Artegall must accept the feminine in order to be her equal.

Although Spenser may appear to affirm this exchange of gender roles, the text moves to restore sexual difference and hierarchy at a crucial moment, in the simile likening Britomart's reunion with Artegall to Penelope's recognition of Odysseus:

> Not so great wonder and astonishment,
>   Did the most chast *Penelope* possesse,
>   To see her Lord, that was reported drent,
>   And dead long since in dolorous distresse,
>   Come home to her in piteous wretchednesse,
>   After long travell of full twenty yeares,
>   That she knew not his favours likelynesse,
>   For many scarres and many hoary heares,
> But stood long staring on him, mongst uncertaine feares.
>
> [5.7.39]

Unlike the similes in the *Odyssey* which affirmed the exchange of gender roles, this simile insists upon strict correspondence along gender lines: between Britomart and Penelope, Artegall and Odysseus. Yet because Artegall has been emasculated, it is Britomart who has been acting as a second Odysseus in completing a journey of her own to rescue Artegall. In hyperbolically likening Artegall's appearance in "womens weedes" to Odysseus' "piteous wretchednesse" after twenty years of wandering, Spenser seems to project his own anxiety concerning Artegall's identity onto Penelope's (and Britomart's) "uncertaine feares." Spenser stresses the temporary nature of this anxiety-producing exchange of gender roles by likening it to carnival inversion—Britomart asks Artegall, "What May-game hath misfortune made of you? (5.7.40)—a reference that serves to reestablish more securely the patriarchal order, as we shall see.[16] Indeed, Spenser's desire in this simile to differentiate his protagonists clearly by gender signals his unease with Elizabeth's rule, for, as Joan Kelly has pointed out, the strict separation of domestic and public spheres along gender lines characterizes patriarchies.[17]

When Britomart slays Radigund in order to rescue Artegall, these analogies between Radigund and herself, on the one hand, and between Radigund and Artegall, on the other, do not allow Radigund's destruction to be read simply as an allegory for the victory of true justice over false. In a "wrothfull" (5.7.34) fury, Britomart "empierce[s]" (5.7.33) her enemy and "with one stroke both head and helmet cleft" (5.7.34). The verb, as in the previous instances in which Spenser used it, underscores the similarity of rather than the difference between the two women. Moreover, Radigund's fatal wound which cleaves her in two finds its reflection in Britomart's own wound, much graver than the flesh wounds she has received up to this point: "it bit / Unto the bone, and made a griesly wound, / That she her shield through raging smart of it / Could scarse uphold" (5.7.33). The two lighter grazes she received in the opening and closing cantos of Book 3 signaled Britomart's vulnerability to the threats posed by Malecasta and Busirane; here the more serious wound implies that her violent slaying of Radigund constitutes a partial self-destruction. Although Britomart had been enjoined to "clemence" in "restrain[ing] . . . sterne behests, and cruell doomes" (5.7.22) at the Temple of Isis, she seems to have forgotten the lesson she was taught there. This moment recalls the similarly problematic final lines of the *Faerie Queene*'s prototype, Virgil's *Aeneid:* like Britomart, Aeneas seems to forget Anchises' instruction to exercise the arts of peace and law by sparing the vanquished (6.851–53), when, overcome by *furia* and *ira*, he slays his enemy Turnus. Spenser underscores Britomart's lack of "clemence" by having Talus follow her lead to engage in a "piteous slaughter" of the Amazons (5.7.35); Talus, earlier the agent of Artegall's violence, becomes Britomart's agent. Britomart here takes on Artegall's earlier cruelty just as she had, in the preceding scene of Radigund's slaughter, assimilated her victim's fury.

In the allegory of previous books, Spenser either maintained a clear distinction between apparently similar figures by keeping them apart (Una and Duessa, Florimell and False Florimell) or by dramatizing a confrontation between antagonists whereby one triumphed over the other (Redcrosse and the dragon, Britomart and Busirane). If allegory is predicated upon the separation of moral qualities and the dialectical resolution of the conflict between them through the victory of one over the other, then in this confrontation between Britomart and Radigund the allegory breaks down, for the opposition between the two poles can no longer be maintained. In the course of the episode, Radigund has gone beyond a simple negation of Britomart, and at its climax, Britomart takes on Radigund's former ferocity. This final encounter between the two viragos dramatizes an ironic doubling rather than an allegorical opposition. Britomart's slaying of her double Radigund, then, does not allow Spenser's heroine simply to exorcize from herself the troubling qualities of tyranny and violence; she annihilates what is vital in herself as well as what is problematic, for the two are inextricably linked.

It is altogether fitting, then, that after slaying Radigund, Britomart gives up her prerogative by instituting male rule in Radegone:

> During which space she there as Princess rained,
> And changing all that forme of common weale,
> The liberty of women did repeale,
> Which they had long usurpt; and them restoring
> To mens subjection, did true Justice deale:
> That all they as Goddesse her adoring,
> Her wisdome did admire, and hearkned to her loring.
> [5.7.42]

The final couplet does little to mitigate Britomart's acceptance of patriarchal assumptions that woman's sovereignty can result only from the usurpation of originary and rightful male rule. This act of self-destruction in repealing woman's liberty repeats and confirms the self-destruction implicit in her slaying of Radigund. As if in recognition of her own contamination by Radigund's violence, Britomart cedes her power to Artegall. Thus the distinction between women in general who are unfit to rule and the exceptional woman who receives divine sanction to rule cannot be maintained, for Britomart undermines her own prerogative and power in destroying Radigund and abolishing woman's rule in Radegone, in the end becoming a shadowy figure like Virgil's Lavinia.

In keeping with the poem's tendency to diminish Britomart, her repeal of women's liberty is followed by her sudden and hitherto unexplained disappearance from the poem at the conclusion of the Radigund episode. Artegall goes forth to pursue his quest of rescuing Irena, leaving behind Britomart, who fades away from the poem in "paine," "sorrow," and "anguish" (5.7.45) over the deferral of her union with him. In Book 3, Britomart's errancy, set off against the imprisonment and subjugation of Hellenore, Amoret, and Florimell, signaled her independence and freedom. Left behind in Radegone, where she herself has instituted male rule, Britomart cedes her role as epic hero to Artegall; this final vision of Britomart presents a much reduced version of her self-sufficient and energetic former self.

Yet the prevailing reading of this episode insists upon affirming Britomart and hence the allegory: it maintains the distinctions between the two Amazons by loading Radigund with negative attributes and Britomart with positive ones. Despite the evidence to the contrary, then, most critics give affirmative readings of the conclusion of Britomart's plot:

> Now she *becomes* Isis ruling Radigund's kingdom with true justice. . . . This final appearance of Britomart in the poem—like Una restored to her kingdom—fulfills that vision of herself as Isis.[18]

> Britomart now has the attributes of a perfect wife. To all intents and purposes, her long journey in the *Faerie Queene* is over. . . . It has led from darkness into the light, from love in nature to love in grace.[19]

I argue rather that the breakdown of allegory, transforming Radigund from a simple negation of Britomart to a complex counterpart or alter-ego, works to diminish and ultimately erase Britomart through her own destruction of Radigund. Britomart cleaves Radigund in two just as the poem itself splits the Amazonian warrior in two parts and has one destroy the other; the half that remains can only be an extremely diminished representation of the militant woman.

The simultaneous conclusion of both the Radigund episode and Britomart's plot dramatizes the disquieting but irreducible fact that the scapegoating of Radigund works ultimately to destroy Britomart as well. For previous readers this scapegoating succeeds (as does the allegory): the "bad" Amazon is purged so that the "good" Amazon can survive. Yet as we have seen, Britomart, the putative "good" Amazon, also disappears from the poem. Victor Turner's description and analysis of ritual sacrifice carries particular significance for our understanding of the workings of the scapegoating of Radigund *and* Britomart:

> A [social or ritual] drama has a kind of circularity of form and intention. There is an intention of restoring an antecedent condition, in this case a condition of dynamic equilibrium between the parts of a society. But any process that involves conflict has its "victims," and any process that reaffirms norms implies condemnation of norm-breakers. It also implies punishment of the innovator as well as the lawbreaker, since the introduction of radical novelty would prevent the ultimate closure of the circle. This "victimizing" and punitive tendency of a cyclical system is reflected in its ritual dramas, for most of them contain a sacrifice. A sacrifice may be regarded as restorative, regenerative; at the moment when the wheel has come a full circle, it sets the cycle going again, the victim is held to be at once innocent and guilty: innocent because the conflicts that have gone before are not the victim's fault, but guilty because a scapegoat is required to atone for those conflicts. In the victim extremes meet.[20]

Just as the reversal of gender roles between Artegall and Radigund follows the ritual of carnival (the "May-game" that Britomart alludes to), so here the slaughter of Radigund corresponds to the ritual of sacrifice of which Turner speaks, for both rituals function to affirm the social order by exorcizing elements that threaten it. The sacrifice of Radigund clearly intends to restore the antecedent condition of patriarchal rule. We have already seen that Britomart's destruction of Radigund allows the victor's restoration of patriarchy or, indeed, makes it all but inevitable. Yet this reaffirmation of norms also entails the condemnation of Britomart as a woman ruler—in Turner's terms, "innovator," if not "norm-breaker" (like Radigund): the poem accomplishes this punishment by having Britomart restore patriarchal rule, and ultimately by erasing her from the poem, despite her "innocence" and her seeming antagonism to the sacrificial victim.

Thus Spenser's blurring of crucial distinctions between Britomart and Radigund leads him to destroy Britomart as well as Radigund. According to René Girard, such a contamination of categories bespeaks a failure of sacrifice: "All victims, even the animal ones, bear a certain *resemblance* to the object they replace; otherwise the violent impulse would remain unsatisfied. But this resemblance must not be carried to the extreme of complete assimilation, or it would lead to disastrous confusion. . . . In order for a species or category of living creature, human or animal, to appear suitable for sacrifice, it must bear a sharp resemblance to the *human* categories excluded from the ranks of the 'sacrificeable,' while still maintaining a degree of difference that forbids all possible confusion."[21] This "confusion" between Radigund and Britomart, the victim and the character whom she replaces, exposes the inefficacy of scapegoating to resolve the problem of the woman ruler, for this scapegoating is supposedly motivated by the overt ideological desire to legitimize one woman ruler over another (or others)—Spenser's so-called "moderate Puritan position" concerning women rulers. But Spenser represents both Amazons as unacceptable rulers. Hence the antecedent condition to which the poem returns after the Radigund episode is not, as most readers have assumed, the legitimate rule of one exceptional woman; rather, through conflating Britomart and Radigund, the text moves to restore the legitimacy of patriarchal rule.

In Spenser's refusal to affirm Britomart, not only by contaminating her with the violence of her enemy but by ultimately effacing her from his poem, we may discern a divergence from his earlier motives, in the sense that Kenneth Burke uses that term.[22] From Book 3 on, Britomart as founder of the Tudor line and ancestor of Elizabeth was the primary vehicle for Spenser's praise of his queen. In the Radigund episode, however, Spenser's changed motive—his faith now turned to disillusionment—finds expression in his subversion of the allegorical mode that he had sustained successfully in the earlier books. This crisis of allegory converges with the failure of sacrifice, for both allegory and sacrifice have in common the need to hold categories apart, and what marks the Radigund episode is the blurring of crucial distinctions; Spenser thereby transgresses the limits of the poetry of praise.

Unwilling to blame Elizabeth overtly, Spenser disguises his criticism of his queen, and his success in doing so is attested to by critics who have interpreted this episode as Spenser's affirmation of Elizabeth's prerogative over that of Mary Stuart.[23] Yet as we have seen, the distinctions between Britomart and Radigund, and hence between Elizabeth and Mary, are difficult to maintain. In fact, Radigund exhibits disquieting similarities with Elizabeth: for example, after the defeat of the Armada, representations both literary and pictoral of Elizabeth as Amazon became commonplace.[24] Radigund's emasculation of her male prisoners recalls Elizabeth's strict control over even the private lives of her male courtiers. In a speech addressed to Parliament during Mary's trial, Elizabeth referred to her reputation for tyranny, a characteristic that links her with the Amazon Radigund:

> I have besides, during my reigne, seene and heard many opprobrious bookes and Pamphlets against me, my Realme and State, accusing me to be a Tyrant: I thanke them for their almes: I beleeve, therein their meaning was to tell me newes, and newes it is to me indeede: I would it were as strange to heare of their impietie. What will they not now say, when it shalbe spread, That for the safety of her life, a Mayden Queene could be content to spill the blood, even of her owne kinsewoman? . . .
>
> I am not so voide of judgement, as not to see mine owne perill: nor yet so ignorant, as not to knowe it were in nature a foolish course, to cherish a sworde to cutte mine owene throate: nor so carelesse, as not to weigh that my life dayly is in hazard . . . but I pray you thinke, that I have thought upon it.[25]

Elizabeth repeatedly calls attention to the danger to her own prerogative and life implied in the execution of another queen, her relative. She thus stresses her similarity to Mary rather than the differences between them—as I have suggested that Spenser does also in representing the conflict between the two queens in Radegone. It is well known that Elizabeth avoided signing Mary's warrant until the last possible minute. Despite Elizabeth's obsession for her reputation as a woman of clemency (and here we may recall Britomart's lesson at Isis Church), she eventually acquiesced to Mary's execution.

Spenser's disquiet over his inability (or refusal) to resolve contradictions in the Radigund episode finds yet another expression in cantos 9 and 10, where Duessa is judged and executed at Mercilla's castle. This episode has traditionally been read as a straightforward and uncritical allegory of Elizabeth's execution of Mary;[26] yet it is Zele who advocates her execution and persuades the reluctant Mercilla, who let fall a "few perling drops" (5.9.50), "ruing [Duessa's] wilfull fall" (5.10.4). It is worth noting, too, that the jury, as it were, renders a split verdict: Artegall characteristically takes

Zele's side, but Arthur is for sparing Duessa. Moreover, Spenser states baldly that "it is greater prayse to save, then spill / And better to reforme, then to cut off the ill" (5.10.2). Here again, Spenser's criticism of Mary's execution is attenuated, but present nonetheless.

As in the Radigund episode, Spenser avoids blatant criticism of Elizabeth as Mercilla, and so the prevailing reading of this episode assumes that Spenser endorsed Mercilla's judgment. For example, T. K. Dunseath asserts that "Mercilla has no choice but to condemn Duessa." Yet his repeated insistence that Mercilla's actions fulfill her name reveals a suspicion that they do not: "She cannot mitigate the punishment, which is to exercise that part of mercy called clemency. The greatest mercy she can show is through the virtue of meekness, or the suppression of wrath. That this is the meaning of Mercilla's judgment and the tears she sheds is obvious from the beginning of Canto X when Arthur and Artegall praise her mercy."[27] Other critics simply read an accepted view of history back into the text: assuming that Elizabeth's execution of Mary met with public approval and that the intent of Spenser's poem was to praise his queen, they conclude that Spenser represents with approbation Elizabeth as Mercilla.[28] Such a reading ignores important elements in the poem which contradict or undermine it; in addition it precludes the possibility that Spenser came to diverge from the dominant ideology.

As Paul Alpers points out, the conflict between justice and mercy remains unresolved at the end of canto 9, and the condemnation of Duessa is deferred to the next canto, "where its context is not the single process of judgment, but a general account of mercy and praise of Mercilla for possessing this virtue."[29] I suggest that Mercilla does not act in accordance with her allegorical name, because the pressures of history do not allow Spenser to sustain the allegory implied in her name. Significantly, Douglas Northrop, though arguing that Spenser defended Elizabeth in his poem, points out that she was coming under attack generally as a woman ruler, as a tyrant, and, specifically, for the execution of Mary:[30] "The numbers and the vehemence of Elizabeth's defenders reveal the importance of the controversy. Shortly after the death of Mary there appeared *A Defence of the Honorable Sentence and execution of the Queene of Scots* (London n.d.). In 1587 appeared Richard Crompton's *A Short Declaration of the ende of Traytors*, and George Whetstone's *The Censure of a loyall Subject*. The burden of them all is the same: the execution of Mary was justified; the Queen is just; the Queen is merciful." Only serious attacks can prompt such strong defenses. Northrop's account paradoxically makes veiled criticism of Elizabeth by Spenser no longer unthinkable. Even if we were to forgo a strictly topical reading of the Mercilla episode, we might still notice Spenser's peculiar obsession with the destruction of female rulers, Radigund and Duessa, who may well function as monstrous doubles or surrogates for Elizabeth herself.

If allegory resolves ambivalence by categorizing and codifying opposing forces, Spenser's departures from allegory in the Radigund and Mercilla episodes expose his ambivalence toward his queen.[31] The unresolved ambivalence, however, generates anxiety concerning his vocation as laureate, his divergence from his earlier poetry of praise. In Mercilla's castle, Spenser describes a self-proclaimed poet whose tongue is nailed to a post for "blasphem[ing] that Queene"; above his head

> There written was the purport of his sin,
> In cyphers strange, that few could rightly read,
> BON FONT: but *bon* that once had written bin,
> Was raced out, and *Mal* was now put in.
> So now *Malfont* was plainely to be red;
> Eyther for th'evill, which he did therein,
> Or that he likened was to a welhed
> Of evill words, and wicked sclaunders by him shed.
> [5.9.26]

In the earlier books of the poem Spenser was confident in his ability to make distinctions between himself and false artists such as Archimago. Here, he can no longer affirm his difference from Bonfont turned Malfont, since he has abandoned unqualified praise for his queen not only in Britomart's slaying of Radigund but also in Mercilla's execution of Duessa. Moreover, by introducing the Mercilla episode with this striking figure of Bon/Malfont, Spenser appears at once to announce that the disgraced poet could very well be himself and to deflect criticism by anticipating it and dramatizing it. Yet Spenser also subtly calls into question the justice of the punishment itself, since underneath the newly inscribed "Mal," the originary "Bon" can still be read; the self-interested and capricious power of the sovereign to rename the poet cannot completely efface his former name. The other emblem of the poet's transgression, his nailed tongue, is also ambiguous: as Michel Foucault has suggested, such punishment marks the victim's body as the vehicle of display for the sovereign's power, although its excessive violence can subvert sovereignty by eliciting solidarity between the people and the victim.[32] The nailed tongue and its superscription thus raise many questions: Is the poet in fact Bonfont or Malfont? According to whose standard? Does Spenser accept the queen's power to rename which rivals or supersedes his own? Does he acquiesce to her power to rename *him* as Malfont?[33]

In the Proem to Book 5, Spenser lamented the degeneration of the world, which has "runne quite out of square, / From the first point of his appointed sourse, / And being once amisse growes daily wourse and wourse" (5.Pr.1). The ultimate consequence of this degeneration is the confusion of opposites:

> For that which all men then did vertue call,
>   Is now cald vice; and that which vice was hight,
>   Is now hight vertue, and so us'd of all:
>   Right now is wrong, and wrong that was is right,
>   As all things else in time are chaunged quight.
>   Ne wonder; for the heavens revolution
>   Is wandred farre from where it first was pight,
>   And so doe make contrarie constitution
> Of all this lower world, toward his dissolution.
> [5.Pr.4]

If, as Helgerson suggests, Spenser's eminence over the other poets of his age resided in his ability to make and maintain distinctions (for example, between Una and Duessa, Florimell and False Florimell), then the blurring of distinctions in the later books (between Britomart and Radigund, Bonfont and Malfont), which subverts his allegory, can be seen as symptoms of Spenser's loss of faith in the course of contemporary history.[34]

It is fitting, then, that as the ultimate breakdown of the distinction between self and Other, at the end of Book 5 Spenser's poem generates the Blatant Beast, a monstrous reincarnation of Slander—and of Malfont. Yet unlike Malfont, who could be silenced by nailing his tongue to a post, this monster threatens, with a multiplicity of uncontrollable tongues, to backbite and destroy Spenser's poem at the end of Book 6.

Notes

1.   Richard Helgerson, *Self-Crowned Laureates: Spenser, Jonson, Milton and the Literary System* (Berkeley: Univ. of California Press, 1983), pp. 55, 91.

2.   David L. Miller, "Spenser's Vocation, Spenser's Career," *ELH*, 50 (1983), 215–16. For similar views, see also Thomas H. Cain, *Praise in the Faerie Queene* (Lincoln: Univ. of Nebraska Press, 1978), pp. 131–32; Michael O'Connell, *Mirror and Veil: The Historical Dimension of Spenser's Faerie Queene* (Chapel Hill: Univ. of North Carolina Press, 1977), p. 13; and Jonathan Goldberg, *Endlesse Worke: Spenser and the Structures of Discourse* (Baltimore: Johns Hopkins Univ. Press, 1980), pp. 166–74.

3.   Robert Ashton, *Reformation and Revolution: 1558–1660* (London: Paladin, 1984), p. 180.

4.   O'Connell maintains, specifically in reference to the Radigund episode, that the mythic power of Spenser's fiction "enable[d] him to respond to the pressure of history without endangering his moral allegory" (pp. 139–40). But see Judith H. Anderson, "'In liuing colours and right hew': The Queen of Spenser's Central Books," in *Poetic Traditions of the English Renaissance*, ed. Maynard Mack and George deForest Lord (New Haven: Yale Univ. Press, 1982), pp. 47–66, who argues that Spenser's representation of Elizabeth is already complexly shaded in Book 3, and in Book 4 is even more critical. The vehicle of such criticism is the distinction and distance between "life and antiquity, historical present and mythic past, current truth and Faerie image" (p. 51).

5.   Angus Fletcher, *Prophetic Moment: An Essay on Spenser* (Chicago: Univ. of Chicago Press, 1971), p. 279. See also the fuller statement on p. 248: "The allegory must show her

relation to her own violence, namely the potential Radigund in her, so that she may experience this violence and reject it for her ultimate marriage to [Artegall]." Similarly, A. C. Hamilton, *The Structure of Allegory in the Faerie Queene* (London: Oxford Univ. Press, 1961) observes: "Radigund expresses Britomart's womanly pride to which Artegall submits" (p. 185); "In terms of the allegory [Britomart] changes from her role as Radigund—one who occasions Artegall's fall—to one who restores his power" (p. 189).

     6.   For example, T. K. Dunseath, *Spenser's Allegory of Justice in Book Five of the Faerie Queene* (Princeton: Princeton Univ. Press, 1968), p. 177, states: "The only physical clash between two women in the poem . . . pits upholders of different principles against one another—love against lust. In the logic of the poem's structure, it is Britomart's final confrontation of the forces of Malecasta. . . . The outcome of the battle is never in doubt." See also *Variorum* 5:221: "[Britomart's] victory is the vindication of social justice against a revolutionary polity."

     7.   James E. Phillips, Jr., "The Woman Ruler in Spenser's *Faerie Queene*," *HLQ*, 5 (1942), 217–18, 233–34. See also his "The Background of Spenser's Attitude Toward Women Rulers," *HLQ*, 5 (1942), 5–32; and Constance Jordan, "Woman's Rule in Sixteenth-Century British Political Thought," *Renaissance Quarterly*, 40 (1987), 421–51.

     8.   See Angus Fletcher, *Allegory: The Theory of a Symbolic Mode* (Ithaca: Cornell Univ. Press, 1964), p. 38. Fletcher considers the essence of allegory to be its abstraction, its "omission of human detail," which neither the mimetic nor the mythic mode omits (p.29n).

     9.   Cain, p. 153.

     10.   Hamilton, *Structure of Allegory*, p. 183, sees the central issue of the Radigund episode to be that of "maisterie" between Britomart and Artegall.

     11.   Rosemond Tuve, "Spenser's Reading: The *De Claris Mulieribus*," in *Essays by Rosemond Tuve: Spenser, Herbert, Milton*, ed. Thomas P. Roche (Princeton: Princeton Univ. Press, 1970), pp. 87–90, explains the "enlargement and deepening of the action," Radigund's development beyond "merely a martial Acrasia," by reference to Spenser's use of Boccaccio's Iole, who was somewhat justified in her humiliation of Hercules because he had caused her father's death. Radigund, whom Spenser compares to Iole, begins to elicit a "sympathy . . . which we ought to feel only for a tragic heroine." But Fletcher sees Radigund as an allegorical figure conforming to his theory of allegory and so interprets this same process differently: "Sometimes, indeed an allegorist will go out of his way to create the monuments of evil and the rationality of madness as when Spenser does . . . when he shows that Radigund, *the absolute antagonist of the good*, has her own laws, her own rights, her own feelings, and her own ideals" (*Allegory*, p. 361; emphasis added).

     12.   Judith Anderson also sees a change in Artegall "from a principle to a person" in his battle with Radigund and notes in this passage "Artegall's fall into a human context, a human condition." She goes on to remark, "Once Artegall sees a human reality outside himself, he becomes aware of his own feelings and, at least to this degree, of himself." "'Nor Man it is': The Knight of Justice in Book V of Spenser's *Faerie Queene*," *PMLA*, 85 (1970), rpt. in A.C. Hamilton, ed., *Essential Articles for the Study of Edmund Spenser* (Hamden, Conn.: Archon, 1972), p. 455.

     13.   Paul J. Alpers, *The Poetry of the Faerie Queene* (Princeton: Princeton Univ. Press, 1967), pp. 127–31, argues that although we note the basic parallel between Artegall's two battles with Britomart and Radigund, critical tact advises against seeking out detailed remembrances.

     14.   Jane Aptekar has noted the paradigm of the "choice of Hercules" between pleasure and virtue as governing Artegall's mistaken "choice" of Radigund. She thus sees Britomart and Radigund, representing virtue and pleasure, as diametrically opposed "choices" for Artegall. *Icons of Justice: Iconography and Thematic Imagery in Book V of the Faerie Queene* (New York: Columbia Univ. Press, 1969), pp. 172–200.

     15.   Kathleen Williams, *Spenser's World of Glass: A Reading of the Faerie Queene* (Berkeley: Univ. of California Press, 1966), p. 134.

16.   On the reversal of gender roles in the Radigund episode, see Lillian S. Robinson *Monstrous Regiment: The Lady Knight in Sixteenth-Century Epic* (New York: Garland, 1985), pp. 337–41, especially her observation that "Spenser explicitly equates the female sex and people who work for wages," placing both in opposition to the aristocratic soldier (p. 341). Natalie Zemon Davis, "Women on Top," in *Society and Culture in Early Modern France* (Stanford: Stanford Univ. Press, 1975), pp. 124–51, argues that transvestism and sexual reversal associated with the carnival were multivalent images that at once affirmed and undermined the status quo. Concerning Radigund, however, she suggests: "Some portraits of [the disorderly woman] are so ferocious (such as Spenser's cruel Radagunde and other vicious viragoes) that they preclude the possibility of fanciful release from, or criticism of, hierarchy" (p. 133). See also Maureen Quilligan, "The Comedy of Female Authority in *The Faerie Queene*," *ELR*, 17 (1987), 167–72, on the Radigund episode's "transgression [of gender roles] deserving the text's violent laughter" (p. 168). Concerning Britomart's restoration of male rule, she writes, "Female authority here is not funny, because it is real" (p. 171).

17.   Joan Kelly, "The Social Relation of the Sexes," in *Women, History, and Theory: The Essays of Joan Kelly* (Chicago: Univ. of Chicago Press, 1984), p. 14.

18.   Hamilton, *Structure of Allegory*, p. 185.

19.   Dunseath, pp. 181–82. Some critics, however, express misgivings about the conclusion of Britomart's plot: Tuve remarks that "there is something oversuccessful about Britomart despite the sop in vii, 36" (p. 90), and Alpers finds unconvincing the contradictions in Britomart's role—"the princess who restores women to men's subjection and then is adored as a goddess" (p. 304).

20.   Victor Turner, *The Drums of Affliction: A Study of Religious Processes among the Ndembu of Zambia* (Oxford: Clarendon Press, 1968), p. 276.

21.   René Girard, *Violence and the Sacred*, trans. Patrick Gregory (Baltimore: Johns Hopkins Univ. Press, 1979), pp. 11–12.

22.   See, for example, Kenneth Burke, *The Philosophy of Literary Form* (Berkeley: Univ. of California Press, 1973), p. 20.

23.   James Emerson Phillips, however, does not discuss the Radigund episode as an example of literary representations of Mary Stuart in his *Images of a Queen: Mary Stuart in Sixteenth-Century Literature* (Berkeley: Univ. of California Press, 1964). But O'Connell sees the Radigund episode as the first allusion to Mary in Book 5, one generous in its portrayal of her, and the combat between Britomart and Radigund as the twenty-year struggle between the two queens (p. 140). Cain thinks that the episode recalls the project of marrying Leicester to Mary (p. 154).

24.   Winfried Schleiner, "*Divina virago:* Queen Elizabeth as an Amazon," *SP*, 75 (1978), 164. He discusses Belphoebe's association with Penthesilea (pp. 176–79). See also Celeste Turner Wright, "The Amazons in Elizabethan Literature," *SP*, 37 (1940), 433–56. Louis Adrian Montrose, "Shaping Fantasies: Figurations of Gender and Power in Elizabethan Culture," *Representations* 1:2 (Spring 1983), 65–68, discusses the Amazonian myth as the culture's "collective anxiety about the power of the female not only to dominate or to reject the male but to create and destroy him." Shakespeare's *A Midsummer Night's Dream*, he argues, "eventually restores the inverted Amazonian system of gender and nurture to a patriarchal norm."

25.   "The Copie of a Letter to the Right Honourable the Earle of Leycester," in *Elizabethan Backgrounds*, ed. Arthur F. Kinney (Hamden, Ct: Archon, 1975), p. 234.

26.   For example, Frank Kermode, "*The Faerie Queene*, I and V," in *Shakespeare, Spenser, Donne* (London: Routledge and Kegan Paul, 1971), p. 58: "*Being herself Justice incarnate as Equity*, [Mercilla] proceeds, as Britomart proceeded to the suppression of Radigund, to the trial of Duessa" (emphasis added). More recent critics note tensions in the episode, though without necessarily concluding that Spenser was critical of Elizabeth. O'Connell sees a Spenser co-opted by Elizabethan policy: "His own vision of mercy . . . becomes no better

than the mercy finally afforded Mary. . . . His devotion to his queen and her cause is evident, even touching, but . . . the Legend of Justice falters" (p. 154). Cain considers the problem to lie in the discrepancy between "the harmony of justice and mercy praised in the icon" and the necessary insufficiency of political action (p. 145). Goldberg sees Mercilla passing judgment as "an exemplary figure of contradiction." See his discussion of the Mercilla episode as the site of a "fiction of sovereign power" in *James I and the Politics of Literature: Jonson, Shakespeare, Donne, and their Contemporaries* (Baltimore: Johns Hopkins Univ. Press, 1983), pp. 1–17. On the correspondences of Duessa and Mary Stuart in Books 1 and 5, see Richard A. MacCabe, "The Masks of Duessa: Spenser, Mary Queen of Scots, and James VI," *ELR*, 17 (1987), 224–42. He holds that Spenser's Mercilla episode is favorable to Elizabeth but also points out that in altering the details of the trial, Spenser makes Elizabeth directly responsible for Mary's execution and actively courts political reaction by representing a subject that had become complex and dangerous: "Those who wished to avoid controversy either left it untouched or attempted to dissociate both Elizabeth and James from the whole affair" (p. 241).

27. Dunseath, p. 218.

28. For example, René Graziani, "Elizabeth at Isis Church," *PMLA*, 79 (1964), 376–89; and James E. Phillips, "Renaissance Concepts of Justice and the Structure of *The Faerie Queene*, Book V," *HLQ*, 33 (1970), rpt. in *Essential Articles*, pp. 471–87. Both argue that contemporaries justified the execution of Mary on the grounds that Elizabeth showed mercy toward her subjects.

29. Alpers, p. 287.

30. Douglas A. Northrop, "Spenser's Defense of Elizabeth," *University of Toronto Quarterly*, 38 (1969), 277–94. The quoted passage is on pp. 280–81.

31. On "Spenserian ambivalence," see Fletcher, *Allegory*, pp. 269–73, who sees personal but not social ambivalence in Spenser, "because his poem is a largely idealized defense of the establishment." He does, however, consider the "taboo of the ruler" (Gloriana) to be at the center of the poem.

32. Michel Foucault, *Discipline and Punish: The Birth of the Prison*, trans. Alan Sheridan (New York: Pantheon, 1977), pp. 3–131, *passim*. Foucault's important study traces the disappearance of public execution and its displacement by private incarceration in late eighteenth- and early nineteenth-century Europe. He argues that in this process, punishment becomes the most hidden part of the penal process, and publicity shifts to the trial and the sentence. Although Spenser describes Duessa's trial at great length, he does not represent her execution; the juxtaposition of the public punishment of Bon/Malfont and the secret execution of Duessa appears to encapsulate the transitional stage that Foucault describes.

33. See Goldberg, *James I*, pp. 2–3, for another interpretation of "Spenser's representation of the relationship of his text . . . to the royal word." He suggests that Spenser submits to Elizabeth's truth in Book 5 generally and specifically in the representation of Bon/Malfont: "The poet . . . authorizes a view of society that denies him authority and makes his text simply a transcription of the social text."

34. Helgerson, p. 65.

Spenser's Giants

Susanne Lindgren Wofford

We hear much of Knights-errant encountering *Giants*, and quelling
Savages in books of Chivalry. . . . These Giants were oppressive
feudal Lords, and every Lord was to be met with, like the Giant, in
his strong hold, or castle. Their dependents of a lower form, who
imitated the violence of their superiors, and had not their castles,
but their lurking-places, were the Savages of Romance. The greater
Lord was called a Giant, for his power; the less, a savage, for his
brutality.

(Hurd, Letter 4, *Letters on Chivalry and Romance*)

But generally the high stile is disgraced and made foolish and
ridiculous by all wordes affected, counterfait, and puffed vp, as it
were a windball carrying more countenance then matter, and
can not be better resembled then to these midsommer pageants in
London, where to make the people wonder are set forth great
and vglie Gyants marching as if they were aliue, and armed at all
points, but within they are stuffed full of browne paper and tow,
which the shrewd boyes vnderpeering, do guilefully discouer
and turne to a great derision: also all darke and vnaccustomed
wordes, or rusticall and homely, and sentences that hold too much
of the mery and the light, or infamous and vnshamefast are to be
accounted of the same sort, for such speaches become not Princes,
nor great estates, nor them that write of their doings to vtter or
report and intermingle with the graue and weightie matters.

(Puttenham, *Arte of English Poesie* III, 6, pp. 165–66)

The connections and displacements between Spenser's allegory of desire—that
is, his psychomachia of the self—and his political allegory can be explored by
means of an analysis of the giants in *The Faerie Queene*. The troubled link
between these two allegories becomes especially problematic in this case
because the giants, who are engaged . . . in the text's representation of the
compulsion exercised by figures, are themselves central to Spenser's reflection

Reprinted from *The Choice of Achilles: The Ideology of Figure in the Epic* by Susanne Lindgren
Wofford with the permission of the publishers, Stanford University Press. © 1992 by the Board
of Trustees of the Leland Stanford Junior University.

on the powers and limitations of allegory. . . . Here the privileging of psychological over political allegory makes possible not only the characteristic swerve away from political critique but a more radical moral analysis. Considering both the classical tradition of giants as figures of rebellion against "lawful" authority, and the more popular tradition—appropriated for civic and royal purpose by Tudor monarchs, especially by Henry VIII and Elizabeth I—in which giants can represent the body politic and the legitimacy of the social order, I argue that Spenser's giants expose an ambivalence about the political system—in the self or in the society—that they either threaten or protect, and signal a concern about the legitimacy of the order allegory is able to represent. The use of the defeat of giants as one of the poem's principal figures for the imposition of political, generic, and sexual stability suggests, furthermore, that Spenser's text exposes the foundations of order as the political suppression of a violent other that nonetheless is necessarily figured as another version of the self. Thus while the submerged politics of these giant allegories hint at the arbitrariness of the power ostensibly authorized by these figures, the psychomachian reading of the giants takes a step further by more openly locating violence and the grotesque within the self.

In *The Faerie Queene* many of the chief threats to personal and political stability are represented as giants, and they are numerous. A list of the more important ones points to the centrality of great size and of the classical myth of the giants' rebellion against the gods in the allegorical scheme: one thinks of Orgoglio in Book I; Disdaine, the gatekeeper of Philotime's court in the Cave of Mammon in Book II; Maleger, who is not called a giant but is described as unusually large in II, xi, 20, and as a son of the Earth in II, xi, 45; Argante and Ollyphaunt in Book III; Corflambo in Book IV; Lust, though he is only "in stature higher by a span," IV, vii, 5; the Egalitarian Giant in Book V, canto ii; Geryoneo in Book V; Grantorto, who is described as "Like to a Giant for his monstrous hight" in V, xii, 15; Disdaine in VI, vii, 41; and Mutabilitie herself, who is described as a giantesse in VII, vi, 13.[1] In Books I, IV, V, and VI Arthur defeats a major giant, and the same pattern occurs in Book II if we consider Maleger a giant. Indeed, as James Nohrnberg has remarked, while the other heroes may face other sorts of battles, Arthur is preeminently a giant-killer.[2] Looking at this giant list, a reader of Spenser would be justified in thinking that *The Faerie Queene* uses greatness of size only as a figure for destructive or rebellious forces within the self or within society.

The House of Alma (Book II), however, is also clearly a giant human body, and Spenser's narrator seems particularly to enjoy the allegorical play by which he makes this symbolism evident.[3] In doing so, however, another tradition is invoked—quite different from the classical myth of the giants, who, following the Titans in rebellion, fought against the gods and had to be suppressed—that the body politic, the body of a society, may be represented as a giant figure. We are familiar with this concept in the doctrine of the King's or Queen's two bodies, which took on new vitality in the dynastic debates of the Tudor period.[4] It appears throughout the sixteenth century in popular festivities, and is represented in such images of Queen Elizabeth as the Ditchley portrait (circa 1590), and in the image of her body made into a giant map (as occurs in a Dutch engraging of 1598, in which Elizabeth's body becomes a map of Europe, itself a parody of Sebastian Munster's engraving "Hispania").[5]

Evidence for the existence and importance of this opposed, popular tradition that also informs Spenser's use of giants can be found in a variety of sixteenth-century English documents in which giants figure prominently in civic pageants, where they appear to stand for the strength and greatness of the body politic. Stow (in his *Survey* of 1618) describes the giants involved with the celebrations of the Midsummer Watch in London. "On the Vigill of St John the Baptist. . . . There were also diuers Pageants, Morris dancers. . . . The Sheriffes watches came one after the other in like order, but not so large in number as the Maiors: for where the Maior had besides his Giant three Pageants, each of the Sheriffes has besides their Giants but two Pageants."[6] The chief burden in the midsummer celebrations was borne, of course, by the guilds, who undertook also the "refresshinge" of the giants—an indication of the pervasive identification of giants with the popular body corporate.[7] Throughout the sixteenth century the giants participated in midsummer pageants: in 1522, the year of Charles V's entry into London, for instance, plans were made to skip the midsummer pageants since so much had already been prepared for his reception, but in the end the tradition was followed. It was decided by the Drapers Guild to "renew all the old pageants for the house; including our newe pageant of the *Goldyn Flees* for the mayr against midsomr; also the *gyant*, Lord *Moryspyks*, and a morys daunce as was used last year."[8] Under Edward the midsummer celebrations were suppressed, but Elizabeth revived them, and there is evidence that the giants continued to play a role throughout the 1580's and 1590's.[9]

These "popular" festivities were also turned to public civic and royal purposes, as we see in Charles V's entry, in the pageantry of which the city's giants had a major role to play. As Charles crossed the drawbridge, he was met with the following representations: "at the enteryng off the gate off the cytee dyd stande ij great Gyauntys one presenting the parson of Sampson and the other Hercules standyng in ryche apparell holdyng betwen a grete cheyn of yron and a table hangyng in the myddys off the chayne wheryn was wrytyn in goldyn lettyrs sett in byce the namys of all the landys and domynyons where the emperour is Kyng and Lorde in tokenning thatt the emperour is able to holde all those domynyons by pour and strength as the seyd gyauntys holde the same cheyne by pourer and strengyth."[10] Here the figures of the giants stand for the power of the King as he draws on the strength of the body politic, and the theme of giant size is also carried over to the dominions of the "empire."[11] The identification of Hercules as a giant has its more scholarly equivalent in the emblem books, where Hercules is represented as a man of enormous height, as he was in the "Hercules Gallicus" tradition illustrated in Alciati's emblem "Eloquentia Fortitudine Praestantior."[12] This emblem alludes to a version of the Hercules story in which he conquers many nations and overthrows tyranny not by force of arms but by eloquence. Through this capacity to persuade, Hercules established good laws and brought the Gallic people to a more civilized life, and thus the emblem is interpreted as a figure of good government. Its valuation of eloquence over military might also made it a favorite of poets and artists for whom it provided a myth of foundation that gave privileged place to verbal power.[13] The little chains ("leuibus . . . cathenis") passing from Hercules' mouth to the ears of his Gallic audience, ironically for my argument, are said in the verse to illustrate the lack of constraint in the moment of verbal persuasion. The popularity of the story of Hercules' victory over the Pygmies, as well as Alciati's emblem of Hercules as a huge figure in the center of twelve miniature representations of his labors, extends this association.

The English tradition of pageant and entry probably goes back farther than does our evidence. There is a record, for instance, of a similar pageant welcoming Henry V home from Agincourt in 1415. On that occasion the King had been met on London Bridge by a "gret geaunt."[14] On the continent, in contrast, Charles more frequently met with representations that alluded to the classical tradition of giants.[15] In spite of humanist influences, however, the English "popular" tradition continued through Elizabeth's reign, and indeed in her entry into London upon her coronation the Queen was met by a similar pageant of giants, this time placed at the Temple Bar and named "Gotmagot" and "Corineus," and again holding tablets inscribed with Latin verses.[16] The names Corineus and Gogmagog, first attached to the London giants in 1554 as far as the evidence tells us,[17] have a historical and biblical echo, suggesting that the giants served as reminders of foundation myths that guaranteed and even extended the power and influence of the city. According to the myth of the founding of Britain, Brutus, the great-grandson of Aeneas, fled from Troy, eventually to arrive in England. One of his band was Corineus, an able warrior; he received the land that would bear his name—Cornwall. There he fought the last of the giants who had inhabited the land, Gogmagog (Spenser calls him Goemot), whom Corineus slew in single combat, throwing him headlong into the sea from a high rock, which was then named after him. Corineus and Gogmagog represent, therefore, the ambivalent origins of the country—both the hero and the giant he slew are represented as giants in the pageant that confirms Elizabeth's rule, both of them serving to assert her legitimacy by linking her with the founding of the nation.[18]

Spenser himself invokes this aetiological myth in his description of the historical origins of Britain in Book II, canto x, where Arthur learns that Britain was first inhabited by giants: "farre in land a saluage nation dwelt, / Of hideous Giants, and halfe beastly men" (II, x, 7). The giants "Polluted this same gentle soyle long time" (II, x, 9), until various eponymous heroes, notably Corineus, defeat them. The giants remain important in Spenser's foundation myth, both as forces to be overcome and pacified, and as bearers of a hovering sense of the greatness of the land itself—its "stature huge and . . . courage bold" (II, x, 7). Corineus, whom Spenser honors as a hero, has, as we have seen, another role to play in the popular processions and festivities where, following this ambivalent tradition, he is himself transformed into one of London's most popular giants.[19]

In these foundation myths, which usually involve some primal violence perpetrated by the giants, the giants must often be purged or destroyed in order to allow the new civilization to flourish. In the popular tradition, however, foundation mythologies also tend to include stories in which giant size characterizes both the attacking ogre and the defending hero. Sometimes this originary giant even takes the form of a threatening monster who is baptized or somehow transformed into a protector, as is the case with the giant Le Reuze, protector of Dunkirk (Le Reuze first appears as a giant in a town procession in the 1550's, although the legends are much older).[20] In these myths, giants incarnate the power and importance of the city itself, and also represent the domestication or containment of the violence that occurred at its founding.

The antithetical function of giants in foundation myths such as these suggests that stories of giants allude to the violent founding of society and therefore can also undermine claims of legitimacy such as those the Tudors consistently strove to reinforce. The giant "Gogmagog" and the hero-turned-giant Corineus represent this antithetical quality: like Dunkirk's Le Reuze, in the pageant they illustrate the aestheticizing of the violence by which "legitimate" order imposes itself, and demonstrate how that violence may be elided and transformed into a myth of legitimacy. While such pageants in Elizabeth's honor may have minimized this antithetical quality, Spenser's allegory cannot do so as easily since his giants inscribe both the myths of legitimacy on which his politics are based and the structure of domination and suppression that permits his allegory to work. This political function is captured well by Bishop Hurd in the passage from his *Letters on Chivalry and Romance* with which I began this section. There Hurd reads giants directly as allegories for "oppressive feudal lords."[21]

Just as Hercules was a giant among men, so, metaphorically, are those of Spenser's heroes who take after him. Such metaphoric association, then, along with the double tradition of interpreting giants, suggests that *The Faerie Queene*'s giant-killers may themselves be more like giants than the fiction ostensibly allows, and that they may thus defend a political or moral order based on a repressiveness similar to that which the giants in the allegory of desire come to incarnate. Hence as figures for the aspects of the self, they may also represent the direction or control of a violence essential to the creation of an ordered self.

Spenser's many benign giants strengthen the association of heroes with giant size by reminding the reader that not all of Spenser's giant figures are valorized negatively. In addition to the two giants who help defend the House of Alma, other "good" giants include Awe, the porter at the gate of Mercilla's court, who sits "with gyantlike resemblance" (V, ix, 22), and Valgo, one of Britomart's descendants: "How like a Gyaunt in each manly part / Beares he himselfe with portly maiestee, / That one of th'old *Heroes* seemes to bee" (III, iii, 32). Both are images of good rule, while the description of Valgo expresses the link, implicitly ignored in many of the classical allusions to the giants, between the giants and the heroes of old. Neither "good" nor "bad" is Daunger, "An hideous Giant" (IV, x, 16) serving as porter or guard on the Porch of the Temple of Venus, a figure taken from courtly romance and allegories such as *The Romance of the Rose*. Spenser is quite consistent in providing a giant to guard many of the text's centers of order and value (the House of Alma, the Court of Mercilla, the Temple of Venus). A more complicated instance in Book III, finally, allies the giants in rebellion with Britomart. . . . When dismayed by the fire surrounding the House of Busyrane, she compares herself and Scudamour to the giants attacking Jove: "What monstrous enmity prouoke we heare," she asks, "Foolhardy as th'Earthes children, the which made / Battell against the Gods? so we a God inuade" (III, xi, 22). This reference is all the more striking since earlier, as she took off her helmet after fighting with Paridell and thereby revealed her hair and her gender, Britomart had been compared to Minerva, removing her helmet after defeating the giants (III, ix, 22). In canto xi Britomart fears that she and Scudamour are invoking a "monstrous enmity," and indeed it is the god they invade who proves to be monstrous, not Britomart in her assault on this figure of abusive authority. A rebellion echoing that of the giants is permitted, it seems, in the allegory of desire, because in that case Spenser can supply deformed or aberrant rulers whose authority "rightly" needs to be overthrown.[22]

Both the formal need for both benevolent and threatening giants and the presence of these specifically "good" ones argue, then, that the giant is a less simple figure than a first glance at Spenser's poem would tell, or that his displacing of the "popular" tradition is not as complete as one might suspect. It further complicates matters, moreover, that this overdetermination itself forms a part of the (relatively independent) exegetical tradition, reflecting in part confusion about the reference to the giants in Genesis 6, which holds that a giant can be a symbol of Christ (as in Psalms 19:5, for instance). William Langland refers to Christ as a giant, and this tradition, with its venerable patristic background, is even found in Luther, who refers to Christ in the moment of crucifixion as "crying with a loud voice like the bravest giant."[23] The Christian reading of the giants conflicts with the classical myth, coming from Hesiod, Virgil, and Ovid, of the rebellion of the giants against the gods, though the biblical giants were also separately connected with the Tower of Babel, with Nimrod, and therefore with the Genesis version of human arrogance. And because giants in the mythographic tradition can also be seen to represent the body, as opposed to the soul, of a human being—as Spenser consistently reminds us with his spelling of *Geants*, from *Gea*, the earth, echoing the creation in Genesis of the body from earth—their story can always evoke either human greatness or the greatest human failings.[24] Their story always narrates, then, to put it in slightly different terms, the impossibility of discriminating between antithetical traditions that coincide in and inform originary figures. Matters are not made easier, either, when we consider that these figures themselves function in the poem to embody, mark, enforce, or guard clearly defined boundaries—cells, bowers, houses, prisons—and thus figure a power of spatial and political discrimination that their own figurative bodies do not share. This discrepancy proves harder than one might expect to contain or displace.[25]

Like Rabelais's Pantagruel, who is discovered to have an entire world within him,[26] Spenser's House of Alma, which represents "man's body" (II, ix, 1), contains a whole society, with its nobility (the emotions around the heart), its intellectuals, and its working people, and thus figures the body politic. Details like the twice sixteen warders dressed in shining steel in the entry porch, a description of the teeth in the mouth (II, ix, 26), or the references to the two doors of the House (sts. 23–24), a beautiful one in front, a not-so-beautiful one behind, make this evocation of the body politic literal and comic. This giant body is itself defended by two giants: "those two brethern Giants did defend / The walles so stoutly with their sturdie maine" (II, xi, 15), a pun on hands ("maine") suggesting which parts of the body might be doing the defending.

Enclosed in its walls, with its virgin ruler Alma, the castle of the body might seem to incarnate the "classic" image of the body as described by Mikhail Bakhtin and elaborated by Peter Stallybrass.[27] It seeks to resist infirmity, contamination, and the results of sin by closing them out, while Maleger, evoking the image of a grotesque body, diseased and out of order, becomes also the giant representative of the "raskall rout" who lay siege to the castle. Maleger and the House he besieges might seem, then, to be two giant figures set in a simple opposition, one giant symbolizing good government of the self and by extension of society, and the other lack of government, chaos, or government by the raskall rout. In his allegorical introduction, however, the narrator proposes that the seeming opposition hides a different type of relationship:

> Of all Gods workes, which do this world adorne,
> There is no one more faire and excellent,
> Then is man's body both for powre and forme,
> Whiles it is kept in sober gouernment;
> But none then it, more fowle and indecent,
> Distempred through misrule and passions bace:
> It growes a Monster, and incontinent
> Doth loose his dignitie and natiue grace.
> Behold, who list, both one and other in this place.
>
> (II, ix, 1)

Spenser's language suggests that the one body can turn into the other: Maleger and his rebellious rout are the distorted or monstrous version of the human body itself, not something entirely "other"—though that distortion appears quite alien in the poem's fiction. The battle between Maleger and the inhabitants of the House of Alma can be read in these lines as a struggle between the classic and the grotesque body, a struggle in which contamination by the grotesque occurs in spite of Arthur's victory. Although the House has been set in order, the gigantic mouth and anus, the enormous stomach with its feasting and its furnaces and caldrons, the elaborate plumbing to help evacuate the waste, all evoke not the perfection of enclosure but the comic, Rabelaisian emphasis on what goes in and what comes out of the body and on the processes of transformation and growth within it.[28] The House of Alma is thus pictured as a classic body that cannot quite escape being parodied or literalized, and thus contaminated, by the grotesque—or again, it is pictured as a figure that cannot help embodying contradictory traditions.[29] By treating this figure of the well-governed body politic so literally, then, Spenser implies that the notion of the body politic is inevitably grotesque, although royal power may depend for its claim to authority on relentless aestheticization, enclosing, and classicizing of the giant that excludes this possibility.

The inevitable joining of these two opposites—"both one and the other" (II, ix, 1)—arises in part from Spenser's moral analysis: that fallen human life cannot evade sickness, death, or the results of sin, that a perfect image of government within the self is an ideal to be sought but not attained. The two apparently opposed giant figures prove to be versions of each other, exemplifying a moral ambivalence characteristic of Spenser's figurative use of his giants: they can be both "good" and "bad," with the plot energy always working to distinguish them while the images continue to reconnect them. Thus Maleger, like other giants, is a son of the earth, Gea, but so is the House of Alma: "Not built of bricke, ne yet of stone and lime, / But of thing like to that *Aegyptian* slime, / Whereof king *Nine* whilome built *Babell* towre" (II, ix, 21). The distinctions between the authorized and the subversive versions are thus made, as Stephen Greenblatt has argued, by a violent process of demonization in which the grotesque or distorted is momentarily excluded:

the "bad" giants are killed off or toppled down, while the "good" ones either help in this process or are purified by it.

It is not surprising, given the homology between such analysis and the construction of the self, to find that the excluded grotesque returns in the antithetical imagery that connects the hero and his or her enemy.[30] The description of the House of Alma thus emphasizes the different implications of these ambivalent giants for Spenser's moral and political allegories. In the moral allegory the double image of the giant body serves to remind readers that, in this internal struggle, the demonized other nonetheless remains a part of the self, a part to be controlled or cleansed, but not something that can be completely purged. But if the duplicity of the image seems to produce instances of complexity in the moral allegory, in the political allegory things work differently. In the ideal society of the House of Alma, there is no place for the "thousand villeins" (II, ix, 13) who put the House under siege, and who appear as trivial to Spenser's scheme as "scattered Sheepe" (II, ix, 14) or "idle shades" (st. 15) or "Gnats" (st. 16). They are "vile caytiue wretches, ragged, rude, deformd" (st. 13), their poverty and class indicated physically as a kind of deformity, and they disappear as their leader is conquered. While the overt political allegory describes just rule putting down a rebellion, utterly destroying or routing the rebellious subjects, the moral allegory posits a more complex relation between the demonized rebels on the one hand and the human body on the other. The moral complexity typifies Spenser's use of giants in a psychomachia, but is reduced when it comes to the political meanings asserted by the narrator. The ambivalent role giants play in the moral scheme stems from their use as figures of alternative versions of the self, and brings the "popular" tradition of the giant as an authoritative image of the body politic into play against the classical mythology.[31]

The shift from the political version of the story as an account of rebellion to a moral or ethical interpretation largely occurs in postclassical interpretations of the myth, such as those proposed by Comes and other Renaissance mythographers who describe the giants either as representing principles of physical science such as earthquakes, or as providing a moral, psychological, or religious allegory. The giants in particular are explained by Comes as representing inner moral struggles of the individual, especially the struggle against the appetites, concupiscence, and lust.[32] Clearly Spenser's Orgoglio, Maleger, and the various giants of desire all belong in this tradition, as has been long noted, and the tendency to view giants as psychological figures occurs also in such places as Donne's *Devotions upon Emergent Occasions*: "O what a *Giant* is *Man*, when he fights against himselfe, and what a Dwarfe when hee *needs*, or *exercises* his owne assistance for himselfe!"[33] Transforming the political story, as these mythographers did, into a moral tale, Spenser's text also makes the battle against the giants an inner struggle. This internalization of a political story still conveys something of that politics symbolically since in Spenser's fiction the giant is treated as an external agent. In linking the submerged politics with a radical moral reading, then, this turn inward conveys the large influence of society in shaping the individual emotional or bodily sphere, and suggests that this sphere has a political significance. This internalization also obfuscates the more disruptive political story being told—a narrative that linked political authority to its demonic opposite—though that story is heard nonetheless in the many incidents in which giants are the cause of enslavement or tyranny.

The recurrence of the theme of thralldom reemphasizes what we find to be the case in Spenser's text more generally: in Arthur's subduing of the rebellion against the House of Alma, the allegory of desire and of the body hides both an allegory of politics (centered on the body politic) and a politics of allegory. As a particularly forceful instance of the workings of allegorical compulsion, the behavior of Spenser's giants of desire figures forth an issue for the writer as well as the moralist. Their action . . . is predictable, though not less onerous for that: psychomachian giants almost mechanically imprison their victims in dungeons or caves, bind them in chains, and in particular make them their "eternall bondslaue" (I, vii, 14) or the "thrall of [their] desire" (III, vii, 37), placing them in eternal bondage (III, vii, 50) or slavery (V, x, 27).[34] The two clear representations of rebellion or revolution in *The Faerie Queene* are the battles fought by "the thousand villeins" and Maleger in Book II, cantos ix–xi, and the reaction of the followers of the Egalitarian Giant in Book V, canto ii, to Talus after he has toppled the giant. In the case of Book II, the political image is tied to a moral one, which is shown to refer to an internal struggle partly because the figures outside who attack the House resemble those described as inhabiting the first chamber of the mind (II, x, 50). This connection between the political theme and the figuration of desire suggests that the poem represents the difficulty of giving fictional form to emotions such as pride and desire by implying . . . that allegorical characterization can be enthralling or enslaving.

The poetry establishes more links between the heroes and the giants than the political allegory would lead one to suspect. As if to distinguish Artegall from other giant-fighters, Book V begins with Artegall's receiving from Astraea the sword that Jove used "in that great fight / Against the *Titans,* that whylome rebelled / Gainst highest heauen" (V, i, 9): this opening seems to affirm that the classical myth of the giants will be given special privilege throughout this quest. The divine sword urges that a violent dividing line be drawn between the hero and those he defeats, yet more similarities exist between giant and hero than this clear division would suggest.[35]

The Egalitarian Giant of Book V, canto ii, can serve as a case in point. As Angus Fletcher observed in *The Prophetic Moment* (p. 157), in this episode Artegall seems to be in dialogue with himself; and as Stephen Greenblatt has gone on to argue in "Murdering Peasants," there is not only an "uncanny resemblance between the Giant's iconographic sign (the scales) and Arthegall's, but . . . [a] still more uncanny resemblance between the Giant's rhetoric and Spenser's own" (p. 20). Spenser intensifies this resemblance—which is called to mind partly by the proximity of the canto to the Proem to Book V—by comparing the giant in his fall to a ship, "whom cruell tempest driues / Vpon a rocke with horrible dismay" (V, ii, 50), so that the shattering and fragmenting of the giant seems the breaking apart of one of the boats that perhaps formerly belonged to the fleet of the poem (as in I, xii, 1 and 42). The Egalitarian Giant is clearly a Bakhtinian collective giant, representing the wishes and thoughts of the "lawlesse multitude" (V, ii, 52) who burst out in open rebellion following his fall (st. 51). The tension that results in the narrative from this ambivalent treatment of the giant and his followers is generated in part by the tension between the moral and the historical (or political) allegories, and is resolved in part by allowing Talus to do the dirty work.

What Artegall in fact does, however, is try to teach the giant to become a figure in a psychomachia, that is, to internalize the issue of justice:

> But *Artegall* him fairely gan asswage
> And said; Be not vpon thy balance wroken:
> For they doe nought but right or wrong betoken;
> But in the mind the doome of right must bee;
> And so likewise of words, the which be spoken,
> The eare must be the ballance, to decree
> And iudge, whether with truth or falshood they agree.
>
> (V, ii, 47)

This statement reiterates the typically Spenserian psychic geography that locates the "sacred noursery of vertue" deep within the mind, but it misses the giant's point in large measure. While Artegall can win on the issue of weighing words, most of what the giant wants to weigh and redistribute is quite physical, and most of it has to do, not with judging right and wrong, but with rendering portions equal. What Artegall does is to depoliticize the giant's message, claiming that such thoughts about leveling and other weighing of the inequalities of life may be perfectly appropriate, as long as they take place within the mind. As mental acts, they may even provide a basis for justice, as long as they do not lead to political consequences. The episode gives, then, a slightly different slant on Spenser's valuation of internal or imaginative life, for in the context of political action, such an inward turn can become an evasion of political meaning. Emphasizing the episode's relevance to Spenser rather than to Artegall, Greenblatt comes to similar conclusions: "Talus' violence, in destroying the Giant, exorcises the potentially dangerous social consequences—the praxis—that might follow

from Spenser's own eloquent social criticism" ("Murdering Peasants," p. 22).
My point, though, is that this exorcism fits also with another move—the
inward turn—that seeks to transform the giant from political to moral
allegory.[36]

This inward turn occurs with many of Spenser's giants, all of whom
are associated with the issue of government (as tyrants or through the
topos of giants as representatives of a body politic), for in all the cases
except those in Book V the allegory transforms what could be a political
topic into a moral one. His consistent shift from the political to the moral,
from the world of conquest and history to an inner world, reveals that the
kinds of oppositions Spenser's allegory represents can be successfully
resolved within his moral framework but not within the political framework he necessarily gives to his poem, and that the model of the self that
Spenser proposes, though submerged, is political. These episodes further
imply that thematic or representational allusions to the political within
these stories can be displaced and suppressed by a depoliticizing turn
inward.

Within the context of the poem's interrogation of poetic modes, the
"inward turn" ceases to be a contingent strategy for evasion and displacement since these versions of the self provide a complicated and at times
disturbing analysis of psychological life that becomes linked through its
giant form with the processes of allegory. Conceived as a mode that dictates
a particular relation of inside and out, allegory would appear to provide a
formal resolution of the psychological and the political, though, as we have
seen, the resolution depends on giving one privilege while displacing the
other and thereby limiting its more disruptive potentiality. It is striking
evidence of the hierarchial tendency within allegory that in the many
instances of opposition or tension between the political and the psychological, the allegory works consistently to submerge and render secondary the
more disruptive interpretation.

A similar ambivalence colors the treatment of gender in these representations of giant bodies politic. Alma, for instance, is a lady and a "virgin
bright" (II, ix, 18), and nothing in the allegory of the body hints at anything
female about it. This nongendered or asexual giant may thus be meant to
represent both sexes, but its lack of gender also allows the text to sidestep
the difficulties that would be encountered were the giant body female. The
situation is very difficult, then, in the case of the giant body that constitutes
the landscape of the Garden of Adonis (III, vi). Here the moral and aesthetic
doubleness of giants is highlighted by a deeper ambivalence about representing female power. As with the literalism that typified the poem's account
of the House of Alma, Spenser is highly specific about the bodily parts to
be found in this landscape, though here he focuses particularly on those
details unmentioned in the case of Alma, on the *mons veneris* that stands

"right in the middest (III, vi, 43) of the Garden.[37] This giant, then, is not only female but sexual and fertile.

Like Spenser's other giants, the body of the Garden of Adonis also has its political resonance, for it draws surreptitiously on the identification of the sovereign's body with the landscape and thereby figures the queen's body politic—the land of England—as the body natural.[38] In spite of its fertility— or perhaps as a related cause of it—this landscape too is marked by hidden or submerged losses that imbue the setting with beauty and animation. In this garden, however, the flowers are not only Ovidian—"And all about grew euery sort of flowre, / To which sad louers were transformd of yore" (III, vi, 45)—but Elizabethan. The landscape is filled with flowers that stand for the permanent frustration or loss of those who loved, while the stanza-long epic catalogue ends on the fate of Amintas, who is associated with the flower Amaranthus and "made a flowre but late" (st. 45); this line is often taken to be a reference to Sidney, whom Spenser had called Adonis in his elegy, but who now has become another flower to adorn Venus's bower. The shift to the allusion to Sidney introduces another disturbing sense in which this garden may be identified metaphorically as the body politic: frustrated suitors and courtiers, whose ambitions and desires were not met, are now scattered "all about" this inner landscape, debris of the power that makes such generativity possible. The figuration of the costs of poetic and of political power marked by the controls, frustrations, and limitations Elizabeth placed on her courtier-suitors come together in the image of the landscape as a body animated by suppressed and aestheticized loss. The poetics of personification in the Garden of Adonis accordingly corresponds to—or displaces—the erotic/political domination by which Elizabeth maintained her power.[39]

This image of hidden death and the frustration of desire contrasts with the partly Neoplatonic mythology of the Garden that surrounds the inner-most bower and *mons veneris*, for in the Garden, although Time threatens and is mentioned specifically as mowing "the flowring herbes and goodly things," life forms constantly die and are reborn as part of a cyclical myth— "So like a wheele around they runne from old to new" (III, vi, 33)—that allows a kind of change apparently not appropriate for the flowers in the innermost bower. Those who "grow afresh" in the Garden are eventually "sent into the chaungefull world againe" (st. 33)—old *Genius* "letteth out to wend / All that to come into the world desire" (st. 32)—whereas the flowers that deck the innermost sanctum, and Adonis himself, seem to be there for good. Moreover, in the Garden, there is no frustration of erotic satisfaction:

> For here all plentie, and all pleasure flowes,
> And sweet loue gentle fits emongst them throwes,
> Without fell rancor, or fond gealosie;
> Franckly each paramour his leman knowes.
>
> (III, vi, 41)

But this special exemption from the constraints felt by lovers throughout the poem somehow fails to apply to the innermost sanctum, where past "sad louers" now seem permanently to have become landscape, and where Adonis must be "hid from the world" and enjoyed not "franckly" but "in secret." These two versions of the Garden embody two competing fantasies: a vision of erotic—and political—satisfaction and creativity on the one hand, and on the other a vision of secret, maternal but also sexual power, protective and able to guarantee safety, but only at the cost of personal freedom and the possibility of acting in "the world"—only by forfeiting, in other words, precisely the heroic power of the constrained and frustrated lovers struggling to fulfill their heroic destinies in the epic action.

This giant too, then, seems to overpower those mortals with whom it comes in contact, for here the language of possession returns, although with a benevolent coloring:

> There wont faire *Venus* often to enioy
> Her deare *Adonis* ioyous company,
> And reape sweet pleasure of the wanton boy;
> There yet, some say, in secret does he ly,
> Lapped in flowres and pretious spycery,
> By her hid from the world, and from the skill
> Of *Stygian* Gods, which doe her loue enuy;
> But she her selfe, when euer that she will,
> Possesseth him, and of his sweetnesse takes her fill.
>
> (III, vi, 46)

Venus and Adonis are at once part of the landscape and separate from it; the "secret" place in which Adonis hides is Venus's innermost bower, yet somehow it is also connected to the flowered spicery of the *mons veneris* (see III, vi, 43), complete with hidden arbor and underground cave, where Adonis's great enemy, the boar, is imprisoned:

> Ne feareth he henceforth that foe of his,
> Which with his cruell tuske him deadly cloyd:
> For that wilde Bore, the which him once annoyd,
> She firmely hath emprisoned for ay,
> That her sweet loue his malice mote auoyd,
> In a strong rocky Caue, which is they say,
> Hewen vnderneath that Mount, that none him losen may.
>
> (III, vi, 48)

Mythologically, of course, the boar destroys Adonis, so that imprisoning him spares the youth. Allegorically, the animal is often interpreted as lust or as a bodily desire that ultimately kills the mortal Adonis (and that links Adonis to Timias, another frustrated courtier); the boar is also connected to the hunt, an erotic image that can figure the active life. The text thus seems to provide an image of permanent *jouissance*—the phallic boar imprisoned "for ay" in a cave underneath the *mons veneris*—that perfectly combines erotic satisfaction and utter constraint. The ambivalent force of the image is in part conveyed by the qualification "rocky": we have seen rocky caves before, and know that they appear in the text in scenes of imprisonment that signal moments of figurative control. Here the threatening image of the all-powerful woman who will "possess" her lover is displaced by or overlaid with the contrasting image of endless satisfaction with its promise of a form of eternal life. This image of erotic satisfaction, with its political connotations, can be shaped only with the darker outline of "possession" behind it, in part because having one's "desire" fulfilled by the Queen also meant complete submission to her. She embodied and practiced the two extremes of power adumbrated in the Garden: the power to satisfy and the power to destroy. As image of the beloved, she was indeed a courtier's "dearest dred."[40]

The love affair of Venus and Adonis can also be read as a story of love between a mortal and an immortal, and thus Adonis might understandably be pictured as overwhelmed by this more powerful presence. The text consistently implies that for a mortal to love an immortal—often a figuration for love of or commitment to an ideal—can be devastating, even if such a love is of the noblest sort. Although Belphoebe excludes herself from this category ("Nor Goddesse I . . . We mortall wights" III, v, 36), Spenser allows her to adumbrate an ideal, and Timias's experience in serving her is as ambivalent as that imagined for Adonis. While presenting the immortal as overwhelming and "possessing" may seem an appropriate evocation of power beyond the human, then, it nonetheless confers a genuine doubleness upon the act of submission to such powers. Spenser's Muse is another female figure who wields over him a power that can be threatening as well as productive, as is indicated by the analogy of the poet and Merlin when possessed by a visionary "spirite." When the union is with one's Muse, the subjection it seems to demand can serve as a figure for devotion to one's vision or inspiration, but the subjection becomes more disturbing—both formally and thematically—in the political language from which such visions prove inseparable in the fiction.

To assert that a political mythology of Elizabeth's union with her land, as well as a political fantasy that links the fulfillment of desire with a deeper subjection, may underlie the myth of fertility and generation in the Garden of Adonis is not to suggest that the latter focus is unimportant or somehow secondary. On the contrary, in this enfolded and protected space Spenser establishes his fiction's authority, claiming for it a generative power that appears to exceed that of the political world. It is striking, however, that even this poetic landscape, which draws on such diverse literary and philosophical sources, also appropriates the Queen's authority and her image of the "body politic," thus risking the danger of coming too close to this body. While imagery throughout the poem communicates an underlying distrust of female power, and while the representation of Venus and Adonis may extend the submerged anxiety in other treatments of female sexuality, the political allusion in the landscape focuses this ambivalence into an ambivalence about Elizabeth herself and a critique of the way she wielded power. This connection is further strengthened by the political connotations in the imagery of erotic "possession" and "enthrallment" characteristic of the poem as a whole. In the Garden of Adonis, the poet at once provides a central myth of fertility derived from a poetic and mythological power, and qualifies it by making it dependent on a principle of female authority figured as satisfying the male only by imprisoning or "possessing" him. The text needs a link to this female, sexual world in order to produce its myth of textual and poetic generativity, for the same reasons that it needs to draw on Elizabeth's power to help establish a social authority, but it nonetheless represents these needs as threatening to the very poetic power that this double mythology should reinforce. The poetic and the political work as partners here to disguise these anxieties about the source of power. The poetic myth promotes a generative interpretation of the female power at the center of the Garden, displacing the darker concerns about submission to the female (in the sexual or political realm) so that the political myth may appear to promote an equally generative understanding of political power. Perhaps because such an explicitly sexual vision of the female body is at stake here, and perhaps because he attempts to represent here the fictional origins of his own poetic forms, Spenser's discomfort with figuring power as female—let alone with relying on a female ruler—seems to come much closer to the surface than it did in his treatment of the ungendered body of Alma. The poetics and politics are not simply mutually reinforcing, then, nor is the poetic myth of the poem's body merged with this image of the body politic without the disclosure of a degree of discomfort—a disclosure that occurs here in the allusions to death and imprisonment, images seemingly out of place in the poet's own myth of imaginative fertility.

Ambivalence about a giant's size seems to be written into the myths themselves: does the creature's greatness lead him or her to great exploits or to a great fall?[41] Since giants can also stand for hyperbole and the high style in epic poetry, this ambivalence also expresses an anxiety that the tropes, styles, and conventions of epic distance, especially those associated with poetic ambition, may endanger rather than advance the poem's moral analysis, or at least render the text "too solemne sad." We have already seen something of this concern in the way the poem uses hyperbole to express chivalric fury while signaling the moment when a character is overtaken by the figure. Such textual disclosures expose unresolvable dilemmas about figurative power and animate a counternarrative that undermines the hyperbolic assertions of the allegorist as it challenges political hyperbole. It is precisely this danger of exposure and criticism that causes Puttenham to urge extra care in the use of the high style:

> But generally the high stile is disgraced and made foolish and ridiculous by all wordes affected, counterfait, and puffed vp, as it were a windball carrying more countenance then matter, and can not be better resembled then to these midsommer pageants in London, where to make people wonder are set forth great and vglie Gyants marching as if they were aliue, and armed at all points, but within they are stuffed full of browne paper and tow, which the shrewd boyes vnderpeering, do guilefully discouer and turne to a great derision: also all darke and vnaccustomed wordes, or rusticall and homely, and sentences that hold too much of the mery and the light, or infamous and vnshamefast are to be accounted of the same sort, for such speaches become not Princes, nor great estates, nor them that write of their doings to vtter or report and intermingle with the graue and weightie matters.
>
> (III, 6; pp. 165–66)

A concern about the abuse of high style gives way in these lines to a general concern about decorum. Puttenham's example is odd because it leaves us uncertain whether the giants—the high style in its more inflated form—are always "Puft vp with emptie wind" (I, vii, 9), as Spenser would put it, or whether it is rather the "underpeering" of the boys that makes the giants ridiculous. Considering the speed with which Orgoglio deflates, the reader of Spenser might see in the underpeering of these boys a reminder of the figure of the dwarf, or even a Redcrosse, peering out from the depths of Orgoglio's dungeon, or of the children gathering around the dragon in Book I, canto xii. Puttenham's word "underpeering" conveys again much of the ambivalence of these midsummer images of authority: the boys under-peer, look under, and thus subvert, the pretensions of the peers, of the realm perhaps, thereby exposing the weakness of the link between popular festivity and governmental legitimacy.

In and through the myths of giants, then, allegory represents its concern with systems of government, and allegory, as we have seen, is associated both with the giants themselves—for the giant overtaking the mortal becomes one figure of the workings of the mode—and with the monarchical body, which these creatures often figure either in its tyrannical or in its benevolent and generative aspect. The persistent connection to the story of Babel is thus not coincidental: giants are associated with the dispersion of languages, having helped to produce the fragmentation that leads allegory to take its drastic steps to recapture meaning. Allegory, the largest of Spenser's giants, large enough to claim to represent the body politic of the poem, can neither contain nor fully control its many antitheses and contradictions. Since it works by positing a system of oppositions and arrogates to itself the hyperbolic power to legislate and to move from one to the other, it finds its monarchy always threatened by rebellious underlings, who call attention to themselves by exposing a different significance to events. In cases such as that of the Egalitarian Giant, and, I would argue, whenever the historical and the moral allegory are potentially in conflict, the rebellion becomes so severe that allegory is driven to reveal its closeness to tyranny, and to the absolutist power that sustains its monarchy. Critical underpeerers may find the serpent of tyranny under the allegorical throne.

In the moment of allegorical tyranny, the reader can always turn back toward the moral allegory, in which more various meanings seem able to coexist, but to turn inward is also to ignore an aspect of Spenser's interrogation of his major poetic mode. When the text finds allegory to have potentially tyrannical powers, then, it is also forced to disclose that the good government it reveres resembles allegory more closely than its politic plots will allow. Spenser's allegorical narrator may feel that this is a price worth paying for order, in the macrocosm or in the microcosm. But his poem is less comfortable with this choice, and leaves its readers unable to decide whether this giant striding along the narrative (allegory itself, the body politic, the body natural) has beneficent or tyrannical intentions and consequences, or whether in fact it is as easy to distinguish order from tyranny as the plot of *The Faerie Queene* would require.

Notes

1. See also V, vii, 10, describing wine as the blood of giants, which the priests in Isis Church cannot drink.
2. See Nohrnberg, *Analogy of "The Faerie Queene,"* p. 264. On Arthur as a giant-killer in the Arthurian legends, see also Hankins, *Source and Meaning*, pp. 125–27.
3. Nohrnberg implies that the House of Alma represents a giant figure, for he comments that the Egalitarian Giant (V, ii) and his adherents serve as a parody of the House of Alma episode. See *Analogy of "The Faerie Queene,"* p. 353.
4. For the appropriation and political manipulation of this concept under Mary and Elizabeth, see Axton, *The Queen's Two Bodies.*
5. I cite these two engravings from Schleiner's article *"Divina Virago,"* plates 1 and 2, pp. 165–66.
6. John Stow, quoted in Withington, *English Pageantry* 1: 37.
7. Cited by Withington, *English Pageantry* 1: 38–39 and n. 5, from the records of the Skinners Guild in 1535–36.
8. Cited by Withington, *English Pageantry* 1: 40, from the records of the Drapers Company for 1522.
9. See Withington, English Pageantry 1: 44.
10. Withington reproduces, in *English Pageantry* 1: 175–78, the account in the manuscript in the library of Corpus Christi College, Cambridge, of "The descrypcion of the pageantes made in the Cyte of London att the recevyng of the most excellent pryncys Charlys the fyfte Emperour & Henry the viij Kyng off englonde," Corpus Christi (Cantab.) MS, 298 (no. 8). This quotation is from Withington, 1: 175.

11. The connection between size and imperial dominion is familiar also from the Ditchley portrait of Queen Elizabeth, where the representation of the Queen as a giant standing on the map of England images an imperial and even a cosmic power. See Strong, *Gloriana*, p. 138.

12. See Alciati, *Emblemata* (1584), Emblem CLXXX, "Eloquentia Fortitudine Praestantior," p. 246 verso. On the Hercules Gallicus tradition, see Nohrnberg, *Analogy of "The Faerie Queene,"* pp. 376–78, and Cain, *Praise in "The Faerie Queene,"* pp. 169–71. Cain does not comment on the attribution of giant size to Hercules.

13. Here is the French translation of the commentary from the 1584 *Emblemata*: "Ceste pourtraiture est prinse d'un traité de Lucian: par laquelle nous apprenons que Hercules tant celebré des auteurs anciens, a esté Gaullois, homme fort bien advisé, & des mieux disans, lequel estant bien fourny des parties qui appartiennent à l'homme propre au gouvernement du public, il reduit par ses sages remonstrances, & establissemens des bonnes loix le peuple Gaullois premierement impoly & barbare à une vie plus douce & civile" (p. 247 recto).

14. Cited by Withington, *English Pageantry* 1: 133.

15. See Jacquot, *Fêtes et cérémonies*, pp. 427 and 459, for examples. Jacquot mentions a painting on the vault of the gate of a city, decorated for a triumphal entry, representing "la Fureur sous les traits d'un géant enchainé," p. 420, echoing the description of the binding of Furor in the opening of the *Aeneid*.

16. Cited by Withington, *English Pageantry* 1: 202.

17. See Withington, *English Pageantry* 1: 58. Anthony Munday alluded to these giants in 1605 as appearing under these same names in the procession on Lord Mayor's Day. See Withington, p. 60, and pp. 59–62 on Gog and Magog.

18. The entertainments for Elizabeth at Kenilworth in 1575 also included giants.

19. See D. L. Miller, *The Poem's Two Bodies*, p. 195, for an account that also stresses a primal ambivalence in giants, this time associated with gender. Miller argues that giants come to be associated with a female contamination also connected to bestiality and the body.

20. See Tilly, *Le Carnaval Dunkerquois*. Le Reuze—the immense processional figure carried first during midsummer celebrations and then eventually moved back to Carnival—was brought out for the founding of the railroad in Dunkirk, an action signaling a cultural assumption that the city's giant should be present for all moments of foundation. A photo in Tilly's book, p. 34, shows the giant standing near the locomotive, which is apparently understood to be his modern cousin by those who organized the festivities. In Belgium and northern France most towns have their protecting giant figures, who played an important role in civic and religious pageantry in the sixteenth century. There is some debate about whether these giants came north from Spain, but evidence suggests in any case that the local legends predate the sixteenth century.

21. See Hurd, Letter 4, *Letters on Chivalry and Romance*, cited by Daniel Devoto in Jacquot, *Fêtes et cérémonies*, p. 314.

22. In all these "positive" examples the characters are "like" giants rather than giants themselves, the comparative structure measuring the distance between radical ambiguity and containable ambivalence that can act as a safety valve.

23. I take these references from Nohrnberg, *Analogy of "The Faerie Queene,"* pp. 273–74. He also gives a list of patristic sources for this interpretive convention, including Augustine, Alanus de Insulis, and Ambrose. The giants were read as being the offspring of the Sons of God and the daughters of men (*Genesis* 6:2–4), and hence as representing the double nature of Christ—part god, part man.

24. As noted by Hamilton. See Seznec, *Survival of the Pagan Gods*, p. 91, on the giants as representing human bodies.

25. See Freud, "Antithetical Sense of Primal Words," for a similar notion of undecidable ambivalence or doubleness of meaning. Freud mentions among others the Latin *altus*, high or tall / low or deep, as an example of such antithesis.

26. See Rabelais, *Pantagruel,* chap. 32; see also chap. 33 for another curative entry into the grotesque body.

27. See Stallybrass, "Patriarchal Territories," pp. 125–31, for an account of how and why the Bakhtinian distinction of grotesque and classic body should be gendered.

28. On the grotesque body, see Bakhtin, *Rabelais and His World,* and, for a useful summary of the difficulties raised by the transgression of boundaries associated with the grotesque body, see Stallybrass and White, *Politics and Poetics of Transgression,* chap. 1.

29. See D. L. Miller, *The Poem's Two Bodies,* pp. 165–83, for the theory that Alma is not left without gender but rather is male, though mention of the male sexual parts is avoided.

30. See Greenblatt, "Murdering Peasants": the "firm boundary between acceptable and subversive versions of the same perceptions . . . is affirmed [in Spenser], as in Sidney and Dürer, by the representation of violence" (p. 21).

31. The allegorical link between the heroes and the giants they fight is especially clear, then, in the cases of giants used in psychomachian allegory: thus Redcrosse's fight with Orgoglio is a fight with an aspect of himself, and such links are evident in the cases of giants such as Disdaine in VI, vii, 41, as well as Care, who "like a monstrous Gyant seem'd in sight" (IV, v, 37). As with the giants Argante, Ollyphaunt, and Corflambo, who serve as figures for lust in Books III and IV, the size of these psychological giants presumably expresses their power over the individual, the capacity of the represented feelings or emotions to overwhelm the self.

32. According to Comes, *Mythologiae,* Bk. VI, chap. 21, "On the Giants," for example, the great size of the giants is included in the myth because "the largest bodies are commonly inclined to give in to lasciviousness, and they stay angry for a long time: they do not easily give way to reason, are less capable of understanding wisdom, and more often give in to their pleasures, desires, and passions, for the strongest and most robust bodies very often have little wisdom or prudence." "As far as I am concerned," Comes continues, "I am of the opinion of Macrobius in the First Book of the *Saturnalia,* chap. 20, that [the myth of the giants] signifies nothing else but the manner in which imprudent people, who let themselves be ruled by their appetites, lusts, and passions, being contemptuous of God, impious, and denying all divinity, are defeated [and turned upside down] since religion is the enemy of all acts that are damnable and to be feared" (my translation).

33. Donne, cited by Nohrnberg, *Analogy of "The Faerie Queene,"* p. 260.

34. On thralls and thralldom see the preceding section in this chapter, and IV, vii, 12; IV, vii, 18; IV, viii, 51–52; VI, vii, 44; VI, vii, 50; VI, viii, 3.

35. See Aptekar, *Icons of Justice,* pp. 146–49. Cited by Hamilton in his edition, p. 598. Aptekar concludes that Geryoneo "represents a perversion or demonic parody of the power of just concord." As Aptekar also points out, Geryon, though evil in Spenser's scheme because he is associated with Spain and Spanish tyranny and because he is an enemy of Hercules, in the emblem books becomes a symbol of concord and united force.

36. See Norbrook, *Poetry and Politics,* p. 151, on the republication of *Faerie Queene* V, ii, as an anti-Leveller pamphlet in 1648.

37. Wells, in *Spenser's Faerie Queene,* pp. 68–69, 75–79, discusses the Garden of Adonis as a "subtle compliment" to Elizabeth, and as a figure of her through appropriation of the *hortus conclusus* tradition. See p. 68 on the identification of Elizabeth with "the garden-like state," and p. 69 for her portrayal as part of the landscape in one of the Progresses: "Elisaes brest is that faire hill." In her treatment of this topic, however, Wells does not discuss the explicitly sexual nature of this garden. On the anatomical geography of the Garden of Adonis, and the specific bodily positions and possibilities of Venus and Adonis, the account of Nohrnberg is especially valuable. See *Analogy of "The Faerie Queene,"* pp. 525–33, esp. p. 526: "If Spenser's Garden is also genital in character, then Adonis preserved within it corresponds to the male member or seed, and the *mons veneris* with its uncut foliage and enclosing grove stands for the female pudenda." See also the important account of Hankins in *Source and Meaning,* pp. 239–55, esp. p. 241.

38. For the politics of poetry drawing in part on this identification, see Helgerson, "The Land Speaks."

39. See Fumerton, "Exchanging Gifts," p. 264, for a different understanding of the allusion to Sidney and of these Ovidian flowers. She sees this stanza as contrasting with rather than helping to characterize the poet's vision of Venus and Adonis.

40. In the dense figuration of these passages, an exchange of male and female characteristics between Venus and Adonis is also adumbrated. See the work of Nohrnberg and Hankins cited above in note 37, and see also Fumerton, "Exchanging Gifts," pp. 262–63. Fumerton notes Adonis's passivity, but sees the exchange of gendered qualities as unproblematic, as if male and female, form and matter, were different but equal. I would argue in contrast that this figurative exchange of qualities is judged and qualified in the representation of its results in the landscape. The Queen's power and symbolic presence in the landscape is only *one* explanation of this darker outline of possession, of course—a psychoanalytic reading of this linking of the maternal body with fears of possession or loss of self would suggest a different wellspring for the episode, and, as we have seen, the text's own critique of the structures of allegory exposes the reliance of this symbolic form on versions of figural domination.

41. As Nohrnberg says, "All giants are subject to this critique of size. . . . It is this potential for diminution that draws them into a hubris myth in the first place," *Analogy of "The Faerie Queene,"* p. 264.

Works Cited

Alciati, Andrea. *Emblemata . . . Latinogallica.* Paris: Jean Richer, 1584.

Aptekar, Jane. *Icons of Justice: Iconography and Thematic Imagery in Book V of the "Faerie Queene."* New York: Columbia University Press, 1969.

Axton, Marie. *The Queen's Two Bodies: Drama and the Elizabethan Succession.* London: Royal Historical Society, 1977.

Bakhtin, Mikhail. *Rabelais and His World.* Trans. Helene Iswolsky. Cambridge, Mass.: M.I.T. Press, 1968.

Cain, Thomas H. *Praise in "The Faerie Queene."* Lincoln: University of Nebraska Press, 1978.

Comes, Natalis. *Mythologiae, sive explicationis fabularum, libri decem.* Padua, 1616.

Freud, Sigmund. "The Antithetical Sense of Primal Words" (1910). In Sigmund Freud, *Character and Culture,* ed. Philip Reiff. New York: Macmillan, 1963. Pp. 44–51.

Fumerton, Patricia. "Exchanging Gifts: The Elizabethan Currency of Children and Poetry." *English Literary History* 53 (1986): 241–78.

Greenblatt, Stephen. "Murdering Peasants: Status, Genre, and the Representation of Rebellion." *Representations* 1 (Feb. 1983): 1–29.

Hankins, John Erskine. *Source and Meaning in Spenser's Allegory: A Study of "The Faerie Queene."* Oxford: Clarendon, 1971.

Hamilton, A. C., ed. *Edmund Spenser: "The Faerie Queene."* London: Longman, 1977.

Helgerson, Richard. "The Land Speaks: Cartography, Chorography, and Subversion in Renaissance England." *Representations* 16 (1986): 51–85.

Hurd, Richard. *Letters on Chivalry and Romance* (1762). Ed. Edith J. Morley. London: Henry Frowde, 1911.

Jacquot, Jean, ed. *Fêtes et cérémonies au temps de Charles Quint.* Paris: Editions CNRS, 1975

Miller, David L. *The Poem's Two Bodies: The Poetics of the 1590 "Faerie Queene."* Princeton: Princeton University Press, 1988.

Nohrnberg, James. *The Analogy of "The Faerie Queene."* Princeton: Princeton University Press, 1976.

Norbrook, David. *Poetry and Politics in the English Renaissance.* London: Routledge and Kegan Paul, 1984.

Puttenham, George. *The Arte of English Poesie* (1589). Facsmile ed. Ed. Baxter Hathaway. Kent, Ohio: Kent University Press, Kent English Reprints, 1970.

Seznec, Jean. *Survival of the Pagan Gods: The Mythological Tradition and Its Place in Renaissance Humanism and Art* (1940). Trans. Barbara F. Sessions. New York: Pantheon, 1953.

Schleiner, Winifred. "*Divina Virago:* Queen Elizabeth as an Amazon." *Studies in Philology* 75 (1978): 163–80.

Stallybrass, Peter. "Patriarchal Territories: The Body Enclosed." In Margaret Ferguson, Maureen Quilligan, and Nancy Vickers, eds. *Rewriting the Renaissance: The Discourses of Sexual Difference in Early Modern Europe.* Chicago: University of Chicago Press, 1986. Pp. 123–42.

Stallybrass, Peter, and Allon White. *The Politics and Poetics of Transgression.* Ithaca: Cornell University Press, 1986.

Strong, Roy. *Gloriana: The Portraits of Queen Elizabeth I.* New York: Thames and Hudson, 1977.

Tilly, Catherine. *Le Carnaval Dunkerquois et les géants.* Dunkirk: Editions KIM, n.d.

Wells, Robin Headlam. *Spenser's "Faerie Queene" and the Cult of Elizabeth.* London: Croom Helm, 1983.

Withington, Robert. *English Pageantry: An Historical Outline.* 2 vols. Cambridge, Mass.: Harvard University Press, 1918.

Tasso on Spenser: The Politics of Chivalric Romance

RICHARD HELGERSON

The argument of this paper depends on three dates and their relation to one another. The first is 1580. In that year two small collections of letters between Gabriel Harvey and Edmund Spenser were published in London. These letters contain the earliest surviving reference to Spenser's *Faerie Queene*, which Harvey had been reading in manuscript and did not much like. The second date comes just a year later, 1581. In that year the first five complete editions of Torquato Tasso's *Jerusalem Delivered* appeared in Italy, to be followed in the next eight years by at least six more Italian editions. This enormously popular poem gave literary expression to a debate that had been raging in Italy for some forty years between opponents and defenders of Ariosto's *Orlando Furioso*, a debate over the proper form of heroic poetry. The last date, nine years further on, is 1590, when the first three books of *The Faerie Queene* were published, books which include at least one extensive borrowing from *Jerusalem Delivered* and many briefer echoes. Clearly Spenser had been reading Tasso and had found the Italian's work relevant to the poem he had shown to Harvey some years earlier.[1]

In addressing the relationship between *Jerusalem Delivered* and *The Faerie Queene* I am particularly interested in the way in which Tasso's poem may have served (and can still serve) as an interpretive guide to Spenser's. Whatever *The Faerie Queene* may have meant in 1580 when Harvey first read it, it is likely to have meant something significantly different in 1590 to anyone who had closely studied *Jerusalem Delivered*, as Spenser had. And this would have been the case were the 1590 *Faerie Queene* no more than a printing, as we know it was not, of the 1580 manuscript. In 1580, Harvey charged that Spenser had let "Hobgoblin run away with the garland from Apollo."[2] What Tasso forces into view and I think forced into view for Spenser himself was (and still is) the buried political significance of Spenser's Hobgoblinism, the meaning in the immediate context of the newly consoli-

From "Tasso on Spenser: The Politics of Chivalric Romance" by Richard Helgerson. *The Yearbook of English Studies*, Vol. 21, 1991. © Modern Humanities Research Association, 1991. All rights reserved. Reprinted by permission of the Editor and the Modern Humanities Research Association.

dated early modern state of what the eighteenth century was to recognize, again with Tasso's help, as the "Gothic" character of Spenser's chivalric romance.

At issue here is less any explicit statement Spenser's poem makes or any thematic "statement" made by its several episodes (though I will refer later to examples of each) than the meaning of the poem's generic form. In Spenser's generation, the generation born between about 1550 and 1565, a large number of men undertook major textual projects that put England at their centre. One might think, for example, of Sir Edward Coke's *Reports* and *Institutes*, William Camden's *Britannia*, John Speed's *Theater of the Empire of Great Britain*, Michael Drayton's *Poly-Olbion*, Richard Hakluyt's *Principal Navigations of the English Nation*, William Shakespeare's English history plays. *The Faerie Queene* clearly belongs on this list. But in each instance England is represented not only by a certain number of assertions that could be pulled out of context and compared to one another, but also by a particular genre, by a discursive "kind." A law report says something about England's legal identity, something about the centrality of precedent, quite apart from anything the individual cases it contains may say. And in doing so, it invests authority in one group rather than another, in judges rather than kings. Each of the genres to which these various works belong performs a similar legitimating act. Each is the implicit advocate of a set of socially grounded interests and of a political ideology associated with those interests. In this *The Faerie Queene* is no exception. Its form had a constituency and a politics, both of which are more easily seen when Spenser's poem is set next to Tasso's. A chivalric romance, like a law report, an atlas, a collection of voyages, or a history play, takes its meaning from an historically located system of differences.[3] For *The Faerie Queene* and its author the most immediately relevant system of differences, both literary and political, was made manifest in *Jerusalem Delivered*.

When eighteenth-century critics called *The Faerie Queene* "Gothic," they referred to its departures from classical epic design and decorum, to its multiple plotting and its fabulous knight-errantry: precisely those features that sixteenth-century Italian critics had already blamed in *Orlando Furioso*.[4] *Jerusalem Delivered* was designed to answer such objections. It does this, however, not by eliminating Ariostan romance but rather by subordinating it to epic. *Jerusalem Delivered* is founded on a conflict that goes far beyond the obvious struggle between Christians and pagans for the possession of Jerusalem. Within the Christian camp itself and within the narrative structure of the poem, the opposed values of epic and romance vie for mastery. Epic finds its prime representative in Goffredo, the divinely chosen ruler of the Christian forces. Romance, as fits its multiplicity of motive and action, has many champions, most prominent among them Tancredi and Rinaldo. Only Goffredo is single-mindedly devoted to the communal cause which brought the crusaders to Jurasalem. The others contribute to that communal cause.

Indeed, its success depends on their participation. But each is at some point led astray by other motives and by other desires: by love, honour, or the romantic quest for adventure.

One episode of many will have to serve to illustrate the strongly political terms in which Tasso presents the opposition between his epic and his romance heroes. In Book v Rinaldo slays Gernando, another of the Christian nobles, in a fight over honour and precedence. Despite the plea of Tancredi, who recalls Rinaldo's "worth and courage" and "that princely house and race of his," Goffredo resolves to punish the offender. "If high and low," he answers,

> Of sovereign power alike should feel the stroke,
> Then, Tancred, ill you counsel us, I trow;
> If lords should know no law, as erst you spoke,
> How vile and base our empire were, you know;
> If none but slaves and peasants bear the yoke,
>   Weak is the sceptre, and the power is small,
>   That such provisos brings annexed withal.[5]

"Sovereign power," "law," "empire," "sceptre": these are the dominant terms of Goffredo's discourse of rule. As the commander of the crusading forces besieging Jerusalem, he governs neither a single nation nor a fixed territory. But he is a royal absolutist none the less. His power was "freely given" him by God, and he refuses to see it diminished. "Since you are all in like subjection brought, / Both high and low," he tells Tancredi, "obey and be content" (v. 38). It is precisely such obedience that Rinaldo denies. Indeed, he refuses even to submit to trial. "Let them in fetters plead their cause, quoth he, / That are base peasants, born of servile strain; / I was born free, I live and will die free" (v. 42). For Rinaldo, the free-born nobleman, submission to the law is a sign of servile subjection. The state and its claims must give way before the higher claim of honour and lineage, and that higher claim is indissolubly linked to the behaviour characteristic of romance. Having defied the law, Rinaldo rides off in search of "hard adventures": "*alone* against the pagan would he fight" (v. 52, my italics). If sovereign power is the mark of Goffredo, solitary adventure is that of Rinaldo.

Tasso leaves no doubt concerning the official allegiance of his poem. It supports Goffredo. (The poem was originally called *Il Goffredo* or, in English, *Godfrey of Bulloigne*.) Where Goffredo's inspiration is divine, the moving forces on the other side are demonic. Satan, acting most often through the intermediary of such pagan women as Clorinda, Erminia, and the enchantress Armida, seduces the Christian champions and leads them into romance. Their recovery not only permits the final liberation of Jerusalem but marks a decisive victory of unity over multiplicity, of historic verisimilitude over the marvellous, of antiquity over the middle ages, and, one must add, of the modern absolutist state over its feudal predecessor. "The old chivalric code is," as one recent critic has remarked, "denied and overwhelmed in an epic world that reorganizes itself according to a new custom, a world where for the concept of 'ventura' (the medieval 'aventure') is substituted that of 'service,' where the role of 'knight errant' is suppressed for that of 'soldier' to a collective cause."[6]

That Tasso's epic allegiance is only official, that his poem betrays a "secret solidarity" with the feudal, romantic ideology that it ostensibly rejects, has been a commonplace of criticism almost since the poem was issued. But if *Jerusalem Delivered* does not make the choice easy, it does make it clear. Here epic stands not only for a supposedly superior literary form but for a whole system of values in which politics has a prominent part. In late sixteenth-century Italy those values were associated with the reinvigorated universalism of the Counter-Reformation church. Elsewhere they would find expression in the absolutist regimes of sixteenth-century Spain and seventeenth-century France. It was in France particularly that critics, though favourably impressed with the unity of Tasso's "fable," refused to forgive "the mixture of the Gothic manner in his work."[7] That mixture and its undoubted imaginative appeal called in question the commitment to absolute authority—aesthetic authority, religious authority, and political authority—on which neoclassicism was founded. Goffredo's obedient assertion of sovereign power had its counterpart in Tasso's acceptance of the classical rules of unity and verisimilitude. Both serve and express what Mervyn James (with particular reference to England) has called "the dominant theme of sixteenth-century political aspiration": "the desire and pursuit of the whole."[8] But the individual aristocratic prowess of Tancredi and Rinaldo, their resistance to royal justice, their solitary feats at arms, their erring loves, belonged rather to the freer world of Ariostan romance, a world in which the ruler was a marginal figure and his imperial project of negligible importance. If Tasso's poem was to satisfy the increasingly repressive and intolerant standards of seventeenth-century neoclassical judgement, that world of romance had not merely to be bounded by the epic but wholly replaced by it.

Tasso himself anticipated this need. Tormented by the thought of his own sinful errancy, he rewrote his poem, transforming the still half-romantic *Liberata* into the fiercely correct and generally unread *Conquista*. But long before making this radically destructive change in his poem, Tasso had responded to similar doubts with a remarkable post-publication addition. As early as 1581, the same year as the first complete edition of *Jerusalem Delivered*, the poem began appearing with a self-protective statement of authorial intention, "The Allegory of the Poem."[9] According to Tasso's allegorical interpretation civic happiness, represented by the capture of Jerusalem, is the goal, and Goffredo, who stands for the understanding of the politic man, is the hero. Solitary enterprise can, from this point of view, only be condemned. Thus, as Tasso puts it, "love, which maketh Tancredi and the other worthies dote and disjoin them from Godfrey, and the disdain which enticeth Rinaldo from the enterprise do signify the conflict and rebellion which the concupiscent and ireful powers" (that is, the love and war of the feudal nobility) "do make with the reasonable," with the newly rationalized and absolute power of the state.[10] If the civic enterprise is to succeed these errant powers must be subjected to their natural master as, to use Tasso's simile, the hand is subject to the head. Thus, however much the values associated with the civic life may be qualified in *Jerusalem Delivered* by an affective preference for romance, Tasso insists that whether one thinks of politics or of poetics, the public side rather than the private, the side of the divinely appointed ruler rather than that of the errant knight, must predominate. In this form and content are at one. The strongly unified epic must, Tasso clearly feels, be a poem of civic life, a poem in which unity of purpose and unity of rule are the guarantors of neoclassical conformity.

All this *The Faerie Queene* lacks. Its principal ruler, the Faerie Queene herself, never appears in the poem and exercises only the loosest and most intermittent control over its action—or, rather, over its actions, for there are many. Redcross, Guyon, Scudamore, Artegall, and Calidore are said to have been assigned their quests by the Faerie Queene, but she does not oversee their progress in anything like the way Goffredo oversees the taking of Jerusalem. Nor are the quests themselves parts of a unified enterprise, unless it be on the allegorical level where magnanimity and glory are said to be central. But in one's experience of the poem such conceptual unity plays little part, if any. Indeed, what readers of *The Faerie Queene* experience is, in this regard, not unlike what they would experience in reading Boiardo or Ariosto: they encounter a large and varied collection of more-or-less independent adventures that serve no common end. That, in effect, is what is meant by chivalric romance, what Italian critics of the sixteenth century and English critics of the eighteenth century meant by the Gothic. As a Gothic poem *The Faerie Queene*, unlike *Jerusalem Delivered*, allows no place for the representation of a powerfully centralized and absolutist governmental order. It acknowledges and celebrates a sovereign lady, but it grants a high degree of autonomy to individual knights and their separate pursuits, and so represents power as relatively isolated and dispersed.

In his letter to Raleigh, a letter that is clearly based on Tasso's "Allegory" and that presents a reading of *The Faerie Queene* informed by acquaintance with Tasso's poem, Spenser acknowledges the limited place *The Faerie Queene* occupies in the epic tradition. Like Tasso, he argues that that tradition has been divided between the representation of private and public virtues and remarks that Tasso himself dissevered these qualities, distributing them between two different characters (or perhaps two different poems), the "virtues of a private man, coloured in his Rinaldo," those of a political man "in his Godfredo." *The Faerie Queene*, or at least that part of it which he had so far written, belongs, Spenser says, entirely to Rinaldo's side, to the private side. Indeed, not only the three books he here presents, but the next nine (only three of which he actually wrote) will be similarly confined. Together these twelve books are to portray "in Arthur, before he was king, the image of a brave knight, perfected in the twelve private moral virtues . . . which, if I find to be well accepted," he says, "I may be perhaps encouraged to frame the other part of politic virtues in his person after that he came to be king" (I. 167–68). Spenser does not refuse the politic in favour of the private, the king in favour of the "brave knight," but he does put the politic and the kingly off to a time that, given the length of the poem, could be expected never to arrive. A similar split and a similar exclusion mark his representation of Elizabeth. As "most royal queen or empress," she is figured by the Faerie Queene, who, as we have noticed, never enters the poem. Belphoebe, who does enter it, stands rather for the queen's private person as "a most virtuous and beautiful lady." Again the private side dominates, and the political is kept waiting for some unreachable narrative prolongation. But that exclusionary deferral is itself an inescapably political act.

Spenser's division of public and private has a long history, going back at least to Aristotle's separate treatment of politics and ethics. Its history as a device for describing the Homeric poems and their various successors is scarcely less long. James Nohrnberg lists some fifteen instances from a period covering two millennia, from the ancient Greek allegories down through Servius and Macrobius to Landino, Scaliger, and Chapman. Nor is Nohrnberg content to stop with this Western, Græco-Roman line. "The Indo-European division of the gods, founder-figures, and castes into a kingly or priestly function (Mitra) and a warrior function (Varuna)" also claims relevance. Even this is too narrow a frame for this capacious tradition. "There seems," writes Nohrnberg, "to be no reason to restrict this [divided] characterization of heroism to Indo-European culture."[11] The effect of such wonderfully expansive scholarship is to naturalize and universalize the formal order of Spenser's poem. Freed from all particular location in time or space, the poem resides in triumph with the immortal archetypes. Though Spenser had heard of neither Jung nor Frye, his own evocation of "all the antique poets historical" aims at a similar elevation. It does something like what E. K. said the antique diction of *The Shepheardes Calender* would do: it brings "auctority to the verse" (ix. 8). But in Spenser a self-protective motive lurks just beneath the surface, a motive he acknowledges in explaining why he has picked Arthur as his hero. "I chose the history of King Arthur as most fit for the excellency of his person, being made famous by many men's former works, and also furthest from the danger of envy and suspicion of present time" (1. 167). The present is dangerous and can be approached, if at all, only by the indirection of a pretended universality.

No poetic form, however, is universal. None can escape the particularity of time and ideology, certainly not chivalric romance. The early English humanists' open opposition to chivalry and chivalric romance (think, for example, of Ascham's charge of "bold bawdry and open manslaughter"), the debate over Ariosto's *Orlando Furioso*, and, most tellingly, the sharp conflict between sympathy and doctrine within *Jerusalem Delivered* all point to the controversial nature of the genre in which Spenser chose to write his major poem. The militant aristocratic autonomy figured by the knight errant was potentially upsetting to reborn classicism, to civic humanism, to bourgeois commercialism, to royal absolutism, and even (as in *Jerusalem Delivered*) to the new military collectivism.[12] Humanist critics and scholars, merchants, ministers of state, and soldiers might thus all find themselves at odds with the chivalric knight. But if chivalry and its representative forms and figures could be highly controversial, they were also powerfully supported by the festive and poetic practices of the Elizabethan court. As Richard Hurd pointed out more than two centuries ago, "tilts and tournaments were in vogue; the *Arcadia* and *The Faerie Queene* were written" (pp. 116–17).

The Elizabethan vogue for tilts and tournaments is one of the best known and most intensely studied aspects of that "romantic" age. From the 1570s until the end of Elizabeth's reign the queen's Accession Day was regularly celebrated with lavish tournaments, and additional tournaments marked other significant court occasions. Indeed, it would not overstrain the evidence to claim that in the last two-and-a-half decades of the sixteenth century the language of chivalry became the primary language of Elizabethan public display, outdistancing even the biblical and classical motifs that had been more prominent earlier. Courtiers became knights, and their queen became a lady of romance.[13] But to recognize the extraordinary importance of the Elizabethan chivalric revival and its part in bringing *The Faerie Queene* into existence is not to dispel the air of potential controversy that, from other sources (including Tasso), we might have supposed to be gathering about Spenser's poem. Elizabethan chivalric display was itself a practice intended to deal with conflict, a way of simultaneously releasing and containing pressures that might otherwise threaten the delicate equilibrium of the Elizabethan state. "Through its conventions of feudal loyalty and romantic devotion, Elizabethan chivalry confirmed," as Richard McCoy has observed, "Tudor sovereignty." But it also gave vent to aristocratic aggression and competition. It thus represented, in McCoy's words, "a precariously incompatible, sometimes contradictory combination of purposes. . . . It allowed a kind of compromise between conflicting interests of the crown and her aristocratic courtiers as well as a mediation of factional and personal conflicts among the courtly ranks."[14]

In a remarkable study of the Earl of Essex McCoy has himself provided an illustration of these conflicting interests and their expression in chivalric display.[15] Celebrated by Spenser as "Great Englands glory and the Worlds wide wonder," "Faire branch of Honor, flower of Chevalrie, / That fillest England with thy triumphs fame,"[16] Essex stood, and died, for the martial and aristocratic values that were essential to chivalric romance. In this stance he and Tasso's Rinaldo have much in common. Each is torn between a private code of honour based on a combination of noble lineage and individual military accomplishment and the public duty any subject owes his sovereign. And each has been seen as central to the last of a particular medieval "kind": Rinaldo the enabling figure of the last Italian chivalric romance and Essex the leader of the last English "honour revolt."[17] Indeed, for each the end closes in before their individual stories are quite finished. In the final books of *Jerusalem Delivered* Rinaldo is reintegrated into the poem's epic design, becomes once again a dutiful soldier in Goffredo's army. And Essex, who through his trial had maintained a posture of defiant steadfastness, collapsed before his execution into abject penance, violating "almost with deliberation . . . all the canons of honour" (James, p. 458). The canons of honour and the canons of romance were rapidly succumbing, as they do succumb in the experience of both Rinaldo and Essex, to a new, more powerfully statist conception of moral obligation, a conception that found support in the unity and verisimilitude of classical literary form. Seen in this way Aristotle's rules (which were really Minturno's and Scaliger's) appear as the literary equivalent of Mervyn James's "desire and pursuit of the whole." The "political culture" of late Tudor England was, in James's words, one "whose stress [fell] exclusively on the creation and watchful maintenance of wholeness: i.e. on the effective incorporation of the individual into the body of the realm, under its head the queen" (p. 460). Change a word or two and this description would equally fit *Jerusalem Delivered* and the Counter-Reformation literary culture that produced it. In both the political and the literary cultures of sixteenth-century Europe wholeness was emerging as a dominant value.

In its Virgilian intimations, its attempts at unity, and its celebration of Elizabeth, *The Faerie Queene* participates in this cult and these cultures of wholeness. But in its adherence to chivalric romance it remains with the errant Rinaldo and the insubordinate Essex on the Gothic side of the great sixteenth-century cultural divide. Spenser came to know the danger of such errancy and insubordination. In Book V of *The Faerie Queene* an incautious poet, who has spoken ill of Queen Mercilla, is found nailed by his tongue to a post. And since Mercilla's court is the poem's nearest representation of Elizabeth's, the warning is particularly telling. Nor is this the only sign of danger. A sense of peril hangs over the whole of the 1596 instalment. Book IV, the first of the newly published books, begins with an acknowledgement that Spenser's own work has found disfavour in high places:

> The rugged forehead that with grave foresight
> Welds kingdomes causes, and affaires of state,
> My looser rimes (I wote) doth sharply wite,
> For praising love, as I have done of late.

And Book VI, the last of the new books, ends with the Blatant Beast of envy and detraction threatening Spenser's "homely verse" which, as he again admits, has already been brought "into a mighty Peres displeasure."

That "mighty peer," the possessor of the "rugged forehead" of Book IV, is universally identified as William Cecil, Lord Burghley, the lord treasurer of England and the queen's principal counsellor. Educated at Cambridge in a college dominated by Ascham and his humanist friends, Burghley was no partisan of the Elizabethan chivalric revival, nor did he much approve those most prominently identified with it. Essex was, for example, at odds with Burghley and with Burghley's son and political heir, Robert Cecil, throughout his public career. Referring to Burghley and Essex, the French ambassador wrote "there was always great jealousy between them in everything, one against the other, and a man who was of the lord treasurer's party was sure to be among the enemies of the earl."[18] In this antagonistic relationship Essex was only taking the place of his political mentor and Spenser's one-time patron, the Earl of Leicester. Spenser himself advertises this Leicester-Essex succession and his own relation to it. Catching sight of Leicester House in the course of his *Prothalamion,* he recalls that it was here "Where oft I gayned giftes and goodly grace / Of that great Lord, which therein wont to dwell / Whose want too well now feeles my freendles case" (l. 138). "Yet therein now," he continues, "doth lodge a noble Peer," the Earl of Essex, whose praises he goes on to sing in words already quoted. From 1579, when he dated a letter to Harvey from Leicester House, to 1596, when he celebrated Essex as "Great Englands glory," Spenser's strongest associations were with the party that opposed Lord Burghley. No wonder Burghley disapproved of his poetry.

"Spenser [was] the poetic spokesman *par excellence* of militant Protestant chivalry."[19] This statement by Roy Strong and Jan van Dorsten in their book on Leicester's Netherlands expedition sums up a widely-held view. What I have been arguing is that the Gothic form of *The Faerie Queene* does more than this. In addition to supporting the militant, interventionist policy of the Leicester-Essex faction, Spenser's image of chivalric multiplicity also represents a form of political organization in which the private initiative and private *virtù* (to use a familiar Italian word that includes both *virtue* and *strength*) of individual aristocratic champions plays an exceptionally large part. Whether consciously or unconsciously, Spenser makes his poem the implicit spokesman for a partially refeudalized English polity. The literary authority of Ariosto might at first have naturalized and thus concealed this political orientation, even from Spenser himself. Ariosto's could, after all, be considered simply the accepted way of writing a long heroic poem in the sixteenth century, whatever your politics. But with the publication of *Jerusalem Delivered,* in which the debate over Ariosto found at once literary and political expression, the mask of Ariostan legitimacy would have slipped badly. Setting Tasso's poem next to Spenser's, anyone could see, as

I think Spenser himself saw, how powerful and how powerfully significant his variance from the epic and its statist ideology really was. Faced with this recognition, he may have felt sufficiently uncomfortable to make some effort to unify and to "Virgilize" *The Faerie Queene*, as many critics think he did sometime between 1580 and 1590. But that effort could not alter the poem's fundamentally multiple and chivalric character. Whatever those qualities had "said," they went on saying, saying perhaps more forcefully for the very acknowledgement that they were not all that might be said. Like Tasso's, Spenser's is a poem divided against itself. But in it the balance comes down more firmly on the Gothic side.

The chivalric character of *The Faerie Queene* is so pervasive that it is almost invisible to any but the most superficial regard. And because literary critics are taught to eschew superficiality, it does not figure in most recent accounts of the poem.[20] In this the eighteenth-century critics had the advantage. They were not yet much given to our kinds of close reading, or at least they laboured under no institutional constraint requiring them to turn their close readings into published monographs. But they were still deeply involved, as we no longer are, in the Renaissance conflict between classical and medieval forms, and they knew that in terms of that conflict *The Faerie Queene* was a very troubling poem, a poem that in various ways resisted the ordering, unifying, and rationalizing tendencies of the previous two centuries. When John Hughes or Richard Hurd call *The Faerie Queene* "Gothic" or when Thomas Warton charges, as he did in his *Observations on the Faerie Queene*, that "Spenser made an unfortunate choice and discovered little judgment in adopting Ariosto for his example, rather than Tasso," they recognize this resistance and reveal that to them it still mattered.[21] This recognition may, as we have noticed, go back as far as Harvey's accusation of Hobgoblinishness, and it continued to be repeated with increasing critical and historical elaboration so long as the dialectic of Greek and Goth remained central to England's self-understanding and self-representation.[22]

But if the mere (and massive) fact of romance design and chivalric action was enough to make a powerful ideological statement, it is nevertheless true that many individual passages of *The Faerie Queene* reveal the ambivalence concerning absolute royal power which underlies the poem's representation of aristocratic autonomy. *The Faerie Queene* is, as many recent critics have insisted, a poem of praise, an important contribution to the cult of Elizabeth.[23] But that praise is variously qualified. Not only is the Faerie Queene herself kept out of sight on the poem's furthest periphery, but those figures of royal power that do enter the poem (all dangerously recognizable likenesses of Queen Elizabeth) inspire more apprehension than allegiance.

This is obviously the case of the "mayden Queene" Lucifera in Book I and her royal look-alike Philotime in Book II.[24] Both represent a demonic perversion of majesty, one that threatens those knights that approach the seat of power with dishonourable subjection. But even the "gratious" Mercilla, who, like Lucifera and Philotime, is first seen "Upon a throne of gold full bright and sheene, / Adorned all with gemmes of endlesse price" (V.9.27), presides over a court that knows nothing of the chivalric honour Spenser's poem is bent on celebrating. The bright armour of Arthur and Artegall "did . . . much amaze" the clamorous mob of petitioners that filled Mercilla's hall, "For never saw they there the like array, / Ne ever was the name of warre there spoken" (V.9.24). And when, later in the episode, two sons of Belge come seeking aid for their oppressed mother, "none of all those knights" belonging to Mercilla's court is willing to undertake the enterprise "for cowheard feare." So it is the stranger knight Arthur, here figuring Leicester, who

> stepped forth with courage bold and great,
> Admyr'd of all the rest in presence there,
> And humbly gan that mightie Queene entreat,
> To graunt him that adventure for his former feat.
>
> (V.10.15)

Mercilla "gladly" grants his request, but both the initiative and the subsequent action are his doing, not hers. If Lucifera and Philotime represent a perversion of honour, Mercilla's court betrays a passive neglect of it, though to say so in any less veiled way than Spenser does would be to risk the fate of the tongue-nailed poet Bonfont/Malfont.

In Book II Mammon tells Guyon that from his royal daughter Philotime alone "Honour and dignitie . . . derived are" (II.7.48). In his proem to Book VI Spenser says something very similar of and to his own "most dreaded Soveraine": "from you all goodly vertues well / Into the rest, which round about you ring" (VI.proem.7). This monarchic claim to a monopoly on honour, dignity, and virtue is precisely what marked the shift from a feudal to an absolutist regime. Spenser's description of Elizabeth as the unique fount of virtue contributes to this shift, but his parodic ascription of similar authority to Philotime questions it. And in the context of Book VI, the Book of Courtesy, even the positive assertion is so qualified that monarchic authority seems to be in competition (sometimes losing competition) with other, more private sources of validation. The book begins "Of Court it seems, men Courtesie doe call," but its narrative finds its prime representatives of courtesy far from court, in the woods and countryside. Indeed, one of the most attractive of those representatives, the old shepherd Melibee, berates the "roiall court" as a place of vanity, delusion, and idle hopes. And at the allegorical centre of the book, in the scene on Mount Acidale, the poet puts his own love in the privileged place hitherto reserved for the queen.[25] He apologizes for the substitution, but he makes it all the same.

Such displacements are anticipated earlier in the poem when the queen herself, in her "private" guise as Belphoebe, is removed from the court and made to speak against it.

> Who so in pompe of proud estate (quoth she)
> Does swim, and bathes himselfe in courtly blis,
> Does waste his dayes in darke obscuritee,
> And in oblivion ever buried is.
>
> (II.3.40)

And, significantly, it is in this private role that she values "deedes of armes and prowesse martiall" most highly. "All vertue merits praise," she says, "but such the most of all" (II.3.37). Where Mercilla presides over a "cowheard" court (the class slur in Spenser's spelling of *coward* is surely no accident) and where even the Faerie Queene recalls the heroic Artegall before his "reforming" work is thoroughly complete, Belphoebe herself bears, if not the instruments of war, at least those of the warlike chase. Divided from her royal power, in her private body, the queen appears as a martial figure, a fit exemplar of Spenser's heroic creed. But enthroned in her public body, she misleads, deflects, frustrates, or simply fails to nourish chivalric valour. It is thus appropriate that Spenser should have chosen to represent the deeds of Arthur as "a brave knight . . . *before* he was king" rather than his achievements *as* king. Kingship in the modern "politic" and absolutist sense is inimical to knightly, aristocratic virtue.

If *The Faerie Queene* expresses much ambivalence concerning the strongly centralized monarchic order that was to a large degree the very enabling condition of its existence, it entertains no similar doubts concerning the aristocratic myth of natural, inborn superiority. Virtuous ploughmen, salvages, and shepherd lasses regularly turn out to be the foundling offspring of nobles and kings, while base-born upstarts are just as regularly betrayed by their pride, insolence, and cowardice. Unlike those humanists who favoured virtue over lineage and who argued that the state might recognize virtue with the reward of noble title (as Elizabeth did for Sir William Cecil), Spenser refuses to envisage the separation of blood and virtue.[26] "Shame is to adorne," he charges, with the "brave badges" of arms and knighthood one "basely borne" (VI.6.36), but "O what easie thing is to descry / The gentle bloud, how ever it be wrapt / In sad misfortunes foule disformity" (VI.5.1). What then are we to make of his claim that "the general end . . . of all the book is to fashion a gentleman or noble person in virtuous and gentle discipline"? This, it must be insisted, is fashioning of a quite limited sort. Spenser does not mean to make gentlemen of what he calls "cowheard villains." That, he supposes, would be impossible.[27] His aim is rather to perfect the well-born in the discipline appropriate to their class.[28] And central to that discipline, as Spenser teaches it, is an aristocratic independence that would make a Leicester or an Essex a dangerous figure in the Tudor-Cecil state, just as a similar romantic and chivalric discipline and a similar insistence on the prerogatives of blood make Rinaldo a disruptive figure in the regime governed by Goffredo. The difference between Spenser and Tasso is that Spenser endorses claims of birth that Tasso admires but ends by reducing to obedience.

That reduction was essential to the making of the modern state and it was powerfully under way in Tudor England. New men and the service of a new monarchy were, as we have noticed, turning the state into the unique fount of honour. Without such changes *The Faerie Queene* would have been quite literally inconceivable. Yet, as much as it is the product of a new monarchic centralism, *The Faerie Queene* resists that centripetal force. It represents an uneasy and unacknowledged compromise between a monarch who gives both poem and nation whatever unity and identity they have and individual aristocratic knights whose adventures are the glory and the safety of the nation. Private virtue, "*ethice*" in the term of Spenser's letter to Raleigh, is made the sole instrument of public action. Instead of a princely Goffredo at the head of a highly organized and complexly equipped army, solitary knights embody England's Protestant destiny in *The Faerie Queene*, destroy the enervating Bowre of Blis, overcome the enemies of Belge and Irenae, capture the Blatant Beast. In a letter to Sir Philip Sidney, Sidney's political guide, the Burgandian humanist Hubert Languet, warned his pupil against independent action on behalf of the Belgian states. "It is not your business, nor any private person's, to pass judgment on a question of this kind; it belongs to the magistrate, I mean by magistrate the prince, who, whenever a question of the sort is to be determined, calls to his council those whom he believes to be just men and wise. You and your fellows, I mean men of noble birth, consider that nothing brings you more honour than wholesale slaughter; and you are generally guilty of the greatest injustice, for if you kill a man against whom you have no lawful cause of war, you are killing an innocent person."[29] In their principal quests Spenser's knights are not guilty of such injustice. Their actions are licensed by the magistrate. But they do enjoy an autonomy that such Elizabethan generals as Leicester and Essex exercised only with peril and reproach. Though tempered by statist ideology, the chivalric form of *The Faerie Queene* strengthens the association that Languet (like many humanists before him) blames, the association of aristocratic honour with "wholesale slaughter," an association that, as Languet realizes, menaces the monarch's authority as the sole dispenser of justice.

In standing against neoclassical order and verisimilitude, Spenser's Gothic image of England stands against the rationalizing tendencies of the modern state, tendencies that determined the form of *Jerusalem Delivered*. This oppositional stance is the constant preoccupation of his various proems. In each Spenser sets what he calls "antiquity," a time that belongs rather to the idealizing historical imagination than to any particular period but whose most prominent features are romantic and chivalric, against the present, with the unfailing proviso that his dread sovereign mistress be understood as exempt from all blame. Indeed, antiquity and the queen are repeatedly presented as the twin sources of his poem. But clearly there is a tension between them, a struggle in Spenser's effort to fit "antique praises unto present persons" (III.proem.3). That tension and that struggle were not, however, his alone. They belonged equally to the militant Protestant faction with which, through most of his career, he was associated: to Leicester, to Sidney, to Essex, and to the many lesser figures who supported them. Bridled by a parsimonious queen and a cautious minister, the members of this faction found themselves, like Tasso's Tancredi and Rinaldo, repeatedly torn between private honour and public duty. By enforcing the claims of duty, both civic humanism and Aristotelian neoclassicism worked to restrict and ultimately deny the aristocratic cult of honour. Spenser's chivalric romance pulls the other way. It enlarges the sphere of honour and identifies private virtue with public obligation. *The Faerie Queene* represents a nation of indistinct boundaries and uncertain political organization, at once British and Faerie, but it leaves no doubt concerning the value of lineage and heroic endeavour. For all its claims to some larger truth, claims that generations of critics have expanded and elaborated, Spenser's poem thus served a quite particular, even partisan, ideology, a Gothic ideology of renascent aristocratic power.

Notes

1. For a list of Spenser's borrowings from *Jerusalem Delivered*, see Veselin Kostíc, *Spenser's Sources in Italian Poetry: A Study In Comparative Literature* (Belgrade, 1969).

2. *The Works of Edmund Spenser: A Variorum Edition*, edited by Edwin Greenlaw and others, 11 vols (Baltimore, 1932–57), x, 472. Subsequent quotations from Spenser come from this edition and are identified by volume and page number with the exception of quotations from *The Faerie Queene*, which are identified by book, canto, and stanza.

3. For an example of an analysis governed by the terms suggested in this paragraph, see Richard Helgerson, "The Land Speaks: Cartography, Chorography, and Subversion in Renaissance England," *Representations*, 16 (1986), 50–85.

4. Eighteenth-century characterizations of *The Faerie Queene* as "Gothic" can be sampled in *Spenser: The Critical Heritage*, edited by R. M. Cummings (New York, 1971), pp. 206, 224, 229, 232, and 260–61. Bernard Weinberg surveys the debate over Ariosto in *A History of Literary Criticism in the Italian Renaissance*, 2 vols (Chicago, 1961), II, 954–1073.

5. *Godfrey of Bulloigne: A Critical Edition of Edward Fairfax's Translation of Tasso's "Gerusalemme Liberata,"* edited by Kathleen M. Lea and T. M. Gang (Oxford, 1981), V, 37. Unless otherwise indicated, subsequent quotations from *Jerusalem Delivered* are from this translation and are identified, as is this one, by book and stanza.

6. Sergio Zatti, "Cultural Conflict as Military Encounter in the *Jerusalem Delivered*," paper read to the Southern California Renaissance Conference (1983). I have also drawn in my

discussion of Tasso on Zatti's book, *L'Uniforme Cristiano e il Multiforme Pagano: Saggio sulla "Gerusalemme Liberata"* (Milan, 1983). The phrase "secret solidarity" in the next sentence is borrowed from Zatti.

7.   Richard Hurd, *Letters on Chivalry and Romance* (1762), edited by Hoyt Trowbridge, The Augustan Reprint Society, nos. 101–02 (Los Angeles, 1963), p. 79.

8.   Mervyn James, *Society, Politics and Culture in Early Modern England* (Cambridge, 1986), p. 460.

9.   Of the twelve pre-1590 editions of the *Gerusalemme Liberata* listed in the British Library catalogue, seven, including the 1581 Ferrara edition and every edition published after 1581, contain the author's allegory. Another, Parma 1581 (British Library 1073.g.31.(1.)), clearly had access to it and used it as the basis for its allegorizations of individual cantos. The allegory is lacking only in the unauthorized and incomplete edition of 1580 and the Parma (British Library 1489. p. 12), Casalmaggiore, and Lione editions of 1581. It is thus probable that in reading Tasso's poem, Spenser would also have read the allegory.

10.   *Godfrey of Bulloigne*, p. 90.

11.   James Nohrnberg, *The Analogy of "The Faerie Queene"* (Princeton, 1976), pp. 61–63.

12.   Arthur B. Ferguson surveys this opposition to the chivalric revival in *The Chivalric Tradition in Renaissance England* (Washington, D.C., 1986), pp. 83–106.

13.   I assume here some acquaintance with the large body of scholarship that has recently been devoted to the Elizabethan chivalric revival. In addition to the work of Ferguson, McCoy, Esler, and James, cited in the notes 12, 14, and 15, see Frances A. Yates, *Astraea: the Imperial Theme in the Sixteenth Century* (London, 1975); Roy Strong, *The Cult of Elizabeth: Elizabethan Portraiture and Pageantry* (London, 1977); Alan Young, *Tudor and Jacobean Tournaments* (London, 1987).

14.   Richard C. McCoy, "'Yet Little Lost or Won': Chivalry in *The Faerie Queene*," paper delivered at Modern Language Association Convention in Houston (1980).

15.   McCoy, "'A dangerous image': The Earl of Essex and Elizabethan Chivalry," *Journal of Medieval and Renaissance Studies*, 13 (1983), 313–29. Similar arguments concerning Essex are made by Arthur Ferguson, *Chivalric Tradition*, pp. 73–74, by Anthony Esler, *The Aspiring Mind of the Elizabethan Younger Generation* (Durham, North Carolina, 1966), pp. 87–99, and by Mervyn James, *Society, Politics and Culture*, pp. 416–65.

16.   *Prothalamion*, ll. 146 and 150–51 (VIII. 261).

17.   Zatti remarks that "*Jerusalem Delivered* closes historically the season of the chivalric poem" ("Cultural Conflict"). The characterization of the Essex revolt as the last English "honour revolt" comes from James, p. 416.

18.   Quoted by Conyers Read, *Lord Burghley and Queen Elizabeth* (London, 1960), p. 538.

19.   R. C. Strong and J. A. van Dorsten, *Leicester's Triumph* (Leiden, 1964), p. 3.

20.   An exception is Michael Leslie's *Spenser's "Fierce Warres and Faithfull Loves": Martial and Chivalric Symbolism in "The Faerie Queene"* (Cambridge, 1983). But even Leslie ignores the broader and more pervasive effects of chivalric romance to concentrate on the moral, religious, and historical significance of chivalric symbolism and knightly combat in specific passages.

21.   Hughes in Cummings, pp. 260–61; Hurd, p. 56; Thomas Warton, *Observations on the Fairy Queen of Spenser*, second edition, 2 vols (London, 1762), 1, 3.

22.   The dialectic of Greek and Goth is central to my essay "Barbarous Tongues: The Ideology of Poetic Form in Renaissance England," in *The Historical Renaissance: New Essays on Tudor and Stuart Literature and Culture*, edited by Heather Dubrow and Richard Strier (Chicago, 1988), pp. 273–92.

23.   This view has been elaborated in two book-length studies: Thomas H. Cain, *Praise in "The Faerie Queene"* (Lincoln, 1978) and Robin Headlam Wells, *Spenser's "Faerie Queene" and the Cult of Elizabeth* (London, 1983).

24. Michael O'Connell discusses these two figures and their likeness to Queen Elizabeth in *Mirror and Veil: The Historical Dimension of Spenser's "Faerie Queene"* (Chapel Hill, 1977), pp. 52–54 and 105–07.

25. I discuss this substitution in *Self-Crowned Laureates: Spenser, Jonson, Milton and the Literary System* (Berkeley, 1983), pp. 92–96. It should be noted that in this passage from Book VI Spenser's resistance to the monarch comes not from the aristocratic position that underlies chivalric romance, but rather from still another position, neither monarchic nor aristocratic, that is Spenser's as poet. Calidore, the chivalric knight, is as unwelcome and disruptive a figure on Mount Acidale as the queen.

26. It would perhaps be more accurate at this point to substitute "*The Faerie Queene*" for "Spenser." On the value of lineage and heroic endeavour, the poet was less certain than his poem. In *The Teares of the Muses*, he mocks those "mightie Peeres" who "onely boast of Armes and Auncestrie" (VIII, 65). Such mockery has no place in *The Faerie Queene*.

27. This impossibility is illustrated by the efforts of the baseborn Braggadocchio to learn horsemanship, "a science / Proper to gentle blood" (II.4.1). Compare young Tristram, whose knightly behaviour shows him to be "borne of noble blood" (VI.2.24) despite his rude upbringing.

28. Frank Whigham exposes the contradictions implicit in such a project in *Ambition and Privilege: The Social Tropes of Elizabethan Courtesy Theory* (Berkeley, 1984).

29. *The Correspondence of Sir Philip Sidney and Hubert Languet*, edited by Steuart A. Pears (London, 1845), p. 154.

Spenser's Late Pastorals

PAUL ALPERS

Spenser, as everyone interested in him knows, began his career as a writer of pastoral. But he also returned to pastoral at the end of his career, and we have not made this fact sufficiently intelligible. This essay begins by interpreting the pastoral cantos of Book VI *as* pastorals, and then draws out the implications of this analysis for *The Faerie Queene* as epic narration and for Spenser's poetry in the 1590s. In particular, I will argue that unlike *The Shepheardes Calender*, which was conceived as a prologue to heroic poetry, Spenser's late pastorals are alternatives to it.

Treating the pastoral cantos as pastoral means paying attention to the old shepherd Melibee and the poet-shepherd Colin Clout. By giving each of these figures his own domain, by involving the hero in a significant encounter with each, and by making these two encounters central to separate cantos of the poem, Spenser indicates that they have equivalent claims on the reader's attention. Critical commentary, however, has not followed the poem's lead. On the one hand, Colin Clout has been viewed as an authoritative presence in the poem. Kathleen Williams called him a "picture of the poet at his task of seeing meaningful order, an ultimate concord, and making it actual and influential in harmonious sound."[1] This is the note sounded again and again by Spenser's interpreters—by Harry Berger, for example, for whom Colin on Mount Acidale exemplifies the poet's "secret discipline," or by Northrop Frye, for whom he is the Prospero of Spenser's epic.[2] Melibee, on the other hand, is treated as always a simple and sometimes even a contemptible case. Berger fluttered the dovecotes many years ago by saying that his praise of the simple life is simply "an excuse for laziness."[3] Other critics, less openly disparaging, still view Melibee as utterly different from Colin Clout. Humphrey Tonkin says that he "inhabits a dream world," whereas "Mount Acidale presents a world of perfect order, visible only to the poet and the seer."[4] Even if Mount Acidale too proves to be in some sense "a dream world," the shepherd-poet at its center remains a privileged presence.

I think we cannot understand these cantos without first recognizing that the poem establishes a balance between Melibee and Colin Clout. Their

From *ELH*, Vol. 56, No. 4 (Winter 1989): 797–817. Reprinted by permission of The Johns Hopkins University Press, Baltimore/London.

237

parity is evident in a shared literary genealogy. Their appearance in two consecutive cantos ultimately derives from the somewhat programmatic juxtaposition, in Virgil's first Eclogue, of two kinds of pastoral song. The exiled Meliboeus represents his more fortunate companion Tityrus as one who "teaches the woods to resound lovely Amaryllis" (*formosam resonare doces Amaryllida silvas, Ecl.* 1.5). In response, the more down-to-earth Tityrus represents his freedom and music-making as "playing as I will on a rustic pipe" (*ludere quae vellem calamo permisit agresti,* 1.10). This last phrase, *calamo agresti,* is an alternative locution for pastoral music to Meliboeus's phrase "woodland muse" (*silvestrem musam,* 1.2). This muse is the lover's, teaching the woods to resound his beloved—or, in the less happy inflection of *The Shepheardes Calender,* "learn[ing] these woods, to wayle my woe" ("June," 95). Accordingly, in Book VI, the woodlands are the domain of Colin Clout. Mount Acidale is "bordered with a wood / Of matchlesse hight" (10.6), and Calidore is first drawn to its summit by the piping and thumping of feet "that through the woods their Eccho did rebound" (10.10).[5] Virgil's other epithet, *agrestis,* comes from *ager*—the "open fields" in which Calidore first comes upon the shepherds (9.4) and where Melibee discovered Pastorella (9.14). The characteristic utterance of this pastoral realm is not what Calidore first hears—"Layes of sweete loue and youthes delightfull heat" (9.4)—but the more astringent wisdom of the *fortunatus senex,* Melibee.

Melibee and Colin Clout can be seen as playing out two versions of pastoral, not only because of this Virgilian genealogy, but also because each derives from a standard figure in Renaissance eclogues. Melibee is a version of the old shepherd who advises or reproves his younger companions, often those who are love-stricken; Colin Clout is himself such a shepherd-lover, whose unfulfilled desire prompts eloquence and song. Each is an admirable, even elevated, example of his type. Though Melibee reproves Calidore, he does so for good reason and without the captiousness of old shepherds like the Thenot of *The Shepheardes Calender* ("February") or the Geron of Sidney's *Arcadia.* Colin Clout breaks his pipe "for fell despight" (10.18) when his beloved and the Graces disappear; but far from indulging his loss and "learning the woods to wail his woe," he bends his eloquence to celebrate the objects of his devotion. The high-minded conception and presentation of each of these figures must have something to do with their appearing in a heroic poem—both because characters in an epic are expected to be exemplary, and because the hero's encounter with each tests or instructs him in some way. Hence we can say that both Melibee and Colin Clout are conceived as figures who speak with pastoral authority.

This will be readily enough granted so far as Colin Clout is concerned, but the case still needs to be made for Melibee. He is prompted to speak when Sir Calidore self-consciously initiates a pastoral discourse:

> And drawing thence his speach another way,
> Gan highly to commend the *happie* life,
> Which Shepheards lead, without debate or bitter strife.
>
> How much (sayd he) more *happie* is the state,
> In which ye father here doe dwell at ease,
> Leading a life so free and *fortunate,*
> From all the tempests of these worldly seas,
> Which tosse the rest in daungerous disease;
> Where warres, and wreckes, and wicked enmitie
> Doe them afflict, which no man can appease,
> That certes I your *happinesse* enuie,
> And wish my lot were plast in such *felicitie.*
>
> (9.18–19, my italics)

Calidore, like many a courtly author, takes the point of the pastoral life to be escape from worldliness and its discontents. His speech encapsulates these motives in the key word "happie," which, as the courtier may well know, has plenty of pastoral authority. Both its meanings are registered here: like Virgil's Meliboeus, Calidore calls the old shepherd he addresses "fortunate," while "felicitie" looks to its root *felix* ("fortunate," but also "fruitful," "blessed"), the word which initiates Virgil's praise of country life in a famous passage in the *Georgics* (2.490ff). But Melibee denies the suggestion of unalloyed pleasure, as he will later deny the implication that it depends on luck:

> Surely my sonne (then answer'd he againe)
> If happie, then it is in this intent,
> That hauing small, yet doe I not complaine
> Of want, ne wish for more it to augment,
> But doe my self, with that I haue, content.
>
> (9.20)

Melibee responds to Calidore's key word "happy" with the idea of contentment. This is, for him a knowing virtue, which corrects the knight by revising his implied account of desire and choice. Melibee's speech leads to and concludes with the story of the false choice he himself made "when pride of youth forth pricked my desire" and, disdaining "shepheards base attire" he sought his fortune at court (9.24). Dismayed by the "vainesse" and "idle hopes" he found there,

> After I had ten years my selfe excluded
> From natiue home, and spent my youth in vaine,
> I gan my follies to my selfe to plaine,
> And this sweet peace, whose lacke did then appeare.
>
> (9.25)

The last line replicates Calidore's ostensible motive for praising Melibee's life, and shows the connection between the knight and the shepherd. But where Calidore feels and expresses his lack sentimentally, Melibee uses the verb "plaine" (i.e. complain) with fine double force. It first registers self-reproach, with "follies" as its object, and therefore expresses just appreciation, not mere regretful longing, for its second object, the "sweet peace" of his "natiue home." Hence Melibee, in his final words, can speak of desire not only chastened by but transformed into moral choice: "Tho backe returning to my sheepe againe, / I from thenceforth haue learn'd to loue more deare / This lowly quiet life, which I inherite here" (9.25).

Melibee's espousal of contentment is neither austerely stoical nor hard-bitten and defiant, in the manner of other old shepherds. On the contrary, his speech has a rather idyllic character—which is what prompts his critics and antagonists to speak of his "laziness," his "dream world," and the "soft pastoralism" of the canto.[6] Remarks like these replicate Calidore's misunderstanding, for the idyllic touches in Melibee's speech are grounded in rural tasks and chosen satisfactions. He defines pastoral content by topoi of golden age poems—the land's self-sufficiency and freedom from foreign trade—but scales them down to a life of conscious simplicity:

> So taught of nature, which doth litle need
> Of forreine helpes to lifes due nourishment:
> The fields my food, my flocke my rayment breed;
> No better doe I weare, no better doe I feed.
>
> (9.20)

His pastoral rhetoric similarly modifies another golden age topos, the spontaneous growth of crops:

> They that haue much, feare much to loose thereby,
> And store of cares doth follow riches store.
> The litle that I haue, growes dayly more
> Without my care, but onely to attend it.
>
> (9.21)

The final phrase denies the absolute meaning of "without my care" and thus revises our sense of what is at issue in pastoral security (*se-curus* = without care). The suggestion of freedom is maintained, but scaled down to the claim that one is without care if one knows what truly to care about—in this case the flocks mentioned in the next lines or the rural tasks and activities detailed two stanzas later (9.23).[7]

To view Melibee this way is to take him seriously as a pastoral speaker—which means to take him seriously as the self-representation of a courtier or a city-dweller. Melibee represents a way of life that Calidore values and desires; he can even be said to represent the knight himself, in that his rejection of the court and return to the country offer a challenging version of the choice Calidore claims to want to make. Colin Clout has a similar relation to the knight, in that his life is devoted to celebrating a "countrey lasse" (10.25) who seems a "miracle of heauenly hew," as Pastorella did when Calidore first saw her "enuiron'd with a girland, goodly graced, / Of louely lasses" and piping shepherds (9.8). Colin Clout, as well as Melibee, holds out to the hero an alternative attitude and role. The effect of his "discourses," as of Melibee's, is that the knight "wisht, that with that shepheard he mote dwelling share" (10.30).

But how can the courtier-hero, who is a surrogate for the reader and the poet, take these alternatives seriously? It is one thing for Spenser to criticize the "shadowes vaine / Of courtly fauour" by considering "the happy peace" and "perfect pleasures" which one finds "amongst poore hyndes, in hils, in woods, in dales" (10.2–3). It is another to translate this awareness of pastoral values into choosing a life so completely defined by a single place and a single round of activities as Melibee's and Colin Clout's. Pastoral envisages this possibility, but its value is not confined to it. The uses of pastoral are also represented by the Shakespearean pattern, in which time spent in a pastoral locale restores courtiers to their homes and to themselves. Since the country is not Calidore's "native home," the question is what in his case can be the equivalent of Melibee's choice.

Spenser's handling of the episode shows his awareness of the problem. Calidore reacts to Melibee's praise of the shepherds' life with what the poet calls "double rauishment" (9.26): he is enraptured with the speech itself and with the country maiden with whom he has fallen in love. These pastoral erotics underlie the sentimental vehemence of his response. After a stanza in which he tries to "insinuate his harts desire" by aping his host's praises of the country,[8] he says:

> That euen I which daily doe behold
> The glorie of the great, mongst whom I won,
> And now haue prou'd, what happinesse ye hold
> In this small plot of your dominion,
> Now loath great Lordship and ambition.
>
> (9.28)

The insistence still on "happinesse," the grand word "dominion" (which represents "small plot" precisely as a form of "Lordship"), and the use of "loath" to express moral recognition show how little the knight has as yet taken in what he has heard. The very structure of the sentence, a sustained period quite unusual in *The Faerie Queene*, suggests that he is not yet able to adopt the style he professes to admire. What Melibee reproves, however, is not this rhetoric itself, but the wish it prompts—that the heavens and fortune would "graunt me liue in like condition" (9.28). Melibee replies that it is vain to accuse the heavens of "fortunes fault" and says: "fittest is, that all contented rest / With that they hold: each hath his fortune in his brest" (9.29). This is a pastoral moral, but so generalized as to be detached from particularities of place or social role, and Melibee's next moral—"It is the mynd, that maketh good or ill" (9.30)—is certainly not confined to pastoral. But its corrective point enables Calidore to find a mode adequate to his situation:

> Since then in each mans self (said *Calidore*)
> It is, to fashion his owne lyfes estate,
> Giue leaue awhyle, good father, in this shore
> To rest my barcke, which hath bene beaten late
> With stormes of fortune and tempestuous fate,
> In seas of troubles and of toylesome paine,
> That whether quite from them for to retrate
> I shall resolue, or backe to turne againe,
> I may here with your selfe some small repose obtaine.
>
> (9.31)

In Melibee's speech, the truth that each man fashions his life takes the form of apothegms—a rhetorical form conventional with the old shepherds of pastoral and expressive of the notion that all men have the same simple needs. Calidore's courtly metaphor, deployed in what would have been called an "allegory," might thus seem once more to miss the point. But unlike his previous mimicry of Melibee's pastoralism, this speech shows that he now understands its point—that knowledge of self is inseparable from knowing and accepting one's circumstances. The image of the ship in the port suggests genuine rest, but does not deny that the courtier spends his life on the high seas. Its poise is confirmed in the moral stance of the final lines. In suspending the choice he knows he will have to make, the knight's understanding takes the form of the "small repose" of this stanza itself. Calidore here achieves his own version of pastoral. Like some speakers of pastoral lyric, he does not represent himself as a shepherd, but the mode in which he speaks has been determined by the literary shepherd whom he has encountered.

   This dialogue of knight and shepherd exemplifies the best of Spenserian and Renaissance pastoral: its critical awareness anatomizes pastoral sentiment and at the same time renews pastoral values. But the nature of its success indicates a dilemma in *The Faerie Queene* itself. For if Calidore has succeeded in understanding his pastoral alter ego, where does it leave him and the poem, beyond this moment of awareness and repose? His speech does not stop there, but continues as follows:

> Not that the burden of so bold a guest
> Shall chargefull be, or chaunge to you at all;
> For your meane food shall be my daily feast,
> And this your cabin both my bowre and hall.

Besides for recompence hereof, I shall
You well reward, and golden guerdon giue,
That may perhaps you better much withall,
And in this quiet make you safer liue.
So forth he drew much gold, and toward him it driue.

(9.32)

The opening line brings us sharply back to the social situation, and the stanza has the effect of retrospectively narrowing Calidore's understanding of what it means for a man "to fashion his owne lyfes estate." The preceding stanza, with its allegory of the ship on the seas of life, suggested that "estate" has its broad sense of "state or condition in general" (OED 1). The knight's power to "fashion" this condition is implicitly no greater than his awareness that a choice, here suspended, will have to be made between withdrawal from and return to the world of the court. But in the next stanza, it very much sounds as if Calidore thinks that the moral power of which Melibee has spoken can be attained simply by choosing the shepherd's "estate" in the narrow sense of "status, standing, position in the world" (OED 3). The speech as a whole is thus divided in its two stanzas, between expressing lyric awareness and stating intended action in the world.[9]

Strictly speaking, one could claim that Calidore's offer of gold simply means to provide for the period of "small repose" of which he has just spoken. But the narrower impression prevails, because the offer of gold gives a literalistic cast to the knight's claim that he can substitute pastoral for courtly realities. Melibee's rejection once more makes explicit the issues of desire and choice in determining a style of life: "But if ye algates couet to assay / This simple sort of life, that shepheards lead, / Be it your owne: our rudenesse to your selfe aread" (9.33). "Couet" turns severely on the knight, as if to say that he can only couch his desires in suspect terms;[10] "assay" too, in this context, may ironically engage the meaning, "test a precious metal." Melibee is as good as his word here. He is entitled to "rudeness" in his speech, because the word also represents the manner of life for which true simplicity is willing to settle.

Then had or had not Calidore learned what Melibee, in their previous exchange, spent ten stanzas telling him? The fact that one can ask this question suggests the present difficulties of Spenser's narration. The offer of gold and Melibee's rejection simply repeat the drama and the issues of the knight's initial encounter with the pastoral world. Repeated spiritual confrontation and instruction are certainly found in other episodes of *The Faerie Queene*, but two things are different here. In the Cave of Mammon, the Bower of Bliss, and the Castle of Busyrane, transitions from one encounter to another often occur without reference to the hero's consciousness. With Calidore, we are aware of motives, calculations, and purposes in acting and speaking. This difference itself reflects a larger difference between these cantos and the "allegorical cores," as Lewis called them, of earlier books. The hero is no longer moving through a large allegorical *world*: the moral and spiritual significance of the shepherds' world is represented less by a full range of symbol, setting, and incident, than it is by the utterance of its main spokesmen. Consider the difference between Melibee and Guyon's Palmer. The Palmer is an allegorical figure, representing part of what the heroic personality is conceived to be in Book II, and his function is to comment *on* the situations which he and Guyon encounter. Melibee, though equally a type figure, is conceived as a human being whose history has made him what he is; far from interpreting alongside the hero, he is what the hero encounters and must deal with. His moral presence does not tell the hero what he is, but rather challenges him with an alternative role. There is a similar mode of narration in canto ten, though Mount Acidale looks at first like one of the earlier allegorical realms. The vision of the Graces, which might seem to be an enduring reality of its world, is made to disappear by the hero's approach; the full representation of its significance then becomes a matter not of allegorical narration, but of the speech of Colin Clout.

The impasse of narration in these cantos is shown by the episode that follows Calidore's offer of gold. He undertakes to woo Pastorella "with all kind courtesies, he could inuent" (9.34)—i.e., presumably, by exemplifying the virtue of which he is patron. But Pastorella, having "euer learn'd to loue the lowly things, / Did litle whit regard his courteous guize" (9.35). Calidore once more, it seems, must learn to "aread" the shepherds' simplicity. This is how he does it:

> Which *Calidore* perceiuing, thought it best
> To chaunge the manner of his loftie looke;
> And doffing his bright armes, himself addrest
> In shepheards weed, and in his hand he tooke,
> In stead of steelehead speare, a shepheards hooke,
> That who had seene him then, would haue bethought
> On *Phrygian Paris* by *Plexippus* brooke,
> When he the loue of fayre *Oenone* sought,
> What time the golden apple was vnto him brought.
> (9.36)

This representation of Paris in a state of innocence is another great moment of Spenserian pastoral. The fatal intimations of the final line, which might be thought to disrupt the idyll, are balanced by fixing the moment just before Paris's choice and also by the golden apple itself, with its physical appeal and its evocation of a glamorous scene that is not unlike what we will see on Mount Acidale—the appearance of three goddesses to a shepherd in love.[11] As in Calidore's speech about the "small repose" he may obtain in the shepherds' world, the effect here is to suspend events and issues that will take the protagonist into the world of heroic action. This is genuinely pastoral writing, but it is discontinuous with the narration that is unfolding in the canto. Unlike the pastoral Arden of Lodge's *Rosalynde*, where Paris and many of his mythological brothers and sisters could be very much at home, the world of Melibee (and probably also of Colin Clout) cannot accommodate the Phrygian shepherd.[12] He can only appear to us in a simile.

This heroic simile is a symptom of the relative fragmentation of narrative in these cantos, and it foreshadows another sign of that fragmentation, the narrator's prominence in canto ten. The separation of the poet's voice from the process of narration is a hallmark of the entire second half of *The Faerie Queene*.[13] But it is not until this canto that the narrating poet includes a representation of himself among the fictional characters, and I want to emphasize the significance of its being a pastoral self-representation. In a sense, no one denies this: who knows not Colin Clout? But on the other hand, commentators want to attribute to this figure imaginative range and power commensurate with what they take to be those of the entire episode. Two things are important to understand, then. The first is that the range and power of the episode, rightly understood, are within the scope of pastoral, rightly understood. But second, the limitations of pastoral (which is to say, of the poet's representing himself as a shepherd-singer) reveal something important about the Mount Acidale episode—and hence, as we shall see, about Spenser's poetry at this stage of his career.

Colin Clout's speech about the Graces is prompted by a loss, and its function is to restore what has been lost. This pattern is characteristic of pastoral, because it foregrounds the motives that have made poets, from Theocritus on, represent themselves as herdsmen. To put it briefly, pastoral is a belated form, conscious of its distance from heroic representations and modes; it seeks to recover what it can of the authentically human and poetic by making herdsmen, not warriors, representative human beings. These motives are especially clear in pastoral elegies, which lament the death of a hero and seek to restore him by memorial ceremonies. These ceremonies, of which the poem recounting them is itself an instance, retain the signs of loss: they are carried out by ordinary humans, who are deprived of the dead hero's presence and who are able to recall him only by what we may call conspicuous representation. Colin Clout's speech about the Graces, which responds to Calidore's request to "tell me, what were they all, whose lacke thee grieues so sore" (10.20), is a pastoral utterance of this sort. For the visionary presence which has gone, it substitutes explanatory discourse. Hence it is introduced by a term used specifically of rhetorical elaboration: "Tho gan that shepheard thus for to dilate" (10.21). Moreover, his discourse emerges from a pastoral exchange, in which the two interlocutors are mutually dependent. Were it not for Calidore's regret for his "mishap" and his request to learn "the truth of all," Colin, "for fell despight / Of that displeasure," would simply have "made great mone for that vnhappy turne"

(10.18). And however authoritative his utterance, its powers are limited. He cannot, as Calidore seems to think (10.19), summon the Graces at will. He is not, in other words, the Prospero of this island, but is in the same position as every other shepherd: he must represent in language what he cannot experience in vision.

It was some such understanding of Colin's speech that made Kathleen Williams say it "has only a limited helpfulness."[14] In her terms, the speech is *rhetoric*, inherently inferior to the poetry of *vision* for which it seeks to substitute. But the narrator of this canto is as much tied to discourse and its limitations as is his pastoral alter ego. The canto begins with the most casuistical passage—weighing the pros and cons of a moral choice—in the entire *Faerie Queene*. The vision of the Graces is first mentioned as a reason adduced in that casuistical discourse—"For what hath all that goodly glorious gaze [i.e. of the court] / Like to one sight, which *Calidore* did vew?" (10.4)—and the narrator proposes to "declare" it "by course," thus indicating the likeness of his own mode to the rhetorical dilation to which he refers in introducing Colin's speech. It is consistent with this beginning that the climax of the Graces' dance does not occur in the ordinary course of narrative, but is displaced onto the simile of Ariadne's crown (10.13). The unusual beginning of this simile (not the usual "Like" or "Such as," but the imperative, "Look," compelling attention) makes it a striking moment of rhetorical intervention, and heralds the fact that it does more independent symbolic work than any other heroic simile in *The Faerie Queene*.

Even if we feel that the narrating poet achieves a kind of visionary breakthrough in this simile, it confirms the tendencies we have been noting in these cantos. In particular, it is consistent with the parity that, I have been suggesting, exists between the narrator and Colin Clout. For there are two more instances of what might be called visionary breakthrough in this episode: both have the effect of taking us outside the narrative itself, and both directly associate the narrator with the shepherd who celebrates the Graces. At the end of his account of the Graces' dance, the narrator finally identifies the shepherd as Colin Clout, and the subsequent gesture of self-acknowledgment ("Who knowes not *Colin Clout?*") leads him to directly address his pastoral alter ego:

> Pype iolly shepheard, pype thou now apace
> Vnto thy loue, that made thee low to lout:
> Thy loue is present there with thee in place,
> Thy loue is there aduaunst to be another Grace.
> (10.16)

This moment is recapitulated at the climax of Colin's speech about the Graces, when his fervent listing of his beloved's characteristics—"Diuine resemblaunce, beauty soueraine rare, / Firme Chastity, that spight ne blemish dare"—concludes with, "She made me often pipe and now to pipe apace" (10.27). This not only returns to the earlier use of piping as an expression of more than verbal intensity, but has the effect, in the clinching phrase, of recalling the presence of the divine country lass: for what else can be suggested by "and *now* to pipe apace"? It is at this moment that Colin's speech most fulfills the pastoral poet's claim of restoring the loss that prompted his song, and it is at this moment that the poet of *The Faerie Queene* and his pastoral self-representation most directly merge:

> Sunne of the world, great glory of the sky,
> That all the earth doest lighten with thy rayes,
> Great *Gloriana*, greatest Maiesty,
> Pardon thy shepheard, mongst so many layes,
> As he hath sung of thee in all his dayes,
> To make one minime of thy poore handmayd,
> And vnderneath thy feete to place her prayse,
> That when thy glory shall be farre displayd
> To future age of her this mention may be made.
>
> (10.28)

Whom do we imagine to be speaking these lines? On the one hand, the rhetorical ardor continues that of the preceding stanza. This is plausibly, then, the voice of Colin Clout, the "dilating" shepherd. On the other hand, the mode of direct address and the identification of "Great *Gloriana*" has the effect of taking us outside the poem;[15] hence the reference to the "many layes" that "he hath sung of thee in all his dayes" makes it impossible not to think that the speaker is Spenser himself. Yet the phrase, "Pardon thy shepheard," not only expresses the poet's diffidence, but also, with its sense of speaking on behalf of someone else, keeps his self-presentation tied to the pastoral fictions of the peom. What is not maintained, however, is the sense of a continuous fiction itself. The last lines of the stanza explicitly look beyond the poem to its afterlife, and the return to ordinary narration in the next stanza gives a slight jolt of displacement—or perhaps we should say, of the undoing of this stanza's displacement: "When thus that shepherd ended had his speach, / Sayd *Calidore;* Now sure it yrketh mee," etc.[16]

So far as *The Faerie Queene* is concerned, the emergence of distinct speakers in the two pastoral cantos tells us something about the problems of heroic narration at the end of the poem. It also tells us something about what happened to *The Faerie Queene* in the final decade of Spenser's life. Between the publication of Books I–III, in 1590, and Books IV–VI, in 1596, Spenser wrote *Colin Clouts Come Home Againe, Amoretti, Fowre Hymnes, Epithalamion,* and *Prothalamion.* With the partial exception of *Colin Clout,* these poems are in genres in which he had not written before. What is common to all of them is that they are large lyric forms and that, as opposed to the poems of the 1580s, collected and published in the *Complaints* volume (1591), they imitate or derive from the love poetry of the European Renaissance. It seems to me that a great deal that we find in these poems—mythological representations, issues of political and courtly service, the experience of love and its relation to love as a cosmic force—could have found a place in *The Faerie Queene.* That is, these poems, taken as a group, represent an alternative body of major poetry to Spenser's epic endeavor. I do not say they are directly due to the weariness with his epic of which Spenser speaks in *Amoretti* 80 and in the first stanza of Book VI. But the mode of expression to which these poems collectively bear witness seems clearly to have been important to him in these years, and I think that the pastoral cantos of Book VI help us understand why. Melibee and Colin Clout seem already on the way to being speakers of what we may call public lyric—the kind of speaker that Colin actually is in the long poem that bears his name. Furthermore, the presence of the courtly figures in these cantos, the hero and the poet, is felt most strikingly in what it seems fair to call lyrical moments, stanzas which detach themselves from the narrative flow of the poem and that have an unusual power of summation—the stanza of "small repose" in Calidore's speech to Melibee, the comparison of the unarmed Calidore to Paris as a shepherd, the simile of Ariadne's crown, the address to Gloriana in which Colin Clout and Spenser merge as speakers.

The narratological character of the pastoral cantos is consistent with the fact that Spenser, in the mid-1590s, felt that authoritative poetry might lie outside the heroic narration of *The Faerie Queene* and in, for him, new forms of lyric. The thematics of these cantos suggest an explanation of this turn in his career. Both pastoral spokesmen represent firm alternatives to life at court, and what is at issue for Calidore is whether to return to that life. Critics who reprove him and speak of his truancy assume that the foundational notions of *The Faerie Queene* hold true this late in the poem—that a knight, by definition, pursues a life of active service to his monarch. Surely it is clear that Spenser himself was questioning this idea in the 1590s, or at least pondering what constitutes true service. The courtier's discontent is prominent in the two "public lyrics" which do not concern the experience and the theology of love, *Colin Clouts Come Home Againe* and *Prothalamion.* In the final stanza of Book VI, the last words of *The Faerie Queene* published in the Poet's lifetime, he bitterly complains of "wicked tongues" maligning his writings and of "a mighty Peres displeasure."

So we may well believe that the alternatives held out by Melibee and Colin Clout are ones that the poet, like his hero, took seriously. And we can ask the same question of the poet of Book VI as we asked of the hero: what kind of choice do these pastoral figures represent? Twenty years ago, Richard Neuse wrote of "Book VI as conclusion to *The Faerie Queene*" in the following terms: "Courtesy . . . combining as it does the profoundly ethical and spiritual with the esthetic . . . , appears as the supreme *poetic* possibility in human existence, and as such represents the perfect point of transition from (poet's) art to (reader's) life. By introducing his 'autobiographical' *persona* into his fiction Spenser seems to say to the reader: So far can I, as poet, take you; here begins your own life—and mine."[17] Neuse suggests that the epic is fulfilled in the poet's emergence from it as an independent figure. Rereading this excellent essay, I wrote in the margin, "What faith we had then!" For this poetic alternative, as Spenser represents it, is not so unambiguous or unencumbered as we, and no doubt he, would have liked to think. Its difficulties become evident in the way Spenser handles the shepherd to whom, so far, we have paid no attention— Pastorella's rejected suitor, Coridon.

Unlike his confrontation with Melibee and his learning to woo Pastorella, Calidore's dealings with Coridon do not count as a pastoral encounter, because they do not make him imagine himself as a shepherd and hence reconsider what he is and what he values. On the contrary, in this context Spenser praises his hero as if he had arrived fresh from court and had never put on shepherd's weeds:

> Thus did the gentle knight himselfe abeare
> Amongst that rusticke rout in all his deeds.
> . . . . . .
> For courtesie amongst the rudest breeds
> Good will and fauour.
>
> (9.45)

In his own person, the knight can only condescend to the rustic. He pats Coridon on the head for his country gifts to Pastorella (9.40)—gifts which can have real charm and erotic expressiveness when represented by the passionate shepherds of eclogue and lyric—and commends his prowess in wrestling when he has in fact just humiliated him (9.43–4). When we go on to canto ten, we find that the poet's own treatment of the rustic is worse than the knight's condescension. Mount Acidale is bounded by a river where "Nymphes and Faeries by the bancks did sit, / In the woods shade, which did the waters crowne, / Keeping all noysome things away from it" (10.7). Among these "noysome things" are not only "filthy mud" and "wylde beastes," but also "the ruder clowne," who cannot "thereto approch." An even more troubling separation of the rustic from the pastoral occurs after Calidore descends from Mount Acidale to resume his wooing of Pastorella. After staging a scene in which Calidore rescues Pastorella from a tiger, while Coridon runs away in fear, the narrator says:

> From that day forth she gan him [Calidore] to affect,
> And daily more her fauour to augment;
> But *Coridon* for cowherdize reiect,
> Fit to keepe sheepe, vnfit for loues content.
>
> (10.37)

These lines reject not only cowardice but the herdsman's condition punningly linked to it. The last line in effect renounces pastoral, whose claim on us is precisely the acknowledgement that our condition in love, as in other fundamental human situations, can fitly be represented by keepers of sheep.

Coridon the rustic is not a genuinely pastoral figure because the courtly poet does not, in the full sense, represent him: in depicting him, he does not speak in his stead or on his behalf. This is strikingly and literally the case in canto nine. During Calidore's sojourn among the shepherds none of them, besides Melibee, utters a word. Their speech (though not very much of it) is reported indirectly (9.6); we are told of their pipings and carolings (9.8–9, 41); we are shown Coridon bringing Pastorella gifts and biting his lip for jealousy (9.38–9); but Melibee is the only shepherd whose speech is directly quoted.[18] To put it most pointedly, this shepherd is able to be a pastoral figure because he has been at court. This detail in the story comes from its source in *Gerusalemme Liberata* (7.12–13), but it is impossible to ignore its connection with Melibee's powers and privilege of speech. Spenser himself is clear about the connection, insofar as it concerns pastoral thematics and poetics. Melibee's having crossed the boundary within which he now dwells makes him conscious of it and the choice it represents. He is even a figure of the poet, for he represents a way of life in the specific sense that he can speak for it. He is also a figure of the pastoral poet, in that his ability to represent himself (which is necessarily to represent himself as a shepherd) enables him to represent the lives of shepherds. But this very relation to the poet and the silence of all the other shepherds reveals what was already suggested by Calidore's relation to Melibee—that Spenserian pastoral is a mode of courtly and humanist self-representation.

One need not view this with indignation: it is no secret that pastoral is of the country, but by and for the city. But it does suggest that the poet shares the dilemma of his hero, Sir Calidore. Fully aware of the trials and discontents of the court, he imagines a world elsewhere and a different style of life in it. But he can only represent this alternative in a way that speaks to the world from which he means to separate himself. Hence he cannot avoid the dilemma that emerges most directly in the apology to Gloriana. He must apologize not so much for praising his actual beloved as, more generally, for finding his inspiration and sense of worth apart from the monarch who should be their source.[19] When we recognize these tensions and contradictions, it is all the more impressive that Spenser conceives Melibee and Colin Clout so coherently. But what I have called their pastoral authority is achieved by identifying each with one locale, the representation of which is the one song he sings. The very clarity with which Spenser presents these pastoral figures suggests that he recognized that he himself, as well as his hero, had to return to the world of the court. The final question I want to address is how the end of Book VI plays out this imperative to return and what it tells us about Spenser's poetic motives in the 1590s.

If leaving the world of the shepherds is meant to be a return to the world of meaningful heroic action, the poet's narration of it is as dispirited and uneven as the knight's fulfillment of his quest is, notoriously, compromised. We can see why the final cantos of Book VI are unsatisfactory as heroic narration in the way Calidore resumes his quest. He does not recognize, as Aeneas does, an obligation greater than love, nor, like the Red Cross Knight, a general imperative to earthly action. Calidore makes no conscious and exemplary choice at all. He is first driven from Mount Acidale by the "enuenimd sting" (10.31) of love and takes up arms again only because a band of brigands destroys the shepherds' world and takes away Pastorella. But if the end of Book VI is unsatisfactory as epic—and in its conclusion something of a poetic shambles—it has considerable vitality as romance. In romance, love does not compromise the hero, but can be accepted as his motive, with all its extravagance, conflicts and humiliations. It is what holds Calidore among the shepherds, but it is precisely his love for Pastorella that cannot be identified with and is not represented by either of the pastoral spokesmen he encounters. This is not surprising in the case of Melibee, who is the kind of old shepherd who opposes love's folly, but it is equally true of Colin Clout. Like Strephon and Klaius, the visionary shepherds of Sidney's *Arcadia*, Colin Clout is devoted to a transcendent love, and his desires, like theirs, are completely transformed into harmonious utterance. This sublimation is not possible for the knightly lovers of either Sidney or Spenser. By the same token, there is more to the poetry of *The Faerie Queene* than Colin Clout's single-minded song. Just as the lyric Spenser of the 1590s is more than a pastoral poet, so in *The Faerie Queene*, the narrating poet is separated from his pastoral alter egos by his identification with the love that motivates the hero.

Calidore cannot abide with Colin Clout, because, as the poet puts it with notable vehemence, the "sting" of love "now gan afresh to rancle sore." The knight must "returne againe / To his wounds worker, that with louely dart / Dinting his brest, had bred his restlesse paine" (10.31). It is the "restlesse paine" of love that undoes the pastoral world of Book VI. The first threat to it comes from the tiger, whose fierce desire for Pastorella represents what the knight must suppress in doing "all dewfull seruice voide of thoughts impure" (10.32).[20] But lawless men can achieve what wild beasts cannot. The brigands invade and destroy "the dwelling of these shepheards" for "spoile and booty" (10.39), but what follows, in canto eleven, is a demonic parody of the scene on Mount Acidale. The brigand captain and the merchants with whom he deals battle to the death over Pastorella, whose beauty, arousing both lust and awe, is described in imagery that recalls the celestial powers of her analogue around whom the Graces danced and even of Gloriana herself (cf. 11.13 with 10.4; also 11.3, 21). Bringing down Calidore from Mount Acidale, taking on the forces of love's "restlesse paine," is Spenser's recognition, in Yeats's words, that "Love has pitched his mansion in / The place of excrement." Not a sentiment that one would associate with Colin Clout, but we may recall that the most extraordinary erotic verse in Book VI is the description of Serena on the cannibals' altar (8.42)—another "lyric" stanza of exceptional intensity.

The courtier-poet's dilemma continued to manifest itself in the final years of Spenser's life. By 1596, he had published the last three books of *The Faerie Queene* and all the major lyrics I have touched on in this essay. His last two works, the *Mutability Cantos* and *A View of the Present State of Ireland*, sharply separate the Queen's servant, analyzing the problems of colonial rule, from the poet, writing a summary fable of life on earth. Here again, Spenser's pastoral writing is an index to his later career. These two final works can be seen as playing out what was ambiguously figured in *Colin Clouts Come Home Againe*. On the one hand, the poet's final return to Ireland, as represented by the *View* of its present state, has even less freedom from the world of power than his long pastoral claimed for itself. On the other hand, the *Mutability Cantos* can be thought to have fulfilled the suggestions in *Colin Clout* of poetic authority and of Ireland as the poet's domain. In that way, they provided, at last, a fitting conclusion to *The Faerie Queene*.

Notes

This essay was presented as the Kathleen Williams Lecture at "Spenser at Kalamazoo," May 1989.

1. Kathleen Williams, "Vision and Rhetoric: The Poet's Voice in *The Faerie Queene*," *ELH* 36 (1969): 144.

2. Harry Berger, Jr., "A Secret Discipline: *The Faerie Queene*, Book VI," in *Form and Convention in the Poetry of Edmund Spenser*, ed. William Nelson (New York: Columbia Univ. Press, 1961), 35–75; reprinted in Harry Berger, Jr., *Revisionary Play: Studies in Spenserian Dynamics* (Berkeley & Los Angeles: Univ. of California Press, 1988), 215–42. Northrop Frye, "The Structure of Imagery in *The Faerie Queene*," in Northrop Frye, *Fables of Identity* (New York: Harcourt, Brace, 1963), 86.

3. Berger (note 2), "A Secret Discipline," 61 (in *Revisionary Play*, 233).

4. Humphrey Tonkin, *Spenser's Courteous Pastoral* (Oxford: Clarendon Press, 1972), 292–3.

5. The text cited is Edmund Spenser, *Spenser's Faerie Queene*, ed. J. C. Smith, 2 vols. (Oxford: Clarendon Press, 1909).

6. The first two phrases are Berger's and Tonkin's (see notes 3 and 4, above). The last is in Isabel G. MacCaffrey, *Spenser's Allegory: The Anatomy of Imagination* (Princeton: Princeton Univ. Press, 1976), 364. In her discussion of Melibee (365–70), MacCaffrey rightly resists the implications of this phrase, but the result is that she has difficulty making his moral authority consistent with the nature of his life.

Judith Anderson's thoughtful commentary at Kalamazoo reiterated the critique of Melibee's naive pastoralism. Consistently with her discussion in *The Growth of a Personal Voice: "Piers Plowman" and "The Faerie Queene"* (New Haven: Yale Univ. Press, 1976), 177–84, she argued that he cannot be taken to be an authoritative spokesman on the central issue, for Book VI, of "the relation of artifice, indeed, of anything essentially 'inward' and mind-made, to forces outside the mind's control." The crucial question raised by her comments is how we evaluate the limitations of the poetic domains of Melibee and Colin Clout. Like many others, Anderson considers that an ironic sense of these limitations, e.g. as expressed by the brigands' destruction of the shepherds' world, is a main point of Book VI as a whole. (It is of course easier to argue for this ironic critique if Colin Clout and Mount Acidale are exempted from it and Melibee is the only culpable pastoralist.) As will emerge, my argument is that both the character of the two pastoral domains and their poetic distinction amidst the uneven writing of Book VI are signs of Spenser's troubled relation to the world of the court and to the imperatives of heroic narration that are assumed to provide a critical perspective on pastoral and poetic "withdrawal."

7.   Similarly, Melibee's statement that "all the night in siluer sleepe I spend" is not advanced as a leading claim (though it is a familiar point in poems praising the country), but appears on the heels, as if the result and reward, of his criticism of ambition and his consequent confidence in "my minds vnmoued quiet" (9.22).

8.   9.27. Calidore's first words are a pastiche of phrases from Melibee's speech. His opening phrase, "this worlds gay showes," is picked up from Melibee (9.22), while key words in the next two lines, "vaine" and "lowlinesse," echo the alexandrines of the last two stanzas of Melibee's speech (9.24, 25).

9.   My account of the relation of the second of these stanzas to the first owes a good deal to the discussion at Kalamazoo, and particularly to points raised by William Oram.

10.   The courtly pastoralist provokes this rebuke by saying, "Your meane food shall be my daily feast, / And this your cabin both my bowre and hall."

11.   The convention, in Elizabethan poems and pageants, of presenting the golden apple to the Queen may even be thought to give a benign cast to its introduction here, where Paris is compared to a knight of Gloriana. Examples of this device in Tudor court entertainments are cited in R. Mark Benbow's introduction to his edition of Peele's *Araygnement of Paris*, in *The Life and Works of George Peele* (New Haven: Yale Univ. Press), vol. 3 (*The Dramatic Works of George Peele*, 1970), 20.

12.   For example, when Rosalynd and Aliena first came to Arden, they come upon Montanus and Coridon singing "a pleasant eglog" in the following setting:

> The ground where they sat was diapred with *Floras* riches, as if she ment to wrap *Tellus* in the glorie of her vestments: round about in the forme of an Amphitheater were most curiouslie planted Pine trees, interseamed with Limons and Citrons, which with the thicknesse of their boughes so shadowed the place, that *Phoebus* could not prie into the secret of that Arbour; so united were the tops with so thicke a closure, that *Venus* might there in her jollitie have dallied unseene with her deerest paramour. Fast by (to make the place more gorgeous) was there a Fount so Christalline and cleere, that it seemed *Diana* with her *Driades* and *Hemadriades* had that spring, as the secrete of all their bathings.

Thomas Lodge, *Rosalynde* (1590), in *Narrative and Dramatic Sources of Shakespeare*, ed. Geoffrey Bullough, vol. 2 (New York: Columbia Univ. Press, 1963), 183. The amorous shepherd Paris is a point of reference throughout *Rosalynde* (cf. 206, 247, 248, 252, 253).

13.   Anderson (note 6). My emphasis, in the rest of this essay, on the uncertainties of narration in the books of *The Faerie Queene* written in the 1590s owes much to the argument advanced by Roger Sale in the last chapter ("What Happened to *The Faerie Queene*") of his *Reading Spenser* (New York: Random House, 1968).

14.   Williams (note 1), 144.

15.   The effect is very different from that, for example, of Guyon's telling Arthur that he serves "the mighty Queene of *Faerie*" (II.9.4).

16.   10.29. A similar shift back to the ordinary course of narration is felt in the first lines of the stanzas (10.14, 17) that follow the simile of Ariadne's crown and the narrator's address to the piping Colin Clout.

17.   In *Essential Articles for the Study of Edmund Spenser*, ed. A. C. Hamilton (Hamden, CT: Archon Books, 1972), 367. Neuse's article originally appeared in *ELH* 35 (1968): 329–53.

18.   Coridon finally speaks in 11.30–32. But this is after the brigands have wiped out the shepherds' world, and his speech recounts their subsequent slaughter of the shepherds, including Melibee and, he thinks, Pastorella.

19.   It would take only a few years after the poem's publication to reveal a similar dilemma in *Prothalamion* (*Spenser's Minor Poems*, ed. Ernest de Selincourt [Oxford: Clarendon Press, 1910]):

> Ioy haue thou of thy noble victorie,
>
> . . . . . .
>
> That through thy prowesse and victorious armes,
> Thy country may be freed from forraine harmes:
> And great *Elisaes* glorious name may ring
> Through al the world, fil'd with thy wide Alarmes,
> Which some braue muse may sing
> To ages following.
>
> (152–60)

By the end of the decade, the Earl of Essex would be Elisa's rival, an alternative source of glory and power. Other poets might find other ways to celebrate this glamorous rebel, but the poet of *The Faerie Queene*, in a last gesture towards his project, seems compelled to imagine a further installment of the national epic sung by "some braue muse."

20.   Cf. 10.35, which begins with Coridon running away from the beast "through cowherd feare":

> But *Calidore* soone comming to her [Pastorella's] ayde,
> When he the beast saw ready now to rend
> His loues deare spoile, in which his heart was prayde,
> He ran at him enraged in stead of being frayde.

The ambiguity of the pronouns in the penultimate line is brought out by the extraordinary doubleness of "prayde." Though commentators (Todd, Hamilton) rightly interpret the meaning to be that Calidore's heart was preyed upon (cf. the same verb used of the brigands at 10.40), the representation of Pastorella as "loues deare spoile" puts the "enraged" Calidore also in the role of the one who preys.

There is a similar "invention" at the end of Book I of Sidney's *Arcadia*, where the lion who assaults Philoclea is slain by Pyrocles/Cleophila, but also, as the description of his pursuit makes clear, figures his desires. Cf. *The Countess of Pembroke's Arcadia (The Old Arcadia)*, ed. Jean Robertson (Oxford: Clarendon Press, 1973), 46–8.

[Iconoclasm in Book 6 and the Mutabilitie Cantos]

Kenneth Gross

The Blatant Beast

The Blatant Beast defines an impasse in the unfolding of Spenser's allegorical quest-romance which brings the six-book *Faerie Queene* to a halt. That the final glimpse we have of the Beast is as a demonic iconoclast, ravaging through corrupt monasteries, should suggest his importance within my own argument, but to fully understand it, that closing must be placed within a broader analysis of the Beast's function in the poem.

This doglike, thousand-headed beast with poisonous tongues (of bears, tigers, and mortal men) and iron teeth emerges at the end of Book V as an agent of Envy and Detraction, who set him on the justicer Arthegall (providing a stark, if evasive, image of the official and unofficial disapproval that followed Lord Grey's harsh rule in Ireland, and that led to his return to England). But the beast becomes truly wounding and virulent only in Book VI, where it wanders through the pastoral world striking almost randomly at unguarded knights and ladies. The Beast attacks Serena as she wanders "about the fields, as liking led / Her wavering lust after her wandring sight, / To make a garland to adorne her hed, / Without suspect of ill or daungers hidden dred" (VI.iii.23); the three villains Despetto, Decetto, and Defetto also use the Beast to wound Arthur's courtly squire Timias, "To draw him from his deare beloved dame, / Unwares into the daunger of defame" (VI.v.15). In such cases it seems as if the Beast represents not the projected revenges of unacknowledged inward sins (like Sansfoy, Orgoglio, or Lust) but rather the sourceless, unpredictable attacks of envy and slander running wild in a world beyond the control of the victim's self. As such the Beast is the goal and enemy of Calidore, the Knight of Courtesy, that quester who is set to purify the public poetics of social relation and social love. Iconographically, this beast of defamatory noise derives very much from Virgil's *Fama*, or Rumor (*Aeneid* IV.173–97), that

inflated monster of public speech which trumpets Dido's romance with
Aeneas and which grows uncontrollably, mingling high and low report and
metamorphosing even truth into something like a lie.[1] Berger argues that the
Beast embodies "the social expression of the malice produced by despair
and self-hatred" ("A Secret Discipline," 42), and he usefully connects it with
the figure of "Sclaunder" in Book IV:

> Her words were not, as common words are ment,
>   T'expresse the meaning of the inward mind,
>   But noysome breath, and poysnous spirit sent
>   From inward parts, with cancred malice lind,
>   And breathed forth with blast of bitter wind;
>   Which passing through the eares, would pierce the hart,
>   And wound the soule it selfe with griefe unkind:
>   For like the stings of Aspes, that kill with smart,
> Her spightfull words did pricke, and wound the inner part.
>
> (IV.viii.26)

The crucial difficulty here is that we cannot disentangle the source of slander
from its aim or victim; indeed, like the self-wounding power of Envy (whose
secret thoughts "murder her owne mynd" [v.xii.33]), slander harms the
perception of the slanderer as much as it defiles its wonted object.[2] Despite
the "publicness" of slander, it has an inward poison; it does not express the
mind, yet it grows from and strikes at the inward parts—though again Spenser
makes it hard to tell whether these belong to the slanderer or the slandered.
The empty, foul wind of slander, Spenser suggests, works by breaking down
our usual distinctions between surface and depth, inner and outer reality. That
is to say, although its venom may appear superficial, slander troubles us
especially in that uneasy space between inward desires and the outward
forms or images that may variously sustain, define, and even originate those
desires.[3] As an extension of envy, it feeds on that separation between subject
and object and between desire and expression which is structured into our
life in the world and in time. Slander lives in the fluid, negative spaces of
discourse that confuse the threshold between the self and the world. Furthermore, the very inevitability of its wounds may suggest the temptations to
reduction and violence hovering in the background even of responsible
allegorical or satirical discourse such as Spenser's own.

   To a culture as invested as that of the Renaissance was in the dynamics
of praise, in the power of rhetoric to transfigure both private and public
experience, slander might appear not simply as a marginal aberration but as an
essential limiting case of language, though also as the revenge of language. The
random poison of the Beast may not even depend on something as definable
as "malice and self-hatred"; rather, it may be the unspoken underside of praise,
prayer, or prophecy, that aspect of the will to define and blame which shifts
into the will to divide and accuse. It may be only the repetition of stories without

ground, cut off from their tellers, yet therefore (like idols) the more able to stick in our minds and mobilize or fixate our desires and fears. Slander and its poison arise at the point where any public or private motives encounter the accidents, inconsistencies, half-truths, and omissions of language. Shakespeare shows us something of this in his picture of how Iago—the victim, scholar, and instigator of jealousy—can take advantage of the common intractability of linguistic reference to do his work. He introduces Othello to the self-born, self-justifying power of the "green-ey'd monster, which doth mock the meat it feeds on" by persuading the naive Moor (so convinced of the simple dichotomies of the moral world and of the unambiguous power of his own eloquence) that none of the words which the two share are transparent, that even words blankly repeated prove unwieldy, duplicitous, and double-edged:

IAGO: I did not think [Cassio] had been acquainted with her.

OTHELLO: O, yes, and went between us very oft.

IAGO: Indeed?

OTHELLO: Indeed? Ay, indeed! Discern'st thou aught in that?
   Is he not honest?

IAGO: Honest, my lord?

OTHELLO: Honest? Ay, honest.

IAGO: My lord, for aught I know.

OTHELLO: What dost thou think?

IAGO: Think, my lord?

OTHELLO: Think, my lord? By heaven, he echoes me,
   As if there were some monster in his thought,
   Too hideous to be shown. Thou dost mean something . . .

(III.iii.99–108)

Playing on the Moor's narrowed commitment to meaning, Iago implicates Othello in an empty, almost unutterable iteration of speech which steals words from their speakers, defiles simple meaning, and yet raises the specter of hidden senses which had not even been thought of. The monster so raised, which means nothing rather than something, or the something that is nothing, is a cousin of the Blatant Beast.

    Reading more strictly for the "historical" allegory, we can say that Spenser intends the Beast to represent a corrupted and corruptible speech that has its habitation in the public world of his poem's reception. The creature is located in the courtly slanders that brought down Lord Grey, in the vile reception that Spenser thought his own poetry received at the centers of power, in the selfish and indecorous spirit of the public which Spenser describes in "The Teares of the Muses" as mocking, disordering, defiling, and ultimately cutting off the true work of poets.[4] The Beast is thus an analytic allegory of slander and a prophetic satire on its more than natural force. His immense scope suggests a kind of paranoia in the poet (can there have been that many slanderers "out there," after all?). And yet Spenser's strategy may be a way of possessing within his poem something that is an uncertain threat to that poem—though not necessarily in order to delude himself that the Beast can thereby be contained or exorcized. We might thus think of the overinflated Beast as a kind of psychic defense against slander as much as an account of slander's actual power. Spenser's picture of the Beast is, broadly speaking, a piece of apotropaic magic; the act of so representing slander exemplifies Wittgenstein's thought that "the contempt each person feels for me is something I must make my own, an essential and significant part of the world seen from the place where I am" (*Remarks on Frazer's "Golden Bough,"* 11e).

Yet in the case of the Blatant Beast it is hard to place such contempt, or to see whether the poet or another truly owns it. The anxious, wandering power with which Spenser invests the Beast suggests that we may want to ask more closely after the motives, means, and costs of thus constructing such an image of outward contempt. (I do not presume, by the way, that Wittgenstein is unaware of such questions.) We might even ask whether one can possess or make over another's contempt without merely mirroring it, or whether to become "an essential and significant part" of the poet's world the slanderer's contempt must correspond to something already in place there.

What I am getting at is an extension of earlier comments on the dangers latent in aggressive images of evil, and the conceptual violence or slander inherent in the act of choosing an idol to be the victim of an act of iconoclasm. Here I need to go further and frame my analysis of the Blatant Beast in terms of two roughly Freudian questions: In what school does the ego learn its postures of aggression and defense? What grounds the ego's introjection of negative or threatening objects of desire? Following through Freud's later hypotheses about an originary complex of sadism and masochism in the ego, one might ask whether the Beast represents not merely a response to an outward threat but also an unfixed violence structured within the poet's self and his poem which is yet directed back against them, a violence that is a constitutive part of the poem's visionary economy. (Such a reading depends, of course, on thinking of the poetic text as a defensive structure, a kind of ego or self in its own right, as well as the self's linguistic expression. Whether or not one accepts this idea as a general possibility, some such hypothesis is required to understand the crisis of slander, which by nature dramatizes the interdependence, however illusory, of the self and its works.) The Beast then could be described as occupying the place of Freud's death instinct, especially as this emerges in the work of some revisionist Freudians as a species of primal envy—like the Beast, a force or instinct of refusal and revenge, an impulse built into the self to defile its objects of desire, a means of outwitting the fear that those objects have always been in danger of being injured or lost.[5] Such a theory posits envy as a delight in disorder and reduction which is yet unavoidably bound up with the expressions of *eros* and turned ambivalently on both the self and the world outside the self. This analogy might illuminate the inevitable way in which Spenser calls up the Beast to shut down his most nostalgic and idealizing of books; it might explain the poet's need always to wound or mar scenes of visionary presence and fulfilled desire with hints of alienation, envy, or idolatry; it might even identify the many-headed Beast as an outgrowth of the extravagance and multiplicity of the poet's narratives, his impulse to trouble all simple centers of purity and authority with ironic mirrors or shadowy doubles. Given that Spenser makes the Beast a poetic and rhetorical more than a clearly psychological entity, the creature would thus represent a power that exists potentially within the poem and its images, rather than merely standing as a symbol for conditions found only in *The Faerie Queene*'s intractable audience.

For the Beast is not only loose in the world; it is loose in the word. Or rather, it grows out of the looseness of words, the capacity of human language for polymorphous, subversive, and yet persuasive babble.[6] The power of the Beast is the power that language takes on in the labyrinth of love, politics, and history. It defines for Spenser an enemy, a sphere of trial, and an inevitable tool. If it does not quite have the tyrannical power of the apocalyptic Beast whose mouth "spake great things and blasphemies" (Revelation 13.5, Geneva Version; cf. *FQ* VI.xii.25), it is all the more unsettling because in accusing it the poet is half accusing himself. For the Beast is ultimately related to the poet's anxious sense of "how doubtfully all Allegories may be construed"; it is the "giant form" of those uncontrollable duplicities, those "gealous opinions and misconstructions" that seem the inevitable shadow of his poetry; it is a force of violation internal to, but also released by, any act of staking out an allegorical vision, especially one with such high spiritual, political, and moral stakes as Spenser's own. Spenser in the opening epistle of his poem defines allegory as a discourse open to slander, but by the end of Book VI he hints more darkly that his iconoclastic allegory shares a space with slander itself.[7]

My argument about the nature of the Beast's poison may be clearer if we look at how Spenser seeks to represent its cure. In Book VI, canto vi, a hermit, himself formerly a knight, heals the obscure wounds of Timias and Serena by telling them to restrain both their will and "outward senses" (vi.7), and at the same time to "shun secresie, and talke in open sight" (VI.vi.14). The regimen, as a way of curing the oddly inward and outward poison of slander, seems aimed at containing both the wanderings of physical desire and the outward "sense" of spoken language, as well as at preventing the growth of poisonous feeling and self-wounding names that the mind nurses in silence. Let us say that it is an attempt to keep hidden thoughts from infecting both desire and speech at once. Ambiguous as such a cure is in itself, it becomes even more confusing when we ask whether it constitutes a likely or literal cure for the poem as a whole—with its unstable forms of secrecy and disclosure, its divagations of desire and praise, its hidden interest in the generative power of alienation and envy. The Hermit movingly expresses the need for "purity of diction." But given the exfoliation of erotic vision and discourse in Book VI, for instance, it is hardly credible that either Calidore or Colin could quite "[his] eies, [his] eares, [his] tongue, [his] talk restraine / From that they most affect, and in due termes containe" (vi.7), as the hermit asks Timias and Serena to do. For there is a sense in which the transgressive idolatry of the knight and the tenuous, celebratory grace of the shepherd continue not only to attract the sounds or wounds of the Blatant Beast but also to feed on the same ambivalences in desire and language which give that creature life. At the end of the poem Calidore seems unable to bind the Beast for more than a short season. Hence, as the narrative moves forward to enclose the poet's own present situation, Spenser himself appears subject to the "venemous despite" and "blamefull blot" of its "wicked tongues," especially as these are embodied in "a mighty Peres displeasure" (VI.xii.41). And yet both the excesses and the defensive moves of Book VI seem strangely calculated to invite such "backbiting," as if the poet wouldn't have it any other way. Hence, Spenser's warning to himself in the last couplet of Book VI may be at best a bitter parody of the Hermit's ascetic teaching: "Therfore do you my rimes keep better measure, / And seeke to please, that now is counted wisemens threasure" (VI.xii.41). Here we have a sign of Spenser's own envy and alienation barely hidden under the mask of wise resignation, and also the traces of an ironic disdain which leave open a space in which the Beast might even take the poet's part.

Spenser hasn't Shakespeare's means to shape the paradoxes of envy and slander into a form of imagination which could work within a wholly human drama. This is perhaps because Spenser is more interested in starker movements of envy proper, the feeling of the subject that would wound the object it lacks, rather than jealousy, that more potentially tragic fear of losing what one already possesses or thought one possessed. But he manages nonetheless to make the dangers of envy terrifying enough, imbuing them both with a religious urgency and with the somewhat less impersonal anxiety of a poet trying to understand the liabilities of his own poetic project. We can see these concerns best, perhaps, in the final vision we have of the Beast—indeed, the final allegorical encounter of the six-book version of the poem. This is a scene that also will draw us back (with a vengeance) into the major figurative terms of my own critical narrative. For we move at the end of canto xii from the high romance of Pastorella restored by Calidore to her long lost noble parents into an almost apocalyptic piece of ecclesiastical satire in which the Beast becomes a strange myth of iconoclasm:

> Into their cloysters now he broken had,
>> Through which the Monckes he chaced here and there,
>> And them pursu'd into their dortours sad,
>> And searched all their cels and secrets neare;
>> In which what filth and ordure did appeare,
>> Were yrkesome to report; yet that foule Beast
>> Nought sparing them, the more did tosse and teare,
>> And ransacke all their dennes from most to least,
> Regarding nought religion, nor their holy heast.
>
> From thence into the sacred Church he broke,
>> And robd the Chancell, and the deskes downe threw,
>> And Altars fouled, and blasphemy spoke,
>> And th'Images for all their goodly hew,
>> Did cast to ground, whilest none was them to rew;
>> So all confounded and disordered there.
>
>> (VI.xii.24–25)

Inverting Calidore's failed attempt to grasp a visionary center, the Beast here seems to expose the empty and corrupt heart of the spiritual order. Indeed, there is a sense in which this last vision rounds off the epic by ironically transporting us back to the center of Book I, where Arthur in canto viii broke through into the bloody, idolatrous sanctuary of Orgoglio in order to save the imprisoned type of true Holiness and Christian faith. And yet in Book VI the Beast seems to engender, feed upon, and perpetuate the very corruption it would cure; the pretense is reformation but the practice is deformation.[8] The sacrileges of the Beast thus recall precisely the work of Orgoglio's seven-headed beast, who also defiled a church and pulled down its holy ornaments. If the later monster seems considerably more strange to us, it is because we see in it a fundamental impulse of the Protestant imagination mirroring so closely the Reformation's own picture of what its corrupt Roman enemy looked like.

But the Beast at this point in Spenser's romance is more than a satire on radical Protestantism (as Jonson thought) or an image of the general distrust of authority which the religious troubles of the sixteenth century could release. The poet knew the relics of Henry VIII's "dissolution" of the monastaries, with its uneasy mixture of political, economic, and religious motives.[9] But if Spenser, writing in the 1590s, complicated his myth of slander with an image of the physical and spiritual violence that half a century earlier had founded the church of the Faerie Queen, it was to remythologize that violence and the ruins it caused for his own purposes. The depiction of the Beast at the end of Book VI is more like a final act of conscience, a gesture filled with both anxiety and presumption. The Beast almost literalizes Spenser's awareness of the complexly iconoclastic motive that runs through his own work (including the impulse to prophetic slander that gives life to Book 1) but that here seems to destroy the work. To find a place for such a Beast within his own poetic temple entails more than a modest poetic skepticism. If the passing vision of dancing nymphs and Graces is the poet's best image of imaginative faith—however much he achieves that image through an ironic recapturing of loss—the Beast is the type of faithlessness and disenchantment become obsessive. He is the poet's confession and catharsis of that aspect of desire which perfects itself in the devaluation, the despoiling, the destruction of desire's objects. He is the demonic triumph of reform preempting even the elegiac triumphs of time. Again, besides being an image of an external force that presses in on the fragile world of the poem, the Beast is an imaginative violence from within, an interior enemy that answers darkly to Colin's interior paramour. The monster that grows within the necessary space between ourselves and our images is as apparently gratuitous in its advent as those presences that attend the singer on Mount Acidale; it is equally the product of the poet's "love." But the Beast is also, alas, considerably less transient than those dancers. Nor will Spenser at this moment allow himself to form the image of an Arthur who might defeat this catastrophic version of what has been called Spenser's "inescapable romance." That Calidore succeeds even partly may be mainly a result of the difficult lessons of Acidale. Having heard Colin's words about grace and discipline, he may also have acquired a sense of the imaginative tact that is needed to live in a world where magic and its passing away, desire and its destruction, idolatry and iconoclasm, are inextricably folded together.

The Triumphs of Hobgoblin

Book VI closes with a diffused, apocalyptic monster that is hurled into the present world, and that finds there no final enemy. The poet's last words in that book suggest a cold, poised resignation, an abandonment of a poetic career. Though it is dangerous to simplify such complex gestures, one might say that the loss of vision on Mount Acidale somehow entails the secret quest of the Blatant Beast, the two events leaving us with a broken poem in a broken world. All the more remarkable, then, that Spenser recovers his voice so strikingly in the Mutabilitie Cantos. Though that poem hardly evades the mutual entanglements of idolatry and iconoclasm, it maps out a space in which the poet can maintain less chilling attitudes of disillusionment and can find a critical irony that sustains some real gaiety. Through these Spenser wins back, if only in parable, some measure of reconciliation between his poem and his world.[10]

My main focus in this section is on the Faunus episode, that digressive etiological fable at the end of the first of the cantos in which the poet explains why Arlo Hill, the site of the trial of the titaness Mutabilitie, came to be abandoned by the gods that inhabited it—the responsibility falling on a comical faun who combines aspects of both Calidore and Blatant Beast. In order to frame my commentary, however, I need first to sketch out a few ideas about Book VII as a whole.

Two points define for me the stress and strangeness of the book, though neither are much spoken of in the available criticism.[11] The first is harder to argue, since it depends on construing the meanings of the story in ways that reverse the poet's more explicit thematic signals. The account of Mutabilitie's rebellion against what she takes to be the illegitimate rule of the Olympian gods, her claims to power over both sublunary and celestial worlds, the conversion of cosmic battle into legal trial under the eyes of Dame Nature, and the titaness's subsequent defeat when the evidence of cyclical, patterned change is presented—all of this suggests that we should read Book VII as a philosophical allegory that seeks mimetically to contain the threat of unbounded, violent, disorderly flux. Yet I would suggest that, to make full sense of some of the poet's strange ironies, we must see that the threat he is fighting off lies as much in order itself—especially order as a facet of human life lived in time—as in disorder or change.

It is the unchangeable facts of the past as much as the uncontrollable accidents of the present which account for the tragedies of human fortune and desire; faith in the fixed idols of anteriority, whether personal or social, serves as well as the ruins of past authorities and times to disorder the choices and powers of present life. In our movements toward an uncertain future, the urge to embrace a usurping order that, one imagines, may change things utterly, can in the end engender greater trouble than the simple loss of stable goals or ordered harmonies. Order itself then—or the will to order, stability, division, equality, closure—may indeed be more effectively catastrophic than whatever is named by idealized myths of unbounded change, decay, entropy, or chaos. The Mutabilitie Cantos tend to repress any direct image of the threatening work of order and defensively project its opposite in the ultimately less disturbing fantasy of the rebellious titaness. The logical emptiness in the arguments of this abstract enemy makes her all the easier to defeat and strengthens Nature's own beautiful and authoritative sophistries, especially those that tell us that all changeable things "by their change their being doe dilate: / And turning to themselves at length againe, / Doe worke their owne perfection so by fate: / Then over them Change doth not rule and raigne; / But they raigne over change, and doe their states maintaine" (VII.vii.58). But the darker wisdom of Spenser's poem is that this will to self-fulfillment can be crossed with a will to self-annihilation. One may then wonder whether Nature's subsequent warning to the ambitious titaness—that she seeks her own decay by trying to fulfill her desire for place and rule—is not something more than a clever joke at the expense of a fragile personification of change unwisely seeking reification. For in human, if not in allegorical agents, the gentle unfoldings of being may end up in repetition or stasis, just as the will to perfect an arbitrary desire may end up in skewed or partial forms of fulfillment or lead to the imposing of that desire as a tyrannical, divisive fatality. Such possibilities may help explain why the poet, invoking a "Sabaoths sight" in the concluding stanzas of Book VII, makes that image of eternal rest at once inevitable and strangely inaccessible. He projects such a rest beyond all human types, as if to remind us that the discourse that would lay hold of apocalyptic vision in any less tentative a fashion would most likely collapse into false prophecy and idolatry. A similar desire to hold lightly onto the blank superiority of order over change may even account for the odd, Lucianic irony that plays over the narrative, making a mockery of both established authority *and* the forces that rebel against it.

My second point is related to this last and concerns the status of the Mutabilitie Cantos as a form of substitute mythology. I have already pointed to one example of such substitution in the way that Mutabilitie herself is introduced as a metonymic evasion of any more explicit myth of the fall, since she is described as the cause of our growing into death instead of life rather than as the effect of creation or crime. On a larger scale, one could say that Book VII is a last vision written "in lieu of" the Book of Revelation.[12] Like the Garden of Adonis, it provides us with a strongly secular apocalypse, or, rather, an apocalypse of the secular. The trial of the titaness issues in a last judgment that tries to locate some sufficient form of restitution, balance, and justice within rather than beyond the cycles of time (even if it does not quite succeed); it also offers an eschatological vision that breaks down the reductively dualistic perspectives or cloven fictions which usually characterize eschatological writing, in particular, as I mentioned above, the coarsely contrastive projection of a demonic enemy as a way of establishing the greater purity of one's own stance. If Spenser's epic unfolds its most overt version of the biblical apocalypse in its very first book, it then closes with an apocalyptic invention that can be said to take the place of any other final vision. Admittedly, there is a gesture toward some more orthodox vision of apocalypse at the end of Book VII, once the cyclical pageant of the seasons has dissolved. Still, it is only a gesture, and we must take seriously Spenser's refusal to fill out any vision of a new heaven and new earth according to the lineaments of Scripture, as well as his refusal to claim that that final image might show a providential order which is intelligibly at work in history. Spenser reduces, schematizes, but also demystifies the dream of Saint John the Divine; neither prophecy, promise, or threat, it becomes largely the shrill cry of the self that longs for an abstracted glimpse of simple rest and changelessness. "If faith is indeed a refuge here, it is a lonely and bitter one. For the poet has no sight of God or of that hearsay Sabbath. He invokes and he waits, but he affirms only the reality of the Titaness" (Greene, *Descent from Heaven*, 323).

As a first step toward developing both of these altered perspectives, I propose to read the Faunus episode as an ironic replacement for that crucial phrase of apocalyptic which occupies itself with the marking and casting out of idolatry. In this reading Faunus is no intrusive Caliban but a prophetic iconoclast. This interpretation of course contradicts the surface evidence that Faunus, in suborning a handmaid of Diana and spying on the naked goddess as she bathes, is caught and cursed for violating a truly sacred presence. The narrative occasion for the inset fable, that of explaining how the Irish hill on which Mutabilitie's trial is held became so barren and wild, also suggests a parallel between the desacralizing of Arlo Hill and the loss of Eden. Likewise, various details of Spenser's story—Faunus's gifts of cherries and apples to the beguiled Molanna, as well as traditional allegorizations of the source myth of Actaeon—seem to identify the faun with the tempter Satan. The evident comedy of Faunus's attempt to get a glimpse of Diana has been noted, of course, but few critics doubt the basically criminal nature of his act or the justice of Diana's punishment (though it is just this punishment that is called into question in Ovid's original version of the Actaeon story [*Metamorphoses* III.253–54]). Yet we need to view Faunus's place within the mythological economy of the Mutabilitie Cantos as a whole, and there he plays a more heroic, if still ambivalent, part.

Faunus banishes from the landscape of Arlo Hill not simply a particular pagan divinity but also a mode of mythic fable. As Richard Ringler has shown in detail, Spenser, despite the generally Ovidian tone of the episode, pointedly stops short of realizing the fiction of metamorphosis ("The Faunus Episode," 292). Alluding to the story of Actaeon, Spenser reports that the unfortunate hunter had indeed been devoured by his hounds, but only "in Hunters hew" (VII.vi.45); the nymph Molanna is punished by being overwhelmed with stones, but she survives as the river we presume she always was; and Faunus himself, instead of being slain, gelded, or transformed, is simply chased across the landscape wrapped in the skins of a deer. Spenser is not, of course, getting rid of the literal belief in metamorphosis, which itself is hardly Ovidian. But he *is* evading the easy fictions of transformation, the habitual depiction of the gods of the landscape, the ironic patterns of punishment, all of which form the literary machinery of Ovid's quite urbane, secularized mythmaking. And he does this, it seems to me, not so much to prove that he is more disenchanted than Ovid as to prepare for the more strenuous and evanescent forms of magic that appear in the vision of Nature and the pageant of the months in canto vii.[13]

It is possible, of course, that Spenser's strategy brings to the surface a more hidden anxiety about the Ovidian tradition. Massey's discussions of the demented literalization of figurative language imposed by the fictions of metamorphosis (*The Gaping Pig*, 26–33), and Harold Skulsky's suggestions as to the epistemological uncertainty generated by the endless, grotesque, and often arbitrary transformations of Ovid's poem (*Metamorphosis: The*

Mind in Exile, 24–61), both indicate directions in which one might pursue this line of argument. My own accounts of both idolatry and iconoclasm show the space these phenomena share with metamorphosis, as well. What Spenser retains from Ovid, however, is his habit of parodying etiological myth. For as a fable of iconoclasm, the Faunus episode presents us not so much with sacred history as with an etiology of disenchantment, a myth of demythologization. It tells a story not of the origins of nature or the gods but of the degradation of both. While it echoes the myth of the fall, its ironizing of Edenic loss sets in questionable light not only myths of divine origins but myths of human failure as well. Its delicately self-conscious ironies suggest the ways in which such myths may at best be rationalizations, by means of a fiction of loss, of a difficult situation in the present, and so inevitably a function of nostalgia for an idealized past. The Faunus episode then, instead of asking us to read *through* the puzzling allegorical surface to some ground in scriptural myth, forces us to see how the surface itself reframes the idea of a fall, even as it manages to reinforce the strongly deromanticized nature of the sacred site. Arlo Hill . . . becomes most haunted in its very warding off of analogies to other sacred hills. This historical height near Spenser's Irish home thus becomes at once more familiar and more strange, no *omphalos* but a place where fiction, myth, and history uneasily cross.

Thus to define the poetic status of Arlo Hill, however, is not the same as showing Faunus himself to be the avatar of the poet's own creatively disenchanting quest, a figure through whom the poet can repossess the blankness of the Irish landscape as more of an imaginative achievement than a curse. One might begin to support such a reading by looking at Faunus's analogies with other characters both within and without *The Faerie Queene*. For example, Faunus, like Britomart and Calidore, violates an apparently sacred place and yet stands as a distanced witness to superhuman presence. Even more interestingly, the Actaeon-like faun recalls the distraught love goddess Venus who comes upon Diana bathing while searching for her lost son Cupid (III.vi.17–19). In all of these cases, the intruding viewer's "interest" in the scene is by no means easy to dismiss as simply idolatrous or corrupt. Nohrnberg's detailed discussion (*Analogy*, 730f.) of the pastoral magician Colin as a composite of the sylvan Pan and his father Hermes—interpreter and imp, thief and psychopomp—could be extended in large part to the guileful faun as well. Indeed, Faunus is really closer than Colin Clout to Gabriel Harvey's famous description of Spenser's poem as "*Hobgoblin* runne away with the Garland from *Apollo*." We could add to this list several fragmentary but quite clear hints of a Christ-like vocation in Faunus, both in his work as ironic subverter of pagan divinity and in his unusual patience at suffering mockery and beating at the hands of Diana's nymphs. (The identification is perhaps reinforced by Spenser's repeated use of the word "foolish" to describe the faun in his lowly, absurd, and transgressive aspects, recalling Erasmus's complex variations on the ideas of human and Christian foolishness in the *Moriae encomium*.)

But such an accumulation of analogy, even when aptly ironic, only fills in part of the picture. One may lose sight of the way in which the poet fragments, juxtaposes, and sometimes suppresses such resemblances, the different "sources" being at times "checkt and changed from [their] nature trew, / By others opposition or obliquid view" (VII.vii.54). Hence one must retreat at least briefly from the all too pleasant excursions of analogy into the more strenuous dislocations of close reading. Here then is Faunus watching Diana from his covert, caught like Mutabilitie in the desire to "see that mortall eyes have never seene" (VII.vi.32):

> There *Faunus* saw that pleased much his eye,
> And made his hart to tickle in his brest,
> That for great ioy of some-what he did spy,
> He could him not containe in silent rest;
> But breaking forth in laughter, loud profest
> His foolish thought. A foolish *Faune* indeed,
> That couldst not hold thy selfe so hidden blest,
> But wouldest needs thine owne conceit areed.
> Babblers unworthy been of so divine a meed.
> (VII.vi.46)

Faunus is at this moment the mythological source of the Lucianic humor that haunts the entire Mutabilitie Cantos, such as is elicited even by the theomachic conflicts of earlier stanzas, where the titaness challenges the power of Jove at the circle of the moon, the threshold of the celestial world, only to have a kind of divine squabbling ensue.[14] The above lines, indeed, anticipate within the poem the laughter that may rise in the reader when, in the next stanza but one, the goddess Diana is compared to an angry "huswife" shaking and threatening a pest that has fouled her creaming pans. Faunus himself, however, seems laughing not so much at the domesticity as at the human nakedness, and especially the sexual nature of pagan divinity. His open laugh indeed strangely reverses the sense of shame and secrecy felt by Adam and Eve upon opening their eyes to their own nakedness. The "some-what" that he spies with so much joy, though not necessarily with desire, is clearly the goddess's genitalia, but the modest, perhaps even prurient evasiveness of Spenser's word—which restores a verbal covering where there is no visual one—does suggest ironies that point beyond a merely physiological demystification of pagan divinity. "Some-what," for all its apparent blandness, may take on an odd resonance of its own, especially when we recall the association of sexual organs with the topography of secret/sacred centers like the Garden of Adonis. I do not mean to suggest that Spenser is happily mocking an ancient image of chastity in the service of a more urbane and sexualized ideal of *eros*, or that the half-human faun is himself not cast as a rather crude form of male sexual seeing or priapic peering. Still, the faun's transgressive laughter, more engagingly mysterious than the goddess herself, wholly problematizes the relation of the eye and its object; the laugh raises questions that unsettle any normative distinctions we might make between what would be sacred and what profane contemplation, what enchantment and what disenchantment, what idolatry and what iconoclasm.

Before going further with my analysis, I want to propose a somewhat unusual "genealogy" for Faunus's laughter. . . . I am interested in a similarity of stance rather than in a definite source, even though here the text is one that Spenser must have known quite well: Boccaccio's *Genealogy of the Pagan Gods.* The passage I have in mind follows from the complex proem to that work, and we will need to pause for a moment over this introductory movement. In the proem, Boccaccio describes himself as a scholarly quester, descending into the darkened landscape of the past and reassembling the fragments of classical fable into a single, renewed body, like Aesculapius restoring the torn *corpus* of Hippolytus.[15] This quest, we must observe, is shadowed by a sense of possible failure and by the fear of envious detractors; there is also a sense of guilt at the violence involved in his reconstructions and interpretations, at the dismemberment that accompanies the act of remembering, as well as a lingering consciousness of the fact that he is still moving within a world of false gods or idols (especially given Boccaccio's lack of interest in the more orthodox accommodations of medieval moral allegory).[16] The landscape of the ancient gods thus proves both sacred and profane while the work of the poetic theologian becomes an uneasy meditation on the errors and absenses of mythographic history as well as on its authentic sources.[17]

The proem culminates in an intricate account of the father god Demogorgon, a chthonic deity that, as Boccaccio may have known, owed its literary existence to a medieval scribal error.[18] He at least knew that the god had no place in any major classical texts, even though he claims that the ancients placed Demogorgon first in their own genealogies "for the sake of a beginning"—adding that it was really the terror of his name which silenced the later authors. Boccaccio's almost certainly comic parable on the problematic authority of classical myth is filled out even more clearly in the opening scene of Book I of his encyclopedia, where Boccaccio presents us with a grotesque theophany of the god:

With greatest majesty of darkness, just when I had described that [genealogical] tree, the oldest grandfather of all the pagan gods, Demogorgon, terrifying by his very name, wrapped in clouds and mist, appeared before me as I was crossing through the bowels of the earth. He was dressed in a sort of mossy pallor, damp and dishevelled, sending forth a fetid and earthy odor, and, declaring rather by the words of others than by his own mouth that he was the father of their unhappy pre-eminence, he stood before me, the contriver of a new work. I confess that I began to laugh when, looking at him, I remembered the madness of the ancients who thought him first and uncreated, the eternal father of all things, and living in the bowels of the earth. (*Genealogy* I.11c; translation mine).[19]

It is altogether remarkable that Boccaccio should stage such a scene of mocked fatherhood at the threshold of his own book of genealogies. Demogorgon is presented as the debunked progenitor of an idolatrous literary mythology; and yet, as a creature of fantasy and a figuration of nostalgia, it may be that the god represents a genuine temptation and threat (especially since the poet's quest must cross into the space where the god himself dwells). The very grotesqueness of the apparition suggests a residue of anxiety in the confrontation. Hence, though Demogorgon is hardly as great a demon of earth and imagination as the catastrophic Orgoglio, Boccaccio feels a need both to conjure and to exorcise him. In this not quite Vichian divination of Demogorgon, the most startling moment is the poet's dramatized memory of his own laughter. For to such an uncertain necromancer as Boccaccio, invoking the demystifying testimony of ancient, ghostly voices, that laugh is both defensive and freshening; it neither quite slanders nor quite sanctifies; it is an enlightened but not coldly sardonic response. Boccaccio's laugh defines rather a regenerating ambivalence in which he who is laughing is, oddly enough, also laughed at or ironized.[20]

Boccaccio's laughter is echoed and intensified in Faunus's. Though the latter resounds at the end rather than at the opening of his mythographic project, Spenser's scene of voyeurism and laughter betrays the same comic fascination with archaic divinity. And though Boccaccio's more nearly Oedipal mockery is replaced in Spenser by an attack on the divine authority of a chaste, queenly goddess, the English poet's retrospective fable achieves a similarly complex lesson about the founding skepticism that places the poet in his spiritual and literary landscape.

But if Spenser *is* the faun, he is more fully exposed to his own mockery than Boccaccio appears to be; the gestures of mockery, that is, are themselves regarded with a greater degree of ambivalence. For we must remember that it is the faun's laugh, not the act of still, silent watching itself, that the poet appears to condemn and that leads to Faunus's punishment. What indicts the wood god is the breaking from rest into motion, from hidden to open, from silence into song. And yet this burden must not keep us from recognizing the laugh's peculiar efficacy. As has often been pointed out, the poet's emphasis on the faun's "silent rest" and entranced sight foreshadows the fragmentary closing of Book VII, where the poet invokes a vision of the reality which stands behind the ever changing, unresting world of Nature, a vision of all things settled "upon the pillours of Eternity" (VII.viii.2). Though the poet seems eager to place this vision beyond all possible images or figures of desire, it is yet mirrored in the faun's "hidden blest" stance of wordless watching. But having noticed the analogy, we must recognize that such watching can at best be read as a parodic prolepsis of Sabbath sight and may even constitute a shrewd warning against the regressive impulses underlying any sort of visionary longing. If the sight that the genial narrator calls "so divine a meed" is after all a kind of mute idolatry, then the intrusive laughter professed so loudly may not be as criminal as it first appears.

Faunus's laugh is indeed the original speech—or the poet's best image of it—that invades the uncertain space infantile voyeurism shares with the desire for apocalyptic vision, breaking the tendency of both to self-absorbed or tyrannical silence. It is hardly a numinous primal word, a prophetic god-cry, a creative *logos*, or a transparent Adamic name. It is strictly speaking "no language," without any illusions of referentiality or ideological effectiveness. Yet Faunus's laughter has the risk and freshness of a human voice, the voice of one who announces his private delights and desires, though neither strictly to himself nor to any calculated audience. Both less and more than human, the demigod is a version of the poet who "areeds his own conceit"—his own poetic figures and continued allegory of praise as well as his own egotism. That laughter may even be the poet's dreamed revenge against the personal and political constraints that led him into bitter, chastened silence at the end of Book VI.

In the opening verses of "The Fall of Hyperion," John Keats wrote that

> . . . Poesy alone can tell her dreams,
> With the fine spell of words alone can save
> Imagination from the sable charm
> And dumb enchantment.
> (*Poetical Works*, 403)

Faunus's laugh is anything but a "fine spell of words," and yet it is a brilliant trope for the troubling magic of Spenser's own poetic idiom, which seeks to disenchant even the dumb enchantment possible in the sounds of language itself. Faunus is a form of the poet at his most exuberant and ambivalent, a figure mocked and mocking, idolatrous and iconoclastic. Thinking of Spenser—for whom every word of desire or praise was a necessary risk, a betrayal of private thought to public chaos; who dilated, distanced, and qualified every divinizing image half a dozen ways and yet was still pursued by the fear of envy and slander—we may recognize that the words that condemn Faunus are strangely directed at the poet himself: "Babblers unworthy been of so divine a meed." The babbler may suffer the fate of Echo and have the expression of his or her desires caught up within nonsense or the alienating repetition of anterior utterance. His poems may wander into or invite the noise, *rumor*, babble, or bleating of the sacrilegious Blatant Beast, the language of desire fulfilling itself in postures of envy rather than grace. Yet Faunus, the poet as Hobgoblin running away with the laurel from Apollo, is also a cousin of that Spenser figured by Raleigh as a "celestiall theife," a more triumphant invader of sacred presence who cast out another chaste poetic goddess from her tomblike temple.[21] Hermetic and Promethean at once, Faunus is a creature who tells the prophetic secrets of the gods, even if those secrets tell us that "Here there are no gods."

Notes

1. The Beast is also related to the three-headed Plutonian dog Cerberus and to the many-headed Hydra, who like the Beast itself (in at least one of its two genealogies) are the offspring of Typhaon and Echidna (Hesiod, *Theogony* 311–14; cf. *FQ* VI.vi.9–12). Orgoglio's seven-headed beast is also compared to the Hydra (I.vii.17).

2. We might point here to Spenser's picture of Envy with her tongue like the sting of an asp and her mouth foaming with poison (V.xii.36), but perhaps even more interesting is Giotto's emblem of *Invidia* in the Arena Chapel: an old woman standing amidst hell fire, with one clawlike hand stretched forth (to snatch or wound?) and the other clasping a moneybag to her side; she has huge ears (to catch tales and slanders), and the snake emerging from her mouth curls back and stings her between the eyes. Here the snake and the slanderous tongue are even more closely identified than in Spenser. Giotto also recalls the poet's play on the question of slander's "sources," his figure suggesting that slander is strangely responsible for (as well as being caused by) the evil eye of envy. (This image appears in Stubblebine, *Giotto: The Arena Chapel Frescoes*, pl. 59.)

3. Cf. W. B. Yeats on the transfiguring power of contempt:

> The finished man among his enemies?—
> How in the name of Heaven can he escape
> That defiling and disfigured shape
> The mirror of malicious eyes
> Casts upon his eyes until at last
> He thinks that shape must be his shape?
> (*Collected Poems*, 266)

4. More specifically, the Beast is an agent of men like Lord Burghley, Elizabeth's treasurer and chief advisor, a figure whom Spenser seems to have identified with the narrow, puritanical spirit at court which could read *The Faerie Queene* only as a seductive, erotic romance (cf. IV.proem.1–2), and so cut the poet off from both patronage and fame (Judson, *Life of Spenser*, 153). Spenser satirizes Burghley rather viciously as a self-serving ape in "Mother Hubberds Tale" (*Poetical Works*, 495–508) and also gives him a disturbing, Urizen-like form in one of the dedicatory sonnets to the 1590 *Faerie Queene*, where he appears as the frozen father-god Atlas, upholding the "grave affaires" of the kingdom on his shoulders (*Poetical Works*, 410).

5. In his aptly titled book of psychoanalytic essays, *A Game That Must Be Lost*, the British art historian Adrian Stokes writes that "the aggression [of the Death Drive] is immediately bound up with loss also: the destroyed object is often the good object attacked in greed, or in envy, the supreme expression of the desire for object-absence fused with libido, since this persecution by the object issues from its very goodness coveted by the subject" (65). Stokes is here writing very much under the influence of Melanie Klein. I should note that I borrow my question about the ego's schooling from Stokes (55).

6.   "Blatant" (sometimes "Blattant") seems to have been Spenser's own coinage and is usually taken to derive from the Latin *blatire*, "to babble." (The OED suggests the possibility of an additional connection with an archaic form of "bleating" which would make the Beast a grotesque relative of those sheep that define the economy of the pastoral world in Book VI.) The invasive power of the Beast perhaps derives from the fact that such "looseness" yet conditions the possibility for the interiority of one's language in the first place, so that the possibility of some distance between self and world, and hence the possibility of desire as such, would seem inextricably bound to whatever the Blatant Beast embodies, most extremely to defilement, to *thanatos.*

7.   Cheney, perhaps playfully unfolding Spenser's word "misconstruction," makes the strange joke that this monster of slander is "what today might be called misreading or deconstruction" ("Retrospective Pastoral," 7). The analogy is, I think, precise enough (if not quite fair to the Beast), but one must recognize that the ironies of representation and the errors of reading or desire which such critical stances may imply for Cheney are not purely imposed on the text. The alien enemy is something that the poem yet recognizes as its own; the Beast is *heimlich* as well as *unheimlich.* It represents a disequilibrium that is a permanent feature of the human linguistic situation (though also much more than that), and especially one that infects Spenser's highly articulated, polyvalent, ambivalent, and complexly perspectivizing work.

8.   This last phrase is taken from a sermon of George Sandys which criticizes the abuses of the queen's "surveyors" (quoted by Kermode, *Shakespeare, Spenser, Donne,* 46).

9.   It may or may not be worthwhile to note that in 1582 Spenser leased lands in County Kildare which contained the ruins of a Franciscan friary, New Abbey, and which had "an old waste town adjoining" (Judson, *Life of Spenser,* 103). Spenser's engagement with the complex poetry of ruins, in both its elegiac and apocalyptic aspects, goes back to his earliest translations in *The Theatre for Worldings* and his splendid rendering of Du Bellay's *Les Antiquitez de Rome* (*Poetical Works,* 606–8 and 509–14, respectively). To focus on the idea of ruins from the perspective of iconoclasm, however, may raise fresh questions about the ways that active violence may intersect with entropy or decay, and the ways that the shapes of ruin may be variously figured as failure or triumph, something inherited or something achieved. It might be interesting to try pushing back to the sixteenth century an analysis of the myths, philosophy, and phenomenology of ruins such as Thomas MacFarland attempts in *Romanticism and the Forms of Ruin: Wordsworth, Coleridge, and the Modalities of Fragmentation,* 3–55 and passim.

10.   I have taken it as a working assumption that the Mutabilitie Cantos are Spenser's attempt to find a form of ending fit for a poem that is preternaturally anxious about the forms and figures of ending, but that otherwise could have achieved no closure besides mere truncation. They are an attempt to come to terms with the personal, literary, and theological burden of ending, to save both ending and endlessness from the infectious iconoclasm of the Blatant Beast. Setting aside the strictly circumstantial and probably insoluble mystery of their late publication in 1609, I would say that the force of the cantos lies in the fact that we must read them simultaneously as a closed, autonomous epyllion and a fragment or fraction of an incomplete seventh book.

11.   Among more conservative readings, perhaps the best is that of S. P. Zitner, contained in the introduction to his edition of the Mutabilitie Cantos. This critic pays very careful but undogmatic attention to Spenser's fundamentally Boethian theories of time, change, and form, and brings out some of the more idiosyncratic facets of Book VII's narrative and allusive mode.

12.   The only critic in whom I find any anticipation of this reading, however sketchy, is Nohrnberg. Commenting on the disappearance of Nature at the end of canto vii, he adds: "It is time to put away expectations of some noisier or more tangible apocalypse. Almost without allowing us to know it, Spenser has his vision, and its crisis is closed. The argument

of the Mutabilitie Cantos will allow of nothing more definitive, and neither will *The Faerie Queene*. That self-balancing progression of becoming and decline and replenishment, through which all of Being is regularly perpetuated throughout Spenser's long poem, rightly issues, not in an apocalyptic cataclysm, but in an apocalyptic homeostasis" (*Analogy*, 86).

13. Berger, reading in Book VII a comic allegory of literary history, speaks of the process of "desymbolization" and "depersonification" by which mythological figures like Mutabilitie and the other gods lose their wonted integrity, a process "in which the referent breaks free from its containing symbolic form. Thus released, it is open to new forms and to new life in later times. This process is already underway as we move from the aggressive pagan individuals of canto vi to the impersonal concord of forces and functions shining more clearly through the figures and emblems of canto vii" ("Archaism and Evolution in Retrospect," 163).

14. The mixture of apocalyptic and satirical elements in Book VII may reflect a deeper generic affinity. Martin Hengel, *Judaism and Hellenism*, 84, suggests that the use of diatribe and satire in late classical literature, and such satiric types as "letters of the gods," "testaments," and journeys to heaven and the underworld may have had some influence on the eclectic creations of late Jewish and early Christian apocalyptic.

15. On the sources of this mythology and its relevance for Renaissance theories of literary history, see A. Bartlett Giamatti, "Hippolytus among the Exiles: The Romance of Early Humanism" (*Exile and Change*, 12–32).

16. On the defense of poetry and interpretation undertaken by the proem and the fourteenth book of Boccaccio's *Genealogy*, see the pointed observations in Ferguson, *Trials of Desire*, 166–68 and 182–83.

17. Boccaccio's famous chiasmus, "Dunque bene appare, non solamente la poesía essere teologia, ma ancora la teologia essere poesia" (*Comento ala Divina Commedia*, 1:43), frames an ideal identification of poet and theologian, but it may also suggest something about the uneasy breakdown of differences between the two vocations that troubles Boccaccio's attempts at both reading and rewriting the narratives of classical myth.

18. On this matter see Maurice Castelain, "Demogorgon ou le barbarisme déifié," and Nohrnberg, *Analogy*, 104, n. 38.

19. I am grateful to the late Robert Fitzgerald for his advice on this rendering.

20. I am drawing here on Mikhail Bakhtin's intriguing typology of medieval and Renaissance laughter in *Rabelais and his World*, 59–144, in particular his description of Rabelaisian laughter as a defensive and yet liberating gesture, a motion that at once asserts and denies, that both buries and revives the object of ridicule. Such laughter ideally frees those who laugh from the violence of both religious superstition and political authority, even while it exposes them to their own irony. Bakhtin, however, associates such laughter with the organized disorder and the publically sanctioned gestures of medieval festival, whereas Boccaccio's and Faunus's laughs seem to project more obscurely private motives.

21. Raleigh's dedicatory sonnet, "A Vision upon this conceipt of the *Faery Queene*," mythologizes the poet's literary ambitions in a scene in which the Faerie Queen intrudes into a shrine that holds "the grave, where *Laura* lay," stealing away the graces and the "living fame" that attend Petrarchan poetry, while "Oblivion laid him downe on *Lauras* herse: / Hereat the hardest stones were seene to bleed, / And grones of buried ghosts the heavens did perse. / Where *Homers* spright did tremble all for griefe, / And curst th'accesse of that celestiall theife" (Spenser, *Poetical Works*, 409)—this last line suggesting that Spenser's poem overgoes classical epic as well as earlier Renaissance erotic poetry.

Works Cited

Bakhtin, Mikhail. *Rabelais and His World.* Trans. Helene Iswolsky. Cambridge, Mass.: M.I.T. Press, 1968.

Berger, Harry, Jr. "A Secret Discipline: *The Faerie Queene,* Book VI." In *Form and Convention in the Poetry of Edmund Spenser,* ed. William Nelson, 35–75. New York: Columbia University Press, 1961.

———. "*The Mutabilitie Cantos:* Archaism and Evolution in Retrospect." In *Spenser: A Collection of Critical Essays,* ed. Harry Berger, Jr., 146–76. Englewood Cliffs, N.J.: Prentice-Hall, 1968.

Boccaccio, Giovanni. *Genealogy of the Pagan Gods.* (*Genealogie deorum gentilium libri*). 2 vols. Ed. Vincenzo Romano. Bari, 1951.

———. *Il comento alla Divina Commedia.* 3 vols. Ed. Domenico Guerri. Bari, 1918.

Castelain, Maurice. "Demogorgon ou le barbarisme déifié." *Bulletin de L'Association Guillaume Budé* 36 (1932): 22–39.

Cheney, Donald. "Retrospective Pastoral: The Returns of Colin Clout." Paper read at the Modern Language Association Convention, New York, 29 December 1981.

Ferguson, Margaret. *Trials of Desire: Renaissance Defenses of Poetry.* New Haven: Yale University Press, 1983.

Giamatti, A. Bartlett. "Hippolytus among the Exiles: The Romance of Early Humanism." In *Exile and Change in Renaissance Literature.* 12–32. New Haven: Yale University Press, 1984.

Greene, Thomas M. *The Descent from Heaven: A Study in Epic Continuity.* New Haven: Yale University Press, 1963.

Hengel, Martin. *Judaism and Hellenism: Studies in their Encounter in Palestine during the Early Hellenistic Period.* 1968. 2 vols. Trans. John Bowden. Philadelphia: Fortress Press, 1974.

Judson, Alexander C. *The Life of Edmund Spenser.* Baltimore: The Johns Hopkins University Press, 1945.

Keats, John. *Poetical Works.* Ed. H. W. Garrod. London: Oxford University Press, 1956.

Kermode, Frank. *Shakespeare, Spenser, Donne: Renaissance Essays.* London: Routledge & Kegan Paul, 1971.

MacFarland, Thomas. *Romanticism and the Forms of Ruin: Wordsworth, Coleridge, and the Modalities of Fragmentation.* Princeton: Princeton University Press, 1981.

Massey, Irving. *The Gaping Pig: Literature and Metamorphosis.* Berkeley and Los Angeles: University of California Press, 1976.

Nohrnberg, James. *The Analogy of "The Faerie Queene."* Princeton: Princeton University Press, 1976.

Ringler, Richard N. "The Faunus Episode," In *Essential Articles,* ed. A. C. Hamilton, 289–98. Hamden, Conn.: Archon, 1972.

Shakespeare, William. *The Complete Works.* Ed. Alfred Harbage et al. Baltimore: Penguin, 1969.

Skulsky, Harold. *Metamorphosis: The Mind in Exile.* Cambridge, Mass.: Harvard University Press, 1981.

Spenser, Edmund. *Poetical Works*. Ed. J. C. Smith and E. de Selincourt. London: Oxford University Press, 1912.

Stokes, Adrian. *A Game That Must Be Lost*. Cheshire: Carcanet Press, 1973.

Stubblebine, James. *Giotto: The Arena Chapel Frescoes*. New York: Norton, 1969.

Wittgenstein, Ludwig. *Remarks on Frazer's "Golden Bough."* 1967. Trans. A. C. Miles. Ed. Rush Rhees. Atlantic Highlands: Humanities Press, 1979.

Yeats, William Butler. *Collected Poems*. London: Macmillan, 1961.

Zitner, S. P. ed. *The Mutabilitie Cantos*. London: Nelson, 1968.

Index

♦